Shaking the Mulga

An Australian family history

Clem Ditton

Brisbane, Australia 2021

Self Published

Front Cover Photo: Mulga blooms – Brisbane Botanic Gardens Mt Coo-tha November 2019
Rear Cover Photo: Hill End, NSW August 2009
Both photos by author

ISBN 978-0-646-82992-0 (hardback)

This work has been compiled with all due dilligence but recognises some errors, inaccuracies or omissions may have resulted. I apologise in advance for any discovered. Corrections can be sent to the author.

Version: 19 Nov 2023

Author contact: clem.ditton@gmail.com

Family history
Australian history
Legal history
DNA detective
Gold rushes
Wool boom
Transported convicts
Potato famine

Contents

Dedicated to Helen, Justin, Hannah and Peg

Preface

Mulga Belt was the family's sheep property I was brought home to as a newborn. I didn't spend much time there, as my parents moved to Brisbane in my first year. However, *Mulga Belt* lived on in my consciousness through my childhood visits to the district and my mother's reminiscences of it. She was still talking about it more than six decades later and she referred to it as home. It was the key location in my thoughts about my Australian ancestral origins. The mulga tree (*Acacia aneura*) is a common species of wattle endemic to much of Australia. It is hardy and spindly and despite that, it is often shapely and quite pretty, particularly when it blooms after rain. Its attractive dense wood is favoured for craft, but that same wood is also poisonous. In contrast, the long and thin grey-green leaves nurture animals, particularly in droughts, and mulga seeds were an important food source for the first Australians. Being 'out in the mulga' means being out in the Australian bush and that resonates with much of what follows. It seemed a worthy starting point for writing about my Australian family tree.

When our first child was born, Australia's bicentennial was in the planning and there was much talk of Arthur Phillip and the First Fleet. It was around this time I remember thinking seriously about my heritage. I did not fully understand why I am an Australian. I was reasonably sure there was no Indigenous heritage in any of my lines, but did our mob play an active part in depriving their mob of all the things they lost out on? Did any ancestors participate in the big events in Australian history? What were the circumstances that drove them to leave their homes to come to this country? Were there any convicts?

I had good oral history about my maternal grandmother's family, who had come from Scotland and that was the go-to story when discussing our non-Australian heritage. I even stayed with distant relatives when visiting Scotland in the early 1980s.

We were all quite comfortable with our Scottish heritage. With the rugged beauty, tartaned clans and barely intelligible accent, it seemed more exotic than England and we happily identified with the culture, to the extent we understood it. There would be a steady stream of picture books, calendars, magazines and illustrated tins of shortbread arriving from relatives still living there. There were some vague stories about my mother's father's family also having a Scottish connection, but little known beyond that. My mother often recounted the family stories. My father rarely did. For my father's family, there were some names, some events and some significant Queensland districts, but the roots were not really understood. An aunt mentioned Ireland, but only years after my father's death and never with any detail.

A little bit of digging, 1980s style, slowly revealed more. That involved a lot of sending away for certificates. Later, as I got a bit more serious – with visits to libraries looking at historical collections and some progress on building the family tree – the most annoying brick walls came more sharply into focus. By the time our second child had arrived, my tree shaking had provided enough bounty to make my bundle of information a 1988 Christmas present to the wider family.

I then spent several decades distracted by my career in IT and nuclear family commitments, with only occasional forays to chip at those brick walls. When I searched again more seriously, the records and the access to them had improved significantly, thanks largely to the Internet. Trove became a thing, and what an amazing thing it became. Then the power of the new tool, DNA, dawned on me. It helped me express my curiosity gene. I realised the best possible outcome would depend on me recruiting some relatives to provide a saliva sample to help with a cross-matching strategy. After some thought and some preliminary results, I deduced the relative value of my relatives' DNA. Close is good, distant is better and old is gold.

Old folk are valuable and not just for their spit. We instinctively know that. Seeking them out gives you the best chance of gathering those valuable memories, oral titbits and photos the previous generation were bound to have but which have eluded you previously. In some cases, they are grateful someone of the next generation has taken an interest, and therefore, part of their story will not go the way most do. Correspondence and collaboration with distant relatives and complete strangers can often throw up vital clues. It pays to be polite, pertinent and occasionally persistent. Sometimes that vital clue is enough to breach the brick wall, and so it was, at several points within this story.

DNA proved to be a strong force. It enabled me to give the family tree a good second shake. Apart from confirming some documented ancestors, it exposed things which were not expected, and it threw up things which were uninvited. It delivered on its potential to reveal long sought-after answers, but all of that came with genuine disruption in other quarters. Four distinct relevant discoveries are described in the text, but an increasing number of significant DNA discoveries are outside the scope of this book. For some relatives, DNA revelations were confronting and for others there was a decision to protect them from the likely truth. The full story to be extracted from DNA, in most families, is still to be discovered.

At the end of this, I was able to give a reasonable answer to the question of, why am I an Australian? I thought it best to write up a considered version of what I had found. The alternative of letting the fruits of all that hard work sit in bits and pieces in boxes and disk drives until it became landfill would just be silly. That was the initial impetus to write a book, and that idea was supported by the realisation that history books are the least likely genre to go out of date. As time went by, I saw there were other reasons to publish. It was an opportunity to explore ideas and themes relevant to family history and history generally, which developed in the course of my research.

Most of the people in this book, myself included, would be considered unremarkable in the context of their own times. Through the prism of another day however, those ordinary lives are worth closer examination because of the stark differences with how things are now and will be in the future. In an ordinary lifespan you can expect several interesting events. On top of that, there were extraordinary things going on around the people in these stories. It is best to keep reminding ourselves about that, so we can appreciate the significantly better current state of affairs. If things go backwards in some areas, then the past can also serve as a reference point for that. I am curious about how the humdrum lives of today will appear when examined in a century or two hence. We have lived through a period of rapid change. There are countless things I took for granted as a child that no longer are as they were.

Like most family histories, this one chronicles the arc from the miracle of birth to the snafu of death. I do chronicle that A begat and B bore C, but hopefully with more context and provenance than some famous tomes that tackle that task. I am also fully aware that too many begats can bore the readership to the point of somnolence. However, some want to see it, particularly if C was their nanna. For the wider readership I explore some themes that stood out during my research. Themes such as health in the bad old days invokes a sense of gratitude that we now have developed remedies to address many issues that were so life threating in the past. With the birth of my own children, there were complications likely to have been fatal if they had been born in the days of yore. Modern medicine enabled both mum and bub to dodge a musket ball. Fateful accidents will always be with us, but from this research I learnt that for Australians, a career in underground mining was more dangerous than being a wartime soldier.

The list goes on: Education is taken for granted today, but not so many years ago, it was a luxury out of the reach of many. Religion had many influences, and not all were good. Our relationship with animals is a multifaceted and constantly evolving story. Alcohol has played a part in enhancing the enjoyment of life and at other times in reducing it to misery. The immigration stories of leaving home to spend months in a cramped, disease-ridden sailing ship should always be remembered, especially when moaning about the twenty-plus hours spent in economy class for a modern overseas vacation. Indigenous Australians should be acknowledged and thanked for not being as belligerent as they have every right to be.

On top of all that, a clear but unexpected, theme showed itself early on. As I wrote the stories, I noticed events and characters brushing up against laws and legal constructs and how those tend to change over time. The non-exhaustive list I have compiled of things mentioned in the story include: age of consent, parental consent, marriage equality, divorce, bigamy, desertion, illegitimacy, wills, intestacy, death duties, orphans and adoption, attempted suicide, gender equality, civil registration, land laws, labour laws, immigration laws, taxation, the death penalty, vagrancy, assault, Indigenous recognition, wildlife preservation, vehicle safety, war precautions, conscription and foreign service, reserved occupations and rationing.

My interest in family history nicely complemented my interest in history generally. I had only limited exposure to history as a subject in school, which probably helped me maintain my interest after my formal education ended. My principal study stream was maths and science. The older I became, the more the Australian story fascinated me. My career also provided a perspective through which to view aspects of history. I was involved in many projects with all the governance mechanisms that necessarily implies. I often thought if they ever did a business case, a risk register and an issue register for the First Fleet, then there would be Buckley's it would get through the first gate. An ethics review committee with 2020 sensibilities would have fallen about in hysterics. Yet here we all are. I am not sure what that says about modern project governance or eighteenth-century British derring-do.

Genealogy is the game of collecting ancestors to see how far back you can go with names, dates and places. It is like collecting anything – the more the better, but with an eye to quality. In this case quality is determined by accuracy, not by how posh the progenitors were. I participate in that game, but I prefer the family history game. That is where you flesh out the bones of past relatives of which you are sure. The further back in time you go, the records get iffier with their scant detail and multiple interpretations. Such sources reduce confidence that you have the right folk in the right boxes. Most people would rejoice in a demonstrated link to an ancient celebrity. The problem with it is, even if you have the extreme good fortune of being able to trust the document trail, then the dilution of any contribution to your make-up from that forebear would be in the homeopathic range. The curse of all published pedigrees is the cumulative doubt that comes from misattributed paternity. DNA studies show current frequencies of misattribution vary in various cultures – e.g. 0.3 percent in Switzerland versus 13.8 percent in Mexico. One to two percent of births is a safe working assumption for historic Britain and Ireland.

One of the fun maths and science facts about pedigree is, as you project back through the generations, the number of ancestors on any given rank is a simple power of two – i.e. two parents, four grandparents, eight great-grandparents etc. These numbers get very big, very quickly. By the time we get to about two to the power of 29, we have exceeded the number of people alive on the planet at the relevant time and that figure would have been reached around 750 years ago. So, clearly something else is going on. If we count only unique ancestors, then after a certain point, the number of unique ancestors starts to run backwards and continues that way as the millennia recede – i.e. the same individuals increasingly appear at different places within the pedigree the further back you go. A graph of the number of unique ancestors would look like a Dutch carrot. This whole phenomenon is called pedigree collapse, and it is essentially down to people taking a fancy to their cousins. Not first cousins necessarily, but predominantly, some kind of cousin. This is not just a hillbilly thing; it is just an old human thing. Small communities, transport limitations and a tribal mentality helped the process along. From time to time, events like migrations or invasions or the Industrial Revolution stirred up the stagnant gene pool.

A related concept derived from the analysis of DNA tells us we can project that, at some point, we all have just one common female ancestor who is called Mitochondrial Eve. On current analysis, she lived around 150,000 years ago in Africa. The male equivalent is called Y-chromosomal Adam (but to stir the possum, I prefer to call him Steve). He is projected to have lived between 160,000 to 300,000 years ago also in Africa. So, on current analysis he is unlikely to be a contemporary of Eve and from that observation it follows that, Eve could not be the first woman. Similarly, it would be way too simplistic to think of Steve as the first man.

The stories are presented in the order that makes the most sense to me and are intended to be read in that order, but as a responsible adult, you can do what you like. The standard advice to family research newbies is to start with the family you know and work backwards. That notion is at work here. The style of this story changes with each passing chapter, as it is driven by the available material or subject under examination. I start with memoirs and oral histories and finish with tales almost completely derived from old records and newspaper reports. If I was more skilful, then

I might have filled in the gaps with stuff I made up and, thereby, have provided a more consistent story. Some authors attempt this, but their skill level undermines the value of the overall product. A few succeed and the result is superb. Conscious of my limitations, I chose the factual approach. The result is, while some chapters may flow nicely, others might resemble a Wikipedia article assembled from an accretion of snippets.

I toyed with the idea of subtitling this book 'an Australian her and his story', but it would be difficult to live up to the promise inherent in that clumsy phrase because of the stark truth that there is a significant gap between the information available for the female and male characters. In general, women were simply less visible within the available accounts. Oral accounts and memoirs have the best potential to redress the imbalance, but sadly, they are rare.

The question of why I am an Australian defined the scope of this book. That's less about me being special and more about a scope being a useful thing. In some cases, more is known beyond the ancestors that came to Australia, but they are only dealt with in a limited way.

A large part of the history of a nation should be the accumulation of the histories of individuals who lived in that nation. Many stories remain untold, and a lot of the compiled family stories are told from a perspective which reinforces certain messages, e.g. bravery in war, pioneer spirit or other triumphs over adversity. So, in telling these stories, I was not wanting to add to those themes unnecessarily. My intention was to tell stories of people living their lives with some emphasis on the interesting bits and their interaction with the themes that interested me. If you get anything out of this book, I hope it is the urge to write about your own family (assuming you have not already).

Acknowledgements

My sincere thanks to the many people who have contributed everything from albums of photographs, newspaper clippings, manuscripts, original documents and oral history gems to those who provided just an obscure tidbit. Some people provided inspiration or perspective or clues or feedback and of course some provided saliva – all of which improved the story. Some helped with the process of publishing the book. All contributions were gratefully received. In alphabetical order:

Douglas Abercrombie, James Barry, Sharon Beck, Joe Bihlmier, Helen Brennan, Brenda Burch, Barbara Caskey, Lyn Collison, Christine Cottrell, Lisa D'Arcangelo, Ivy Dare, Mary de Jabrun, Joanne Dever, Allan Ditton, Arthur Ditton, Bob Ditton, Hannah Ditton, Justin Ditton, Lola Ditton, Peg Ditton, Ralph Ditton, Tom Drohan, Thomas Ebersoll, Lanny Edey, Nancy Edwards, Helen Evans, Joan Everitt, Deb Favier, Janette Fenwick, Sarah-Jayne Fenwick, Alwyn Foott, Jill Fyffe, Sean Gobey, Mary Graham, Rosemary Guertin, Delma Haack, Graham Haack, Patti Hacket-Hunter, Christine Hawkins, Anne Hickey, Doug Hill, Lyndal Hill, Susan Hughes, Christine Jones, Ian Kelly, Margaret Kelly, Lesley Knezevic, Becky McCauley, Heather Millar (editor), Duncan McGonigal, Peter McGonigal, Mitchell & District Historical Facebook group, Fiona Moffat, Beth Mowry, Lyn Murphy, Kaye Nardella, Meredith Newman, Ruth Nicholson, Stuart Nicholson, Jay Nicol, Sonya Nicol, Charlie Noon (NSW), Charles Noon (Qld), Don Noon, Eric Noon, Ian Noon, Jodie Noon, John Noon, Julia Noon, Les Noon, Mike Noon, Danny O'Neill, Paul O'Neill, Kirsty Ogden, Mary Barbara Oberst Orr, Christine Phillips, Kath Ramsey, Maureen Reinders, Barbara Rex, Janice Robinson, Grahame Roebuck, Beverley Schweers, John Schweers, Phil Sheridan, Robyn Simpson, Denise Sweeney, Margaret Szalay, Sandra Tier, Rosaleen Underwood, Shirley Walmsley, Carol Weber, Jack Welsh, Barbara Wilde, Amy Williams, Margaret Wood Fitzgerald, Orreen Yates.

A special mention is reserved for the Queensland Family History Society, particularly the Family History Writing Group which has provided a valuable forum for me to test out my writing adventures. Without such a supportive group, I doubt that I would have made the leap to publish.

My ancestors, significant others and I have lived on lands traditionally owned by Indigenous peoples and I acknowledge their continuous connection with those lands. Those traditional owners and indicative relevant current place names, included for context, are listed below in alphabetical order: Agwamin (Lyndhurst), Badtjala (Maryborough), Barunggam (Toowoomba, *Corranga*), Budjari (Eulo), Bundjalung (Warwick), Darumbal (Rockhampton), Dharug (Lithgow, Newnes, Prospect), Djirbalngan (Innisfail), Eora (Sydney), Gija (Bowen), Gugu-Badhun (Charters Towers), Gungarri (*Mulga Belt*, Mitchell), Gureng Gureng (Calliope, Gladstone), Iningal (Aramac), Kamilaroi (Goonoo Goonoo), Kuku-Yalanji (Cooktown), Mandandanji (Mitchell, Roma), Ngunawal (Canberra), Nyawaygi (Townsville), Tharawal (Wollongong), Turrbal (Brisbane) Waka Waka (Caboolture), Wangan (Clermont), Wiljali (Broken Hill), Wiradjuri (Hill End, Pipers Flat), Yangga (Conway), Yilba (Cape River), Yuggera (Brisbane), Yuin (Bega) and Yuwi (Mackay). Primary reference: The AIATSIS map of Indigenous Australia, David R Horton, 1996

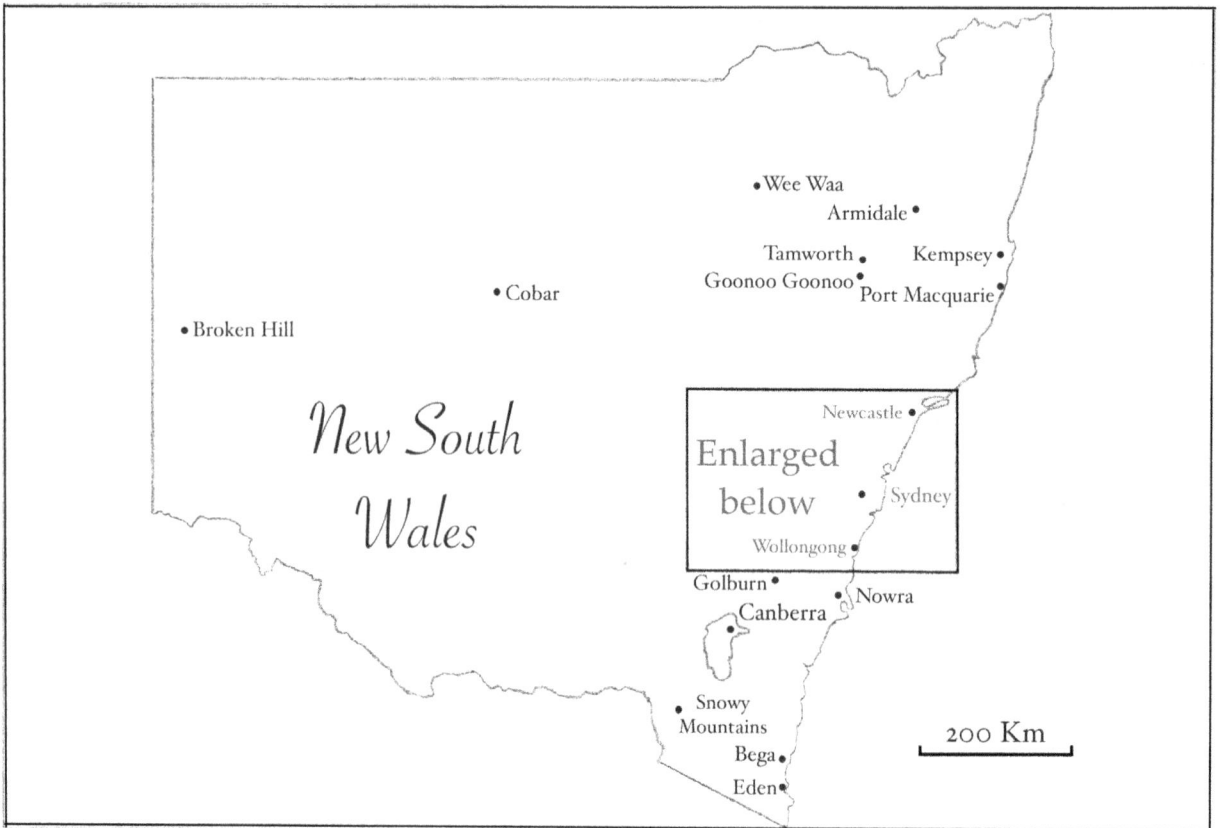

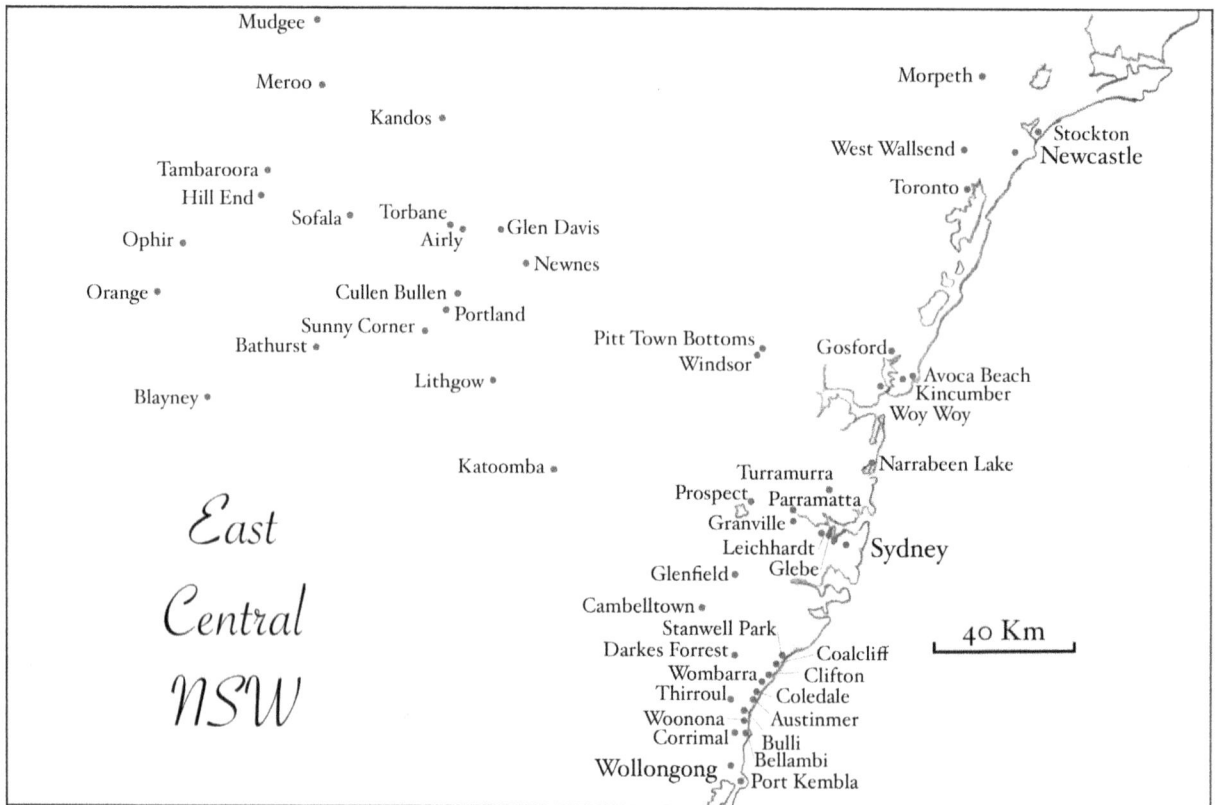

Milne Bay (PNG)

Queensland

300 Km

Cooktown

Mitchell River
Palmer River

Cairns
Atherton   Yungaburra
Innisfail
Tully

Burketown

Townsville

Lyndhurst Station

Reid River   Bowen
Charters Towers   Longford Creek
            Ravenswood   Prosperpine
            Walkerston
Cape River Pleystowe   Mackay
Conway Station
            Mirani   Sarina
            Mia Mia
            Homebush
            Sandy Creek
Winton   Clermont

Boulia   Aramac   Rockhampton   *Tropic of Capricorn*

Longreach   Mount   Gladstone
Barcaldine Alpha   Morgan
            Emerald Calliope
                            Cania Gorge   Hervey
                            Monto   Bay
                                    Maryborough

Charleville Mitchell   Roma   Gympie
                              Kingaroy   Kilcoy
Quilpie   Corranga   Bracalba
                     Mulga Belt Jimbour   Caboolture
                              Dalby   Ipswich
                         Toowoomba   Dunwich
Thargomindah Eulo   St George Pittsworth Brisbane
                              Drayton   Gold
                              Clifton   Coast
                              Warwick Laidley
                                    Stanthorpe

Maps of Queensland and New South Wales showing most locations mentioned within the stories

xi

Chapter Chart

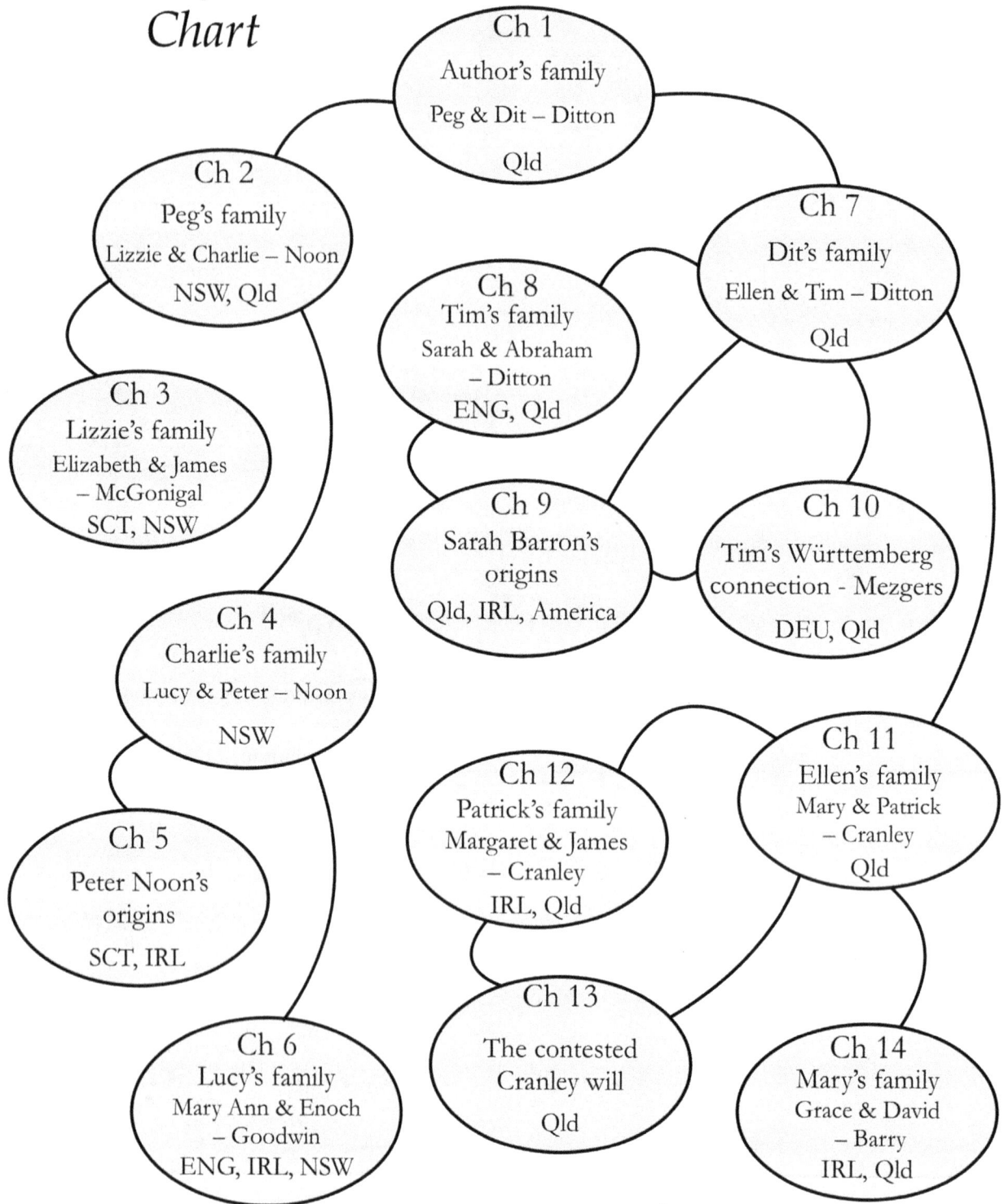

Ch 1
Author's family
Peg & Dit – Ditton
Qld

Ch 2
Peg's family
Lizzie & Charlie – Noon
NSW, Qld

Ch 7
Dit's family
Ellen & Tim – Ditton
Qld

Ch 8
Tim's family
Sarah & Abraham
– Ditton
ENG, Qld

Ch 3
Lizzie's family
Elizabeth & James
– McGonigal
SCT, NSW

Ch 9
Sarah Barron's
origins
Qld, IRL, America

Ch 10
Tim's Württemberg
connection - Mezgers
DEU, Qld

Ch 4
Charlie's family
Lucy & Peter – Noon
NSW

Ch 11
Ellen's family
Mary & Patrick
– Cranley
Qld

Ch 12
Patrick's family
Margaret & James
– Cranley
IRL, Qld

Ch 5
Peter Noon's
origins
SCT, IRL

Ch 13
The contested
Cranley will
Qld

Ch 14
Mary's family
Grace & David
– Barry
IRL, Qld

Ch 6
Lucy's family
Mary Ann & Enoch
– Goodwin
ENG, IRL, NSW

This chart depicts how the chapters relate to each other. A pedigree chart is provided at the end of the book

Chapter 1

A post-war marriage

Peg and Dit – Ditton

The Second World War (WWII) interrupted everyone's lives to varying degrees.[1] When it was all over, there was enormous relief and lingering grief. It took some time before normality was restored and when it was, it was different to what had been before. Lives had been put on hold and with peace came the space to think about the future. The pregnant pause of the war had given birth to the baby boom. In Australia, the birth rate almost doubled from what it had been in the depression and war years.[2] This chapter is about the post-war family of my childhood. My parents are Peg Noon and Arthur (Dit) Ditton.

Before the marriage – Arthur

Arthur Cranley Ditton (Dit) was the second child born to Ellen Cranley and Tim Ditton. He was born at home in Paxton Street, Townsville, Queensland (Qld) in December 1916.[3] Tim was a federal public servant and Ellen was a stay-at-home mother. In 1917, the family was transferred to Maryborough and from there to Brisbane in the early 1920s. Young Arthur attended St James Catholic Primary in Spring Hill and in 1929 was sent to St Joseph's College, on Gregory Terrace or 'Terrace', as it was known for his secondary education. Arthur made a good impression with his all-round cricket prowess and was made twelfth man of the First Eleven when he was still in Junior.[4]

Arthur was gifted academically, but he clashed with some of his teachers. Most significantly, a Christian brother falsely accused him of cheating in an oral Latin exam. He was able to provide the answer sought, but the unbelieving teacher felt the need to search his book for the notes that Arthur must have secreted. Even with no notes found, no apology was offered and the accusation still stood. He was strong willed and the sense of injustice that could not be righted caused him to cease all association with the school. He did not return to any school after that. Unfortunately, what awaited Arthur in the outside world were the early days of the Great Depression.[5] It soon became apparent that the lessons to be learnt outside school were significantly more useful than fluently demonstrating the love of tables in a dead language.

Bewilderingly, I also was taught Latin for three years. By tradition, the first verb learnt in Latin was *amo* (English: to love) and the first noun learnt was *mensa* (English: table). Endless lessons were devoted to the multiple variations of verbs across their multiple conjugations.[6] Then there were the multiple declensions of nouns across six or seven cases.[7] To succeed at Latin, you needed to lovingly commit tables of word endings to memory. This was where an academic ideal collided with lumpen adolescence. Latin seemed to bring out the worst in

Arthur, bottom left as an altar boy circa 1926

Arthur, on a night out in Brisbane mid 1940s

teachers. I witnessed these frustrated pedagogues resorting to scruff grabbing and physical manhandling of students in a vain attempt to impart the lessons more effectively. For a student this was a kind of torture, neatly summed up by the scene from Monty Python's *Life of Brian*, where the centurion puts the point of his sword under Brian's chin and forces him to review his grammatically incorrect Latin graffiti.[8]

Tim had given his children some extra tuition at home. From an early age, Arthur and his younger brother, Paul, were given newspapers and told to read out aloud selected articles. Tim's idea was this would improve their reading and diction, which would place them ahead of the pack in the competitive world awaiting them. I suspected Tim also did the same with arithmetic, as I remember my father giving me quick mental sums to complete when I was just starting school.

Tim had arranged a job for Arthur at a bank, but he declined that in favour of finding his own way in the world. Many struggled to find work at this time, but Arthur seemed to have a knack for staying employed. He tried his hand at many things. He was a jackeroo on a property owned by the Tullys near Quilpie and Eulo, west of Charleville.[9] He worked on a farm on the Darling Downs. At one point he had a job drying bones. Later he gravitated to wool classing and worked for the Brisbane office of the Australia-wide firm, Wilcox Mofflin & Co (WMC).[10] Whilst working at WMC, he kept up his interest in cricket and was selected to participate in the Qld Practice Squad. This was the squad of about forty players the Qld Sheffield Shield team was selected from.[11] The consensus was Arthur would have made the state side had it not been for WWII – certainly his early form showed lots of promise.[12]

Early in the war, before the fall of Singapore, Arthur expressed his opinion at a party, saying, the Japanese were the ones Australia had to worry about.[13] His mate, Paddy Bowes, almost threw him out for suggesting that, as Paddy subscribed to the common opinion that no Asian country was any real threat to British people and Singapore was considered an impenetrable fortress.[14] The rapid Japanese advance in South-East Asia alarmed the Curtin Government and eligible able-bodied men were being called up into the armed forces. Arthur was called up in early 1942. He was billeted at the Roma Street railway yards where there were many tents pitched.[15] He spent five months in the army before his uncle and co-worker, Tom Waters, applied to have him withdrawn under the Manpower Regulations.

Manpower was a scheme which exempted workers in reserved occupations from being conscripted or prevented them from volunteering for armed service. These jobs were essential for the war effort or the strategic economy. Since Australia had been riding on the sheep's back, jobs in the wool industry were just such jobs. The difficulties were, under the published guidelines, Arthur was not old enough to be considered an automatically exempted wool classer, as the exemption age was set at 'over 30' and he was 25.[16] Another work category was wool appraiser, where the exemption age was '25 and over'. Particularly valued employees of a business could be protected via the catch-all category of 'Leading Hands', as they were exempted at any age.[17]

There was some commentary in government correspondence about how inconsistently exemptions were being applied. So, Arthur's exemption was not straightforward. It was a result of lobbying by his uncle, Tom Waters, on behalf of WMC who employed them both.[18] If Arthur had completed six months of military training, then he would have some entitlements regarding his service. Since that milestone had not been reached, he was allowed the exemption and his service record was extinguished.[19] It is believed his unit would have been part of the 7th Australian Infantry Brigade, which comprised battalions raised from Brisbane and surrounds.[20]

Arthur, Tim and Paul circa 1938

Conscripted men typically went into militia battalions, but they could opt to join regular army battalions.[21] In the end, even the militia battalions were shipped to Milne Bay in New Guinea in July 1942, where they saw heavy action with significant casualties. Prior to the militia's deployment to New Guinea, there were many derogatory labels applied to the militia. The most famous was 'chockos', short for chocolate soldiers who were expected to melt when any heat was applied. Another worth retelling was 'koalas', which reflected their

L to R: Tom, Joe, Jack, Grace & Maureen Waters circa 1924

perceived protected species status. A label that I can remember my father using, which gave a distinct flavour of the time, was 'cut-lunch commandos'. It referred to military personnel with desk jobs and reservists. Arthur had left the army just prior to the New Guinea deployment and remained conflicted about the situation, as he had been prepared to fight, and he was not the one who sought his own exemption from military service.

During the war, the Manpower provisions also stopped people from leaving or changing jobs if they were in reserved occupations. These workers had to work long hours. They did not wear special uniforms or insignia. Similar to the WWI experience, some of these workers were anonymously sent white feathers, to shame them out of their perceived cowardice.[22] Modern-day trolling is not as new as

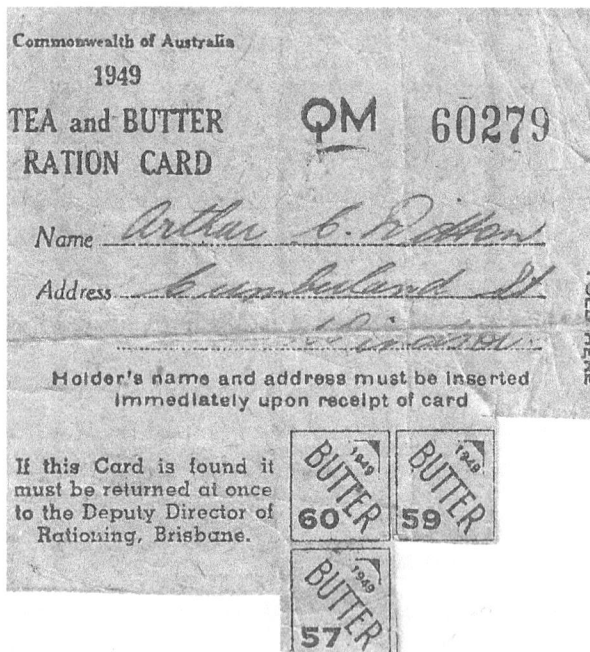

Arthur's ration card from 1949

some lament; the ignorant souls who sent these feathers demonstrate a clear antecedent. Arthur had just Saturday afternoon and Monday night off. On Saturday afternoon, he worked at the racetrack as a bookie's penciller for his sister Ursula's father-in-law, Ernest P. Freney. That is a job which requires good fast mental arithmetic. One evening in July

1942, he got home late, as usual, to find a note on his pillow about his brother, simply saying, 'Paul was married today'.[23] By the end of the war, Arthur was sick with bronchitis, as the long hours and the dusty workplace had taken their toll.

Both his father, Tim and his uncle, Tom Waters died in 1944. After the war, Arthur was looking for a change, so he left WMC and teamed up with a friend and for a year, took contracts building stockyards around Normantown and Georgetown in the Gulf of Carpentaria. One of his workplaces was Lyndhurst Station. The venture lost money and his health was still not the best. He got his job back at WMC and between March to October 1947, he was posted out to Mitchell in south-western Qld. Some of his duties were to buy animal hides from local businesses. It required a good knowledge of product quality and the likely market conditions at the time of supply. For the next few years, he was based out of Toowoomba, travelling all over the Darling Downs and further west, trading in skins and livestock. When staying in Mitchell, he took a room at the Hotel Mitchell and in Toowoomba he lived at the Crown Hotel. Life was austere at the end of the 1940s as the aftermath of the war was still being felt. Basic foods and commodities were still being rationed, with coupons needed to buy controlled items.

There was a sizeable Aboriginal population in Mitchell, and it would be fair to say, at best, they were treated like second-class citizens. It could be argued the government did not consider them to be citizens at all. It was not until the 1967 referendum that Aboriginal people were counted as inhabitants and the federal government could legislate for their benefit as opposed to their control.[24] Prior to that, their status was not equivalent to fauna as is sometime popularly stated, but arguably much worse.[25] Aboriginal people were subject to highly restrictive state laws which controlled many aspects of their lives. Restrictions which these days, no person of any background would, could or should tolerate being imposed by government.[26]

An Aboriginal man saw Arthur in the Hotel Mitchell bar and realising he was new in town, asked if Arthur could shout him a beer. Not wanting to offend, Arthur obliged. The white men in the bar scolded him. From then on, he avoided a repeat of this situation whilst in Mitchell. Arthur was sympathetic to the plight of Aboriginal people, but race relations in Mitchell were typical of country towns across Australia with a deeply racist attitude entrenched as the default. Arthur was not strident about Aboriginal disadvantage, but I can recall he occasionally related an anecdote or even told a joke where the clear message was, they were getting a rotten deal.[27] Despite Arthur's issues with the school that he had attended, he had retained his Catholic faith and he took it seriously. Catholic teaching put a high value on fairness. Catholic practice, however, often fell short of those lofty heights.

Within a week of arriving in Mitchell, Arthur had met a local his own age, Jim Noon. They got to talking about cricket and Jim asked him if he would like to umpire a game in Mitchell on the coming weekend. Arthur agreed, and it was there that Peg Noon, Jim's sister, saw him for the first time. As she and four other young women arrived at the cricket oval in a car, she and the others all asked in unison: 'Who's that?' Mitchell was a small town and the arrival of a stranger was cause for comment. Peg liked what she saw and so did Arthur. A romance developed, with Arthur doing most of the chasing.

Before the marriage – Peg

Elizabeth Peggy (Peg) Noon was born in June 1928 to Lizzie and Charlie Noon. She was the fourth child and first daughter of the family. Her much older brothers, Peter, Jim and Bert, made a bit of a fuss of her, as did her father. Her mother, the disciplinarian, was less forgiving of her antics. Her parents had moved to their sheep property, *Mulga Belt*, in 1922. Peg spent her first few years on the property with her family. Her older brothers were away at boarding school or out working a good deal of the time. She saw more of Jim and Bert than she

saw of Peter. There were few children of her own age in the district. She had a next-door neighbour, Aldyth (Bub) Timmins, who was just one year older than her, and they became best friends. It must be said that next door, named *Newikie*, was several kilometres away. A trip to the Wollongong district in New South Wales (NSW) to visit her grandparents resulted in the following newspaper article which stretched some of the facts:

An interested visitor to the Corrimal School yesterday was little Peggy Noon, of Mitchell River, Nth. Queensland, who before she came to Corrimal last week on a holiday to her grandparents, Mr. and Mrs. McGonigal, had never before seen more than two or three children together, and had never heard a concert in her life. Consequently, a class of children was a novel sight for her, and she was delighted with the singing lessons. She said she had only read of such things before. She lives on a lonely station on the Mitchell River, and had to travel many miles to reach railhead at Mitchell township. She is being taught by a governess. Her mother and brothers are accompanying her.[28]

The journalist had confused, the town of Mitchell in Southern Qld with the Mitchell River on Cape York in Far North Qld. The property was remote, but not that remote. The arrangement with the governess was never a success because as Peg tells the story 'either she was in tears or I was'. Her mother declared, 'The girl needs an education'. Without any further discussion, in 1937, aged eight, she was sent to board at the convent in Mitchell. It was the closest option to home which catered for girls. Peg has a lifelong memory of her first day. After wondering why she had arrived at this place, she was confronted by a row of metal washbasins and lockers on opposite walls. It was a spartan environment with few creature comforts. In the first few years she was the only Protestant, and in those days, there was a genuine divide between the Catholics and the Protestants. Peg did not feel particularly welcome. Not that she had any strong grounding in religion – she rarely saw a church outside her schooling days. Her father was not particularly religious, and her mother's religious observance was not a priority, whilst living in the bush. As time went by, she did make friends at

Peg aged approximately ten circa 1938

Peg aged 21, 1949

school, one of whom was Marg Caskey, who would go on to become her sister-in-law.

After seven years, she completed scholarship and then was sent to Glennie Anglican Girls College (Glennie) in Toowoomba for two years.[29] She remembered Glennie with much more affection and formed some deep friendships. These years were the last two years of WWII. There was a military hospital next door to the school with lots of recuperating young men.[30] The Glennie girls were prevented from going within ten yards of the boundary fence on pain of immediate expulsion. This rule was relaxed for VE Day when the girls went dancing in a conga line through the wards.[31] On VJ Day, the Toowoomba Grammar boys gathered outside Glennie at two am and celebrated with loud cries of 'The war is over'.[32] The girls all got up and went to the chapel to pray in thanks for the welcome news.

An anecdote, which Peg often repeated about Glennie was the time when she was seated at dinner with ten other students and the headmistress who had rotated to their table. Miss Gwen Dowson had studied at the University of Brussels and she had an accent which suggested a fine upbringing.[33] A fly had settled on the jam, and Miss Dowson asked one of the girls to take the jam back to the kitchen. A student from Thargomindah, said 'Oh don't worry about that Miss; out home, we just pick them off'. To which, Miss Dowson raised her little finger to just below her eye and with a startled expression replied, 'How extraordinary!' Her response had etched itself into Peg's memory so much so, it could still be recalled in her nineties. Miss Dowson was one of Peg's favourite staff members and she appreciated the gesture when Peg's brother, Jim, came up to visit her before he was redeployed to New Guinea in late 1944. Miss Dowson said to Peg, 'This is important. You must spend some time with your brother' and offered her private rooms so Peg and Jim could spend some quiet time together.

An incident which had a deep impact on Peg was when one of her classmates expressed concern for her younger brother who was boarding at Toowoomba boys' prep. Polio cases were reported at that school. Shortly after expressing her concern, the girl herself was taken ill and late that evening taken down to Brisbane. The news reached Glennie the next day that the girl had died. There were further outbreaks of this cruel disease in Australia in the early 1960s. The Sabin oral vaccine was first used in Australia in 1966. The disease is now effectively eliminated in the developed world and the Western Pacific region.[34]

After completing Junior, Peg went home to help out with bookkeeping and household duties with some occasional outside work. With her parents' encouragement she bought and sold cattle and made a tidy profit. Some went towards buying a piano, as she was fond of playing classical music. Mitchell was the main town they went to for commercial and social activity. And that is how eighteen-year-old Peg Noon got to meet the thirty-year-old Arthur Ditton at that fateful cricket game. She did not like the name 'Arthur', as she thought it sounded a bit too stiff and formal, so she christened him 'Dit'. Subsequently, that was her preferred name when talking to him or about him. Peg appreciated that Dit also liked classical music, and his reading choices reflected a more cultured mind than what had been previously on offer. She also thought he had a fine voice, which meant Tim's strategy with the newspaper reading was paying dividends in other fields.[35] At the Mitchell Show Ball, Peg had her first in-depth chat with Dit and without knowing his background fully, she made the statement 'Well, one thing I know for sure is that I will never marry a Catholic'.

The courtship and the wedding

Dit stayed in Mitchell until October 1947 and that allowed for some relatively easy social contact with Peg. Her peers were counselling her with statements like, 'He is too old for you, Peg'. However, she told them she spent most of her time with her older brothers and boys her own age seemed like twits. A young man in the district fancied himself as Peg's suitor and she would have none of it. It didn't hurt that her brother Jim, who was the same age as Dit, had taken a fancy to her friend Marg Caskey, who was eighteen months younger than Peg.

Dit returned to work in Toowoomba and journeyed to all points west, as part of his job. Peg and Dit wrote letters to each other and Dit made long-distance phone calls to Peg. This was an expensive luxury and required a bit of organisation. *Mulga Belt* was on a shared party line serviced out of the switchboard at *Cedarvale*.[36] Dit booked a regular evening call at the same time each Wednesday and Saturday. Sometimes Peg would give instructions to the switchboard operator that she would be on a neighbouring property and to put the call

Left: Dit and Peg at Windsor c 1949 Centre: 17 April 1950, St Columba's Mitchell Right: about to honeymoon

through to there. Peg and Dit sometimes holidayed together in Brisbane, staying at his mother's place. The couple needed to be chaperoned, to maintain decorum. Any suggestion of intimacy between an unmarried couple would be a scandal in Australian society in the late 1940s. Even the status of fiancée provided no dispensation.

Dit and Peg announced their engagement at Peg's 21st in 1949, and they set a wedding date for the following year. There had not been a proposal as such – just an understanding. The impending 21st birthday party was the catalyst for Peg to ask Dit whether they should announce their intentions on that occasion. *Mulga Belt* was the venue and many in the district attended.[37]

Father Robert Flynn performed the marriage ceremony at St Columba's Catholic Church in Mitchell in April 1950. Peg decided to convert to Catholicism.[38] As Mitchell was a small close-knit community, Peg said they faced the dilemma of inviting no one to the reception or inviting everybody. They invited everybody. Luckily, this was corresponding with the start of the wool boom, so the added expense was easily managed. Peg's bridesmaids were Daphne Cornish from *Walangra* and Marg Caskey from *Avalon*. Dit's best man was Peg's brother Jim, and Tim Manns from *Tartulla* was his groomsman. Dit's mother Ellen, his Aunt Tottie, his sister Mary and his niece made it out to the wedding. His younger brother, Paul, was getting married for the second time that same day in Brisbane. Peg and Dit only became aware of Paul's wedding with their own date looming.[39] Peg and Dit had their honeymoon at Southport, on the Gold Coast. They tripped out to the hinterland at Springbrook and then they settled into married life in Toowoomba for their first year. Their first house together was in Braemar Street. This street is about fifty metres away from a block which Dit's maternal great-grandfather, James Cranley, purchased and farmed in Toowoomba's earliest days.[40]

In 1951, the wool boom was in full swing and Peg's father, Charlie, asked if she and Dit would like to manage *Mulga Belt*. Her brothers had all married, and the family had acquired more properties which her brothers were working and living on. Charlie and Lizzie were looking to wind back a little and the wool boom was providing plenty of work for everyone. In May 1951, they moved back to *Mulga Belt* and lived in a second house about a hundred metres west of Peg's parents' house.[41] Dit's experience as a jackeroo and his earlier job as a wool classer would see him a useful addition to the workforce. One of the Aboriginal workers

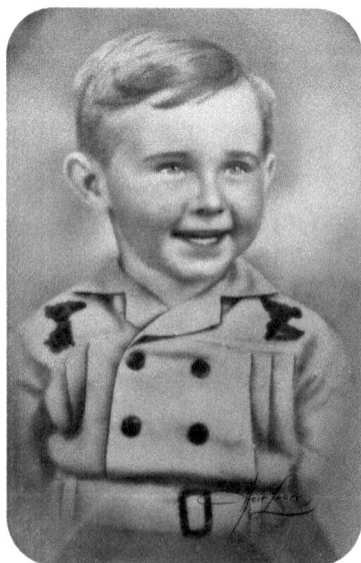

Ralph circa 1954

Peg and Dit with baby Ralph 1951

Beth circa 1954

on *Mulga Belt* remarked on how well Dit sat in a saddle.[42] Dit got on well with Charlie and they both liked and respected each other.

Just a few months after returning, in early August 1951, Peg went to the hospital in Mitchell to give birth to her first child, Ralph.[43] Unfortunately, Dit had fallen ill to appendicitis. He was brought into town on a Friday with severe stomach pain and taken to hospital where there was only a locum available. He was operated on with the nursing matron, Marg Frawley, present. It was later intimated to Peg, Marg completed the operation, as the locum was too green. Ralph was born on the following Tuesday. Dit's appendix had burst and peritonitis had set in. Peritonitis was responsible for the death of Dit's uncle, Tom Waters, in 1944, so Dit would have known what he was facing. Dit was ill in hospital at the same time that Peg and newborn Ralph were also in there. Antibiotics were relatively new, and the government strictly controlled their use. A police sergeant had to sign documents to allow them to be used for Dit. He steadily recovered and it was doubtful he would have survived without the antibiotics.

A second child, Beth, was born in 1953 and a third, Clem (author), was born in 1955. Peg found looking after three small children hard work. As she liked to say in later years, 'I loved them more each year that they got older'. Ralph was the hardest work, as he was into mischief the moment he was mobile. He will never be allowed to forget the day his new shoes went missing and were only found when the dam level dropped in the dry weather.

Peg started to suffer some health problems around 1953, which was diagnosed as a thyroid problem. The lack of iodine in the bush diet was a likely contributing factor. She was developing a goitre, which is a problem she had shared with her grandmother, Lucy Goodwin and some of her cousins in NSW. She had her thyroid removed in Brisbane around 1954. Following the operation, Peg had to take one pill a day to compensate.

Dit was a participant in a Qld Department of Agriculture program to plant buffel grass in the district. It was planted on several family properties. A hardy, drought-resistant perennial from Africa, it was superior to native grasses as a stock feed, particularly during droughts, and responded well to light rain. The program was so successful, there are now calls of alarm that 'this invader is now a threat to biodiversity'.[44] In Central Australia, it is considered a disaster of cane toad proportions, and it needs to be managed by frequent burning as it threatens to overwhelm the native vegetation, such as the incredibly hardy spinifex.

Sheep dipping involved running the sheep through a trough of chemical solution. The chemicals were toxic to parasites such as lice, but also were not entirely safe for humans and animals. One of the chemicals used was arsenic. Dit associated the red rash on his ears with the times he pushed sheep through the dip. Several issues started to mount for Dit with his work at *Mulga Belt*. Charlie's health was failing and there was the issue of what to do about the children's education. He received an enticing job offer from his old workplace at WMC. He was offered around £10 a week, which was good money in those days.

Dit with in-laws: Bert, Lizzie, Jim and Charlie

The year in Brisbane

In early 1956, the family left *Mulga Belt* and moved to Alderley, a suburb in north-west Brisbane. The next-door neighbours, the Lovelocks, were welcoming and provided some respite for Peg with the little ones. They memorably had guinea pigs, which were an attraction for the young children. Ralph attended school locally. A neighbour across the road was in the same class and made the mistake of not inviting Ralph to her birthday party. Ralph camped on their front fence eyeballing the comings and goings during the party, until an embarrassed Peg retrieved him.

Peg's share of the family company and its land holdings was sold off to the rest of her family in a complex transaction. Dit felt the WMC work was not what he was really looking for and thought another change would be necessary.[45] He applied for a state public service job after seeing an advertisement in the paper. The job was with the Queensland Agricultural Bank (Ag Bank).[46] He was successful in February 1957. The position, titled as 'Inspector', involved providing loans to farmers and graziers at favourable rates and with tailored conditions. He obtained a Valuer's Certificate and became a Justice of the Peace. His first posting was to Monto in Central Qld.

Monto

In Monto, the family first lived in a housing commission home, which Peg hated. One of the next-door neighbours had a backyard strewn with chook feathers. He would get drunk on the weekend and the kids would run around the yard with no pants on, much to Peg's disgust. After a few months, Dit and Peg purchased a house at 35 Bell Street across the road from the water tower, which was much more to Peg's taste.[47] The next-door neighbour to this house was Gerry O'Conner, the editor of the local newspaper, the *Monto Herald*. So, the neighbourhood met with Peg's approval. The sale was handled by the local solicitor, Henry

Bandidt.[48] The locals used to jokingly say: 'Bandidt by name and bandit by nature'. Later another solicitor, Andrew Biggar, bought into the practice and it became *Biggar Bandidt*, which amused the townsfolk even more.

The yard had a large garden trellis made of lattice, which ran from the tank stand near the house past the outhouse on the left and past a large wooden cubby house on the right, onwards to the garage at the eastern end of the block. The house had no hot water outside the kitchen, which was typical for houses then, so water for a bath was heated with a portable electric element in a metal bucket. The house had no town sewerage or septic system. All the wastewater from the kitchen went into two halves of a 44-gallon drum cut lengthways stationed outside the sleepout and kitchen. Each Saturday, Ralph was given the job of emptying out the two containers onto the lawn and trees. The outhouse had a pan which was collected as 'night soil' once a week.

Peg obtained her driver's licence whilst at Monto, which opened up some possibilities. The whole family piled into the car to drive the short distance down to the police station. As children could be left unsupervised in a car without guilt in those days, Peg and Dit went inside and came out a few minutes later with Peg's driver's licence. All she had to do was to answer a question about the meaning of colours on traffic lights. The closest traffic light was hundreds of kilometres away in Brisbane. The sergeant had seen Dit instructing Peg whilst she drove around town. That was good enough for him. The family bought a Holden hydramatic sedan, which was easier for Peg to drive than the manual Ford Zephyr, which they had previously. Dit also had a Holden for work, but there were strict limitations on any family use. A family car meant the family could go on Sunday drives to places like Cania Gorge. Annual holidays meant a drive along the inland route to Brisbane.[49] That involved quite a few dirt roads. Seat belts, child seats and restraints were all things for a future day.

In these days before electronic gadgets, the whole family would participate in games such as *I spy*, to relieve the tedium of the trip.

Beth started school in Monto in 1959, and I started in 1961. All three children attended St Therese's Catholic Primary School, which was less than a kilometre from home. The kids walked that distance together or alone both ways. As paper was a relative luxury, pupils used slates in class to provide answers to tests or questions asked by the teachers. The school shared its grounds with the St Therese's church. One day Peg was volunteering at the church and had the young Ralph in tow. Ralph saw this as his opportunity to act out his youthful impression of a priest. He ascended the pulpit and announced to the small congregation of volunteers: 'I want your money'.

I have a memory of my parents attending an evening function at the town hall, which was only a few blocks away. No babysitter was needed in this small country town. The five-year-old me woke up and missed my parents, so I wandered off in my pyjamas to find them. I was relieved when I found them, but they were not as happy, as that meant an end to their evening.

Dit kept a few cans of beer in the fridge and the rest of the carton in the garage. One day Ralph and Beth decided to try a warm can for themselves. They went across the road to a vacant block near the water tower and hid in the long grass. They offered to give me a taste if I would get a can-opener from the kitchen.[50] When Peg asked why I needed a can-opener, I could not tell a lie. Peg sent all three children to the bathroom. The next few hours were spent awaiting Dit's return from work and anticipating what would be his idea of a suitable punishment. After stifling a few chortles and allowing the stay to continue a little longer, Dit had Peg let the children out and nothing more was said. Never again did the children sample any beer, without parental oversight.[51]

The drink which all the family was meant to enjoy was homemade ginger beer. A batch would be made at home with a ginger beer bug which had been kept active by regularly feeding it ginger and sugar. The batch would be poured into cleaned out beer 'tallies' and closed with a Crown seal. They would be placed somewhere cool for the chemistry to work its magic. Under the tank stand was a traditional place, but the temperature variation plus

Beth and Ralph with swans, Monto, circa 1960

Clem in grade 1, Monto, 1961

a little too much sugar would typically result in a few exploding bottles over the maturation period.

Occasionally cats would visit the family and, on several occasions, liked the attention they received so much they decided to adopt the family. Dit was not so fond of cats. Dogs were out of the question too, it seemed. So, the standard solution to an unwanted cat was to take it out to a remote bit of bushland like the Cania Gorge, put some butter on its feet to provide a distraction and drive home minus the cat. One cat was a bit more resourceful than expected. After a few weeks, it managed to navigate the thirty-plus kilometres back to Bell Street and camped out on the tank stand, to everyone's surprise.

One day a cat with a bit more class than the rest of them, a female Persian, arrived. The family took a shine to her and named her Farrah. She was happy with her new home, but when it was time to leave Monto, Dit went through with the routine of a one-way trip to Cania Gorge. As a sign we cared for this one a bit more, Dit left it a cooked lamb chop, as well as the butter on its feet. Today's feral cat problem would have had some of its origins in such practices.

Innisfail

In January 1962, Dit was transferred to Innisfail, in Far North Qld. The family arrived on *The Sunlander*, an air-conditioned passenger train service. As the family stepped out into the monsoonal January air, they wondered how they would function in this omnipresent sauna. The first week or so was spent in a hotel in the town centre. One evening in that first week, the family looked out into the street to see a large dead saltwater crocodile on a trailer.[52] That was the only salty seen in all the time we were in Innisfail. The much-less-dangerous freshwater Johnstone River crocodile was seen occasionally.

The family lived in four houses whilst there, all in East Innisfail. The first, in Bourke Street, was home for only a few weeks as Peg detested it.

There were Mickey and Minnie Mouse portraits painted on the walls, which was rather lowbrow in Peg's assessment.[53] The land was flat, waterlogged and close to bushland. It was cane toad heaven. In the January humidity, mosquitoes and other insects invaded the home. The house was on stilts, but the moisture still reached into the house. The children memorably turned over a rug on the lounge-room floor, which had a strange feel to it, only to discover the underside swarming with beetles. The next house was more comfortable. It was an interesting Art Deco home on the corner of Cargill and Hickey streets and the house which the last child, Anne, was brought home to from hospital in 1963.

Innisfail has a famously wet, wet season. Only the nearby town of Tully surpasses it. In the dry season, the empty paddock east of Cargill Street would catch alight and the fire brigade would come to put it out. The burnt-out block would show the remains of bandicoot nests. One day Ralph asked me to lift a sheet of corrugated roofing which was sitting on a vacant block on the western side of the house. With some suspicion, I flipped the tin over and saw a black snake quickly sliding away. A juvenile taipan, he later informed me.[54] Any of Ralph's subsequent suggestions were assessed with that experience in mind.

Childhood activities remembered from Innisfail include go-carting down an unsealed and heavily eroded Church Street. The poorly built go-carts would carry multiple passengers and they would invariably crash after hitting a washout. Several small bodies would be thrown out of the tea chest or crate cabins. After each crash there would be running repairs and then the process would be repeated until the multiple gravel rashes became too much. Leaky homemade canoes with corrugated-iron hulls were used with some success in watery paddocks, but with much less success in the river.[55]

After the lease ran out at Hickey Street, the family moved to a house on Mourilyan Road. It was a bit of a come down in terms of comfort. A few

Hickey Street house, Innisfail circa 1963

Anne, Innsifail 1964

months later, the house which the Ag Bank owned in Innisfail became vacant, as the senior officer, George Gould, had been transferred south. The family moved to 57 Ryan Street, on top of a hill with views to Mount Bartle Frere, Qld's highest mountain.[56] The house was a large airy Queenslander with plenty of space inside and outside in the yard. There were trees to climb and space for chooks and endless games. Fences between properties were the exception rather than the rule. The neighbourhood was filled with children of the baby boom, and everyone's front yards and backyards, as well as the nearby rain forest, became one big playground. There were frequent unsupervised barefooted excursions into the bush. We armed ourselves with cane knives. What could possibly go wrong? How the children escaped the snakes, cassowaries and other multiple hazards of the bush remains a mystery. Green tree ants were the only creatures to have gotten the upper hand of an encounter.[57] Mosquitoes were of course the other main pest which followed us into our home and tried to feast on us at night. Mosquito nets were essential for a peaceful night's sleep. Air-conditioning and insect screens were not yet available options, but we did get through a lot of mosquito coils. One day, some children found some thick roots in the bush which they believed to be yams. They cooked them up and offered them around. All who ate them had reason to regret their decision and their misplaced

faith in their mate's bush tucker knowledge. Luckily, recovery from the unknown poison only took a day or two.

The children attended the Catholic schools in Innisfail. They rode their bicycles the two kilometres to and from school. I had an old black second-hand fixed wheeler which was muscle and character building. The Sacred Heart Convent was co-ed until grade three and then girls only after that. The older boys went across the road to the Marist Brothers Good Counsel College. The Dittons could not help noticing people who lived all their lives in the North had some speech patterns which were not remembered from the South. The most noticeable traits were the slower pace of talking and the 'ay' which trailed each sentence. The 'but' sentence ending seemed to turn up later, as it was not noticed during our time there.

There were also a lot of children of Mediterranean heritage. When the South Sea Islanders stopped being 'recruited' for work in the cane fields, folk from the Mediterranean filled the gap. The Innisfail district was a favoured destination for the post-war waves of Mediterranean migrants as well. A large community had been built up. In the Catholic schools particularly, more than sixty percent of the children had surnames which indicated Mediterranean origins – Italian being the most common. Some Chinese families also stayed on in the North after the goldrush days.

Clem's class at Good Counsel College, Innisfail circa 1964. Clem is centre of the image

The customs and foods of Far North Qld were much more diverse than southern parts of Qld at this time, which helped everyone's education and palate. Baby Anne had her second name tweaked from Mary to Maria, to honour the Mediterranean population of Innisfail.[58] Ralph studied Italian at school and shared some of his lessons with his siblings. Counting to ten in Italian was a lesson I retained long enough to use on visits to Italy many decades later.

Two doors down Carmel Street was the Hogan family. The Dittons were often at the Hogan's as they had children which matched each of the Ditton's ages and genders. There would be endless games, indoor and out. Beth and Cheryl would stage plays and concerts, drafting the rest of us into their production. We would all listen to an old wind-up gramophone, which played 78 rpm wartime favourites, like *Johnny got a Zero* or some Andrews Sisters' songs. Peg would summons her brood to dinner by standing at the top of her back stairs and ringing a brass bell that could be heard at the Hogan's. Anne was still too young to wander free range through the neighbourhood, but her older siblings made a fuss of her when they got home. To keep Anne from wandering too far, Dit had erected a Masonite barrier at the front and back doors.[59] It could be slid out of the way or stepped over. One day, a recently arrived English kid came to the front door. He had a grievance with Ralph over some incident. The gist of what he was saying was, he was going to get his father to come and speak to our father about the matter. Unfortunately, the phrase he used for his father was 'my old man'. To which Ralph tunefully replied, 'My old man's a dustman'.[60] That's when the trouble started. If it wasn't for the Masonite barrier, there would have been blood.

Dit would give us a real treat on most Saturday afternoons by dropping all three older children at the movies with the necessary funds and then pick us up after the show had finished. This was a win-win situation, as the older children were up to date with popular culture and Dit got to spend some quality time with Peg on the weekend, which helped to explain the arrival of Anne, the welcome afterthought.

Dit took some memorable home movies whilst in Innisfail.[61] That was his most prolific period. It was at Ryan Street in late 1964 that the Dittons got their first TV. It was rented for the Christmas school holidays. The family had hired TVs on annual holidays at the Gold Coast and Brisbane. The nearest TV station was 250 kilometres away in Townsville with mountains and a turbulent atmosphere in between. The signal was weak, and the images competed with the 'snow'. I often wondered if the transmission of my favourite show, *My Favorite Martian*, was coming from Mars. In the summer, Dit would arrive home from work and immediately switch the TV to the cricket and who would argue with that?

Ralph related an incident from 1965 when aged fourteen, he visited the dentist and the dentist suggested a matching set of gold fillings. Ralph agreed and returned home with a flash solution to his childhood caries and a bill for £80 (more than $2200 in today's money). The normally calm and collected Dit hit the roof. After some discussion, the bill was paid. My current excellent dentist assures me, such a thing could not happen today.

Dit's health was not good. Innisfail's warm and humid climate took a toll. He lost his sense of taste and smell in the later years at Innisfail. Part of his work involved approving loans for new tropical agricultural ventures as far afield as the Atherton Tableland. He fostered the growing of tobacco, tea and pecan nuts. Sugar cane and bananas were the main stay of the agriculture in the region. His work involved a lot of car travel on pretty ordinary country roads. Cars then had no air-conditioning and one car he was assigned was jet black, so although he theoretically had a desk job, he did get to sweat a lot. He once had three broken windscreens within ten days with his government car. The private car also suffered a few. This was in the days of toughened glass, not laminated. A highway in the region was christened the *Crystal Highway* because of all the piles of broken glass littering the side of the road. A chicken-wire windshield was the solution used for the private car on the long trips south from Innisfail to Brisbane. That trip typically took four days one way, with stays in motels along the way. The trip had to be completed before the start of the wet season as floodwaters could cut the road. When the family took their holidays in the south, Dit would catch up with his mother and siblings in Brisbane, and then spend some time on the Gold Coast enjoying the milder weather and a spot of surf fishing.

On the final trip south in January 1966 to take up the new posting in Toowoomba, the car was loaded on a trailer and an enterprising farmer and his tractor pulled it across a flooded creek for the extortionate fee of £2. The following month, Australia switched over to decimal currency and children were immediately robbed. In any corner-store, a sixpence would buy a dozen assorted lollies, but its replacement, the five-cent coin, would buy only ten. The memory of this outrage has always served as a reminder to me as to just how sheltered and problem free my childhood was.

Peg did most of the cooking, but one thing Dit took responsibility for was the cooking of fish. He would grill white-fleshed fish with lemon juice and butter. He was quite good at it. Dit was not a heavy drinker, but he did enjoy a beer of an evening and often a rum with a beer chaser.[62] When table wine became popular in Australia in the early 1970s, Dit experimented with the new fad. The types tried were white and quite sweet by modern standards. Dit also liked a flutter on the horses. Never any more

Dit with akubra surf fishing at Burleigh Heads circa 1964

than could be afforded and he had some modest success. He used to look for improving form.[63] He once won $300 on a double. He had a similar win from a weekly habit of buying casket tickets. His one habit which did not do him any favours was his smoking. He, like most men of that generation, would smoke about one pack a day. His brand was appropriately named – Craven A.[64]

Dit's devotion to Catholicism meant he attended Mass religiously. He had high moral standards and was a stern but loving father. Smacking was within his armoury on the rare occasions he thought it warranted, but its use disappeared when reason became more effective. He rarely swore and almost never argued with Peg. He would lead the family in the rosary in the evenings after dinner. Even the introduction of TV into the home did not disrupt the routine of the family kneeling and reciting the repetitive prayers as each bead passed through the fingers. Dit's religion also influenced his politics. His affiliation was to the Democratic Labor Party (DLP)[65], which grew out of the famous Labor Party split in the 1950s.[66] The split was prompted by the perception, communists were infiltrating the party. Catholics dominated the DLP and it was influenced by BA Santamaria's National Civic Council (NCC), which Dit paid attention to.[67] He liked to keep up with current affairs with newspapers, radio and TV. The ABC was his preferred information source, a preference which some of his children inherited.[68]

Ralph remembers attending a meeting with Dit, which was held at St Theresa's Convent in Monto. The meeting was for concerned citizens who wanted to discuss the developments in Asia as a result of the rise of Communist China. Dit was on the head table with members of the DLP and NCC. He did some of the talking and answered some questions. The fear at the time was about the march of communism and the threat that it posed to other Asian countries and then to Australia itself. Ralph was impressed his dad was so knowledgeable about the topic and that the community were taking

heed of his message to be on guard. Subsequent to that meeting, there was the Cuban missile crisis, and China's victory in its border skirmish with India, both in 1962. That was followed by developments in Vietnam, Indonesia and Malaysia which all bolstered the prediction, communism was about to drag the world into the sorts of conflicts which had been so costly in the previous decades. The US-led intervention in Vietnam then became a self-fulfilling prophecy.

On the work front, Dit contributed to some of the debates which raged within the agricultural industry. In the 1960s and 70s there was a common cry for farmers to, 'Get big or get out'. In response, Dit wrote an article for his organisation's newsletter arguing the more appropriate call would be, 'Get efficient or get out'. He had an interest in agricultural practices which helped preserve the land for future generations. One of his interests was the Keyline Plan, a land management and contouring strategy which improved soil fertility and protected against erosion.[69] He helped me out with some useful material when I participated in a debate at school. A fellow student with a conflicted pinko hue to his thinking had chosen the debating topic: 'Farmers are parasites who live off the subsidies paid for by the workers'.[70] Turns out, in Australia, they mostly weren't.[71] Europe was a different story, however.

Toowoomba

The family arrived in Toowoomba in January 1966. The first week was spent at the Globe Hotel in Ruthven Street in the city.[72] After renting at 84 Mary Street for six months, the family purchased a newly built three-bedroom brick-veneer house at 6 Cedar Street for $12,000.[73] Toowoomba's more southerly and elevated position was a more favourable climate for Dit's health. It also had better education options for the children, as they got older. Ralph and I were sent to St Joseph's Christian Brothers College and Beth was sent to St Ursula's College. Anne had not yet started school, but when she did in 1969, it was at Mater Dei Convent.

Cedar Street was a cul-de-sac, established in the 1960s. The neighbours got on very well and formed a close-knit community. Next door at number 8 was the Baptist Manse. The pastor John Knights and his family once went on vacation and asked the Dittons to look after the house whilst they were away. Dit had made a batch of ginger beer, which was poured into recycled beer bottles. He thought it would be a good idea to use the Knights' fridge to temporarily store the batch. The teetotalling Knights came home early to find their fridge full of beer bottles.

Around 1970 the *Toowoomba Chronicle* reported Dit had been awarded a silver tray, valued at $21, for winning the 'guess the weight of the bullock' competition. The Toowoomba Royal Show held the competition. Nine people had submitted the correct weight of 973 lb. Dit had his name pulled out of a hat and was declared the winner. The only trouble was, he had no memory of having entered the competition. He suspected someone had entered on his behalf. He was always wary of prospective clients offering him any produce or anything which might be construed as an influence on the decisions he had to make in his job.

Dit was talked into playing in a father and son cricket match at St Joseph's around 1969. His skills were clear, but his lack of fitness meant he needed a runner as his run total climbed. He was dismissed run out. That was the last time he ever played cricket. Dit's health was still not great, but he would never take any time off work. He was diagnosed with polycythaemia vera, a blood disorder, resulting in too many red blood cells. He was of average weight and tried to look after himself with some light exercise and, for the time, a healthy diet. He also had a sensitive stomach. As soon as he got home from work of an evening, he would take a dose of Mylanta to calm his stomach. He suffered other ailments as well; Peg remembers him leafing through a paperback, *A–Z of Diseases,* and when he got to 'syphilis', commented; 'Well, that's at least one bloody thing that I haven't got'. During the late evening of Tuesday, 19 September 1972 after a full day's work, Dit suffered a fatal heart attack. He was 55.

Ralph was now working in the CBC Bank at Parramatta in NSW. Beth was in her second year of teacher's training at Queensland University. I was in my senior year at St Mary's Christian Brother's

Left: Peg and Dit at home circa 1972 - Photo by author. Right: Ralph's 21st family dinner, Weis restaurant, August 1972 L to R: Ralph, Peg, Dit, Anne, Clem and Beth[89]

College in Toowoomba and Anne was nine years old, a student at Mater Dei primary school.

Life after Dit

Dit was a state public servant and so a modest pension was payable to Peg as his widow. Peg also had an even more modest private income from having invested her payout from *Mulga Belt*. She had been a stay-at-home mum, with only volunteer work for school or church undertaken outside the home. Her generation was the last where such an option was the default. Up until 1966, a woman had to resign from the Commonwealth Public Service once she married. Australia passed the *Sex Discrimination Act* in 1984. This was the green light for everyone to follow their dreams. It was of some note that for all of the year 2011, the Premier and Governor of Qld, the Prime Minister and Governor-General of Australia and our foreign head of state were all women.[74] Almost all of these acquired their position by competition and/or merit. The one who clearly did not has worked hard to compensate for the fact her position came via a hereditary lottery. My sister, Beth, was confident. Some called her 'bossy'. She had a good radar for injustice and would not hesitate to point it out. She continued her advocacy for rectifying all sorts of injustice into her adult life. She inherited my father's embrace of religion as demonstrated by her earning a degree in divinity, whilst raising her family and working in the parish.

In 2016, she lost her personal chemical and nuclear war against that cruel aggressor, breast cancer.[75]

In 1974, Peg and Anne left for a European vacation. This was Peg's first time outside the country. They spent some time in Scotland catching up with relatives who Peg had corresponded with for decades. After returning, Peg did some volunteer work in the library at St Joseph's College. The principal, Brother Brian Saward offered Peg the job of the school secretary. She accepted and worked in that job until 1992. She joined a professional association of school secretaries and took a brief study tour of the USA in 1982. She served several school principals and they all maintained contact with her long after she retired.

In January 1976, a severe hailstorm significantly damaged the house. Many concrete roof tiles were smashed, and water poured down walls damaging the plasterboard and carpets. Those at home at the time huddled within the hallway, as tile shards and hailstones punctured the ceiling. They feared the damage would be even more severe. Over 5500 houses in Toowoomba were damaged, including 2500 which were damaged severely.[76] The Ditton's home was one of those.

In 1998 Peg, aged seventy, was driving home from her regular classes in folk art at the University of the Third Age (U3A).[77] A car came through a give-way sign and collided with her flimsy Hyundai

Anne as an eleven-year-old in London, 1974

Beth in the early 1970s

sedan. The worst injuries resulted from the seatbelt breaking her collarbone, indicating it would have been much more serious if not for the seatbelt. In Australia, the compulsory wearing of seatbelts was phased in from 1969. The car was a write off and she bought a more substantial second-hand Subaru Liberty, which she drove until giving up her licence in 2015.

The Baptist Manse sat unoccupied for many years until it became the private home of the memorable Bev and Mark Thornton. Mark was a senior policeman and Bev was a nurse. Bev had a big generous personality and hosted a menagerie of different animals in her backyard. She and Mark joined the ranks of all the other close friends Peg had made amongst her neighbours. Bev and Mark passed away within ten days of each other in 2014, both from cancer. That had come just two years after her neighbour at number 7, 77-year-old Col Brady had a fatal fall from his roof.[78] Col used to mow Peg's lawn for a modest fee and help with other yard work. Peg was quoted in the *Toowoomba Chronicle* saying of his death: 'It has rocked us to our bootlaces'. Peg lived on at Cedar Street until December 2015, when she sold the house and moved to a retirement village in Brisbane. She had lived in Cedar Street for almost fifty years. The cul-de-sac had been a wonderful supportive small community where everyone had looked out for each other. Peg died in a Brisbane nursing home in July 2022. She was 94.

Ralph dodged the bullet of the birthday lottery which sent young men to Vietnam. At the time he was prepared to go, as he, like many, saw it as an opportunity. Few of those returning viewed it that way afterwards. His bank career saw him move around country NSW including a stint at Wee Waa. Whilst there, a flood ravaged the town and he had the job of keeping the bank secure as water ran through the whole town. He and a colleague perched up out of the water where they observed snakes swimming through the building. They used the bank's revolver to hurry them along.[79] A stint in the audit branch brought him a short posting in Leichhardt in Sydney, where he confronted an armed robber. It left a lasting impression. He was posted to Perth where he married and raised a family. The technology driven rationalisation of banking operations meant Ralph left banking to run his own small business.

In 1973, I took up a place at Queensland University studying for a science degree. This was the era of that wild and crazy Gough Whitlam Government, where tertiary education was entirely free, and they awarded me a Commonwealth Scholarship to pay for my living expenses. After graduating, I found employment in the Commonwealth Public Service in Canberra, with its overly generous working conditions. I utilised the parental leave, the leave without pay, the part-time and the flexitime to the hilt. My work and life were in perfect balance. After fourteen years, I plied my trade in the real world, but I remain grateful I was a beneficiary of that Gough-inspired insanity and muse whether we will ever see its like again. The current conventional wisdom is, rather than emulating the lunacy of the past, it is more prudent

Beth, Anne, Clem, Peg and Ralph, Brisbane 2001

19

Peg (seated) surrounded by relatives and friends at her 90th birthday party in 2018, Brisbane. Photo Sean Gobey

to sink taxpayer's money into submarines likely to be obsolete before making a splash.[80]

Anne's teaching career took her to Beaudesert and Longreach, then Brisbane and the Gold Coast. She then turned her attention to raising a family on the Gold Coast. As a sideline, she expanded on her childhood fascination with fortune-telling, which was greatly assisted by her natural talent as a storyteller. Anne's embrace of the twilight zone and Ralph and Beth's embrace of conventional religion, in contrast to my more science-inspired view, never stopped our appreciation and respect for each other. The only God I feel comfortable with is the Great Originating Detonation[81], but my belief system includes the conviction that others should choose whatever works for them. Thank God, we are not all the same.

A Catholic education in the 1960s and 70s

Despite its shortcomings, I enjoyed school and it suited me. Catechism and dogma aside, I found most aspects of the Catholic ethos to be positive, particularly the emphasis on honesty, compassion and fairness. Of course, the more anyone pursues lofty ideas, the more they expose themselves to the risks of hypocrisy, but some good things do rub off in the process. On the occasions that I meet up with old classmates, I am often struck by their positive qualities. Patrick White[82] in his autobiography, *Flaws in the Glass,* suggested that most Australian artists, himself included, bought up as Protestant would reluctantly admit that they missed out by not having a Catholic childhood. He believed that even lapsed Catholics 'luxuriated'.[83] Even with only a tenuous claim to artistry, Patrick's observation resonated with my own perceptions and they reinforced my conclusion that the religion 'baby' was of debatable value but that there was wider agreement that the bathwater around it produced wholesome stock.[84]

Despite the technicality that a Catholic school is a private school, there was nothing elitist about the education I received. Our schools suffered the same lack of resources as any state school. My abiding memory of school is a 'one size fits all' approach and clearly kids are not all one size. Sure, after primary there was some subject streaming, but within those subjects there did not seem to be much latitude. I got impatient in maths and science and other subjects, as I absorbed the lesson quickly and was frustrated that we were still repeating the topic; whereas in English, I struggled when Shakespeare was thrust at me. I wanted to like it, but I found it heavy going. I get it now, but not then. Other students had a different view – my sister Beth's concerns were the reverse. None of these frustrations were ever sufficient reason to avoid school. The only day I can remember wagging was that day in July 1969 when *Apollo 11* landed on the moon. There was no way I was going to miss a second of that TV broadcast.

Segregation of the genders strikes me as a bad option, because it creates more problems than it solves. A larger pool of students would help with a diversity of educational offerings.[85] In addition, rather than regarding members of the other gender as mystifying aliens they would be seen without prejudice, as just fellow students. I won't even mention the binary bias inherent in the division.

As well as wasting most people's time on things like Latin, there was a general aversion to teaching subject matter with a high probability of being useful in later life. I recall, just before year ten, the state education board decided the subject Christian Doctrine, taught in Catholic schools, was not worthy of the ranking of a regular subject. I was in complete agreement with the board and not just because I was rubbish at it. As a result, the school had to beef up our syllabus to have sufficient real subjects to allow us all to pass the Junior exams. The subject chosen was Citizenship Education. It was a subject designed to prepare non-academic students for the world they were about to be ejected into. The school taught the two-year syllabus in one year. What a brilliant subject I found it to be – something which is actually useful. I do appreciate the subjects that expand the mind, but there are also many topics which would have been beneficial to explore, e.g. safety, first aid, hygiene. Then there are practical skills like managing money, cooking, growing food, using tools, etc. And what about the other three Rs: relationships, respect and rubbers. There would need to be profound climate change in Hell before a Catholic school would take on that last topic. I am also aware of the current thinking that less is more, as a way to emulate the success in Finland, but my point is simply, there should have been greater preference for practical content over some of the dross I was taught.

Luckily, I had no exposure to the sort of abuse canvassed in the child abuse royal commission.[86] However, I did have plenty of exposure to the abuse called corporal punishment, which involved striking a child with a cane or strap. Nuns, brothers and lay teachers used it. Apart from being cruel, it was arbitrary and largely ineffectual. It showed a lack of imagination and fed the sadistic fantasies of those who should never have been teachers. There was a nun in Innisfail who earned the slur, 'the little red bull'. She was far too quick to use the handle of her feather duster for the slightest slight, until she accidently poked a child in the eye, which immediately invoked a response of concern and regret. The most shameful and idiotic episode I experienced firsthand was in 1970, when a teacher used a strap to deliver four 'cuts' to all forty students in an unsupervised room because some students had talked to each other.[87]

I deduced there were some advantages in being in the middle of the road. A distant female Ditton cousin and her sister, attended an upmarket school, They were a bit further advanced with their English literature and were studying Rupert Brookes' poem *The Old Vicarage, Grantchester.* A line in the fourth verse reads: 'And Ditton girls are mean and dirty'.[88] That line haunted them for the rest of their days, at that posh school.

Endnotes to Chapter 1

1 World War Two (WWII), for Australia lasted from 1 Sep 1939 until 2 Sep 1945.

2 The birth rate was 2.1 births per female in 1931 and 3.5 in 1962 www.abs.gov.au 4102.0 – Australian Social Trends, 2004.

3 Qld Birth Certificate (BC) 1917/3501 19776, 20 Dec 1916, Paxton St., Townsville, Arthur Cranley Ditton

4 The First Eleven is the team of the best available cricket players and is typically made up of all seniors or talented sub seniors. To be given the position of twelfth man (first reserve & assistant) as a junior (year 10) is a significant honour.

5 The Great Depression lasted from Aug 1929 until Jun 1938 – Wikipedia.

6 e.g. the 3 persons: amo, amas, amat – I love, you love, he/she/it loves, then the plural. The 6 tenses were: present, future, imperfect, perfect, future perfect and pluperfect. Also, active and passive versions. There are 4 distinct conjugations and then the irregular verbs. Other Romance languages (e.g. French) use similar constructs.

7 The cases were Nominative, Genitive, Dative, Accusative, Ablative, Vocative and less commonly, the Locative.

8 *Romanes eunt domus* is corrected to *Romani ite Domum* (Romans go home!).

9 The Tully family story is detailed in: F Lehane, *Heartbreak Corner*, self-published, Beaudesert, 1996

10 A heritage-listed Wilcox Mofflin building still stands in Longland St, Newstead.

11 In the 1930s it was played between NSW, Vic, Qld & SA. During WWII, it was suspended.

12 Sporting (54 runs retired), *Beaudesert Times*, Fri 3 Nov 1939, page 2 http://nla.gov.au/nla.news-article216092707 & From defeat to victory, *The Telegraph* (Brisbane) Tue 5 Feb 1935, page 17 http://nla.gov.au/nla.news-article182791395

13 On 15 Feb 1942, the British in Singapore surrendered to the Japanese, which meant up to 80,000 British, Australian and Indian soldiers became prisoners of war. They joined the 50,000 captured earlier in the Malayan peninsular campaign. Winston Churchill described it as the worst disaster in British military history – Wikipedia.

14 Australia was a British dominion then and by extension, Australians were considered British.

15 Oral history as remembered by myself from conversations with my father. Ascot racecourse was another campsite.

16 Reserved occupations, *The West Australian,* Mon 16 Mar 1942, page 3 http://nla.gov.au/nla.news-article47184849

17 Reserved occupations, *The Herald* (Melbourne), Wed 6 Nov 1940, page 11 http://nla.gov.au/nla.news-article244582214

18 Tom was married to Arthur's aunt, Grace (Tottie) née Cranley. Tom and his son Jack worked for Wilcox Mofflin & Co.

19 There is no record of his military service in the publicly available archived military records.

20 Ralph's information on the 7th Brigade was that it consisted of the 9th, 25th, 61st 15th & 47th battalions with the last 2 reallocated to the 29th Brigade in May 1942.

21 Militia were initially intended as home defence units, but as the war progressed, that role fell to volunteer reservists. Conscription had existed in Australia since 1909. Conscripted forces could not be sent overseas until Jan 1943 when the area they were allowed to serve in was extended into the South West Pacific, however, because Eastern New Guinea was administered by Australia, militia units were sent there in Jul 1942.

22 White feathers were more common in WWI, particularly where the Australian overseas forces were all volunteers. In popular culture, women were the origin of most of these acts, but as it was anonymous, we can never be truly sure.

23 Paul married Dorrie Green at St Bridget's, Red Hill in 1942. A daughter was born, but the marriage faltered a few years later whilst the war was still on. The family blamed it on the Yanks (over paid, over sexed and over here).

24 The referendum removed section 127 and deleted part of section 51 (xxvi) of the Constitution which were used to justify an assimilationist approach used by the states. That approach effectively stripped them of their unique identity and self-determination. An upside of the assimilationist approach was that some concessions had occurred prior to this, e.g. Indigenous people became eligible for pensions in 1960 on the same basis as non-indigenous Australians, provided they were not 'nomadic or primitive'. Some Indigenous people were given the vote in 1949, particularly those who had acquired a formal education or those who had served in the military. The downsides were legion. Indigenous people had lost control of how they could live their lives and a stolen generation was born. https://www.dss.gov.au/sites/default/files/documents/05_2012/op12.pdf

25 The darkest notion associated with being treated as fauna is that there would be no justice in the event of homicide. In fact, there were occasionally prosecutions of non-Indigenous for killing Indigenous Australians, even in colonial times. A famous example of this was the aftermath of the Myall Creek Massacre in 1838, when 7 settlers were tried and hanged.

26 State governments determined where they could live, if they could own property, what their pay level could be, whether they could drink alcohol, whether they could vote, who they could marry and whether they could be the legal guardians of their own children. reconciliation.org.au

27 A remembered joke related to a boss suggesting to his Aboriginal offsider how they should divide up the birds from their hunting trip. The offsider pointed out to his boss that every option suggested included the duck in the bosses share and the crow in his share.

28 Visitor from N. Qld, *Illawarra Mercury,* Fri 4 Dec 1936, page 11 http://nla.gov.au/nla.news-article132564182

29 Scholarship was year 8 (end of primary at that time).

30 *The Toowoomba Chronicle,* Tue 15 Aug 1995, page 4 had the reminisces of a Glennie pupil, Una Fallon. In that article she said the hospital was the requisitioned Glennie Junior School. The article has more detail on celebrations on VJ day.

A post war marriage

31 VE day, 8 May 1945. The day victory was declared in Europe.

32 VJ day, 15 Aug 1945. The day Imperial Japan surrendered in WWII.

33. C Henderson T*he Glennie. a work of Faith a History of the Glennie Memorial School Toowoomba 1901-1981* Rank Xerox, Sydney c. 1983

34 https://en.wikipedia.org/wiki/Polio

35 When my daughter heard my father's voice for the first time (on a recording which I had made shortly before he died) her first reaction was 'very Aussie'. The Australian accent has changed over the decades. The recording was of an impromptu horserace call which he made up on the spot and it flowed quite seamlessly.

36 The exchange was named *Cedarella*. Cousin, Don Noon, owned and operated *Cedarvale* as a cattle station until 2018.

37 In 2018, a neighbour who was a teenager at the time told me how big an occasion it was and nobody wanted to miss it.

38 Peg said there was no pressure from Dit. It was entirely her decision. Because Peg had attended the convent for many years, Father Flynn didn't think any additional instruction was necessary.

39 Paul was marrying Joan Essen and his divorce from his first wife had only recently come through. Whether the same day was chosen deliberately or accidently was not remembered. It is believed Paul's sister, Lola, attended Paul's wedding to Joan.

40 The block he purchased in 1857 is bounded by South, Hume, McCook & Geddes Sts. Cranley St runs east west through the middle of what was his farm. These old farming blocks were being redeveloped into suburbs of workers cottages in the post-war expansion.

41 The second house was sold and moved to the Bodkins' property (*Kameruka*) when their house burnt down.

42 There were at least 4 Aboriginal men employed on *Mulga Belt*.

43 Peg stayed in Mitchell for about 3 weeks awaiting the birth, as it was too risky to do a last-minute dash.

44 https://www.sciencedirect.com/science/article/pii/S01401963311003399

45 Edna Hynd's brother, Cecil, also worked at WMC at that time. Edna was Peter Noon's (b. 1910) wife.

46 The Agricultural Bank started in 1902 and became the Queensland Industry Development Corporation (QIDC) in 1986, which was folded into Suncorp along with the Metway Bank in 1996 – Wikipedia. A small portion of QIDC, the Government Schemes Division, was retained outside of Suncorp. It is now called the Queensland Rural and Industry Development Authority. Its functions are steadily evolving to assist in ways that the Ag Bank did before.

47 The purchase price was approximately £2400.

48 Henry Bandidt (1906–1990), an honest man, was the member for the House of Representatives seat of Wide Bay for 1 term (1958–1961). He represented the Country Party. He lost to the Labor Party candidate in the cliff-hanger 1961 election.

49 The family went to Monto via train. The car was freighted on the train. The same was done for Innisfail.

50 Drink cans did not yet have a ring pull. You used a can-opener to put 2 triangular-shaped holes in the top of the can. A hole for your mouth and another for the air.

51 The children were given small beers or shandies at evening mealtimes at irregular times. I'm yet to be convinced it was a bad thing.

52 Saltwater crocodiles were legally hunted for their skins in Qld up until 1974. At that point, they had become quite rare. After they were declared a protected species, their numbers recovered. Innisfail is on the Johnstone River, which has its own species of less dangerous and somewhat shy freshwater crocodile.

53 Despite Peg missing her true calling as a princess, she is a wonderful human being and admired by all her family including her ten grandchildren and increasing numbers of great grandchildren. At a friend and neighbour's funeral in 2016 the eulogy given by an ex-priest included remarks on Peg's unfailing optimism and good spirits.

54 Ralph distinctly remembers Dit running over another taipan with a lawnmower after it startled him. Dit did a little involuntary dance when it appeared near some banana trees growing over a septic tank.

55 After heavy rain, various paddocks (e.g. in Carmel St.) would have large stretches of standing water which just invited children's play. Modern nanny-think would deem it too dangerous for children.

56 Mt Bartle Frere in the Wooroonooran National Park is 1622 m high and is 26 km from Innisfail. The summit is often obscured by cloud particularly in the wet season. Tourist buses would stop outside the house as the view from that location was unobstructed. The house was on the corner of Ryan and Carmel sts and was rembered as 59 Ryan St., but now known as 57 Ryan St (double block).

57 They would drop down on passers-by and give a nasty bite. They swarmed over the tree which they lived in so if you saw them first, you avoided their space. I like to think they are the inspiration for the fictional 'drop bears'.

58 Peg employed an Italian woman and later a Spanish woman one day a week for housework and was impressed with their work ethic.

59 Tradename for an engineered hardboard, popular before chipboard and MDF became more widespread.

60 Britain's Lonnie Donegan had a big hit with his 1960 song 'My old man's a dustman'. It reached number 1 in several countries around the world, including Australia.

61 Movies were shot on standard 8 mm which was derived from 16 mm film. Half the film was exposed then turned over.

62 Early on, his preferred rum was 'Old Soldier Rum' a blend from Dalgety's using Normanby Rum (from Strathpine) and Beenleigh Rum. As those brands disappeared, he switched to Bundaberg Rum, which seemed to dominate the Qld market from about 1970.

63 He gave an example of looking for a horse which placed 6th and then 4th in its last 2 races.

64 Apparently named after an Earl of Craven, but it did reflect the addictive nature of tobacco.

65 After Jun 2013 it became the Democratic Labour Party (spelling change) – Wikipedia.

66 The principal issue at stake was the influence of the Communist Party on the labour movement. The split effectively meant the Labor

Shaking the Mulga

Party was kept out of office for almost 20 years, which the DLP considered a worthy aim. Such was the fear and hatred of Communist influence during this Cold War period, they preferred the rule of the conservative coalition than that of their former comrades.

67 Bartholomew Augustine Santamaria (1915–1998), Melbourne advocate for social conservatism and anti-communism.

68 The ABC was the Australian Broadcasting Commission until 1983. Afterwards, it became the Australian Broadcasting Corporation.

69 PA Yeomans, *The Keyline Plan,* self-published, Sydney, 1954

70 The topic pits agrarian socialist ideals against the interests of the proletariat.

71 At the time (1970), some Australian wool and wheat producers were receiving subsidies intended to be 'temporary'.

72 Hotel on the eastern side of Ruthven St north of the intersection with Margaret St. Now demolished.

73 Decimal currency started in Australia on 14 Feb 1966. One pound became 2 dollars. One shilling, 10 cents.

74 The women were, respectively, Anna Bligh, Penny Wensley, Julia Gillard, Quentin Bryce & Elizabeth Windsor. Incidently Australia's richest citizen at that time (and also now) was also a woman, Gina Rinehart. Similar to Elizabeth, birth played a big part in Gina's crown.

75 Discovered early, incised with good margins, the triple negative variant defied 3 courses of strong chemotherapy and radiation therapy. We can only hope, gentler, more effective treatments are developed for this scourge.

76 https://www.thechronicle.com.au/news/lessons-learned-from-infamous-1976-hailstorm/3266638/

77 U3A is an education movement for seniors originating in France in 1968 and adopted internationally.

78 Man dies after roof fall *The Chronicle* (Toowoomba), 13 Sep 2012. https://www.thechronicle.com.au/news/man-dies-roof-fall/1543099/

79 They perched up in the voucher loft where the old records were stored. One morning they were out in the bank residence attached to the bank waist deep in water. They saw a snake swimming in the water and used the revolver to take pot shots at it.

80 Since writing that, the policy has changed to something involving greater expense and a absolute reliance on an unstable superpower and a has been empire.

81 The Big Bang is now recognised by most cosmologists as the origin of this iteration of this universe.

82 Incidentally, Patrick White's maternal uncles were named Ralph and Clem which is the only the second time outside our family where I had heard those names paired. The other instance was when a family chose them as names for their dogs.

83 P White, *Flaws in the Glass, A Self-portrait,* Penguin Books, UK, 1983 page 244. Patrick said it better, but I didn't want to steal his words.

84 Alluding to the age-old idiomatic expression, 'Don't throw the baby out with the bathwater.'

85 One of my old schools, St Joseph's Christian Brothers College in Toowoomba realised they could do better and began the switch to co-education in 1983.

86 The full title was the Royal Commission into Institutional Responses to Child Sexual Abuse 2012–2017.

87 The teacher had left the room to attend another matter and issued instruction to the 40 students to be quiet. He returned 15 minutes later and heard a number of students chattering. Corporal punishment was banned from Qld government schools in 1995, but technically remains legal in private schools to this day.

88 Rupert Brooks (1887–1915) wrote the poem in Berlin in 1912 and was reminiscing about his time in Cambridge. Ditton girls refers to the girls from the village of Fen Ditton near Cambridge. Rupert was described by WB Yates as the handsomest man in England. He died from sepsis on a military hospital ship whilst participating in a military campaign in WWI – Wikipedia.

89 This Polaroid photo is the only known photo with all six family members together. Dit died six weeks later.

[3]

Chapter 2

Sheep Jockeys

Lizzie and Charlie - Noon

The federation of the Australian colonies was formalised on the first day of the twentieth century. The Commonwealth's prosperity steadily increased as it struggled out of recession. Much of the increase was due to the country riding on the sheep's back. In the decades that followed, the country endured the two world wars. One could be summarised as a tragic failure of leadership and the other as a serious existential threat. Just five years after the exhausting struggle of WWII, the Allies were again at war. The Korean War triggered the phenomenal Australian wool boom. This chapter tells the story of the family that nurtured my mother, Peg. Her parents were Lizzie McGonigal and Charlie Noon.

Before their marriage

Charles Peter (Charlie) Noon was born on a farm at Pipers Flat, NSW in March 1890.[1] He was the second child and first son of parents, Lucy née Goodwin and Peter Noon. The family had moved to the farm around 1889. It was about three kilometres south of the town of Portland, NSW.[2] Charlie's father worked the farm, but also took mining jobs in the district as required.[3] It can be inferred Charlie worked on the farm with his father, as around 1900, Peter placed an advertisement trying to sell a 'Forest Devil' stating, he and a boy (probably Charlie) had cleared seven acres of bush with it.[4]

Charlie went to school in Portland, but did not advance beyond about grade five, which was common for children in those days, as they often had to get to work to help the family.[5] As was seen in his later life, he had had a good grounding in practical skills from farming, building and mechanics. Around 1907[6], the family moved to the oil shale venture which had started up in the nearby town of Newnes, and Charlie found work as a miner either excavating the shale or the coal.[7] Some coal was converted to coke and some was used to heat extract the oil from the shale.

Elizabeth (Lizzie) Currie McGonigal arrived in Newnes in 1908 with the rest of her family. They had only stepped off the ship from Scotland a few weeks beforehand. Lizzie, the second oldest daughter, was born in 1888 at *Bridgecastle* cottages, Torphichen, West Lothian, Scotland.[8] She had a twin brother Robert. The family had moved around various locations since her birth. In 1890 and 1891, they were living at Bathgate, West Lothian.[9] From 1893 to 1899, they lived in the towns of Tarbrax and Wishaw, both in the County of Lanarkshire.[10] From 1900 until their departure for Australia, they had lived in Whitburn, Livingstone and Bathgate, all in the County of West Lothian.[11] Lizzie's parents paid for her to be taught cookery at *Bridgecastle,* a grand house close to her home in Bathgate and even closer to her birthplace.[12]

The McGonigal family stayed in Newnes between 1908 and 1912, but Lizzie only spent a relatively short time there as by 1910 she had taken the train to Sydney to work in the Presbyterian Ladies College as a cook.[13] Lizzie, Robert and her three eldest sisters were in Newnes long enough to all find romance there. Three McGonigals married three Noons.

Marriage and the early years

Charlie had written letters to Lizzie in Sydney, but they were not turning up. Meanwhile the postman at Lizzie's end was taking an interest in Lizzie himself, and so that was thought to be the explanation for the missing letters. Charlie came down to Sydney to investigate why Lizzie had not replied. From that visit they decided to get married.[14] The wedding was in the suburb of Waterloo on Melbourne Cup day in 1910. Because Charlie was not yet 21, he had to get the permission of his father.[15] They returned to Newnes, and their first son, Peter Charles, was born in September of the following year.[16]

Early in 1912, the Newnes operation faltered due to a combination of reasons. The initial one was, the retorts to extract the oil were built to the design used in Scotland where the oil shale was not as rich. At Newnes the high oil content resulted in inefficiencies, damage to the retorts[17] and injuries to workers.[18] The labour was also agitating, as conditions were being cut to handle the increasingly tight financial position of the company. It was

Lizzie in her finery circa 1910

A young Charlie circa 1910

around this time that Charlie and Lizzie started to look elsewhere for opportunities. They headed over to the booming Broken Hill mines where Charlie worked underground for about a year. The conditions there were difficult as underground work was dusty and dangerous.[19] The dust adversely affected Charlie's health. A friend, Freddy Whitlock, suggested they try their luck together up in Qld. Freddy was a bachelor.[20]

They got into their sulky and headed up to Aramac in Central Qld.[21] There, they set up camp a distance out of town and proceeded to shoot and skin kangaroos. One day, they noticed the smoke of a distant bushfire but thought it too far away to be a problem. Charlie and Freddy left to do their shooting, leaving Lizzie and young Peter at the camp. Lizzie was expecting her next child. Conditions changed and it was clear the fire was headed for the camp. Lizzie, the young woman raised in Scotland, had learnt her Australian bush craft well. She cut a firebreak and secured the hides they had already collected by covering them with soil. She then took herself and Peter to a waterhole in the creek and stayed until the fire passed. She had saved their lives and their livelihood, but she had miscarried as a consequence and suffered poor health for a time afterwards. Whilst at Aramac, a woman Lizzie knew gave birth in the hospital, but then was in poor shape herself. She asked if Lizzie would take the baby if anything happened to her. She thought about it; however, Charlie was against it. The woman died shortly afterwards.[22]

The roo-shooting venture was a success and it gave them seed money to buy into their next enterprise – a sawmill much closer to civilisation, at Caboolture in South East Qld. Freddy was a partner in that operation as well. This was around the period when the clamour started for all able-bodied men to do their bit for the mother country. Charlie was now a family man and so any commitment to becoming a soldier would have been a difficult call for the family. Freddy resisted the call as well, which at least demonstrates not every single man rushed

off to the big adventure on the other side of the world. As that adventure turned into a murderous debacle, fewer men made the decision to enlist. The jingoistic Prime Minister, Billy Hughes, tried to make the decision easier by holding a plebiscite[23] to get the electorate's support for committing Australian conscripts to overseas service.[24] It narrowly failed in 1916 and more emphatically in a softer version in 1917. A sizeable proportion of the soldiers, already in Europe, helped to vote it down.[25] Of those who answered the call, fewer than half came back alive and physically uninjured. Many of the rest had issues which emerged once back in civilian life.[26] For various reasons, over sixty percent of eligible men decided to stay at home. From all we know now about WWI, that choice was the wiser one, but it would not have been a simple or easy choice to make at the time. In retrospect, it was clear that what was needed to avoid this calamity was serious diplomacy and effective leadership.[27]

During their time at the sawmill, Elizabeth was expecting her next son, James Currie McGonigal (Jim). She decided to stay with her parents at Scarborough, NSW for the birth in November 1916.[28] Jim was just going to be called James, but the story goes, Lizzie's father registered the birth and he took it upon himself to add two more names to the registration.[29] To get to NSW, Lizzie took a ship with Peter, as Charlie stayed at home to look after the business. Lizzie was prone to seasickness, and on one of these trips, she was so sick that she called out to Charlie. Only to have a man respond, 'I'm a Charlie, but probably not the one you want'. Peg cannot recall Charlie ever calling Lizzie by her name. Other people called her that. Charlie's favourite name for her was 'Ducky'.[30]

Sometime after 1916, Charlie and Freddy sold the sawmilling business and then went into banana growing at Bracalba, which was about fourteen kilometres north-west of Caboolture on the D'Aguilar Highway. Whilst there, Charlie and Lizzie took their first holiday together at the beach. They had left their banana harvest in the care of

Jim, Bert (seated) and Peter circa 1920, Brisbane

Lizzie and Peg circa 1938

others. The rail freight had been paid, but due to the heat, the bananas had sweated and were ruined. A third boy, Bertie (Bert/Buddy), was born at Kilcoy hospital in August 1919. Their dressmaking neighbour, Florey McLean, became a family friend, who they maintained contact with for decades. Florey made dresses for special occasions for the Noons, including Peg's wedding dress. Despite the setback with the ruined harvest, the bananas proved to be a great success and the venture raised enough money to step up to their next enterprise. This time around though, Lizzie insisted, it just be Charlie and herself. So, the partnership with Freddy Whitlock ended.[31]

Mulga Belt

In the winter of 1922[32], Charlie and Lizzie bought the stocked 4781.5-acre (19.35 km²) sheep property named *Mulga Belt*[33] located about sixty kilometres SSW of Mitchell in South West Qld.[34] It was whilst there that Elizabeth Peggy (Peg), the unexpected addition and last child, turned up in June 1928.[35]

Anecdotally, *Mulga Belt* had been split off from the much larger *Bonus Downs,* but land records tell a different, more complicated story.[36] Mr EC (Charles) Lambe sold *Mulga Belt* in June 1922 to Mr Rudkin who quickly on sold it to the Noons (referred to as a 'Brisbane buyer').[37] Many in the district thought Charlie paid too much for it, as it was a 'tough little block'.[38] *Bonus Downs,* itself was 330,000 acres (1335 km²) and devoted to cattle raising, when 76-year-old Irishman, Sir Samuel McCaughey, purchased it in 1908. He switched its use to sheep and made many improvements. He employed over one hundred people and later sold off some portions.[39] *Bonus Downs* had previously been owned by two sets of owners, Eric Ledbetter and JC & WR McManus. Both had walked off the property due to lack of water.[40] So, water was always going to be an issue to be managed. Tanks and dams were the key to capturing the unpredictable rain, but they were a significant expense and had to be placed judiciously.[41]

One of the acquaintances Charlie and Lizzie made was Albert Rattenbury, a WWI Light Horse veteran. Albert built dams with a team of horses pulling a bucket. However, when there were no dams to build, Albert decided to camp in the shearer's quarters at *Mulga Belt*. His horses also felt quite at home on the paddocks of *Mulga Belt*. Charlie was always a softie and he let his uninvited guest stay and employed him from time to time when he needed an extra hand in the mustering. Albert got the benefit of Lizzie's cooking as well, as he would dine with them of an evening. Charlie got annoyed with Albert once, as he was not good with following orders and sacked him. Albert's answer to that was to join the mustering uninvited and put himself back on the payroll. His difficulty with following orders is understood to have gotten him into trouble in WWI when he hit an officer over the head with a saddle. When anyone was going to town, Albert would give them some money to buy him a casket ticket. His persistence paid off when he won £3000. That brought his forgotten relatives crawling out of the woodwork.[42]

Charlie was made a Justice of the Peace in 1933.[43] His neighbours sought and valued his opinion. Ian and Darcy Paul,[44] neighbours from *Greenoaks*, remarked, you could almost hear Charlie's brain ticking over when thinking about a problem. Making the tough little *Mulga Belt* a going concern is testament to his ability.[45] Charlie was good with his hands. He built sheds, holding yards, a sheep dip and even a summerhouse for Lizzie. The summerhouse had many wooden louvres on all four sides to help catch the breezes. He built a tennis court using ant bed and an effective charcoal meat safe before the era of refrigeration.[46] He and his boys were very capable at woodcraft and carpentry. Peg remembered the boys had to redo some cladding on a shed because Charlie, the perfectionist, said it wasn't straight. He once stitched up his son Peter with kangaroo gut after a bull gored him in the yard.[47] When the shearing

Freddy Whitlock is the taller gentleman at rear, on a rare visit to *Mulga Belt* in the late 1930s. The full group is, L to R: Peter, Lizzie, Charlie, Freddy, Jim, Elma Brown, Alfie Brown, unknown, Esmay Brown, Bert. The Browns were cousins to Edna Hynd, Peter's wife. Elma and Esmay were twins.

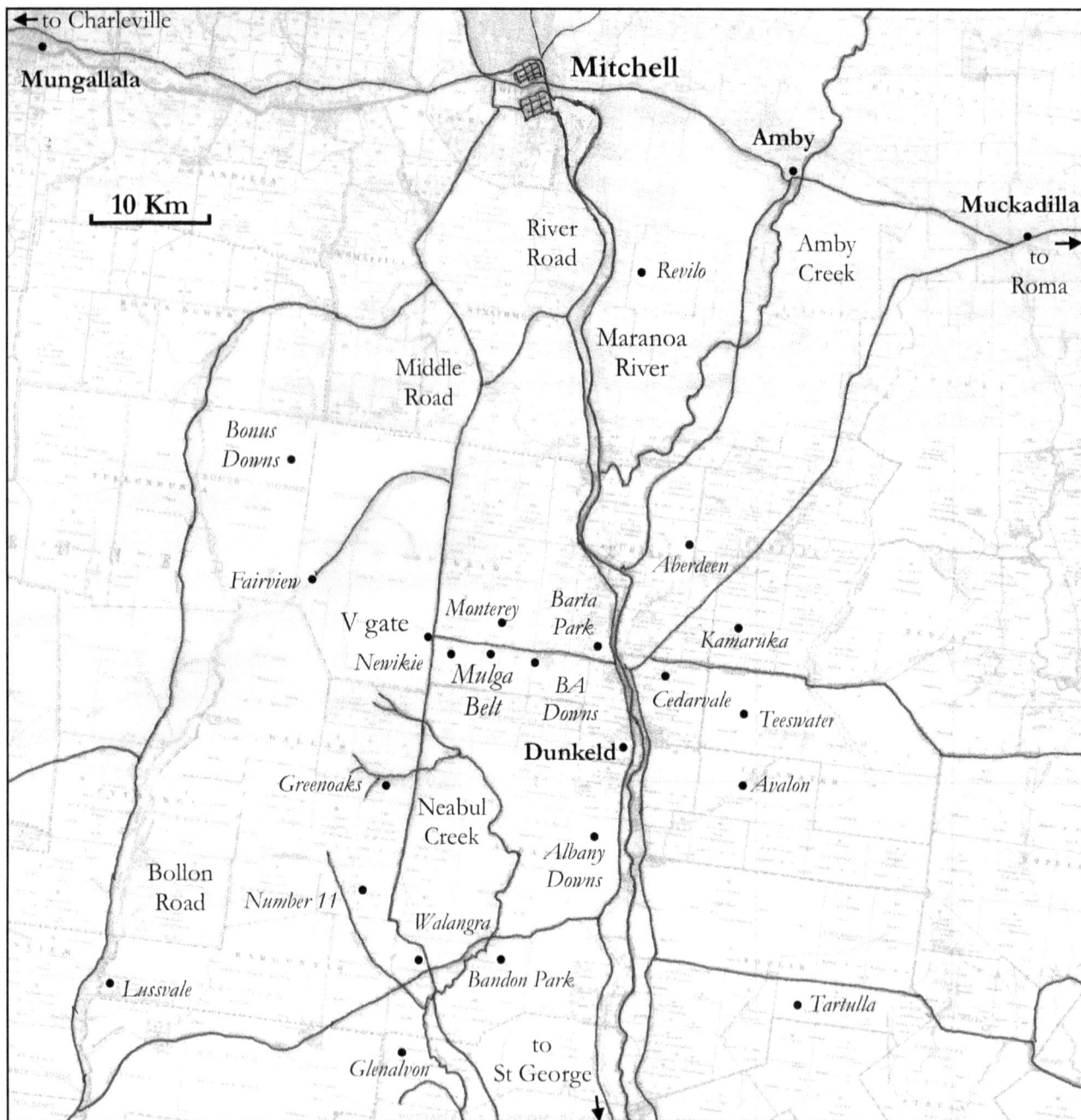

Map of the district with *Mulga Belt* at centre, with a collage of cadastral maps from 1947 – 1953 as background

was to be done, a crowd of men would turn up and Lizzie's cooking skills would be employed to please the crowd.[48] Lizzie was renowned for turning on a good feast at a moment's notice. Neighbours would turn up to use their sheep dip, and Charlie would invite them to stay for dinner and they would invariably accept.[49]

Several years after buying into *Mulga Belt*, the wool price doubled to 25 d/lb.[50] At the end of the 1927–29 drought, Charlie and Lizzie purchased a property from Mr McFarland. The property, *Bandon Park*, was to the south of *Mulga Belt*.[51] In the 1930s, Charlie and Lizzie put in for a draw of leasehold land and they won another property, which on the

The main house on *Mulga Belt* circa 1950. Photo from the collection of Charles Noon.

schedule, was simply called '*Number 11*' and that was the name that stuck.[52]

Mulga Belt was accessed via a lane which ran between the Middle Road and the River Road (Mitchell – St George Road which followed the Maranoa River).[53] Their immediate neighbours were the Timmins family at *Newikie* to the west and Jim Cowlishaw at *BA Downs* to the east.[54] On the other side of the lane were the Farmers at *Glenorchy* (later *Monterey*) and the Footts at *Barta Park* to the east.[55] As you would expect in a remote community with relatively large properties, neighbours became important for socialising and helping out at times of need. Peg's best friend, Bub Timmins, suffered a hard loss when her father, Bill Timmins, died in 1939. Charlie was the executor of his will and assisted the family for some time after. In 1949, Peg was one of the Bub's bridesmaids and Charlie had the honour of giving Bub away.

The neighbours considered Jim Cowlishaw, who lived alone at *BA Downs*, a little mad. He was tight with his money, despite coming from a wealthy family. His family owned the gasworks in Brisbane. He had sisters who visited him who took overseas holidays, which was a clear sign of wealth in those days. Jim never turned down an invitation to dine with the Noons, especially if he mentioned, he had 'run out of food'. He was so tight that, when he went away and asked Albert to mind the place, the neighbours suggested he counted out the tea leaves he would leave for Albert to make a brew. He was also rumoured to be listening in on the party line when the telephone rang for someone else.[56] People thought they could hear him, and besides, how did he know some of the things that he knew? Peg often recounted the story of when she was five years old, and Jim and her parents were sitting on the verandah at *Mulga Belt*. She threw her arms around Jim's neck and said, 'You're not mad, are you, Jim?' He must not have taken offence as he gave Peg the gift of a heifer when she was a child.[57] Jim sold *BA Downs* to Len Munchow from Stanthorpe around 1940 and moved to Brisbane.[58] Len sold *BA Downs* to the Noons in 1945.[59]

Noons on their fishing trip Easter 1936, L to R: Peter, Jim, Charlie, Peg, Bert and Lizzie.

The neighbours sometimes did things differently to how Charlie and Lizzie would do them. When slaughtering an animal for meat, Charlie would kill selected stock of high quality and would then share some of it with neighbours.[60] Some meat would be salted to help it keep for longer. Englishman Bill Farmer, across the lane at *Glenorchy*, had a different view of the quality of animal that was suitable for home consumption. It would be an animal that was expendable because it was not doing so well. So, when it came time to share with Bill, Charlie opted out.

Peg remembered, there was a certain formality at home. Charlie would come home from working out in the paddocks or sheds around 5.30 pm. He would have a wash and change into decent clothes. They would have a drink and then dinner would be served. Charlie would always sit at one end of the table and he would carve the meat. Lizzie would sit at the other end and serve the dessert. There was a lot of lamb (or hogget to be more precise) eaten at home – for breakfast, lunch and dinner in many

Bandon Park sheep pens with three Noon boys on the roof – Bev and John Schweers Collection

Left: Dunkeld group: Front: L to R: Marg Caskey, Aldyth (Bub) Timmins, Marg Walden Back: L to R Mary Walden, Peg Noon, 'Chicky' Harris, Patty O'Conner c 1947 Right: Boys swimming at Neabul L to R: Jimmy Timmins, Billy McDougal, Jim Noon, Tim Manns, Len McDougal

cases. Fresh vegetables were hard to come by and not easy to grow due to the water situation. So, the diet lacked some of the things considered healthy these days.

The neighbourhood got together for socialising at their own properties. They would have tennis matches or go fishing together at Easter time.[61] On Sundays, they would get together at Dunkeld, a little further south on the River Road. Before the war, there was just a bough shed there.[62] Some key families[63] pooled their funds and efforts to build a hall which was completed in 1951 and over 500 people attended the opening.[64] This then allowed for dances and other activities.[65] Tennis and cricket were also played there.[66] A golf course was built in 1966[67] and a primary school opened in 1967.[68] Dit got involved with the social cricket played at Dunkeld, which were among the last games of cricket he ever played.

Droughts came in unpredictable cycles and were always a challenge. They required more work keeping feed and water up to the stock. Sometimes that feed was cut mulga or it might be hay which suddenly became more expensive as everyone needed it. Prices for stock dropped as everyone affected was trying to reduce their herds or flocks and of course shot up again when the drought ended,

as everyone wanted to restock. Fires were a major concern for the community.[69] It was something that would immediately unite the district. They would drop everything and get together to fight any fires as needed. There was also the possibility of flooding rains, which brought hazards and damage as well as the welcome bounty.

Another hazard associated with spending your life outdoors, which is not often considered, is the risk of lightning strike. One day, in the 1920s, Charlie rode his horse from *Mulga Belt* to neighbours at *Coultra* (now part of *Monterey*), tied his horse up under a tree, went inside and immediately afterwards a lightning strike killed the horse.[70] A family from *Toomoombilla* that the Noons socialised with had lost one of their relatives, Florence Penhallurick. In 1912, lightning had killed her alongside her horse.[71]

Charlie and Lizzie had made special friends with a brother and sister named Arthur and Elsie Keable. Arthur was another Light Horse veteran from WWI.[72] They lived on *Walangra*, a property to the south. A sister of theirs, Mabel Cornish, had died in childbirth leaving a young girl, Daphne, in need of a home.[73] Arthur and Elsie raised Daphne, but her older brothers Ron and Percy were raised elsewhere. Percy later came to *Walangra* and spent a lot of time there. The Noons and the Keables

Sheep in pens with swollen creek, *Bandon Park* – Bev and John Schweers Collection

would take it in turns to host Christmas and New Year for each other and visited at other times for tennis matches. Elsie was Aunty Elsie to Peg. They had a white cockatoo which was able to distinguish the sound of the Noon's car approaching and that was its cue to say: 'The Noons are coming! The Noons are coming!'

Charlie and Arthur both liked to party and were often the last to leave. An oft-told story was the time they had had a session in Mitchell, around show time, and it came time for Charlie to leave with Lizzie. Arthur was staying on in the town, and as Charlie started driving home, he said, 'It's no good, Ducky, I can see four guideposts' (instead of the two that were there). 'We had better go back.' So back they went, where Charlie, the scamp, continued the session with Arthur. Charlie's father, Peter, had been a leader of the Temperance movement in Newnes, but Charlie and his brother, Frank, would slip down to the Newnes Hotel when the Temperance meetings were on. Because Arthur could get a bit angry whilst on the grog, Elsie tried to moderate Arthur's drinking by banning OP rum from *Walangra*. To thwart his sister's best intentions,

he secreted a stash on the end of a fishing line in the creek. One of the floods from the 1950s sent an armada of empty rum bottles down the Neabul Creek to neighbouring *Glenalvon*.

Roads were basic, with bitumen only a dream. Gates crossed the road, which had to be opened and closed. Cattle grids would only become widespread in later decades. Cars were typically driven with windows down to keep cool, which meant dust and, in turn, a change of clothes needed when you got to town. They wanted to look smart when they strolled around town. Standards have slipped a bit at Mitchell since those days. It didn't rain often, but when it did, it meant creeks could quickly flood, and if you had to be somewhere for a date that you couldn't miss, like having a baby, then you travelled days before. A mail truck would come once a week, on Saturday, and later twice a week. If you needed anything from town, you would phone through and order it and the mail truck would deliver it, whether it be groceries or a new sheep dog. The truck would return a day later to pick up letters or items like wool bales for the return post.

Bill Farmer had a problem with one of his gates, which was not in the best of repair. It irritated him that it was being left open on a regular basis. He suspected the mailman, Roy Mutton. So, one Saturday, Bill secreted himself in position to watch the expected arrival of Roy. Roy arrived, opened the gate, drove through and then closed the gate. Bill jumped out of hiding and startled Roy. 'So, you are not the culprit, after all,' Bill exclaimed. Roy professed ignorance of the matter, but later intimated to the Noons he didn't know what possessed him to close the gate on that occasion.[74]

There was always something to do on the property, and it was rare for Charlie and Lizzie to get away for a break, especially in the early years. Charlie even missed Peter's wedding because the property was in drought, and the flock and stock needed survival feed. Lizzie, Jim and Peg were able to get to the wedding. Lizzie visited her family in NSW several times with her younger children. Charlie could not get away and it seemed to suit him anyway. He had lost touch with his family back in NSW. His father had died in 1915 and his mother remarried in 1917. The feeling within the family was the new husband was 'no first prize'.[75] Frank, his closest brother from his early days, was reportedly upset with Charlie's much reduced contact. The family back in NSW were not having an easy time of it, and they could have done with more help. A teenage brother, David, known as Dick, had come up to Qld to work with him whilst he was in Aramac. Dick caused some unspecified mischief and was sent packing, so Charlie decided that his family was the one he had with Lizzie and that was enough for him. Charlie never spoke to Peg about his family. Anything Peg learnt about his family came from Lizzie. Her parents rarely fought in Peg's recollection, and if they ever did, it was probably about her.[76]

Peg was very fond of her father. Lizzie had a short fuse and would often scold Peg for her shenanigans, but it was 'water off a duck's back'. However, if Charlie ever pulled her up for something, it was as if she had been mortally wounded. Lizzie sometimes shut Peg in the bathroom when she was being naughty. Charlie would open the bathroom window when he got home for lunch and lift her out. That's the sort of thing Lizzie would get annoyed with Charlie about.

Peg said her father did not treat her like a child. He would talk to her like an adult. She recounted the story of when they came across a ewe that was near death. Charlie put the ewe out of her misery and opened her up, showing the eight-year-old Peg that the ewe was sick with nodule worm. He then talked to her about what needed to be done to prevent the disease.

L: Christmas at *Walangra* c. 1947 R: Terry Sweeny (bank manager), Arthur Keeble, Charlie Noon c. 1950 Mitchell

35

Charlie was not particularly religious, but he had standards. Charlie was asked if he would like to join the Masons in Mitchell. He asked what was involved and the proposer said, 'All you really need is a belief in God'. Charlie, who had a low opinion of the man asking him, thought – if a belief in God allowed you to behave as you do, then no thanks.[77]

All the boys had started their education via correspondence.[78] Peter won a scholarship to spend three years at Gatton Agricultural College in January 1926.[79] Jim and Bert spent some time boarding at the convent in Helidon, which catered for boys. Jim stayed until scholarship, but Bert finished up a bit earlier. Bert's distaste for formal education probably started when he took a belting from the nuns in his first week, after he lay down on the floor for his habitual nap after the evening meal.[80]

Lizzie kept her Scottish traditions alive in the things she cooked (e.g. shortbread and Aberdeen sausage), what she celebrated and in how she talked.[81] Her children also used some of her curious expressions. She kept up correspondence with her parents and siblings in NSW and her cousins, Effie Smith and Bessie Ross, in Scotland.[82] She encouraged Peg to also correspond with the next generation. So, Peg had Anne Campbell and Sarah Mercer as Scottish pen pals.[83] Lizzie often suffered from hay fever, with grass pollen as the main suspect. Whenever she saw Rhodes grass in flower, she was bound to suffer. Hay fever could bring on severe headaches.[84]

Country kids make their own fun. Bert and a friend were doing just that when they were filling the valves from old tractor tyres with gunpowder. They would hammer the open end closed and then throw the resulting cartridge into an incinerator. Bang! Oh, what fun! Until one detonated at the hammering stage. It took off half a finger and the top of another. A bit of shrapnel shot into Bert's stomach and another into his neck, narrowly missing his artery. Lizzie prohibited any such nonsense in future, with a threat to kill him if he survived a repeat.[85]

Tennis party at *Mulga Belt* c. 1938 F: dog, Lizzie, Charlie, Peter, M: Jim, B: Daphne Cornish, Arthur Keable, Bert

Bert was the principal prankster of the family. He saw an opportunity to exercise his talent when he came across a nest of bats within a tree he had felled with his neighbour, Jimmy Timmins. He gathered the bats into a bag and carried them home to join a gathering of ladies Lizzie was hosting at *Mulga Belt*. When Lizzie asked Bert what he had in the bag, the scallywag answered by releasing his catch into the room occupied by the tea, scones and shrieking ladies.[86]

Wildlife was abundant in this vicinity and a pleasure to observe for anyone so inclined. Even the beloved koalas were sometimes seen.[87] However, some sections of the wildlife were viewed as threats to livelihood. Various species at differing times posed differing kinds of danger. Dingoes and, to a lesser extent, eagles preyed on the sheep. Rabbits competed for pasture. Kangaroos posed a similar threat, but also made car travel hazardous before the era of the sturdy roo bar. Later pigs and goats entered the scene. Time and effort had to be expended to keep the populations under control. There were incentives to hunt the kangaroos as their skins and meat could provide extra income or at least food for the working dogs. In this district, the working dogs were typically kelpies. They would be chained up to hollow logs close to the homestead. One of their duties was to act as watchdogs. They loved their main duty, which was to push sheep from place to place. The double act of dog and grazier remains one of the most captivating spectacles of country life. It is truly remarkable – so much can be accomplished with just simple voice commands, a few whistles and the occasional profanity.

Things that are taken for granted in modern urban life were simply not available in the lifestyle lived out at *Mulga Belt* in the early years. Water for drinking and washing at *Mulga Belt* came from only two large rainwater tanks. Conserving water was always front of mind. Seniority played a part in deciding who got to use the bath water first. After that, the garden got its share. Some properties pumped water for washing from dams or creeks.

The colour was such that a visitor from the city would take some convincing they would be cleaner after using it.

When electricity finally arrived in the 1940s, it came from diesel generators and car batteries in a 32 volt configuration, which had to be stepped up for most appliances.[88] Before electricity, there were carbide and kerosene lanterns to provide light. Wood stoves were a boon on a frosty winter's morning, but a compounding component of discomfort on a summer's day. Ironing clothes required a relay of mother pots heated on the stove.[89] If you were feeling lucky, you could use a dangerous petrol iron. Before electricity, laundry was all done by hand, and surprisingly, whites stayed white.

In these pre-TV days, evenings would be occupied with the women knitting and the men practising their woodcraft.[90] Motor vehicles, telephone lines and the wireless all helped to reduce isolation, but they were primitive compared with today.[91] Still, the sense of isolation had reduced significantly since the days of earliest European settlers. Of course, this was a world away from the existence the Indigenous Gunggari people experienced in the same locality for the countless millennia previously.

After first contact with the explorer Thomas Mitchell, in 1846, relations between the traditional owners and the newcomers were on a downward trajectory. Many bad things, including mass murder, were done with government complicity, but the Aboriginal inhabitants continued to resist.[92] A new Commonwealth law in 1901 allowed for Aboriginal people to be rounded up and sent to reserves on land they had little or no connection to.[93] Many remained behind. The landmark 1992 Mabo High Court decision overturned the doctrine of *terra nullius* and in response, the Commonwealth Government passed the *Native Title Act of 1993*. The 1996 Wik High Court decision clarified the relationship between native title and existing pastoral leases, stating they could co-exist on the same parcel of land.[94]

In 1996, a claim was lodged on behalf of the Gunggari people. In 2008, after much negotiation with over 200 respondents and some amendments to the original claim, the Qld Government recognised Gunggari Native Title for some land in the Dunkeld area. The negotiations continued, and in 2012, the Gunggari people proved additional claims in the Federal Court of Australia to various parcels of land, south of Mitchell. In September 2019, A third claim of over 8,122 km² was accepted in the Federal Court and supported by the Qld Government.[95] That claim extends north and west of the town of Mitchell. Their rights are non-exclusive, meaning they are able to use the land for approved purposes, but also must share it with existing landholders via the negotiated agreements.[96] The Gunggari claim was the first native title claim recognised in Southern Inland Qld. The Noons employed some Aboriginal workers in the 1940s and 50s and beyond.[97]

The War and the Boom

Peg can remember Jim standing between two beds in the boys' bedroom and saying, 'Someone has to go'. The boys had gotten together to discuss the start of WWII and that was the decision they agreed on. Jim enlisted in the army in July 1940 and became a gunner trained on anti-tank guns.[98] He was sent to Palestine and he saw some action against the Vichy French in the Middle East. In 1942, Prime Minister Curtin then wanted some Australian troops back home to defend Australia against the Japanese. The convoy was waylaid at Colombo, Ceylon, for three months because of the threat of Axis submarines.[99] His sometimes neighbour from *Walangra*, Percy Cornish, was with him through the whole war.[100] Percy's brother Ron Cornish was a journalist and is most likely the author of this following bit of propaganda/fiction, which was published in quite a few newspapers.

Few Australians, if any, remain among the guerilla forces, which are constantly harrying the Germans in Crete, said Private R. Noon, of Mitchell. Most of the A.I.F. who were left on the island when it was captured were rescued by a British destroyer, which approached the island during darkness and sent boats to bring the men off. Most of the Australians knew the destroyer was coming to take them off, he said, but he would not tell how they found out. Guerillas took heavy toll of the German occupying force, but they were helped greatly by the Cretans themselves. Private Noon and his brother, Gunner J. Noon, who have returned to Australia, met once for only a few minutes. Up to that time neither knew where the other was because Gunner Noon was taken prisoner in Greece. He remained a captive for only a week, however, escaping and making his way through Turkey to Syria, which had only just been occupied by the Allies. He was captured with a lieutenant and five rankers. He said it was the lieutenant who organised the escape. 'We just managed to find a weakness in the compound and dug our way under the netting during the time the guards were at the end of their beat at night. Hundreds of others were able to do the same thing. Making their way into a Greek village, they were given old clothes in which to make their get-away. You can't tell me they are not a grand people, those Greeks, he said. Sneaking across the Turkish frontier at night, they found that a surprisingly large number of Turks had more than a smattering of the English language. It took them four days to reach the Syrian border, where they announced themselves as escapees from the Germans. After hours of cross-examination the English officers believed their story. 'I had three hours cross-examination myself,' said Gunner Noon. During the week in which he was held a prisoner he was treated rather well, but suspected that it was only a Nazi ruse. [101]

An Allied ruse, more likely; there was no Private R Noon and Jim's war was eventful, but not quite to this colourful degree. It was the sort of fare readers of newspapers in those days wanted to read because the real news, before this, had been quite grim. The news steadily started to get better from the second half of 1942 with Allied land successes in the Pacific theatre at Milne Bay, Kokoda and Guadalcanal. The African campaign turned the corner for the Allies with the battles of El Alamein.

Jim's battalion arrived home safely from Ceylon and was then deployed to New Guinea in late 1942 where Jim saw some action. After a year, he was back in Australia as he had been suffering from dysentery.[102] Percy had hearing problems as a result of working with the anti-tank gun, which on top of other things, made sentry duty problematic. As there was not much call for anti-tank skills in New Guinea, Jim was assigned to an ambulance unit aiding the wounded. He was posted to Wewak

Percy Cornish and Jim Noon in uniform at *Mulga Belt* circa 1940 just before they were sent to the Middle East

in early 1945. Jim was discharged in October 1945, but he had contracted malaria as most of the diggers in New Guinea did.[103] That was still with him for some years to come.[104] After returning home from the war, Jim purchased the property *Glenalvon* from Bob Marlin in 1951.[105]

Jim souvenired some Japanese Occupation currency that was intended for use in a conquered Australia. He liberated it from a Japanese doctor prisoner of war (POW). He passed on some of that currency to his nephew, Ralph, who collected banknotes. Those notes were later donated to the Macarthur Museum in Brisbane to assist with the education program on WWII run for school children.[106] Charlie and Bert joined the army

reserve and were part of the home guard.[107] Their duties were not onerous, but if the Japanese had succeeded in New Guinea, then there was the genuine expectation, and therefore fear, that the militia would be called upon to defend Australia.[108]

In 1945, when victory in the war against Japan appeared likely, Charlie and Bill Timmins jnr placed a tin 'V' for victory sign on the gate at the junction of the lane and the Middle Road. It was tied to a tree after the lane was fenced and the gate was not needed anymore. In the 1990s, a local schoolteacher with a nose for history, John Dale, heard about this unique and authentic relic of those times, and organised the council and the Rotary service club to preserve the sign and mark it with a

Japanese Occupation Currency souvenired by Jim Noon and now in the McArthur Museum in Brisbane.

THIS TIN "V" WAS PLACED ON THE FORMER MONTEREY/NEWIKIE DOWNS BOUNDARY GATE IN 1945 BY MR. C. P. NOON AND MR. W. J. TIMMINS. THE "V" SIGNIFIED VICTORY BY THE ALLIED FORCES IN WORLD WAR II. WHEN THE ORIGINAL GATE WAS REMOVED, THE SIGN WAS RELOCATED TO AN IRON BARK TREE, THEN LATER TO ITS CURRENT POSITION BY THE MITCHELL ROTARY CLUB, BOORINGA YOUTH COUNCIL AND BOORINGA SHIRE COUNCIL. IT NOW STANDS AS A REMINDER OF THE ELATION AND RELIEF EXPERIENCED BY ALL AUSTRALIANS AT THE END OF THE WAR.

THIS MONUMENT WAS OFFICIALLY UNVEILED BY
DR. W. J. WILSON
MAYOR OF BOORINGA SHIRE
AND
MR. B. NOON
ON
15th AUGUST, 1998

Left: V Gate plaque   Right: Clem and Justin Ditton on a visit to the V-gate lane monument September 2002

plaque.[109] It now takes pride of place at the entrance to the officially renamed 'V-gate Lane'.

Peter met Edna Hynd from Brisbane who was visiting her aunt and uncle, the Browns, who lived in Mitchell. Maria Brown was the sister of Edna's mother Wilhelmine. Peter and Edna married in October 1940, at Clayfield Gospel Hall in Brisbane.[110] Edna was born in 1918 and was raised in Brisbane.

Her father, John, was a Brisbane-born tramway man.[111] Her mother Wilhelmine Ockenfels[112], born in Germany, would have been doubly devastated when her son, Eric, a sergeant in the RAAF, was killed in a 'flying battle' over Germany on 26 June 1942.[113] Wilhelmine was strictly old school when it came to discipline and decorum – as in, rise before the sun and no lounging around in pyjamas.[114] It

Peter & Edna's Brisbane wedding in October 1940: The wedding party included: John Moore, Olive Harrington, Eric Hynd, Merle Moffat, Peter and Edna, Gracie Hynd, Jim Noon and Peg Noon.
Edna lost her brother, Eric, to the war and her sister, Gracie, to TB in 1948.

was a significant change for Edna when she came to live out west. The discipline was useful, but the city comforts were thin on the ground. In 1948, Peter and Edna built a homestead on *Bandon Park* and moved in shortly afterwards. Peter also spent time shearing on neighbouring properties, during and after the war.

In the early 1940s, Bert's eye was taken by the young Jessie Cocks, who lived with her parents across the river on *Aberdeen*. She was the daughter of Henry (Harry) Cocks[115] and Elizabeth Grieve.[116] The Cocks were part of the social group at Dunkeld. Bert and Jessie married in Mitchell in June 1942. They moved next door from *Mulga Belt* to *BA Downs* in 1946.

Marg Caskey, Peg's friend from the convent days, lived with her parents Tom Caskey and Janet née Kinchington at *Avalon*, which was nearby on the other side of the Maranoa River.[117] Marg came to *Mulga Belt* to stay for a week, and from then on, Jim and Marg started to see more of each other, often at Dunkeld. The big flood of 1950 destroyed the bridge over the river just before Peg's wedding and so Marg had to be pulled across the river in a bathtub to get to the big event. The lack of a bridge also posed a challenge to the continuance of Jim and Marg's romance. Jim formed an alliance with Bob Sullivan on the other side of the river who was dating Doreen Foott from Jim's side. Jim and Bob rigged up a flying fox over the river and arranged to swap cars so both couples could continue their courtships. Marg said, riding the flying fox was one of the scariest things she ever did in her life.[118] Jim tied the knot with Marg after her 21st birthday in April 1951. Bob and Doreen followed suit in September 1951.[119]

At that time, most graziers in this district ran sheep on their properties with some cattle as a second string. The price of Australia's wool during the WWII years was constrained by contracts that had been signed with America and Great Britain. As the war ended, demand for fine wool rose. By 1949, it had risen to more than double its wartime price. The Korean War started in June 1950 and the Americans sought to tie up the Australian wool clip with another comprehensive contract.[120] Prime Minister Robert Menzies resisted and after the United Nations troops experienced their first Korean winter, the price of wool exploded. Many people have heard the price of 'a pound a pound', but in May 1951 the top price achieved in Australia hit 375 pence a pound (i.e. £1 11s 3d a pound [lb]).[121] The seesawing fortunes of the war meant it lasted much longer than anyone anticipated. It dragged on for three bitterly cold winters and for several years, the price remained much higher than it ever had been. This was combined with good rains in the district in the early 1950s, so that meant the district was at maximum production. That resulted in a flood of money for the Noons and their neighbours.[122] Some

Left: Peg and Lizzie in front of *Mulga Belt* with Merino rams.   Right: Mail truck laden with wool bales

people went crazy with this windfall and did not make the wisest of choices. The boom generated plenty of work and Charlie made his offer to Dit and Peg to join them on *Mulga Belt*.

Shortly after the peak of the boom, an act of absolute treachery ensued from the political party that claimed to represent people on the land. Arthur Fadden, the leader of the Country Party and treasurer in the Menzies Government announced, in May 1952, the introduction of Provisional Tax.[123] The government was desperate for funds because of war expenditure. The top marginal personal income tax rate (after £4000/per annum) was already 75 percent.[124] This new proposal introduced the requirement to pay tax in advance for the current year based on your income in the previous year.[125] So just as you had calculated your liability for your highly successful last year and were preparing to pay that, you were required to make a distorted estimate and pay tax for the current year as well.[126] The graziers' perception was the government was trying to fleece them, even before they had shorn their sheep. Under this arrangement, the Noons were initially assessed as needing to pay £90,000 in tax for the two years, from their income of £60,000 in the financial year 1952–53.[127] Charlie got advice from solicitors in Roma and formed a company, which ensured a more practical tax bill could be arranged.[128] However, many in the district did not and they were ruined.[129]

Another consequence of the wool boom was that it provided an added incentive to find alternatives to wool. Synthetic fibres steadily improved and with that there was a fluctuating but steady decline in the price of wool. This was just another challenge for the families who spent their lives gambling on the vagaries of primary production. In August 2018, the wool price peaked at $21.16 a kilo, which if expressed as pence per pound would be about 1152 pence (i.e. £4 16s).[130] However, inflation since 1951 has risen by 2,030 percent. So, in 1951 real terms, the recent peak price would be equivalent to 57 pence a pound then. This is the highest real price wool has reached since the 1950s. Put another way, the top 1951 price achieved by the Noons of 236 pence a pound would equate to about $88 a kilo in today's money.

One piece of clear evidence for Charlie and Lizzie's prosperity and generosity was when 22-year-old Mitchell shoemaker, Tom Ringlestein, lost his left leg in a freakish tackling accident during a game of Rugby League at Mitchell in July 1952. Charlie pledged a bale of wool to a fund set up for Tom's benefit.[131] Charlie had been a notable supporter of football in Mitchell. In 1950 he had donated £10 to the local football club and provided a further £1 a week so the club could employ a coach.[132]

The family company, Noon and Company, teamed up the interests of the offspring. Bert was teamed with Peg and Jim was teamed with Peter.

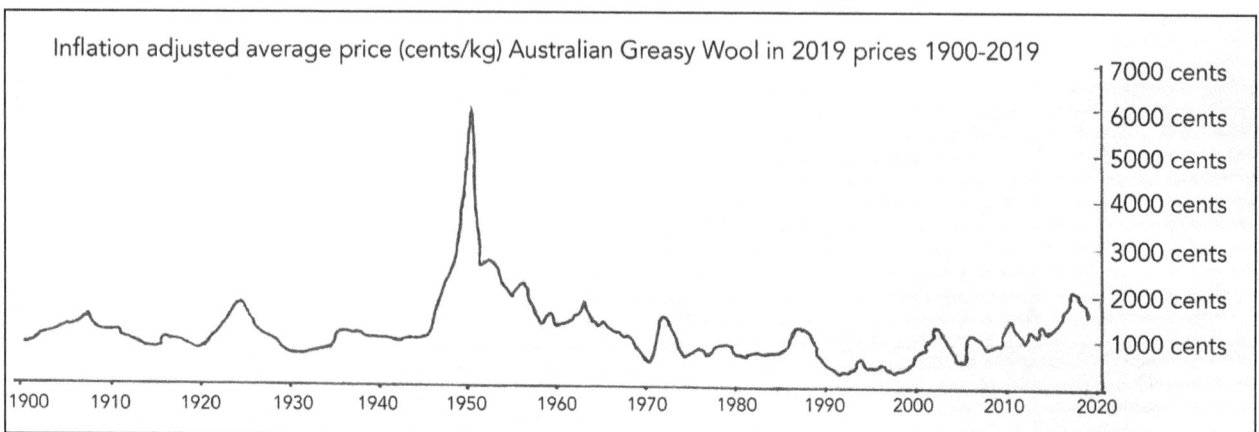

The 50s wool boom in context – Sources: ABS 1301.0 S16.3 (wool industry) Australian Wool Industry Secretariat Dr Peter Morgan via the ABC and Journal of Department of Agriculture, WA Series 4 Vol 38 No 1 Article 7

By the 1950s, Peter was on *Bandon Park*. Jim was on *Glenalvon*. Bert was on *BA Downs* and Peg was on *Mulga Belt* with her parents. *Number 11* was managed with visits every three weeks or so to move sheep between paddocks to disrupt the parasite cycle.[133]

The wool boom meant the Noons could afford a few luxuries like trips away. They also appeared in the social pages of the newspapers when they reported some of their coming and goings, such as:

Mr. and Mrs. C. P. Noon of Mulga Belt returned to Mitchell on Saturday morning after holidaying in Brisbane.[134]

In town for some shopping this week was Mrs. C. P. Noon, 'Mulga Belt', Mitchell. Made the Belle Vue Hotel her headquarters while she was here.[135]

Around 1955, Charlie's health deteriorated and he had to go to the hospital in Mitchell more often. Lizzie bought a house in Mitchell as a place to stay when in town. Charlie's time in the mines was catching up with him. His pipe smoking would not have helped the situation. He died in Mitchell from chronic bronchitis, pneumoconiosis and congestive heart failure in October 1956.[136] Some of his last words were his advice his sons should not buy into the meat works in Roma.[137] His mind was ticking over even until his last breath. His estate was valued at just over £80,000.[138] His executors were Jim Noon, Arthur Ditton and Douglas Pack the Roma solicitor. The complicated property and company arrangements, putting land holdings in partnerships of individuals with a company shareholding structure sitting on top, counted against the estate as it invoked a large death duties bill.[139]

The land was a mixture of freehold and Crown leasehold selections.[140] Freehold was always preferred to leasehold although the latter

Lizzie and Charlie in Sydney c. 1949

Charlie & Lizzie at *Mulga Belt* in late 1940s

was easier and cheaper to acquire. The difficulty was the government could unilaterally change the lease conditions, such as increasing rent, or take the lease from you as they did to the Loughnans, the leaseholders at *Lussvale*. The government broke off portions of *Lussvale* and Peter acquired a block which adjoined *Bandon Park* and Bert got a block which adjoined *Number 11*. All properties were converted to freehold in the 1960s and 70s.[141]

Lizzie mostly stayed on at *Mulga Belt* but was quite restless after Charlie's death. She spent some time in Mitchell and with Peg in Monto and then with Jim at *Glenalvon*. She paid a visit to her sisters in NSW in 1959. Around the end of that year, she suffered from severe headaches, which she thought were associated with her hay fever. Subsequently, she was diagnosed with a brain tumour and her health declined. Eager to avoid a repeat of the problems with Charlie's estate, the family arranged a restructure which only needed Lizzie's signature. She practiced a signature successfully and then attempted to sign the papers for real. It was at that point she lost her ability to sign her name and so the family had another massive death duties bill.[142] Lizzie was flown to Brisbane where she was immediately operated on, but she did not regain consciousness after the operation and died in the Brisbane Mater Hospital in March 1960.[143]

Afterwards, Peter managed *Mulga Belt* and *Number 11* along with *Bandon Park*. Edna and Peter had seven children together. Edna died in Charleville in 1969 and Peter died in Mitchell in 1982. Later, one of Peter's sons managed *Mulga Belt* and in turn one of his sons, Ian Noon and his partner Jodie took over after him. *Mulga Belt* celebrated a centenary of Noon stewardship in August 2022 with a big event. As well as now being a working goat and sheep property, it is developing as an impressive event venue. Much investment has improved water security for the property, even to the point that beautiful homestead gardens can now be sustained. *Mulga Belt* has passed through four generations of Noons management, and so far, six generations have been there.

Bert and Jessie had two children. Jessie died in February 2007 in Mitchell and Bert died ten weeks later in Mitchell also. Jim and Marg had three children. Marg was the last of that generation when she died in 2023, aged 93. Jim had died in 1996 from a heart attack aged almost eighty. He had just played a few ends of bowls at Mitchell and was enjoying a beer with Bert when he said he wasn't feeling too well. The consensus was, it's a pretty good model for how to exit the world.

Queensland bottle tree and windmill in Mitchell, 2002. Photo: author

Endnotes to Chapter 2

1 NSW BC 1890/19393, Pipers Flat, 8 Mar 1890, Charles Peter Noon

2 Portland, NSW, is known as 'the town that built Sydney' as it was the site of Australia's first cement factory and much of that cement was used in the construction of buildings in Sydney.

3 Fire near Piper's Flat, *Lithgow Mercury*, Tue 11 Dec 1900, page 3, http://nla.gov.au/nla.news-article218631577

4 Advertisement, *Lithgow Mercury*, Fri 22 Jun 1900, page 5 http://nla.gov.au/nla.news-article218634379

5 Oral history from Peg Ditton née Noon. That was despite the NSW *Public Instruction Act 1880* requiring school attendance until age 14.

6 Gladys May was the last child born at Pipers Flat in 1906. The Noons bought land at Newnes in 1908.

7 NSW Marriage Certificate (MC) 1910/13867, Waterloo Sydney, 1 Nov 1910, Elizabeth McGonigal & Charles Peter Noon

8 Pronounced 'tor-ficken'. Scottish Statutory Birth (SB), 1888/671/31, 17 Jul 1888, Elizabeth Currie McGonigal.

9 Sister Jean's Scottish SB 1890/662/010241 and the 1891 Scottish Census. Scottish county boundaries have been redrawn since the McGonigals time. Bathgate was in Linlithgowshire.

10 Sister Margaret's Scottish SB 1893/010069 and sister Janet's Scottish SB 1899/628/000470.

11 Scottish census 1901 & sister Sarah's Scottish SB 1903/669/000081 & sister Janet's recollection (1907).

12 Oral history from Peg Ditton née Noon

13 Peg thinks she also worked at Burwood College (or maybe even Methodist Ladies College).

14 Stories of letters etc is oral history from Peg Ditton: The MC has her residence as Scarborough (Wollongong district) and her occupation as home duties. Also, to arrange parental permission implies it was not really a spur of the moment thing. So maybe, she had to resign her position when she announced she was getting married, which was the way things worked back then. The marriage was performed in the Congregational Church (now Uniting Church).

15 NSW MC 1910/13867, Waterloo Sydney, 1 Nov 1910, Elizabeth McGonigal & Charles Peter Noon

16 NSW BC 1911/46609, Numietta St, Newnes, Peter Charles Noon, 30 Sep 1911

17 GJ Taylor, *Newnes, History of a Blue Mountains Oil-Shale town*, Australian Railway Historical Society, Redfern c 1987 page 13

18 Serious accident at Newnes, *Lithgow Mercury*, Wed 2 Aug 1911, page 3 http://nla.gov.au/nla.news-article219536580

19 Over 800 men have been killed in the mines at Broken Hill since the 1880s – Miner's Memorial Broken Hill.

20 Oral history from Peg Ditton née Noon

21 Oral history from Peg Ditton and Ivy Dare, daughter of Charlie's brother, Frank Noon, 2016.

22 Oral history from Peg Ditton née Noon. Electoral Roll gives Charlie & Lizzie's address as Kerr St, Aramac

23 Historically it was referred to as a referendum, but it was a mechanism to get popular support for legislation which was stalled in a divided parliament. Passage of the vote would not have changed the constitution, which is what a genuine referendum would do. Hughes' tactics were heavy handed during the campaign, with dissent against the proposal being shut down by government and police action on the grounds it was treasonous. This earned him the sobriquet of a dictator from his opponents and is seen as a likely contributing factor in the loss of the vote.

24 https://www.abc.net.au/news/2014-12-30/berg-testing-times-make-for-great-and-awful-leaders/5992730

25 https://en.wikipedia.org/wiki/1916_Australian_conscription_referendum. In the 1916 plebiscite, 44.9% of the Australian Imperial Forces formal votes were against the proposition whereas in 1917 it had risen to 47.5%. Although neither of these was a majority, the relatively large opposition vote tended to negate the argument that the troops already over there were desperate for more men from home to help them on the battlefields.

26 331,000 embarked from Australia. 308,000 served in a theatre of war. 62,300 died during the war. Over 125,000 were discharged medically unfit and 60% of the rest applied for pension help in the post war years. *Sydney Morning Herald* 30 Apr 2014.

27 e.g. http://jalalhussain.com/2017/12/17/the-failure-of-leadership-and-its-legacy-the-outbreak-of-world-war-one/

28 NSW BC 1916/43728 Scarborough, Bulli Shire, 4 Nov 1916, James Currie McGonigal. That part of Scarborough is now Wombarra.

29 The only problem with the story is that the birth entry was certified by Lizzie.

30 Oral history from Peg Ditton née Noon

31 Oral history from Peg Ditton née Noon: Florey later lived at Holland Park in Brisbane.

32 A newspaper clipping from local paper of 30 Oct 1956, Death of Mr C. P. Noon (obituary) gives an Aug date, but some family members remembered the anniversary being celebrated around the winter solstice (late Jun) The newspaper reported the sale as 16 Jun 1922..

33 *Mulga Belt* was a name used by the previous owner. It is not yet known when the property was first named that. Mulga Belt is also a term used for the SW section of Qld starting at Mitchell, which has an abundance of Mulga. *Mulga Belt* consisted of portions 15 of the Parish of Dunkeld, County of Kennedy (2941.75 acres) in combination with portion 10 of the Parish of Albany, County of Kennedy (2240.75 acres). This is based on recollections and the fact these 2 blocks were both owned by CFW Kleeman in 1913. Also, the leasehold section (section 10) was held by EC Lambe in 1918 when he was before the land court for the determination of what rent was to be paid for the block (aka No. 2994). His name was on the grant of land for section 15 (freehold) in the Land Court in 1920.

34 Mitchell is named after the explorer Sir Thomas Mitchell who passed through the area in Dec 1845. One of Mitchell's claims to fame is that it is the birth place of Australia's shortest serving Prime Minister, Frank Forde (b. 1890) who was the Labor leader for the seven days following John Curtin's death in July 1945. He was replaced by the more charismatic Ben Chifley.

35 Qld BC 1928/13950, Mitchell, 1928, Elizabeth Peggy Noon

36 Peg Ditton's recollection of *Mulga Belt's* origins. Close, but not quite accurate. An 1893 cadastral map shows one portion of *Mulga Belt* as being part of the *Dunkeld* run, but with no ownership details. The other portion was part of the *Glenormiston* run. The *Dunkeld* run borders *Annie Vale* to the west which is marked as part of Bonus Downs Holdings (1954 map). A 1897 map shows the blocks as part of the *Albany Downs* resumption and the *Tomoo* (Portion B) resumption. A 1920s Qld tenure map shows that the western portion of the *Dunkeld* block is now owned by *Bonus Downs*. So, the story about once being part of *Bonus Downs* appears to true for neighbours to the west. The blocks which now constitute *Mulga Belt* were created by a survey captured on survey plans KE3 and KE10 dated 1909. *Mulga Belt* can be seen on a 1913 cadastral map with the owner then listed as CFW Kleemann. DNRME museum. No evidence these are "soldier settler" blocks.

37 Pastoral property sale, *The Brisbane Courier*, Sat 17 Jun 1922, page 17 http://nla.gov.au/nla.news-article20541216

38 As it was assessed by others in the neighbourhood compared to sweeter country in other directions. 'Little' is an assessment in relation to neighbouring properties. The carrying capacity of the land and the economies of scale meant a viable property in this district would preferably be larger than *Mulga Belt* (e.g. at least 2500 hectares). Charlie recognised that early on and is thought to have used agistment before acquiring more land. If *Mulga Belt* had been a perfect square then each side would measure 4.3 9 kms (2.73 miles), so it is not really 'little' if compared with coastal farming land.

39 http://bonusdownsfarmstay.com.au/history/

40 http://www.queenslandcountrylife.com.au/story/4412886/restoring-homestead-history-all-a-bonus/

41 Artesian water played a part also, but not all properties had access to it. Not used on *Mulga Belt* at that time. It was typically around 400 metres down and boring that deep would cost over $100,000 in today's money.

42 Oral history from Peg Ditton née Noon. In those days lottery winners had their names published in the newspaper.

43 Justices of the Peace, *The Charleville Times*, Fri 14 Apr 1933, page 10, http://nla.gov.au/nla.news-article76388542

44 The Paul brothers were young men from NSW, sent by their parents to make a go of running a sheep property. On one occasion they ran out of food and found their way over to *Mulga Belt*. The Noons were out but arrived home to see smoke coming out of the chimney, which was the Paul boys cooking their dinner.

45 The anecdote is EC Lambe had not left *Mulga Belt* in good shape as he struggled to make a go of it. (He was not a returned WWI soldier as some suggest.) The block had a lot of prickly pear, which was still being eradicated into the 1940s. The Cactoblastis moth had been introduced in 1925 and it was still working its way through the infestation around *Mulga Belt* for a long time after.

46 Ant bed was clay from termite mounds that was better quality than clay in the ground. The charcoal was held in thick panels on 3 sides of the enclosure and wetted down regularly, so the evaporation cooled the contents of the safe. Kerosene fridges (using the absorption method) were adopted in the 1930s, but there were dangers of explosions and the pilot light blowing out.

47 The kangaroo gut was from a recently killed roo. He also stitched up a neighbour after he was attacked by a kangaroo.

48 In later years, the shearing teams employed their own male cook.

49 She would also whip up a batch of scones at short notice – oral history from Peg Ditton née Noon.

50 Reports by the brokers, CP Noon; Mulga Belt, Mitchell, AAA w 25½ d.(/lb.), *The Telegraph* (Brisbane), Fri 10 Feb 1928, page 4 http://nla.gov.au/nla.news-article179750804

51 Portion 15 of the Parish of Wallam, County of Kennedy, 6454.35 acres.

52 Portion 11 in the Parish of Wallam, County of Kennedy, District of Roma, 6879.5 acres. Leases were awarded to people in the district with some land already (but not too much) to improve viability.

53 The Middle Rd was between the River Rd and the Bollon Rd (the road to Bollon from Mitchell).

54 Pronounced 'Bar Downs'. 5720 hectares on 4 titles.

55 The property name was changed to *Monterey* after the owners of *Glonorchy* came to grief financially.

56 Party lines were telephone lines shared with a set of neighbours (typically around 6 or 7). Distinctive Morse code like ring sequences would determine whom any incoming call was for. *Mulga Belt's* call was 3 shorts. Only one party could use the line at a time. Outgoing calls could only be made if the line was not engaged. Distance calls would typically have to be booked in advance. The operator of the manual exchange which serviced *Mulga Belt* was at *Cedarella* (Cedarvale homestead).

57 Oral history from Peg Ditton née Noon

58 Jim joined the army and fought in the war. After the war he married ('well') and settled in Brisbane. Some of the information is from written notes provided by Bert Noon to earlier family history researchers & Peg's recollections.

59 *BA Downs* comprised portions 13 & 14 of the Parish of Dunkeld, County of Kennedy (2386.75 acres, 2537.75 acres respectively) in combination with portions 9 and 19 of the Parish of Albany, County of Kennedy (2241.25 acres, 6946.75 acres respectively). Portion 19 (named *Hopefield* on a cadastral map) was not contiguous with the rest of *BA Downs* and was referred to by the Noons as the *Neabul Block*. Portion 13 (Dunkeld, Kennedy) was owned by WG Page in 1913, whereas portion 14 was owned by GF Bartholomaeus. According to the land transfer documents portion 14 had a new homestead, a men's dwelling and a wash house. Portion 13 had no buildings.

60 Charlie mostly killed sheep. He would kill a beast (steer – young neutered male [*Bos taurus*]) in the wintertime.

61 The fishing was best in some waterholes on the Maranoa River, south towards St George. The Easter fishing trip was a nod to the Christian tradition of not eating 'meat' on Good Friday – oral history Peg.

62 Six round posts in the ground supporting a roof of tree boughs with dead leaves providing shade.

63 Balsille, Blackett, Batterham, Caskey, Gillespie, Kinchington, Noon, O'Sullivan, Paul, Sullivan, Timmins, Wade, Walden.

64 Dunkeld Memorial Hall Opened, *Western Star* (Roma), Fri 6 Jul 1951, page 4 http://nla.gov.au/nla.news-article97541739

65 Before this, some properties used their shearing sheds to host dances. Today there is a dedicated dance shed on *Mulga Belt* itself. The Dance West studio caters to rural students of dance. http://www.dancewest.com.au

66 e.g. Mitchell Tennis, *Western Star* (Roma), Fri 30 Apr 1954, page 4 http://nla.gov.au/nla.news-article97556640 & e.g. Dunkeld I Victorious …, *Western Star* (Roma), Tue 21 Nov 1950, page 2 http://nla.gov.au/nla.news-article97539189

67 From information given during Barry Caskey's eulogy 2018. The 'greens' were made of sand and the 'fairways' were hard to distinguish from the 'rough'. Hazards included kangaroos.

68 From a clipping thought to be *Toowoomba Chronicle,* Oct 1985 – Mitchell camped in Dunkeld area.

69 Fires Sweep Maranoa, *Western Star* (Roma), Tue 2 Oct 1951, page 1 http://nla.gov.au/nla.news-article97542602

70 Oral history from Peg Ditton née Noon. Mitchell & District History Facebook group provided some information on *Coultra*.

71 Penhalluricks were related to the Keable family by the marriage of Elsie's sister Rita to John Penhallurick. Struck by lightning and killed, *Bundaberg Mail and Burnett Advertiser*, Mon 4 Mar 1912, page 3 http://nla.gov.au/nla.news-article215777198

72 Their parents were John Knight Keable & Agnes Martin. Arthur Charles Keable served in WWI in the 2nd Light Horse and was wounded in the shoulder in action in Palestine in Apr 1917. His horse was killed in the incident. His service record also details bouts of VD, malaria and some mischief in Jerusalem in 1919. He died in 1958. His tractor had rolled, but it was suspected he had had a heart attack.

73 Qld MC 1905/C/2234, 1 Nov 1905, Mabel May Keable & Frederick George Cornish.

74 As told by Bert Noon in a speech when celebrating the restoration of the V-gate (notes supplied by Barbara Caskey).

75 From oral history passed on by Amy Williams, daughter of Charlie's brother George

76 Oral history from Peg Ditton née Noon

77 In a small country community like Mitchell, everyone knew each other's business.

78 Oral history from Peg Ditton née Noon – incidentally, the School of the Air started in 1951.

79 To Gatton College, *Warwick Daily News*, Sat 16 Jan 1926, page 4 http://nla.gov.au/nla.news-article175723611

80 From oral history provided by Don Noon and corroborated by Peg Ditton

81 Aberdeen sausage is a tasty meatloaf based on minced meat and bacon. She never cooked haggis or any other offal-based recipe, e.g. New Year's is a much more significant celebration than Christmas in Scottish tradition. Lizzie spoke with a Scottish accent and her speech used many phrases rarely heard today in Australia.

82 Effie's mother was Lizzie's aunt Jane née McGonigal, Bessie was originally Bessie McGonigal, a daughter of James' brother John.

83 Anne's married name was Innes. Her grandfather was James' brother Tom McGonigal, who died in South Africa. Sarah married Jim Smith who, after being a shepherd in the Lammermuir Hills, became the groom to the Duke of Roxburge at Floors Castle, Kelso, Scotland.

84 Oral history from Peg Ditton née Noon

85 Oral history from Peg Ditton née Noon – repeated story even told at his funeral.

86 Oral history from Don Noon and Barbara Caskey

87 They were most commonly seen in trees on the creek bank at *Glenalvon*. They were heard more than they were seen.

88 Shearing at *Mulga Belt* under the Noons management was always done with mechanical shears powered by an engine which drove the shears. Manual shears (click click) were only ever used out in a paddock for small jobs.

89 The flat iron is heated on the stove and picked up with a detachable handle and then used. It would cool down quickly requiring it to be swapped for a new hot one. Repeat often. 'Mother pot' may have been an informal local term as on-line historical sources don't mention it.

90 Whittling or carving or making furniture or tools such as axe handles.

91 Wireless was the term always used for the radio. It is an example of a relatively modern word changing meaning.

92 The woolydays.wordpress site states: 'at least 75 Aboriginals were killed along the Maranoa River up to 1862'. In 1880, a former premier of Qld, George Thorn, boasted that inland Qld Aboriginal people were 'pretty well shot down and got rid of'.

93 *Aboriginal Protection and Restriction of Sale of Opium Acts 1901*

94 https://en.wikipedia.org/wiki/Native_title_in_Australia

95 Native Title Tribunal determination areas can be seen at: https://www.nativetitle.org.au/find/pbc/7725

96 https://woollydays.wordpress.com/2012/06/24/gunggari-people-get-native-title/ The AIATSIS map of Indigenous Australia shows the Mandandanji lived on and around *Mulga Belt* and the Gunggari were further to the west although the map does have a caveat – that not all groups agree with what is depicted and it specifically should not be used to support native title claims. The much-celebrated rugby league player, Jonathan Thurston, has Gunggari heritage via his mother.

97 Percy and Joe. Percy had some ancestry from India. He was in a relationship with Joe's mother (Peg's oral history). There were 2 others who were employed as well in Don Noon's recollection.

98 Noon, James Currie McGonigal: Service Number – QX16430: Place of enlistment – Toowoomba, Qld. He was in the 2/1 Australian Tank Attack Regiment – source: recordsearch.naa.gov.au.

99 Ceylon was renamed Sri Lanka in 1972.

100 The 2 others in his gunnery team were Charlie Derwent and ? McCaffery. Charlie Derwent was a resident of Mitchell and lifelong friend. McCaffery's son, nicknamed 'Shorty', became the postman in the district for 30 years.

101 Mitchell A.I.F. men escape, *Western Star and Roma Advertiser* (Toowoomba), Fri 25 Sep 1942, page 8 http://nla.gov.au/nla.news-article98101406

102 National Archives of Australia – WWII, Noon James Currie McGonigal Service Number QX16430

103 Digger is a term used for Australian soldiers since WWI.

104 Oral history from Peg Ditton née Noon

105 Portion 2 of the Parish of Retreat, County of Maranoa (15165 acres). Vendor name from a family history info from Jim c 1980

106 Ralph supplemented Jim's gift to make a complete set. Peg presented them and a photo of Jim to the museum in May 2016.

107 Noon, Charles Peter: Service Number – Q229049: Place of enlistment – Mitchell, Qld

& Noon, Bert: Service Number – Q229048: Place of enlistment – Mitchell, Qld

108 Japan had abandoned its plan to invade Australia even before its setback at the Battle of The Coral Sea (insufficient manpower).

109 *The Chronicle* (Toowoomba), Fri 6 Nov 1998, page 11, John died of a heart attack after being struck by one of his pupils.

110 Maria Charlotte Ockenfels married Alfred George Brown in 1918 (Qld Marriage Index (MI) 1918/B22276).

111 John Hynd, born 2 Feb 1891, Brisbane, Qld – died Jun 1981, Brisbane, Qld.

112 Wihelmine Ockenfels, born circa 1891, Bohlm on the Rhine, Prussia – died Jan 1967, Brisbane, Qld.

113 https://www.awm.gov.au/collection/R1719436

114 Corroborated by Peg and Shirley Walmsley, née Noon, who stayed with her grandmother for her early years.

115 Henry (Harry) Cocks, born 1886, Lincolnshire, England – died 12 Jul 1970, Mitchell, Qld

116 Elizabeth Grieve, born Nov 1880, Kirkpatrick Juxta, Dumfries, Scotland – died 31 Oct 1979, Mitchell, Qld

117 Finlay Thomas John Caskey, born 27 Jan 1896, Clifton, Qld – died 4 May 1970, Qld. Janet Kinchington, born 25 Jul 1906, *Revilo*, Qld – died 20 Dec 1998. Janet was raised on the property named *Revilo*. The history of *Revilo* is detailed in the book by MJ Fox, *Fox's history of Queensland: Its people and Industries*, States Publishing Co., Brisbane, 1923 page 200 & 201

118 Oral history from Jim & Marg's son, Don

119 Sullivan-Foott wedding, *Western Star* (Roma), Fri 12 Oct 1951, page 6 http://nla.gov.au/nla.news-article97542731

120 At that time Australia supplied 80% of the world's fine wool (suitable for high quality clothing).

121 https://quadrant.org.au/opinion/qed/2012/09/woolly-headed-socialism/

122 The highest published price achieved by CPN/*Mulga Belt* was 236d for AAA w (wether) classed wool in Feb 1951. & Brisbane wool sales, *Queensland Country Life*, Thu 15 Feb 1951, page 25 http://nla.gov.au/nla.news-article97122944

123 New provisional taxation system, *Morning Bulletin* (Rockhampton), Fri 23 May 1952, page 1 http://nla.gov.au/nla.news-article57101928 Provisional Tax was abolished with the GST reforms of year 2000. It was replaced with the Pay As You Go (PAYG) Tax. Arthur Fadden is reported as telling his rural constituents that the taxes would have been higher if not for his efforts. F Lehane, *Heartbreak Corner*, self-published, Beaudesert, 1996, page 191

124 http://www.abc.net.au/news/2015-04-01/tax-facts/6361050

125 http://adb.anu.edu.au/biography/fadden-sir-arthur-william-10141

126 Income tax for primary producers had previously used a rolling five-year average.

127 As the peak of the boom was in 1951–52, it inflated the estimate for the following financial year.

128 Noons were clients of the Roma-based solicitors Dyball and Pack..

129 Oral history from Peg Ditton née Noon

130 Wool price pure gold for farmers, *The Courier Mail*, Sat 23 Feb 2018, page 27 (no current on-line reference) & https://www.farmonline.com.au/story/5817537/milestones-for-wool-in-2018/

131 Footballer loses leg in freak injury, *Western Star* (Roma), Fri 18 Jul 1952, page 1 http://nla.gov.au/nla.news-article97546470 & Bales weights vary, but 280–320 lb is a guide. Based on its position in the donation list, value was at least £150. & Injured footballer fund, *Western Star* (Roma), Fri 25 Jul 1952, page 6 http://nla.gov.au/nla.news-article97546577

132 Football match, *Balonne Beacon* (St George), Thu 23 Mar 1950, page 2 http://nla.gov.au/nla.news-article215370314

133 Later drenching products (administered via a metal nozzle down the sheep's throat) improved significantly, which allowed parasites to be controlled chemically and without the need to rotate paddocks as frequently.

134 Mitchell roundabout, *Western Star* (Roma), Fri 20 Feb 1953, page 8 http://nla.gov.au/nla.news-article97549799

135 Social pages, *Truth* (Brisbane), Sun 10 Oct 1954, page 38 http://nla.gov.au/nla.news-article201192947

136 Qld Death Certificate (DC) 1956/7461 5408, Mitchell, 30 Oct 1956, Charles Peter Noon. Pneumoconiosis is a lung disease caused by the inhalation of dust, often in mines and from agriculture – Wikipedia.

137 Oral history Peg: Charlie said to Dit a day or so before he died, 'Make sure the boys don't go into the meat works'.

138 Affidavit submitted to the Supreme Court in 1957. Current equivalent is approx. $2,500,000 (RBA calculator).

139 Oral history from Don Noon. If they had been in a company name, then it may have affected eligibility for future leasehold land.

140 From an indenture outlining the terms of the partnership of Noon and Company 1958.

141 Information from Eric Noon, son of Peter Charles Noon.

142 Inability to sign is oral history from Don Noon, son of Jim & Marg Noon. Death duties were abolished in Qld by the Bjelke-Petersen Government in 1978 and every other Australian state quickly followed. The Bjelke-Petersen Government was the long-lived but ultimately corrupt government which had Johannes (Joh) Bjelke-Petersen at its head from 1968 until he was ousted by his own party in 1987. His longevity was due in most part to a blatant gerrymander, but he was popular amongst his rural base. The Fitzgerald Royal Commission 1987–89 exposed government corruption and abuse of power and corruption throughout all levels of the police force.

143 Qld DC 1960/36789, Mater Brisbane, 5 Mar 1960, Elizabeth Currie Noon. Medical flights were rare at that time.

Chapter 3

Canny do Scots

Elizabeth and James – McGonigal

The inhabitants of Britain had been migrating to Australia in fits and starts since the First Fleet. There was a downturn in this activity between 1892 and 1906, where the numbers were only a small fraction of what they had previously been. In net terms, Australia lost people to emigration during this period.[1] A deep recession had hit the world in 1890 and Australia experienced the Federation Drought from 1896 to 1902, which slowed Australia's recovery.[2] By contrast, America and other countries saw a rapid rise in their industrial power. America was the preferred destination for those seeking a new life. More than thirteen million people arrived in the USA between 1900 and 1914.[3] Australia's fortunes turned the corner in 1907 and it was once more in favour as a destination, although only a few thousand turned up in that year. This is the story of the family that raised my maternal grandmother, Lizzie McGonigal. Her parents were Elizabeth Douglas and James McGonigal.

From Scotland to Australia

James Currie McGonigal and his eldest son, Peter, travelled to Australia from London on the steamer *Oruba,* landing in Sydney on 6 September 1907.[4] The next day James celebrated his fiftieth birthday. He had taken this calculated risk at this stage of his life to assess the prospects for his family in Australia. His native Scotland offered only limited opportunities for the foreseeable future. He had been a journeyman blacksmith moving between jobs and accommodation in a cluster of localities west of Edinburgh.[5] The family had however, in true Scottish form, managed to save some money as James and Peter had arrived as unassisted immigrants. They also had some resources to invest in their next venture in their new home.[6]

From oral history accounts, the McGonigal family had earlier plans to migrate to South Africa. James' brother, Thomas, had gone to South Africa to join the Natal Volunteer Ambulance Corps to assist in the Boer War.[7] Back in Scotland, he was a loch keeper. The Corps was disbanded in 1900 and the Boer War had ended in May 1902. He returned to South Africa in December 1902 with the intention of migrating. Once settled, he would send word of the conditions there and when best to follow. Unfortunately, Thomas died of cholera on Boxing Day, 1902 at Newcastle, South Africa, just weeks after returning.[8] The McGonigal's emigration plans were put on hold.

On arrival in NSW in 1907, James and Peter found their prospects were indeed better. James then sent for the rest of the family and Peter beckoned his fiancé, Fanny Philip. There is a family anecdote that a young woman in Australia had caught Peter's eye, and after James saw him talking to her, he asked: 'Well make up your mind young man, is it this one or the one back in Scotland?' Fanny and Peter had been corresponding by mail and they had both saved the stamps, which Fanny then pasted onto plates. The plates survive to this day.[9]

Fanny and the rest of the McGonigal family arrived in Sydney aboard the steamer *Ayrshire* in October 1908. It had left Liverpool seven weeks earlier having come via Cape Town and Melbourne.[10] James' wife, Elizabeth Smaile McGonigal (née Douglas), had accompanied her six daughters and her other two sons as well as Fanny. James and Peter were there to meet them. Peter, 21, married Fanny,

25[11], on 6 October 1908 in the Congregational Church in Castlereagh Street, Sydney.[12] This was the very same day, she and the McGonigal family had landed in Australia. According to the family story, the wedding took place at the insistence of Peter's mother. Elizabeth would not even wait until Fanny's trunk cleared the wharf, so she could unpack her wedding dress. Fanny was a dressmaker and it was probable that she, herself, had made the dress.[13] Part of the motivation to ensure the couple were made respectable, as soon as possible, may have been related to experiences with Elizabeth's sisters. Both her older sister Mary, and her immediately younger sister Margaret, had children out of wedlock whilst they were domestic servants

A portrait of the McGonigal family believed to been taken in Edinburgh circa 1902. L to R with birth years: Elizabeth jnr (1888), James snr (1857), James jnr (1897) Mary (1884), Margaret (1893), Peter (1886), Elizabeth snr (née Douglas) (1864), Janet (1899), Robert (1888), Jean (1890). Sarah (not present) was born in 1903. Elizabeth jnr and Robert are twins.

Wolgan Valley view with Newnes at left circa 1917 – National Library Australia[175]

in Scotland.[14] Elizabeth had also been a domestic servant before her marriage, but she managed to escape the occupational hazard which typically ended your career and compromised your standing in the community.

Shortly after they arrived, James took the family to Newnes, NSW, the site of an oil shale mining venture. James and the family pitched a tent on the side of a hill. Water had to carried from the creek. The tent initially had a dirt floor, but Elizabeth demanded a wooden floor, which was quickly organised.[15]

Oral history suggests the McGonigals were aware of the Newnes project prior to leaving Scotland, and it was that, specifically, which drew them to Australia. The Commonwealth Oil Corporation (COC) operated Newnes. It started on a grand scale in 1905 and was primarily financed out of London.[16] The town and mine had been named after the principal financier, the London-based publisher, George Newnes. It was situated amidst the spectacular timbered and mountainous landscape of the Wolgan Valley about 35 kilometres north of the coalmining and industrial town of Lithgow. The site now sits within the Wollemi National Park. Large amounts of infrastructure had been built and the processing plant had been devised based on that used to process oil shale deposits in Scotland.

James' neighbours in Bathgate in 1891 were oil shale miners.[17] Increasing numbers of Scottish workers with relevant experience were arriving at Newnes, with their families. It is likely James had used his blacksmithing skills within the industry, and consequently, he would have had

relevant experience. The family story is they had invested most of their savings in the project. Given the nature of their circumstances, this is probably referring to the investment of their own time and effort and relying on savings awaiting returns via wages. It is highly unlikely they invested directly in the COC operation. The first production of oil did not begin until 1911. Unfortunately, the enterprise foundered in early 1912 due to technical, logistic

Three McGonigal sisters at Newnes circa 1909. L to R: Maggie, Lizzie & Jean[176]

Staff at the Bellambi brick works circa 1919. James is second on left.[177]

and capital raising issues. Added to that, from late 1911, there were prolonged strikes over coal hewing rates and a proposed reduction in ironworkers' conditions.[18] Production ceased in February 1912 and the enterprise under that management was dissolved in 1913. Newnes did go into production under different arrangements between 1914 and 1923 and a subsequent operation in the WWII years with an operational shift to nearby Glen Davis.[19] However, the McGonigal family joined the 1912 Newnes exodus and decided on a different course.[20] They had lost the savings they had sunk into Newnes.

After that episode, James and Elizabeth spent a few years at Pitt Town Bottoms, a few kilometres east of Windsor on the southern bank of the Hawkesbury River. They were known to have dairy cows as James advertised for the sale of two

James McGonigal shoeing a horse. The back caption reads: 'Father hadn't known that I took it down'[178]

cows and gave his address as Oakville.[21] They may also have grown vegetables or tried blacksmithing.[22] Subsequently, James and Elizabeth moved to Bulli, a coalmining district north of Wollongong. Some of the family had already moved there by 1910.

In late 1915, James took up vacant blacksmithing premises in what was then known as Scarborough. The business was situated near the cemetery on the coast side of the Main South Coast Road. His newspaper ad suggested residents should: 'Encourage your local blacksmith by bringing along your work, satisfaction guaranteed. Sulkies repaired and tyreing done'.[23] Their residence was part of the premises also. Oral accounts have them living about two houses north of the entrance to the cemetery.[24] The Commonwealth Electoral Roll of 1917 lists James, Elizabeth and their son Robert, living at *Bonnie Braes*, Scarborough.[25] This locality is now within the suburb of Wombarra. A later residence was in the neighbouring suburb of Coledale.

Coke works to process coal from nearby Bulli No 2 Pit were built in Coledale in 1905. The McGonigal's neighbours typically worked in the mine or the coke works or associated industries. In the years between their time at Wombarra and their time at Coledale, they moved to a residence at Owen Park Road, Bellambi, about fifteen kilometres south of Wombarra and closer to the centre of Wollongong. James was working at the Bellambi Brick works around 1919–1920.

The McGonigal children's stories – Lizzie's siblings

In the years between their arrival in Australia and their relocation to the Bulli district, the older children had started to make their own lives. James' suggestion to his daughters was reputed to be: 'Find yourself a Scotsman and you will be all right'.[26] Only one daughter, Mary his eldest, followed his advice and it was Mary who was to have the hardest time of it.

Mary Nimmo

Mary Nimmo McGonigal married a Scotsman, Charles Calder, in March 1910 at Woonona near Bulli.[27] He was a coalminer and twenty years her senior. Charles and Mary met at Newnes. Charles was living there in 1909[28] and in 1913 the couple were still residing at Newnes[29], but they moved to West Wallsend, NSW shortly after that.[30] The marriage produced four children: Elizabeth (Betty) (born 1911), Margaret (Peggy) (b. circa 1912), Robert (Bob) (b. 1913) and James (Jim) (b. 1915). Peggy died at the age of seven.[31] The marriage ended when Charles died in the Gladesville Mental Hospital in July 1923.[32]

Mary married another Scotsman, Hugh Innes, in 1924 in Sydney.[33] He was also twenty years her senior, but unfortunately, Hugh was not free to marry, as his first wife, Matilda Boyce, was still alive in Victoria. In these days, prior to the *Family Law Act 1975*, divorce was a luxury, affordable only by the rich.[34] In April 1925, Hugh received what was the typical sentence for bigamy at that time, three months hard labour in Goulburn Gaol (and two sets of hostile in-laws).[35] It appears the relationship did not continue after that setback.

Her teenage son, Bob, caused her some trouble requiring her to declare him an uncontrollable child in May 1930.[36] Oral accounts stated her children had to be put into care, as Mary was not able to look after them. However, it appears she maintained contact with at least Betty. Mary did not chance her luck again with Scotsmen, or men of any other stripe for that matter. She was a frequent and welcome visitor at her sister Jean's place at Avoca Beach. On all occasions, she was on her own.[37] She did not get on well with her youngest brother, Jim, who identified her in court proceedings as 'the mischief-maker of the family'.[38] Mary died in a nursing home in Charlestown, Newcastle, NSW in January 1973.[39]

Mary Nimmo Calder née McGonigal[179]

Bob, Betty and Jim Calder circa 1920[180]

Peter

Peter and Fanny had moved to Lithgow and had a son, James Currie (Jim), in 1909.[40] Peter was working in a local colliery.[41] However, with a large measure of homesickness on Fanny's part, they decided, Australia was not for them. They returned to Scotland on 2 May 1911 on board the *Suffolk*.[42]

They returned to the same region in which they had previously lived. Peter found work as a shale miner in the Blackburn/Bathgate district in West Lothian, echoing his time at Newnes. Peter and Fanny went on to have three more children born in Scotland: Fanny (b. 1913), Peter (b. 1915) and Elizabeth (b. 1924).[43]

A grandson of Peter, also named Peter McGonigal[44], related the following anecdotes of Peter's working life back in Scotland. Peter worked in No 3 Seafield shale mine. On 10 February 1915,

he was caught in a fall of stone from the roof. A stone fell on him injuring his back. In another incident, a horse taking Peter and another man into the pits stopped and would not move. The experienced oversman saw this and told them to get out. Shortly afterwards rocks fell from the roof. When he worked in the Westwood shale pit and he was making up shots, two cans of gunpowder went up where he was sitting. His skin was hanging off his fingertips and his arms were also burnt. His co-workers put thick machine oil all over his arms and hands. The doctor gave them hell for doing it, as it had to be scraped off. There were 'trees' nine inches thick which were burned in the blast. Peter continued to work in the mines after recovering from his injuries. His son, Peter, and grandson, Peter, also worked in the pits in their time. Peter snr died in 1961 at Seafield, Blackburn, West Lothian and Fanny snr died in Bathgate in 1964.[45]

Left: Peter and Fanny in a belated wedding photo shoot – wearing the dress she should have worn.
Centre: Fanny and Peter in their early days at Lithgow, NSW. Fanny referred to Australian houses as 'chocolate boxes', as she considered them flimsy compared to what she knew from Scotland.
Right: Peter back in Scotland with grandchildren David, Ruth & Les Dalglish.[181]

Robert Douglas

Lizzie's twin brother, Robert, continued the link with the Noon family by marrying their eldest, Mary Ann, in December 1911 at Newnes.[46] They had a boy, James Currie born in 1912, but he died the following year.[47] William (Andy) was born in Granville, west of Sydney, in 1916 whilst Robert was working as a 'fuel man'.[48] Mavis was born in September 1919 but died in August 1920.[49] Tragically, shortly after her confinement with Mavis, Mary Ann succumbed to a syphilis infection in October 1919.[50] From available records, it appears Robert and Mary Ann were estranged around the time of Andy's birth, as Robert was living in Scarborough with his parents and Mary Ann returned to Newnes.[51] Mary Ann's story is examined in a little more detail within the chapter dealing with her parents.

Robert was at a loose end for several years. It is understood he left his only surviving child, Andy, in the care of his parents as he searched for the next move. He joined his twin sister in the Bracalba district in the D'Aguilar Ranges north-west of Brisbane. An anecdote which survives his time there was, when he left, the horse he used to ride would stop at the Bracalba Hotel automatically whenever anyone else rode the horse. The horse would take some convincing to continue the journey.[52]

In October 1924, the issue of the child minding came to a head. Elizabeth snr took her son, Robert, to the small debts court in Bulli. The complexities of the situation are best presented in the words of the original newspaper report.

Robert McGonigal working with a winch clearing trees which may put him in Bracalba, Qld circa 1918 – from the collection of Peter McGonigal

Elizabeth McGonigal, of Bellambi, proceeded against her son, Robert McGonigal, claiming £8/10/ alleged to be balance due for looking after defendant's son (aged 8). Plaintiff's evidence was that she had kept the child at her home. Defendant had given her £5 and had promised to give more, but failed to do so. The plaintiff's daughter corroborated. For the defence, the defendant, his brother and another sister deposed that defendant had endeavoured to get the child away, but his (defendant's) mother would not let him. At length he surreptitiously took the child away. Defendant's father had written him stating they did not want any money for looking after the child. Constable Armstrong deposed that defendant came to him some months ago, and asked for advice on the matter. In the court there was much wordy warfare between the parties. His Worship entered a verdict for defendant.[53]

Robert married Elizabeth (Betty) Methven in January 1925 in Turramurra, Sydney.[54] They moved to Lithgow, NSW. Andy had a half-sister, Joan (b. c. 1928). Betty, the daughter of a coalminer, was from Fifeshire, Scotland and was ten years younger than Robert.[55] She had emigrated from Scotland, alone at the age of 23, two years before marrying Robert. At the time of Joan's birth, Robert and Betty were living at 5 Brook Street, Oakey Park.[56] By 1937, they had moved to 94 Macauley Street in Morts Estate.[57]

Robert suffered a back injury at his work while trying to lift a heavy load at the steelworks colliery in March 1931.[58] On a happier note, Robert and Betty hosted a wedding reception at their home in January 1933, where Joan was a flower girl and his blind cousin, Andrew, was the organist.[59] That connection is explored further at the end of the chapter.

Robert's granddaughter, Janice, remembered him as a terrible torment, often playing practical jokes on her, such as tying her apron strings to a chair. Robert had moved to 10 Walker Street, Five Dock, Sydney in his later years and was living with his daughter, Joan and her husband, Lyle Wrightson.[60] From firsthand accounts, Robert was suffering from acute shortness of breath attributed to 'dusting' received in the mines.[61] He died at the age of 83 in 1972 in a convalescent home in Summer Hill.[62] Betty died in a nursing home in 1989.[63]

Margaret Lauder Douglas

Completing the union with the Noon family, Margaret (Maggie) married Charlie Noon's brother, Frances (Frank) Noon, in September 1913 at Petersham, Sydney.[64] Maggie and Frank spent their early life at Petersham. Their first child, Stanley (Stan), was born there. By 1915, the family had moved to Clifton, NSW, where their next child, Elizabeth (Bette) was born. Clifton is about twenty kilometres north of Wollongong. This is the point where the escarpment to the west of Wollongong, angles NNE to meet the Pacific coastline, resulting in dramatic coastal scenery. Maggie's parents had recently moved to the district and at this stage were quite close by, with their residence at present-day Wombarra. Frank was a coalminer in the Bulli pit. A number of Frank's siblings (David, Veta, Gladys, Leslie and Arthur) lived close by at various times. Frank registered as a Justice of the Peace in December 1933.[65]

Their next child, Harry, was born in 1919, followed by Dorothy (Dot) in 1923 and Ivy in 1925. Ivy recalled an incident from her childhood when Frank, took Dot and Ivy into the coalmine where he worked. Even they had to duck down to get into the confined workspace. Frank operated the machine which carved the coal from the coalface.

Frank and Maggie on their wedding day in 1913

Maggie, Bette and Frank circa 1919[182]

The Noon house at Reef Avenue, Wombarra – from the collection of Peter McGonigal

Grahame Roebuck, a grandson, related the anecdote that he had fond memories of the ritual of going to his grandparents on Christmas Eve. Grandfather Frank was always absent on these occasions, with the explanation from Maggie he was up in the Scarborough Hotel, which was his favourite drinking hole.[66] Santa always made an appearance on these occasions. It was only after his childhood years that Grahame made the connection between Frank's absence and Santa's presence. The family established a home at the modern address of 1 Reef Avenue, Wombarra. [67] Its beach frontage and dramatic backdrop is so spectacular a location by modern standards that the current owners rent it out at $800 a night.[68] A sum which, if you ignored inflation, would buy the entire property in the days when it was built. During the Depression years, the property had a gantry that allowed for the sawing of bush logs, which were used by neighbours to build houses, sometimes on land squats within the nearby bushland.[69]

His nephew, Les Noon, remembers when he was eight, he wanted a sled and his father took him to Uncle Frank's workshop (on the ocean side of the house). After Frank's efforts, he emerged with a beautifully crafted work of art and all the other kids just had several bits of timber cobbled together.

Anecdotally, Frank and Margaret won a substantial cash lottery prize in the later stages of their life. The Coledale Co-operative ran the lottery. It came at a particularly welcome time and relieved some financial pressures.[70] Frank died in August 1955 at the Coledale hospital from a lung disease associated with mining.[71] In his later years he had to sleep on the veranda to assist with his breathing. Maggie was said to have had a phenomenal memory, particularly for relatives' birthdays. Maggie, who was affectionately remembered by all who knew her, died in May 1962 at their beach-side home in Reef Avenue, Wombarra.[72]

Jane (Jean)

When aged 20, Jean had a relationship with Joseph (Joe) Coleman, in Newnes, which resulted in a daughter, Ruby Doreen (Dora).[73] Joe Coleman, a 36-year-old bachelor, was working there as a prospector and road contractor.[74] The marriage was prevented by parental objection primarily because Joe was a Catholic.[75] This prohibition was very real and widespread at that time. Over time, attitudes within the McGonigal family softened, as just ten years later, their youngest daughter, Sarah, married a Catholic. Joseph never married.[76] Dora's story is examined in more detail at the end of the chapter.

Jean went on to marry Bill Bryant, an Australian-born bricklayer, stonemason and orchardist at Turramurra, NSW in May 1913.[77] Maggie McGonigal and Frank Noon were the witnesses to their wedding, and four months later Jean and Bill returned the honour at Maggie and Frank's wedding.[78] Dora became big sister to William (b. 1916), James (b. 1917), Elizabeth (Kathleen) (b. 1919), Arthur (Tod) (b. 1921), Jean (b. c. 1924), Celia (Heather) (b. 1925), Mary (Nancy) (b. 1927) and Thomas (b. c. 1937). A daughter, Margaret was born in 1914 and died the same year. They also fostered children, one of whom, Bob Wilson, married their daughter, Kathleen.[79]

The Bryants lived at Turramurra in the early years. They spent some time at Lithgow and then lived at Round Drive, Avoca Beach near Gosford in a house named *Bonnie Brae*,[80] which Bill built.[81] A granddaughter, Carol Weber, recounts how Jean was a good cook and Sunday dinner was always an open joyful affair for all workers in the local area. Dinners were always well attended. Echoing the McGonigal-Noon linkage, three of Jean's daughters married three Muldoon brothers. Jean married Albert. Heather married Keith. Nancy married Leslie.[82] Bill died at Gosford in October 1965 and Jean died at Gosford in June 1970.[83]

Janet Douglas

The family had had an earlier child named Janet Douglas, born in August 1895, who sadly only lived for eight days. Thankfully, the second Janet was in much better health. Like her sister Lizzie before her, she worked at the Presbyterian Ladies College, in Sydney. Her main job was ironing students' uniforms, and as a result, she was a fastidious ironer for the rest of her life. She was the next to marry. At age 18, Janet married 28-year-old Englishman, James (Jim) Hayes, in December 1917 at Bulli. For some unknown reason, Jim changed his surname unofficially from Hay to Hayes during his emigration from England in 1913.[84] In 1924, he was caught up in a bitter battle with his volatile brother-in-law, Jim McGonigal, which is explored later in this story.

L to R: Bill Bryant, Janet Hayes, Lizzie Noon, Dora Hicks, Jean Bryant and Maggie Noon Avoca Beach circa 1959

L: The Hayes children, Jean, Wal and Jim on the family sulky with 'Sun' the horse. R: Janet Hayes, Jim Hayes and Lizzie Noon at *Mulga Belt* in the 50s – both photos from the collection of Ivy Dare and Brenda Burch

In June 1941, he was working as a 'wheeler' in a Scarborough coalmine. A wheeler led the 'wheel horse' dragging the loaded skips to the surface.[85] Jim owned and cared for his horses at Bellambi. Jim learnt about the care of horses from his father who owned and trained horses in Islington, London for use in Hansom Cabs.[86] One day at work in 1941, a skip ran over his right hand, crushing his fingers.[87]

Janet and Jim had three children Jean (b. c. 1918), Jim (b. c. 1920) and Walter (Wal) (b. c. 1923).

They also raised their granddaughter, Beverley (Bev).[88] In later years, they moved to 10 Princess St, Corrimal.[89] In 1938, he advertised for the sale of two land allotments near Corrimal Station and for a silky oak sulky in first-class order.[90] Oral accounts remember Jim as being fastidious – requiring a neat and tidy living space – and Janet is remembered as being quite happy with Jim taking on the housework to achieve that.

Left: Janet (Centre) in Scotland in 1973 with her nieces Fanny (L) and Lizzie (R) from the collection of Bev and John Schweers. Right: This is the last residence of the McGonigals in Scotland. It was called Hopefield House/Cottage in Blackburn: Original handwriting on back of photo reads: 'This old house has red tiles roof. One sister in front could be left out. Evergreen trees in front. Would like it in colour'. The cottage is now demolished.

Jim died in October 1962 in Wollongong.[91] Janet returned to Scotland on a visit in 1973 where she was interviewed for an article in a local Scottish newspaper. She gave her reminisces of her time there 64 years previously. Most of the town of Blackburn had been altered since her departure and not attractively. The pleasant sight of the dykes and the green fields stirred her memory. She recalled living in a large house called *Hopefield*, which was derelict at the time of her visit. She recounted the family's early struggles to build up their homes in Australia.[92] When Janet died in February 1989 at Wollongong, she was the last of the McGonigal family that had come out from Scotland.[93]

Sarah Stafford Bell

The youngest, Sarah, aged 17, married Maxhem (Max) Gorbach in October 1920 at Bulli.[94] He came to Australia in early 1914.[95] He had been born in Moscow and trained as an engineer. He stated he had worked as an engine driver in Russia.[96] He worked at the coalmine at Corrimal until September 1924, when he accidently fell from a skip at work whilst installing a slab in the ceiling. He severely injured his back and hip, and consequently, he was unable to work in any capacity for several months.[97] Max identified as a Catholic, so the earlier McGonigal objection to marrying into that faith had apparently softened from their early years. However, he probably started life as Russian Orthodox and changed to Catholicism in Australia, as that was the closest denomination available.

He was referred to as having been a White Russian – however, the Russian Civil War, pitting the Whites against the victorious Reds, started in 1918, after he had left Russia.[98] After he recovered sufficiently from his accident, he worked as a specialist masseur in his residence at Rothery St, Corrimal until August 1930.[99] He moved his practice to Catherine St, Glebe in Sydney. In later years, he used the title 'Doctor'.[100] The family lived at 220 Glebe Point Road, Glebe, Sydney. Sarah and Max had two children: Joyce (Joy) (b. c. 1925) and Noel (b. c. 1927). Max died in Balmain, Sydney in November 1960 and was buried according to the rites of the Catholic Church.[101] Sarah died in Croydon, Sydney in 1970.[102]

James Currie junior

The last to marry was James (Jim) jnr, a coke worker. He married Edith Delaney in her hometown of Lithgow on Boxing Day, 1923.[103] It is fair to say Jim, in 1924, was an angry young man. He was at war with his parents over a property they shared. He was at war with his sister, Mary, and his sister, Janet, and her husband, Jim Hayes, and he was at war with the council over perceived incompetence and injustices. He tried to pit the council against his

L: Sarah and Max R: L to R: Frank Noon, Maggie Noon, Jim McGonigal and his wife Edith née Delaney[183]

parents. This conclusion is drawn from the number of newspaper items, letters to the newspapers and letters to council. It is hard to piece together whether any of his belligerence was based in real troubles or whether mountains had been made out of molehills. He seemed to be on good terms with his brother, Robert. The newspaper article, best encapsulating his state of mind, is the following from 12 September 1924.

Bulli Court: Malicious Language. Jas. McGonigal proceeded against James Hayes of Bellambi, for breach of the peace, to wit, using violent and malicious language. Mr. d'Apice for the defence. Complainant deposed that he was cutting some wood in his yard when defendant came along and abused him, using the words the subject of the charge. It was a family quarrel; defendant was his brother-in-law. To Mr. d'Apice: Was married last Christmas time; he claimed part of his parents' home as his; did not threaten court proceedings against his father. There had been several arguments about the property; did not tell defendant he (witness) would 'fix him'; there was bad feeling between witness and his mother; did not say to his mother, 'I will fix you and your fancy son-in-law'; did not say 'I was going to make it impossible, for Jim Hayes to live'; the boot was on the other foot. Defendant never attempted to strike witness. James Hayes (defendant) deposed he was cutting fodder in the yard at the time of the argument; McGonigal said, 'I will fix you up so that you won't want to go to any court.' Witness replied that somebody had already fixed him up by poisoning two of his fowls, and giving his pony a dose of some kind; did not say that he would put some gelignite under complainant's dossel[104] and blow him and his bag up.[105] After hearing further evidence by defendant's wife, Mrs. Mary Calder and Mrs. McGonigal, his Worship dismissed the information. No costs were allowed.[106]

The seeds of some of the trouble seemed to have been sown with a property arrangement initiated in August 1919 when Messrs Hayes & McGonigal jointly acquired Lot 28 of Owen Park Estate, Bellambi.[107] Permission to build another house was granted to J McGonigal at Bellambi in April 1923.[108] The friction started with a fence built in 1922 and things had been getting worse since his wedding. Jim McGonigal and his wife were in a house between the houses of his parents and the house of Janet and Jim Hayes. Jim Hayes claimed: 'I did him a good turn over a block of mine. I also lent him some money for the upkeep of his house

some months ago when he met with an accident'.[109] Jim claimed part of his parent's property as his own. He tried to sell five acres of land and a three-roomed fibro cottage at Bellambi ('cheaply') in April 1924.[110] He advertised in a Lithgow paper as well a local one.[111] In the court proceedings, he admitted, he prevented his mother getting out with her cart past his place because she had abused his wife. He said of his sister, Mary Calder: 'I know her to my sorrow. She is the mischief-maker of the family'.[112]

These snippets are from the battles between Jim and his parents, which involved the council:

Correspondence. From Jas. McGonigal, senr., stating that his son disputes the right of entry to property as per agreement with the Council. — Referred to the Mayor and Town Clerk for inquiry.[113]
Correspondence. From J. McGonigal, junr., re the trouble between himself and his parents over a roadway. He demanded an apology from them before giving a road of access.[114]
Correspondence. From J. McGonigal, junr, intimating he intended to fence certain land at Bellambi. — To reply that the Council would not permit any land belonging to it to be fenced. ... Works. Committee's Minutes: Recommended — That J. McGonigal senr. be refused permit to construct bridge in Owen road.[115]

In 1925, Jim wrote a letter to the *Argus* headed, 'Kept in the dark', complaining he is required to pay rates for lighting and water when neither are supplied for his street in Bellambi. A reasonable complaint — however, the letter goes much further than it needs to.[116]

Sometime over the next few years, Jim joined his brother Robert at Oakey Park, Lithgow. Whilst there, he was a delegate for the Labor Party to a Municipal Assembly.[117] He was on the board of the Zig Zag School P & C and an active and moderately vocal member of the community.[118] He was also a successful and competitive vegetable grower. He shared top honours in the vegetable section at the Lithgow Flower Show in January 1938.[119] The energies he expended in warfare at Bellambi were more purposefully channelled. During the WWII years he worked for the munitions factory at Lithgow. His profession was listed as boiler attendant at that time. In 1942, he was transferred to Orange, NSW, and he received a gift from the community in appreciation of his civic efforts.[120] He returned to Lithgow shortly after and was working as an engine driver in 1949 and 1954 according to the Commonwealth Electoral Roll.[121] His obituary in 1955, however, said he was working at the Terry's Brewery at the time of his death and had been for several years. He was secretary of the brewery's social club. His obituary used the words 'well known and highly respected' and 'quiet but friendly disposition', which confirmed the transformation of his public persona at least.[122]

Edith and Jim raised five children who survived them: Dora (b. 1927), Hazel (b. 1928), Nellie (b. 1931), Rita (b. c. 1932) and James Currie (b. c. 1943). Five other children had died during James' lifetime. Oral accounts recall their youngest, James, was disabled and needed ongoing care. Jim died after a brief illness in 1955 at Oakey Park, Lithgow and Edith died in Lithgow in October 1960.[123]

James and Elizabeth, continued

Returning to the parents' story – around 1927, James and Elizabeth acquired a four-roomed cottage with a verandah, named *Glen Cottage*.[124] It was on the northern corner of Garlic Street[125] and the Main South Coast Road, Coledale.[126] The property had a sulky shed and a workshop where James pursued his blacksmithing work.[127] A substantial creek ran through the property,[128] with a recreation reserve on the other bank and the house looked out onto present-day Sharkey's Beach.[129] Coledale and Wombarra, their earlier address, are both spectacularly situated on the Pacific Ocean shoreline with a narrow flat section and then a hillside rising steeply to a vertical escarpment. The area suffered some dramatic landslips in 1950[130] and in 1988.[131]

James and Elizabeth marked their fiftieth wedding anniversary on 31 August 1933 with their picture in a local paper.[132] They put their Coledale

Main South Coast Road, Coledale circa 1905, the locality, James and Elizabeth moved to in later years[184]

Celebrating Golden Wedding - 1930

Mr and Mrs G. McGonigal, of Glen Cottage Coledale, Illawarra Line. Recently celebrated their Golden Wedding. Fifty years ago they were married in Kirklonds, Sinlithgowshire Scotland.

L: L to R Elizabeth, Lizzie, James, Peter, Robert and Mary circa 1890 R: Elizabeth and James from a newspaper.

cottage on the market from September 1934[133] through to May 1936.[134] The market was not strong as the Bulli coalmine closed in 1926 and the country was still suffering from the Great Depression of the 1930s. They did manage to move in 1936 where they re-established their residence at Bellambi[135] and advertised for a new home for their dog.[136]

In retrospect, 1924 had been their horror year with the public 'wordy warfare' with their sons Jim and Robert, Max's career-ending accident and Mary's bigamist marriage. Now, in their twilight years, these issues were essentially resolved and just a memory.

After learning of the death of his brother Peter in Scotland in 1935, James wrote of his concern in a letter to his son, Peter that the family Bible should pass to his son rather than to his brother John, revealing some old family tensions back in Scotland.

With family members working in the mining industry, they would have had mixed feelings about strikes that were gradually making conditions better, but also causing much disruption. In a letter to his daughter, Lizzie (who was very fond of her father)[137] dated 2 April 1940, James wrote: 'The Coal Stryk is in full swing and I think miners will be sorrow that they will get nothing but might lose something'.[138] It is estimated that at this time, a coalminer in NSW with an intended 40-year career, had a one in 24 chance of accidental death and a one in five chance of suffering a serious debilitating injury.[139] The all-too-common lung problems were not counted within those statistics.[140] Miners strikes during the early part of WWII led to accusations of treason by the then Menzies Government, which linked strikes to communist activities. There were communists within the mining unions, but the unions' militancy was mostly associated with legitimate grievances –

e.g. the underground dangers over a career exceeded the risks experienced by Australian enlisted men during WWII.[141] A fact that refutes the communist-plot argument was that the rate of strikes increased over the course of the war, despite the election of the more sympathetic Curtin Labor government in October 1941 and Communist Russia's entrance into the war in June 1941 on the side of the Allies.

James died at his residence in October 1940, aged 83.[142] In her later years, Elizabeth had a pronounced fleshy lump on her shoulder, which she refused to have seen to, as she considered it would be an unnecessary expense. Others were more concerned for her than she was herself. Her granddaughter, Ivy, remembered her with much love for her care and kindness. In contrast, her daughter, Lizzie, remembered her mother scolding her when she was caught reading a book. 'I don't want dolly daughters, there's work to be done,' she would say. After her husband's death, Elizabeth moved to Sydney to be cared for by her daughter, Sarah, as dementia was starting to take hold.[143]

In March 1943, a letting agent took action on her behalf as her Bellambi house tenant skipped without paying rent.[144] In April 1943, Elizabeth died in the Buxton Private Hospital, Glebe.[145] Her son James had made his peace with her as he was the informant on her records. In the same month, the home in Bellambi was put on the market.[146]

As with their own large family, by current standards, both James and Elizabeth had come from large families also. This was quite the norm for these times. James parents, Peter McGonigal and Elizabeth née Currie, had seven children who grew to adulthood.[147] Three died in infancy. Elizabeth's parents, Robert Douglas and Mary née Nimmo had nine children who survived infancy.[148] The family story regarding Elizabeth's parents was that Mary was from a wealthy family and Robert was not. Mary's parents were farmers who employed servants.[149] Robert was at times a labourer, a shale miner and a railway fettler.[150] The Nimmo's objected to the marriage and 'disowned' Mary after she married Robert.

Left: Jim and Sarah Smith circa 1974 Centre: The Mcgonigal brothers L to R: John, Tom, James, Peter circa 1880, Edinburgh Right: Bessie McGonigal is top right with brother John with parents John and Janet circa 1910

Scottish relatives Left: Fanny McGonigal Jnr Centre: Jim McGonigal, centre, the Australian born son of Peter with his dapper pals. Jim is remembered as having a very good baritone voice. R: Anne Campbell (later Innes), in her WRNS uniform. She served in an intelligence unit in WWII.[185]

Contact was kept up with the families who remained in or returned to Scotland. Letters and gifts were exchanged, and as modern communications and transport improved, other options became available. An example of that is when Lizzie, and then her daughter, Peg, corresponded with four Scottish cousins for several decades. Shortly after WWII ended, Lizzie sent their Scottish cousins food parcels via the wool company they dealt with. There were still severe shortages and harsh rationing in Britain for several years after the war.[151] In the late 1960s to early 1970s, air travel between Australia and the UK became affordable for folk of average means. So, several Australian relatives including Janet and Peg visited Scotland. Scottish relatives also came out to Australia for visits. One, a son of James McGonigal, the child born to Peter and Fanny before they returned to Scotland, came for a six-week holiday in 1971. He delayed his return and eventually met and married an Australian girl. They settled in Qld.[152]

Peg's pen pal, Sarah Smith (née Mercer) and her husband Jim, came to Australia for a visit in the late 1970s. Jim, rightly, took much pride in his Scottish heritage and traditions. He worked as the groom to the Duke of Roxburghe at Floors Castle. He decided to wear his kilt whilst exploring Toowoomba. Predictably, some local yobs catcalled from their truck with cries of 'I like your dress'.

An episode demonstrating the divide between Scottish Catholics and Protestants was when Peg was visiting her cousin, Bessie Ross (née McGonigal), in 1974, Peg mentioned that she should go to Mass and asked directions to the nearest Catholic church. Bessie replied, 'Oh well, you can either go with the Devil or go with the Lord'. Bessie was a tad voluble, so much so that whilst on a Highland bus tour with Peg, an American tourist observed. 'That woman could talk the leg off an iron pot'. Peg overheard that and said, 'Be careful, that's my relative you're talking about'. To which he replied 'Well, I wouldn't brag about it, honey'.

Peg also corresponded with her second cousin, Anne Innes (née Campbell). Several of us enjoyed a visit with her at various times. She was easy to like, with her gentle but slightly wicked sense of humour. She was a descendant of Tom McGonigal who died in South Africa in 1902. Her maiden surname, Campbell, is a polarising name in Scotland as a result of the 1692 massacre at Glencoe and the Jacobite defeat at Culloden in 1746.[153] A father of one of her childhood friends in Scotland once told her, she wouldn't have been allowed into the house if they had known her surname. I was hitchhiking in Scotland in 1980, and a man who gave me a lift shared his local knowledge with me. As we passed into the area around the Mull of Kintyre, he said 'This is Captain Campbell country'. I asked if people still cared about that, to which he replied, 'Not as much as they should'.

McGonigal is a name of Irish origin, associated with County Donegal.[154] James' paternal grandfather, Peter, was an agricultural labourer who was born in Ireland in 1786.[155] He sought a better life in Scotland and so James and his family continued that journey. James is understood to be the only one of his family to emigrate from Scotland apart from Thomas' ill-fated attempt. In addition to Elizabeth's brother Andrew migrating to Australia (see below), one of her sisters, Mary, migrated to Canada in 1904 with her husband, John Barnes, and their children. Her youngest sister Janet married John Flint and migrated to the USA. She died in Santa Barbara, California in 1942.

The McGonigals are just one of many thousands of families who have made Australia their home during this period. Most families shared the story of the gamble on the long one-way journey in search of a better future, primarily for the younger family members. The themes of hard and hazardous manual work, tragic child mortality and family disputes probably plays out in many other families also, just the details are different. Thirty-seven grandchildren survived James and Elizabeth.

Contrasting beach scenes. Left: Jim Hayes jnr, Jean Hayes and William (Andy) McGonigal on the beach at Corrimal. (Australian style) Right: Fanny and Peter at the beach (British Style).[186]

Dora's story

The wider family talked about Dora Bryant, Jean's first child, because it seemed like her story had a Cinderella flavour to it. A bit of research showed it had a sad and complicated tinge as well. Dora had an accident in her teens, resulting in her walking with pronounced limp. She had remained in contact with her biological father, Joe Coleman. Around 1928, Dora moved from her family home at Avoca Beach to Sydney. There, a pregnant 17-year-old Dora married her baby's father, John Millerick, a 48-year-old widower with three young children. John's first wife, Caroline, had a few months earlier taken her own life by hanging herself.[156] Dora had two children with John, Margaret (b. 1929) and Sydney (b. 1930), but Margaret died at the age of two. The marriage with John broke down after four years.

In early 1932, Dora left with her two-year-old son, Sydney, to live with her ailing father, Joe. He lived in a red brick mansion in Stockton, NSW, which he shared with Joseph Thomas, a Congregational clergyman. Joe had never married, and Dora was his only child. Joe died in November 1932, leaving his property portfolio valued at £3000 to Dora, at a time when – during the Depression – an average house cost about £300. There was a complication requiring judicial adjudication, in that the will was provided on a form and two contradictory sections were filled out. One section provided for a thirty-shilling weekly allowance for fifteen years with the remainder of capital then transferred. There were also provisions for her son, Sydney. The other section allowed for immediate transfer of all funds directly to her. The judge decided the allowance construct was the just entitlement.[157]

Two years later in November 1934, John Millerick took his own life, also by hanging.[158] John's sister reportedly raised the three Millerick orphans. Just eleven days after John's death[159], Dora married Alf Hicks, a farmer's son, who was of a similar age.[160] Joseph Thomas officiated at their wedding.[161] Dora's son, Sydney, died in 1936, aged six. Dora and Alf had a happy and adventurous life with three boys and a deep interest in travelling, gardening, rock collecting and birds. The English–Irish comedian, Spike Milligan, when staying at nearby Woy Woy, is reported to have enjoyed their company because of their shared interests, particularly bird watching.[162] They lived on a large secluded property at Kincumber near Avoca Beach named *Wildwood*, which had feeding facilities for the over seventy species of birds which regularly visited the property. An undated local newspaper cutting featured the garden during one of its public openings in the 1960s and 70s.[163] Dora lived to the age of 98.[164]

Andrew Douglas and family

One of Elizabeth snr's younger brothers, Andrew Douglas, migrated to Australia in 1928.[165] He brought with him his wife, Anne, and seven sons (Andrew, Robert, James, Alexander, William, George and John).[166] A son, Drummond, had been killed at the age of 24, in a shale mine accident at Kirkliston, Scotland in 1919.[167] They settled in the Lithgow district to be neighbours with their relatives, Robert, James and Jean McGonigal. After arriving in Australia, Andrew snr worked as a gardener and then the caretaker at Hoskins Memorial Church. The local newspaper described the Douglas family as 'particularly musical'.[168] They lived at 121 Vale Road.[169] Anne died in 1939 and Andrew snr in 1940.[170]

Andrew and Anne's son, John, was accidently killed in 1934 at the Port Kembla steelworks. He was instructed to remove some clamps from the moulding of what should have been a solid ingot of fifty tons of steel. The ingot was suspended, within its moulding, about two feet off the ground and about to be lowered into a pit. Due to a lapse in supervision, the ingot was still molten and as the first clamps were removed, the liquid broke free from its moulding, engulfing John as he lost his footing, killing him instantly. Six others were also burnt with one other later dying of his burns.[171]

Andrew and Anne's son, Andrew, played the organ at the 1933 wedding hosted by his cousin, Robert McGonigal.[172] Andrew had been severely blinded in a childhood accident. Another child had accidently poked Andrew in the eye with a stick. An infection spread to both eyes. Consequently, he was taught to play pianos and organs at an institution in Edinburgh. He was also taught how to tune and repair them. Blind people were considered particularly suited to this task as their hearing sense was often accentuated to compensate for the lack of sight. This became Andrew's profession in the United Kingdom, which eventually led him to that role in China for fifteen years. In 1922, he was employed in this role at the palace of China's last Emperor, Henry Pu Yi. He remembered him as 'a likeable and even-dispositioned youth' who sometimes drew up a stool and played beside Andrew.[173] Andrew left China in 1929 as the Sino-Japanese conflict was starting. He died at the age of 61. He was survived by his wife, Annie and his daughter, Noela.[174]

Hoskins Memorial Church and garden, Lithgow, September 2016. Photo: author

Endnotes to Chapter 3

1 An average of just over 1000 assisted immigrants arrived in Australia per year between 1890 & 1905. Between 1892 & 1906, an estimated 25,000 citizens were lost to Australia due to net migration. *Australian Historical Statistics* – Ed: W Vamplew, Pub: Fairfax Syme & Weldon Associates NSW 1987.

2 https://en.wikipedia.org/wiki/Federation_Drought

3 https://www.gilderlehrman.org/history-now/essays/progressive-era-new-era-1900-1929

4 All NSW, Australia, Unassisted Immigrant Passenger Lists 1826–1922

5 The Scottish addresses recorded for James and his family are:

Uphall, Ecclemachan Parish, County Linlithgowshire (1883) Scottish Register Marriages (RM) 1883/666/1, 31 Aug 1883

Kirknewton, East Calder, County Edinburgh (1884) Scottish SB 1884/690/000063, 20 Aug 1884, Mary

Ecclemachan Parish, County Linlithgowshire (1886) Scottish SB 1886/666/8, Peter

Bridge Castle Cottages, Torphichen, County Lothian (1888) Scottish SB 1888/671/30, Robert

Bathgate, County Linlithgow (1890) Scottish SB 1890/662/010241, 28 Dec 1890, Jane

29 Deane Row, Bathgate, Linlithgow (1891), Scottish Census 1891 662/1 8/ 18

Tarbrax, Carnwath, County Lanark (1893, 1895, 1897) e.g. Scottish SB 1893/010069, 21 Mar 1893, Margaret

200 Caledonian Rd, Wishaw, County of Lanark (1899) Scottish SB 1899/628/000470, 9 Jun 1899, Janet

114 Stoneyburn, Whitburn (1901) Scotland Census 1901 673/01004/00025, 31 Mar 1901

74 Seafield, Livingstone, County Linlithgow (1903) Scottish SB 1903/669/000081, 8 Aug 1899, Sarah

Hopefield house, opp. Redhouse school, Bathgate (c. 1907) (Janet's recollections).

6 Oral history recounted by Peg Ditton, daughter of Lizzie

7 From information supplied by Kath Ramsey, Scotland (descendant of Thomas) in Jan 2017.

8 Oral accounts and details supplied by Ruth Nicolson, Scotland

9 Oral history by Ruth Nicholson, Scotland Dec 2016

10 All NSW, Australia, Unassisted Immigrant Passenger Lists 1826–1922

11 Scottish SB 1883/672/000103, Uphall, Linlithgow, 10 Apr 1883, Fanny Philip

12 NSW MI 1908/12348, Waterloo, Fanny Philip & Peter McGonigal

13 Oral history related by Beverly & John Schweers (Hayes Line)

14 Mary had a son in 1884 at Kirklands (Scotland SB 1885/666/000002, 19 Dec 1884, Alexander Douglas) and Margaret had a son in 1889 at Bridgecastle (Scottish SB 1889/671/000007, 18 Feb 1889, James Douglas). Both women subsequently married and had other children.

15 Oral history related by Beverly & John Schweers (Hayes Line)

16 http://users.tpg.com.au/newnes/h/histo.htm

17 Scotland Census 5 to 6 Apr 1891, Bathgate, Linlithgow 662/1 8/ 18

18 Our industrial troubles, *Lithgow Mercury*, Mon 12 Feb 1912, page 2 http://nla.gov.au/nla.news-article218742174

19 *Australians Events and Places*. Ed: G. Aplin, S.G. Foster & M. McKernan Pub: Fairfax, Syme & Weldon, NSW 1987

20 The Newnes exodus, *Lithgow Mercury*, Fri 8 Mar 1912, page 4 http://nla.gov.au/nla.news-article218743739
& The Newnes exodus, *Lithgow Mercury*, Fri 28 Mar 1913, page 4 http://nla.gov.au/nla.news-article218663425
& The Newnes exodus, *Lithgow Mercury*, Wed 24 Apr 1912, page 3 http://nla.gov.au/nla.news-article218737377

21 For sale two good milch cows, *Windsor and Richmond Gazette*, Sat 28 Dec 1912, page 6 http://nla.gov.au/nla.news-article85850258
& repeated the following Saturday Jan 4, 1913, page 9

22 Oral history related by Beverly and John Schweers (Hayes Line)

23 Advertising, *South Coast Times and Wollongong Argus*, Fri 19 Nov 1915, page 15 http://nla.gov.au/nla.news-article141647292

24 Oral account by Ivy Dare, daughter of Maggie Noon – the approximate current day address is 573 Lawrence Hargrave Drive.

25 *Bonnie Braes* is Scottish dialect for beautiful hillsides. Commonwealth Electoral Roll 1917, Illawarra, Sub-Division of Bulli.

26 Oral history recounted by Peg Ditton, daughter of Lizzie

27 NSW MI 1910/7073, Woonona, Mary M McGonigal & Charles Calder

28 Newnes IOG Templars, *Lithgow Mercury*, Mon 9 Aug 1909, page 1 http://nla.gov.au/nla.news-article218479740

29 Commonwealth Electoral Roll 1913, Division of Macquarie, Sub-Division of Wolgan

30 NSW Birth Index (BI) for Robert: 45135/1913 & James: 47285/1915 has West Wallsend as the birth district location.

31 NSW DI 1919/5318, Annandale, Margaret A Calder

32 NSW DC 1923/010020, Mental hospital, Gladesville, 11 Jul 1923, Charles Calder

33 NSW MI 1924/13940, Sydney, Mary N Calder & Hugh Innes

34 *Family Law Act 1975* was implemented by the Whitlam Government's Attorney General, Lionel Murphy (before he became a suspect character). The changes were substantial, e.g. it removed the previous fault-based divorces with a single ground of Irretrievable Breakdown.

35 Quarter Sessions, *Sydney Morning Herald*, Thu 23 Apr 1925, page 6 http://nla.gov.au/nla.news-article28067383

36 *NSW Police Gazette*, 14 May 1930. Research suggests this may have resulted in Robert going to reform school.

37 Oral history from Lyn Collison, descendant of Jean

38 A family matter, *Illawarra Mercury*, Fri 12 Sep 1924, page 9 http://nla.gov.au/nla.news-article138374565

39 NSW DC 1973/80151, Amaroo Lodge, Charlestown, 20 Jan 1972, Mary Calder

40 NSW BI 1909/38101, Lithgow, James C McGonigal

41 A postcard exists from 1909 which was addressed to Peter at Torbane, a mining town, about 50 km NNW of Lithgow.

42 NSW, Departing Crew and Passenger Lists 1898–1911, Peter & Fanny McGonigal, 03/1911 *Suffolk* for London

43 Information supplied by Ruth Nicholson, Scotland, granddaughter of Peter

44 His father's name was also Peter McGonigal.

45 Scottish Statutory Register Deaths (SRD) 669/02 0014, Seafield, West Lothian, 4 Aug 1961, Peter McGonigal
& SRD 662/1 47, Bathgate, West Lothian, 3 May 1964, Fanny McGonigal

46 NSW MI 1911/14809, Wallerawang, Mary Ann Noon & Robert D McGonigal

47 NSW DI 1913/646, Annandale, James C McGonigal

48 NSW BC 1916/41518, Abbott St., Park Hill, 11 Dec 1916, William Charles McGonigal. Andy was also called 'Bill' on occasion

49 NSW BI 1919/42698, Wallerawang, 20 Sep 1919 Mavis I McGonigal
& NSW Death Transcription (DT) 1920/15105, Newnes, 18 Aug 1920, Mavis Irene Lucy McGonigal

50 NSW DC 1919/024066, Newnes, 25 Oct 1919, Mary Ann McGonigal

51 Commonwealth Electoral Roll Bulli 1917, Robert McGonigal

52 Oral history recounted by Peg Ditton, daughter of Lizzie

53 Bulli Court, *South Coast Times and Wollongong Argus,* Fri 17 Oct 1924, page 4 http://nla.gov.au/nla.news-article142455708

54 NSW MI 1925/2075, Chatswood, Elizabeth Methven & Robert D McGonegal/MacGonegal

55 Scottish SB 1898/436/11 Largeward, Kilconquhar, Fife, 16 Apr 1898, Elizabeth Methven

56 Commonwealth Electoral Rolls, 1930, NSW, MacQuarie, Lithgow

57 Commonwealth Electoral Rolls, 1937, NSW, MacQuarie, Lithgow

58 Brevities, *Lithgow Mercury*, Tue 31 Mar 1931, page 2 http://nla.gov.au/nla.news-article221857436

59 King-Cook (A pretty wedding) *Illawarra Mercury*, Fri 6 Jan 1933, page 8 http://nla.gov.au/nla.news-article132888758

60 Oral account from Janice Robinson, granddaughter of Robert

61 Oral account from Ralph Ditton who visited Joan and family several times 1969–1972.

62 NSW DC 1972/041966, Summerview, Summer Hill, 27 Jan 1972, Robert Douglas McGonigal

63 NSW DI 12595/1989 & oral history from Janice Robinson. Betty was the informant on Robert's death record.

64 NSW MI 1913/9791

65 Searchlight, *Illawarra Mercury*, Fri 15 Dec 1933, page 11 http://nla.gov.au/nla.news-article132439487

66 Oral history: this was in the days of 6 o'clock closing and men drank in pubs rather than at home.

67 Known earlier as 3 Reef Avenue, Wombarra.

68 https://www.airbnb.com.au/rooms/10753154?s=nqWKUAb5 (accessed on 25/7/2016)

69 Oral history from Ivy Dare, daughter of Frank & Maggie

70 Oral account by Ivy Dare and Brenda Burch – the prize was referred to as a 'Star Bogart'.

71 NSW DC 1955/23746, Illawarra Cottage Hospital, Coledale, 11 Aug 1955, Francis Enoch Noon

72 NSW DC 1962/15762, Reef Av, Wombarra, 6 May 1962, Margaret Lauder Douglas Noon

73 NSW Birth Transcription (BT), 18 Belmore St., Sydney, 24 Apr 1911, Ruby Doreen McGonigal

74 Social at Newnes, *Lithgow Mercury*, Fri 2 Apr 1909, page 3 http://nla.gov.au/nla.news-article218482498

75 Oral history recorded from Peg Ditton in notes dated from 1988

76 NSW DC 1932/19756, 48 Fullerton St, Stockton, 6 Nov 1932, Joseph Coleman

77 NSW MI 1913/6072 Marriage was at St James Anglican Church, Turramurra, NSW 25 May 1913

78 Information was supplied by Lyn Collison, from the Bryant line.

79 Oral history from Lyn Collison

80 It is unknown if the name was influenced by the name of Jean's parents' house in Scarborough/Wombarra.

81 Information from Lyn Collison & Carol Weber – granddaughters of Jean

82 Information supplied by Carol Weber 2016

83 NSW DI 1965/35131, Gosford, William Henry Bryant
& NSW DC 1970/35069, Roma private hospital Gosford, 28 Jun 1970, Jean McGonigal Bryant

84 Oral history related by Bev & John Schweers (Hayes Line)

85 The wheel horse was the lead horse if in a team. Carol Weber, from the Bryant line explained the role of the wheeler.

86 Oral history related by Bev & John Schweers (Hayes Line)

87 Accidents, *South Coast Times and Wollongong Argus*, Fri 20 Jun 1941, page 14 http://nla.gov.au/nla.news-article142204475

88 This occurred when the marriage between Janet's daughter, Jean, and William Cram ended. Bev married John Schweers.

89 NSW DC 1962/37649, Wollongong Hospital, 6 Oct 1962, James Hayes

90 Advertising, *South Coast Times and Wollongong Argus*, Fri 18 Feb 1938, page 11 http://nla.gov.au/nla.news-article141731827

91 NSW DT 1962/37649, Wollongong Hospital, 6 Oct 1962, James Hayes

92 Home after 64 years in Australia, newspaper clipping, newspaper & precise date (c 1973) unknown.

93 http://austcemindex.com/m/inscription?id=1143129

94 NSW MI 1920/17592, Bulli, Sarah S B McGonigal & Maxim Gorbach

95 Advertisement naturalisation, *Illawarra Mercury*, Fri 12 Aug 1927, page 13 http://nla.gov.au/nla.news-article135888739

96 Compensation claims, *Illawarra Mercury*, Fri 24 Jul 1925, page 7 http://nla.gov.au/nla.news-article138377299

97 Workmen's compensation, *South Coast Times and Wollongong Argus*, Fri 24 Jul 1925, page 18 http://nla.gov.au/nla.news-article142844279

98 Oral history recounted by Peg Ditton. The term 'White Russian' was a term used to emphasise he was not a communist.

99 Advertising, *South Coast Times and Wollongong Argus,* Fri 15 Aug 1930, page 17 http://nla.gov.au/nla.news-article142613257

100 Subscription list, *The Catholic Press* (Sydney), Thu 28 Oct 1937, page 7 http://nla.gov.au/nla.news-article106338462

101 NSW DI 1960/30883, Balmain, Maxham Gorbach

102 NSW DC 1970/003766, Croydon, Western Suburbs Hospital, 23 Jun 1970, Sarah Stafford Bell Gorbach

103 NSW MI 1924/4001, Lithgow, Edith Delaney & James McGonigal

104 English slang meaning 'bed', implying 'bag' in sentence means wife. Charming!

105 He also allegedly added: 'I'll slash you across the face with this hook'.

106 Bulli Court, *South Coast Times and Wollongong Argus*, Fri 12 Sep 1924, page 10 http://nla.gov.au/nla.news-article142458436

107 Week by week, *South Coast Times and Wollongong Argus*, Fri 29 Aug 1919, page 8 http://nla.gov.au/nla.news-article142450856

108 North Illawarra (NI) Council minutes, *Illawarra Mercury*, Fri 6 Apr 1923, page 4 http://nla.gov.au/nla.news-article133021137

109 A family matter, *Illawarra Mercury*, Fri 12 Sep 1924, page 9 http://nla.gov.au/nla.news-article138374565

110 For sale, South Coast, *Lithgow Mercury*, Fri 11 Apr 1924, page 4 http://nla.gov.au/nla.news-article220704737

111 Advertising, *South Coast Times and Wollongong Argus,* Fri 11 Apr 1924, page 11 http://nla.gov.au/nla.news-article142457694
Jim gave his address as Pleasant St.

112 A family matter, *Illawarra Mercury*, Fri 12 Sep 1924, page 9 http://nla.gov.au/nla.news-article138374565

113 NI monthly meeting, *Illawarra Mercury*, Fri 5 Sep 1924, page 5 http://nla.gov.au/nla.news-article138375021

114 NI Council, *South Coast Times and Wollongong Argus*, Fri 10 Oct 1924, page 18 http://nla.gov.au/nla.news-article142456764

115 NI Council, *South Coast Times and Wollongong Argus*, Fri 5 Dec 1924, page 10 http://nla.gov.au/nla.news-article142457001

116 Letter, *South Coast Times and Wollongong Argus*, Fri 7 Aug 1925, page 10 http://nla.gov.au/nla.news-article142842187

117 Lithgow. A.L.P., *Sydney Morning Herald*, Tue 16 Feb 1937, page 8 http://nla.gov.au/nla.news-article17301869

118 Oakey Park, *Lithgow Mercury*, Mon 4 May 1942, page 3 http://nla.gov.au/nla.news-article220769200

119 Flower show, *Lithgow Mercury*, Mon 31 Jan 1938, page 4 http://nla.gov.au/nla.news-article220867028

120 Oakey Park news, *Lithgow Mercury*, Wed 14 Oct 1942, page 4 http://nla.gov.au/nla.news-article220770564

121 Commonwealth Electoral Roll 1949 & 1954

122 Oakey Park personality dies suddenly, *Lithgow Mercury*, newspaper clipping from 1955, (no on-line reference).

123 NSW DC 1955/4735, 108 Bells Rd, Oakey Park, 26 Jan 1955, James Currie McGonigal
& NSW DI 1960/3646, Lithgow, Edith Cecilia McGonigal

124 Commonwealth Electoral Roll for 1926 has the Bellambi address. The 1928 roll has the Coledale address.

125 Sometimes written as Garlick St. The current address of the property is 2 Park St. The original house was replaced.

126 Coledale compact cottage home, *Illawarra Mercury*, Fri 22 May 1936, page 9 http://nla.gov.au/nla.news-article133085858
& Garlic St. is now called Park St. Source: Parish Map of Coledale – Wollongong Library and Oral History Ivy Dare

127 Oral history from Ivy Dare: He did his blacksmithing work at his home.

128 Advert, *South Coast Times and Wollongong Argus*, Fri 18 Jan 1935, page 13 http://nla.gov.au/nla.news-article143512800

129 Bulli Council, *South Coast Times and Wollongong Argus*, Fri 25 Oct 1935, page 4 http://nla.gov.au/nla.news-article143512838
They also owned a vacant block 200 feet x 75 feet, which stretched from the Main South Coast Rd to 'Coledale beach'.
Advert, *South Coast Times and Wollongong Argus*, Fri 10 May 1929, page 17 http://nla.gov.au/nla.news-article143122140

130 Evacuate, *South Coast Times and Wollongong Argus*, Thu 6 Apr 1950, page 20 http://nla.gov.au/nla.news-article142870549

131 http://users.ipfw.edu/isiorho/G300LandslidinginUrbanAreapdf.pdf

132 Unidentified newspaper and publish date. 1930 date on image implies error. Scottish SM 1883, 31 Aug 1883, Ecclesmachan, Linlithgow

133 Advert, *South Coast Times and Wollongong Argus*, Fri 21 Sep 1934, page 11 http://nla.gov.au/nla.news-article142636669

134 Coledale compact cottage home, *Illawarra Mercury*, Fri 22 May 1936, page 9 http://nla.gov.au/nla.news-article133085858

135 The Commonwealth Electoral Roll identifies their residence as being in Pleasant St, Bellambi.

136 Watch dog, *South Coast Times and Wollongong Argus*, Fri 7 Aug 1936, page 11 http://nla.gov.au/nla.news-article142640504

137 Oral history from Peg Ditton, Lizzie's daughter

138 Letter in possession of Peg Ditton, viewed 2016

139 http://honesthistory.net.au/wp/coal-miners-during-world-war-ii/

140 A study from Montana, USA in 1914 found 40% of miners had chronic respiratory illness.
& https://www.ncbi.nlm.nih.gov/pmc/articles/PMC4556416/

141 In WWII, 926,000 Australian men enlisted in all services. 30,700 were killed (1 in 30) and 25,700 were wounded or injured (1 in 36).

That made it safer to fight in WWII than spend a career in a coalmine. WWI was a different story.

142 NSW DC 1940/24592, Owen Park Pd, Bellambi, 17 Oct 1940, James Curry McGonigal

143 Oral history recounted by Peg Ditton, daughter of Lizzie

144 Tenant abandons house, *Illawarra Mercury*, Fri 5 Mar 1943, page 1 http://nla.gov.au/nla.news-article132567853

145 NSW DC 1943/9183 Buxton private hospital, Glebe, 11 Apr 1943, Elizabeth Nimmo Douglas McGonigal

146 Advertising, *Illawarra Mercury*, Thu 22 Apr 1943, page 5 http://nla.gov.au/nla.news-article132578118

147 Peter McGonigal born 24 Jul 1813, Ratho, Lothian, Scotland – died 20 Nov 1887, West Calder, Lothian, Scotland
& Elizabeth Currie born 14 Jun 1821, West Calder, Lothian, Scotland – died 8 Oct 1910, West Calder, Lothian, Scotland.
& Details of children from census and birth records.

148 Robert Douglas, born c 1838, Kirkliston, Linlithgow, Scotland – died 1 Aug 1912, Bathgate, Lothian, Scotland
& Mary Nimmo, born Mar 1837, Muiravonside, Stirlingshire, Scotland – died 26 Sep 1902, Broxburn, West Lothian, Scotland.
Details of children from census and birth records.

149 1851 Census of Scotland

150 From marriage certificate, children's birth certificates and death certificate

151 Oral history from Peg Ditton

152 Information provided by Duncan McGonigal, Stanthorpe

153 Wikipedia: Massacre of Glencoe, 1692 & Battle of Culloden, 1745

154 surnamedb.com McGonigal. Scotland's worst poet is famously one: William Topaz McGonagall (2 ls). His crowning glory was the poem *The Tay Bridge Disaster*. Unfortunately, or fortunately, no familial link can be found to this celebrity.

155 Scotland Census 1861 from the village of Ratho.

156 NSW DT 1928/2605, 92 Little Simmons St, Enmore, 8 Mar 1928, Caroline Millerick

157 Estate of £3000, *Newcastle Sun*, Fri 31 May 1935, page 7 http://nla.gov.au/nla.news-article166083021
& Legal advice – Justin Ditton: The convention when contradictions occur is the more detailed option is favoured.

158 NSW DC 1934/18682, 140 Wilson St, Redfern, 12 Nov 1934, John Thomas Millerick

159 The *Commonwealth Marriage Act 1961* introduced a requirement that a marriage have a minimum of 1 month's notice.

160 Alf later became a real estate agent – oral history from the Bryant branch.

161 NSW Marriage Transcription (MT), 11 William St, Stockton, 23 Nov 1934, Ruby Doreen Millerick & Alfred Robert Hicks

162 A book by Spike Milligan is believed to exist with pictures of Dora, Alf and the birds – not yet located.

163 Oral history recounted by Carol Weber 2016

164 Ryersonindex.org, Hicks, Ruby Doreen, death notice, 27 Jan 2010, 98, Veronica Nursing home, late of Kincumber

165 Scottish SB 1869/665/000009 Newbigging, Dalmeny, Linlithgow, 2 Apr 1869, Andrew Douglas

166 Their only daughter, Lucy, had died in infancy.

167 Scottish SRD 1919 667/36 Parish of Kirkliston, County Linlithgow. Cause: crush injuries.

168 Shocking death, *Lithgow Mercury*, Wed 4 Apr 1934, page 2 http://nla.gov.au/nla.news-article219606224

169 Commonwealth Electoral Roll 1937

170 Mr. Andrew Douglas, *Lithgow Mercury*, Wed 13 Nov 1940, page 2 http://nla.gov.au/nla.news-article220780621

171 Steelworks fatalities, *Illawarra Mercury*, Fri 6 Jul 1934, page 14 http://nla.gov.au/nla.news-article132433478

172 King-Cook (a pretty wedding), *Illawarra Mercury*, Fri 6 Jan 1933, page 8 http://nla.gov.au/nla.news-article132888758

173 Lithgow's blind organist, *Lithgow Mercury*, Wed 1 Jun 1932, page 1 http://nla.gov.au/nla.news-article219678791

174 Funeral of Mr. A. Douglas, *Lithgow Mercury*, Mon 30 Aug 1954, page 2 http://nla.gov.au/nla.news-article220817446
& Death of Mr. A. Douglas, *Lithgow Mercury*, Fri 27 Aug 1954, page 2 http://nla.gov.au/nla.news-article220818704

175 EB Studios (Sydney, N.S.W.) (1917). Panorama of Newnes Oil Works, New South Wales, 6. NLA, out of copyright

176 Caption on back: 'From left to right, 2 blue eyes 1 brown eyes. Costume: white silk blouses. V black skirts with silver belts'.

177 W Hapgood, *Deep Valleys, Tall Trees, Tough Men and Women: Pioneering stories of 'Bulli' and some local History,* self-published Bulli 1992, ISBN 0-646-10901-4 Photo is in Chapter 14. The full caption is L to R. Tom Fritz, J. McGonigal, E.G. Cram, C. Warner, S. Wanson, A.E. Cram, R.B. Cram. Bellambi. Chapter 14 deals with the Cram family who ran the brick works and several other enterprises. William Cram, a member of this family married Jean Hayes, daughter of Janet née McGonigal. Jean and William's daughter, Bev Schweers, and her husband John, have generously contributed key information and photographs for this story

178 Photo from the collection of Ivy Dare and Brenda Burch

179 Photo from the collection of Bev and John Schweers

180 Photo from the collection of Bev and John Schweers

181 Photos from the collections of Duncan McGonigal, Peter McGonigal & Bev and John Schweers respectively.

182 Both photos from the collection of Ivy Dare and Brenda Burch

183 Photos from the collections of Douglas Abercrombie and Ivy Dare & Brenda Burch respectively.

184 85/1284-30 'View at Coledale', Kerry and Co, Sydney 1884-1917 - Used with permission of Museum of Applied Arts & Sciences

185 Photo left from collection of Bev & John Schweers Photo centre from collection of Peter McGonigal

186 Both photos from the collection of Bev & John Schweers

Chapter 4

Mining paradise

Lucy and Peter – Noon

Mining by Europeans in Australia started around 1790 with a coalmine near Newcastle. With the announced discovery of gold in the 1850s, Australia quickly became a serious mining nation. Over time, significant capital was poured into mining operations chasing everything that had a commercial value. That included oil shale. This chapter is the story of the family that raised my maternal grandfather, Charlie Noon. His parents were Lucy Goodwin and Peter Noon.

Peter Noon's origins are dealt with in the next chapter. For now, it is sufficient to say he was born in Scotland and was one of my most frustrating brick walls. Peter, a miner, married Lucy Louise Grace Goodwin, a servant, at the St Matthias Catholic Church in the mining town, Mitchell, NSW.[1] A year or so after their wedding in May 1885, the town formally took on the name of the gold and silver mine, Sunny Corner, which was the reason for the town's existence.[2]

Lucy was the seventeen-year-old daughter of Enoch Goodwin and Mary Ann (née Smith). Lucy was born at Spring Creek, Walhallow Station near Goonoo Goonoo in NSW in 1867.[3] Her father had been an alluvial goldminer, but Lucy was born during the period when Enoch was a shepherd after the easily won gold ran out. The family returned to the goldfields about 1868 when underground mining expanded. Most of Lucy's childhood memories would have been formed in the mining town of Hill End. We do not know much about Lucy, but we do know her origins. Peter and Lucy lived at a time and place where life was recorded in detail. However, the record was mostly concerned with the activities of men. We can infer many things about the trail Peter left, however we only get glimpses of Lucy and most of the other women in this chapter. We only see Lucy organising and attending functions and meetings and supervising children at children's social events.[4]

Panoramic view of Sunny Corner mine and smelting works in 1899[155]

Peter and Lucy had their first child, Mary Ann, at Sunny Corner in April 1888.[5] They moved about twelve kilometres east from there around 1889 and leased two adjoining blocks to make a 104¼ acre (42.2 hectares) farm at Pipers Flat.[6] The farm was about three kilometres south of the town of Portland and convenient to the Piper's Flat train station.[7] The farm evolved to have twenty acres under cultivation, two acres of orchard and the remainder of land was pasture and bush used for the grazing of horses and cattle. In 1903 Peter registered his brand for horses and cattle.[8] The property had a four-roomed house, a hayshed, a stable and a cart-shed. The crops they harvested were hay, potatoes and fruit. The land was subjected to long dry spells and sometimes bush fires.[9]

The family grew whilst at Pipers Flat. After Charlie in 1890 came Francis Enoch (Frank) in October 1892.[10] George was born in August 1895 and David Cecil (Dick) arrived in July 1898.[11] In January 1899, Lucy was recovering from an illness, and Peter placed an ad in the local paper thanking Mr & Mrs Whiteford and Mr & Mrs Dennis and the many other friends and neighbours for the assistance they provided.[12] Their next daughter, Veta Edna, was born in September 1900 and Allan Stanley was born in April 1903.[13] Allan died nine months later and was sadly mourned, with Peter and Lucy expressing their thanks to neighbours and friends for the kindness and sympathy shown to them in their bereavement.[14] Their next child Aimee (Amy) was born in April 1904 at Pipers Flat, followed by Gladys May in April 1906 at Portland.[15]

The farm appears to not have been sufficient to comfortably support the family, as Peter worked at coalmining jobs in the district to supplement

Retouched studio portrait of Peter Noon and Lucy Noon (née Goodwin) circa 1914[156]

A panorama of the Newnes oil shale works circa 1920 – National Library of Australia[157]

the family income.[16] In December 1900, he was temporarily working at Zig Zag in Lithgow when a suspicious fire started near the farm's stable. The family put the fire out with the help of neighbours.[17] A bushfire a few months later also required assistance from his neighbours. Subsequently, he advertised, the farm was available for lease for the sum of £16 a year.[18] He also advertised for the sale of a spring cart and a harness. He placed a similar ad in 1904.[19] The family was prosperous enough to allow a generous donation of £1 s2 6d to the Lithgow hospital in 1901.[20]

According to a family anecdote, Peter could be a firebrand at times, particularly if he thought people were taking advantage. He supposedly changed religion from Catholic to Protestant when a priest sold him a dud horse. A version says he was excommunicated for his reaction. The religion change was real, but no documentary evidence has yet been found to support the excommunication. However, when selling a horse himself, in 1901, he thought it wise to include in his ad, the words 'Thoroughly staunch. Will give a trial'.[21]

Around 1907 the family moved to a new opportunity opening up thirty kilometres to the north-east of their farm. An extensive and rich oil shale deposit in the Wolgan Valley was being developed in earnest. The town of Newnes was developing at the site to house the workers required to build and operate the mine and plant. As well as the brick retorts, the enterprise utilised coke ovens to convert the local coal. Tall chimneys provided efficient and safe gas flow. Large oil and paraffin

tanks were needed to store the end product and operations and administration buildings were also constructed over an extensive site.

By 1907, the railway had been extended into the Wolgan Valley to support the enterprise. It was a significant engineering feat to facilitate the track's descent of 2200 feet (677 m) onto the valley floor.[22] The tracks were laid in spectacular locations such as at the base of towering sheer cliffs and the train provided scenic vantage points along the necessarily slow journey. As a consequence of this enterprise, bricklayers, ironworkers, oil-workers, coalminers, quarrymen and all sorts of other tradesmen were needed in the valley. People with oil shale industry experience from Scotland, such as the McGonigals, were also arriving in increasing numbers as the venture grew.

From available accounts, the workers initially pitched tents on vacant land, including mining lease land. The government developed a town plan on the Crown land and sold land plots in commercial and residential zoned areas. This allowed more substantial structures to be built and a small well-ordered town rose up within the valley centred around the train station. Peter Noon, Lucy Noon and their eldest child, Mary Ann, each bought an adjoining plot in section 28 of the Newnes town plan in June and July 1908.[23] The plots they bought ranged in price between £6 and £6 10s. In 1908, Peter took part in a discussion about the establishment of a school of arts for Newnes. He wanted a library even before that was established. Others agreed, but some argued it would be premature.[24]

a floor space of 60 feet by 34 feet with a 15-foot-deep stage with two anterooms.[27] The enlargement allowed him to operate the hall as a skating rink when not needed for functions.

The first function, held within the hall on 3 March 1909, was a meeting of the IOGT branch with almost one hundred people in attendance. It was formally opened on 12 March with a concert organised by the IOGT. Peter provided the hall free of charge for the occasion. The proceeds of the occasion went towards establishing a dramatic club.[28] The first play that they staged was *The Shaughraun*, in which Peter played the role of the villain, Cory Kinchela.[29] In May 1909, Peter Noon was elected as secretary of the IOGT.[30] Events, other than lodge meetings and drama evenings, reported to be held within the hall within the first year included the following: a bachelors' social evening[31], several wedding receptions[32], a musical evening[33], a Robert Burns night – Caledonian Society social[34], a surprise birthday party[35], a smoke concert[36] organised by the local GUOOF[37] lodge[38], a civic action meeting[39] and a boxing contest.[40] Picture shows[41], more civic action meetings[42], entertaining lectures[43], children's entertainment[44], dances, balls and dancing competitions[45] were just some of the many other activities the hall was used for during its existence.

The hall was located about 150 metres from the railway station. Its roller-skating rink was patronised nightly. The Newnes Public Hall was also used as a skating rink.[46] Skating carnivals were held in both halls, where young patrons adopted fancy dress and skated for pleasure and prizes.[47] Members of the Noon family were reported wearing various costumes,[48] which reflected the popular characters

Wolgan Valley Train, 1910 - Powerhouse Museum[158]

A public hall and a small church hall were already within the town, but Peter and Lucy saw an opportunity for a private hall. In Portland in 1904, Peter had been one of the prime movers to establish a branch of the Independent Order of Good Templars (IOGT), which was a lodge associated with the Temperance movement.[25] That appears to be the principal reason for him building the hall on their newly purchased land. However, he also saw other opportunities. The initial hall, an iron building measuring 40 feet by 24 feet, was completed in March 1909. There was a stage at one end.[26] He enlarged the hall in April 1910 to have

Noon's Hall and home at bottom right. The train line runs across centre of image with the train station and post office at left. The Wolgan river is behind the train line and the shops are on opposite bank (centre).[159]

or childhood interests of the time. In 1910, Peter Noon leased out the operation to Messrs Brown & Pascoe. They ran a competition with a medal awarded for winning efforts. In April 1910, the holder of the medal was Peter's son, Frank.[49] In June, Frank successfully saw off a challenger for his Wolgan Valley title for the half-mile.[50] A gold medal was won for his skating in August 1911.[51]

The Noon family continued to grow with the birth of Leslie (Les) Raymond in March 1909 and Arthur Robert (Syke) in February 1912.[52] As well as being an entrepreneur within the community, Peter had a day job as a quarry man within the COC operation. He was also elected vice-president of the Newnes Industrial Co-operative Society. The goal of the organisation was to open a co-operative store at Newnes.[53] He was elected chair of the organising committee for the town band, in which he also played.[54] In May 1910, he relinquished his role as secretary of the IOGT branch to his wife, Lucy.[55]

In November 1910, Peter held an 'indignation meeting' in his hall regarding the postal department shifting the post office onto private land away from the central site which had been reserved for it in the town plan. It was claimed the annual rent of

£150 would in three years have fully paid for the required building on its originally designated site. A petition with over 500 signatures was sent to the local MP to get the Post Master General to carry out the wishes of the people of Newnes.[56] This sounded reasonable however he had overreached when he accused the Newnes Progress Committee of 'conniving' to get the post office established on private land. The Progress Committee tactically resigned en masse in early 1911. The opening manoeuvres of the rival groups are best reported in the words of the original newspaper reports:

Matters in connection with the Progress Committee question have developed rapidly. As soon as it was publicly known that the late committee had resigned the following notice appeared in prominent places: — 'Notice — A public meeting will be held in Mr. Noon's hall on Sunday, 15th January, 1911, at 3 p m. Business – To elect a Progress Committee in the interests of the C.O.C.'s and Government township. Pro. James Carmichael, R.M.' Shortly afterwards another notice appeared beside the above, worded as follows – 'Notice – A public meeting will be held in Newnes Public Hall on Monday, 16th January, at 7:30 p.m. Business: To receive report and balance sheet of the Progress Association – for past half-year and elect a committee for the ensuing term. A. G. Rheinberger, hon. Secretary' The first-mentioned meeting duly eventuated, and, prompted possibly by the idea that there might be some 'fun', the public attended in fair numbers — nearly one hundred putting in an appearance. Mr. Carmichael, as convener, stated that as the late committee was defunct, he had been approached by several prominent residents and requested to call a public meeting for the purpose of electing a new committee. He had done so, and with a view to getting to business at once, he moved that Mr. P. Noon take the chair. This was seconded by Mr. Heslin, and carried unanimously. ...[57]

Both camps were present at this meeting with the representatives of the old committee displaying superior tactics. After some discussion, James Carmichael sided with the old committee in preventing the meeting proceeding to the business of electing a new committee. The second meeting proceeded the following day at the Newnes Public Hall with superior tactics again displayed by the supporters of the old committee. A slightly edited version of the newspaper report of that meeting is as follows:

The Progress Committee matter came to a head on Monday night at a public meeting in Newnes Hall — a meeting called by the secretary of that committee. As showing the interest that had been aroused in the matter, the attendance exceeded that of any public meeting ever held in the valley, there being fully 250 men present. Mr. P Noon was proposed as chairman, but declined the honor. Mr. P. Doyle, president of the committee, was then unanimously chosen to preside. The chairman, in his opening remarks, stated that he was extremely pleased to see such a big attendance. The committee was on its trial, and should that meeting, after hearing the report and balance-sheets read, decide against the committee, he, as a member, was willing to take his gruel in good part. He invited those who had had so much to say to come forward like men and substantiate their statements. He then called on the secretary, Mr. Rheinberger, to read the report and balance-sheet for the past term of six months. This was done, and the report showed that the committee had attended to a large number of matters of especial interest locally. The balance-sheet showed the committee to be in a surprisingly good position. The main charge against the late members was that they had been conniving to get the post-office erected on Jones' private township, but the documentary evidence brought forward proved conclusively that the committee had unanimously protested against such being done, and had advocated the erection of the building in question on the site reserved for it on the Government township. ... Mr. P. Noon then rose and charged a member of the committee with having signed the petition, which was got up against the post-office being on private property, in another party's name. He gave the name, which he alleged had been signed. Immediately a gentleman in the body of the hall rose and stated that the rightful owner of the name had signed the petition himself in his (the speaker's) presence. He, the signee, was present in the hall, and could substantiate his statement, if necessary. The meeting showed unmistakably, that it was not necessary. Mr. L. G. Jamieson then took the floor. He said that during his residence in Newnes he had gone about with his eyes and ears open, and he could conscientiously say that if there was a body in the town that deserved well of the public it was the Progress Committee. The members had worked most unselfishly, and in the post-office matter he knew that some of them had sunk their own personal interests for the benefit of the town. He could not understand how men, some of whom occupied positions of some importance as heads of business concerns and dispensers of literature, could descend to such tactics, which would be a disgrace to a second-class schoolboy, or even a 60th rate lunatic. Mr. Noon took the last part of the remark as a personal insult, and a wordy-duel ensued, in which one of the duellists had decidedly the advantage over the other. The report and balance-sheet were unanimously adopted, on the motion of Mr. Riley, seconded by Mr. Strangell. The president then formally tendered the resignations of the members. Mr. McDonald said that now that the whole affair had been threshed out, he thought that the best way to test the feeling of the meeting was to ask those present to send the whole committee back in as a body or turn them right out. He moved that the late committee be asked to withdraw their resignations and complete their full term of office. The chairman ruled the motion out of order, at the same time expressing doubt as to the correctness of his ruling. The committee seem determined, if possible, to force the matter to a ballot and one of them, Mr. C. O'Brien, moved that the resignations be accepted. This was seconded by Mr. E. Muir, another committee man. The whole of the committee, with their more ardent supporters, voted for the motion, as of course, did the malcontents, but the general public, evidently was quite satisfied as to the committee's bona fides and the motion was defeated by 75 to 54, a large number refraining from voting either way. Before the meeting closed, Mr. P. Noon rose and said that without 'smoodging' to any man, he must say that after hearing the report read he was quite satisfied that he had been misled, and that the committee had certainly not been idle during their term of office. Re the post-office matter, it was evident also that they had been working in the best interests of the general public. The president then invited the public to take more interest in the P.A., attend the meetings and listen to the business transacted, when they would be in a position to thoroughly understand matters for themselves. Discussion at times got warm but the chairman never for a moment lost his grip of the audience, and it was entirely due to his judicious conduct of affairs that personalities were almost entirely eliminated from the discussion. It is to be hoped now that the friction, which has existed will cease, and that all parties will work hand in hand for the general good.[58]

The post office ended up being established on the railway station platform, which is understood to be neither of the two competing locations.[59] However, Peter had lost some public stature from that episode and he was not so prominent in public affairs for a period after that. He again rose to a leadership role when industrial relations had deteriorated at Newnes in early 1912. There were industrial troubles on several fronts. The COC had reduced the coal hewing rates. and the rates for ironworkers were also subject to proposed reductions. Operations at Newnes ceased on 12 February 1912.[60] Peter and a colleague, Mr Alexander Luchetti, had been appointed as union delegates.[61] Their duties were to visit other mining districts to raise funds in support of the striking workers. Peter had visited Portland, Torbane, Airly and Lithgow. He had got a 'good reception with the workers at those sites realising the men of Newnes had a good case in fighting the proposed reductions'.[62] Meetings were held to approve the application of levies. The numbers affected by the strike actions were listed as '52 men, 40 women and 130 children'. Following this report, he ventured onto Sydney and Glenbrook to continue his fundraising efforts on behalf of the miners and oil workers.[63]

These industrial troubles combined with technical, logistical and finance raising difficulties resulted in the winding down of operations at Newnes. The town had suffered a similar downturn of several months in the middle of 1909, but this one was more severe, and many more workers drifted away from Newnes.[64] Typically, the men would leave their families at Newnes whilst they looked for work elsewhere.[65] In July 1912, Peter opened his hall and offered the use of skates for no charge to host a skating carnival on condition the proceeds went to the benefit of wives and children of those on strike. The event was well attended and was hailed a great success.[66]

The interest in the local branch of the IOGT had waned by February 1912 to the point that its affairs needed to be wound up.[67] In fact, the aims of the lodge were not even shared throughout the Noon family. Whilst their parents were attending lodge meetings repeating their messages to the faithful on the evils of drink, Charlie and Frank would be enjoying a drink together.

Newnes shops with footbridge across Wolgan River circa 1910.[160]

The Noon family at their house in Newnes circa 1917.
Photo by: E. Breedon[161]

Peter and Lucy's family were growing up and moving away. As recounted previously, Charlie, married Lizzie McGonigal in 1910 and Mary Ann married Lizzie's twin brother Robert McGonigal and Frank completed the hat-trick by marrying Maggie McGonigal.

Peter and Lucy maintained their connection with Newnes through the exodus, as they had their business interests there. The mining operation got under way under new management in 1914, and it started to produce oil in profitable quantities shortly afterwards. Peter Noon is listed as a resident of Granville in a 1915 street directory, so he may have split his time between Newnes and the western Sydney district.[68] We know Peter spent time at Newnes as he exercised on his own skating rink, but this contributed to his death on 8 May 1915[69], as seen by the following newspaper report:

An inquest was held by the coroner (Mr. E. P. Richards, J.P.), at Newnes on Sunday, concerning the death of Peter Noon, proprietor of the skating rink there. It appears that on the previous evening deceased was seen to fall, whilst skating was in progress. Immediate assistance was rendered by Const. McKenna, and Messrs. McDonald and Morton, but death had already taken place. Dr. W. D. Kirkland certified at the inquest that death was due to acute dilatation of the heart.[70]

Peter left an estate to Lucy of 'about £350'.[71] The value of the Newnes land and hall would have been a significant part of that, but it appears the

Detail of above: L to R: Gladys, Amy, Syke, Lucy, Les with dog, Mary Ann and her unknown new beau (not Robert McGonigal).

hall was not sold to realise its value. Peter had tried to sell it in 1911 but did not get any takers.[72] The hall was still being used by the community after Peter's death. A social was hosted in the hall on 19 July 1916 for the benefit of Lucy and her family. 'The weather prevented a bumper house, but a large number of tickets were sold' providing a satisfactory result.[73] In November 1917, Lucy aged 49, married William Henry Rochester, aged 57, a carpenter and a widower, at Lithgow.[74] Some of the older Noon family were not so happy for the new couple and it partially contributed to some family ties not being as strong as they previously were. Lucy died in Hill End on 25 March 1927.[75] She was buried in the Tambaroora cemetery.[76] She had previously resided at Tyldesley near Cullen Bullen ('Cullen' for short). One of the contributing causes of death, cited on her death certificate, was a goitre. Goitre and other thyroid issues, requiring surgery, were subsequently reported in a number of Lucy's descendants across the various branches. William Rochester died in Granville in July 1936.[77]

As the Newnes operation again wound down in 1927, Peter's son, George Noon, demolished the hall and the materials were taken to nearby Cullen by 'motor lorry' to build a home for the younger Noon family. Newnes was then without a hall.[78] The land was not sold, probably because there were no buyers at that time. The Lithgow council continued to send out rates notices to the owners of the blocks in the ghost town. As late as 1992, notices were sent to 'Estate of P. Noon c/- George Noon'. George had also passed on by this time and there was no incentive to pay the accounts. Subsequently, the council sold as many blocks as it could in an auction to recoup its arrears. A private owner purchased the blocks previously held by the Noon family. He has erected a rough timber and tin shelter amongst the brick foundation ruins and the bush which has reclaimed the blocks.

The town had a brief revival from mid-1931 when the government financed an initiative to provide employment in the Great Depression. This ended with a change in government the following year. In 1938 operations were moved over the mountain to Glen Davis, with some materials being salvaged from Newnes for that move. That site successfully operated during the WWII years when a domestic supply of oil was a logistic and strategic necessity. Newnes had become a ghost town by the 1940s except for the Newnes Hotel, which still operated as a hotel for a few decades more. What was left of the town was deliberately demolished in the 1960s for a mixture of salvage and safety reasons. The hotel is the only building which remains of the original town. In 1989 the Newnes Hotel building was moved about 200 metres to a site less vulnerable to floods. It no longer operates as a hotel. It is used as a museum and an information kiosk. The spectacular natural environment,

L: Newnes coke oven ruins R: Foundations for stock tanks. Both images by author, September 2016

Some of the current day residents of Newnes. Both photos by author, September 2016.

abundant fauna and the historical ruins attract many modern-day visitors.[79] Similarly, many of the mining buildings were demolished. Chimneys were removed and other buildings partially demolished, but some of the infrastructure was too extensive, to completely demolish and substantial ruins, now protected by the National Parks management, still exist. The bush is steadily reclaiming the ruins, but they are likely to still be recognisable for centuries to come.

Anthony (Tony) Luchetti was the son of Peter Noon's fellow union delegate, Alexander Luchetti. After retiring as the federal member for Macquarie, he wrote an account of the early days of Newnes in his 1976 publication on the oil shale industry (in NSW).[80] He described how the oil shale works at Newnes resulted in the 'despoliation of a beautiful valley'. The fire under-writers required that trees be cleared for a mile around the works. The abundant wildlife, including koalas, were all displaced, and in the case of wallabies, chased to their deaths by men and their dogs.

Human society has changed it values since those days and it now recognises the significance of places of outstanding natural qualities such as the Wolgan Valley. The wildlife and the trees are reclaiming Newnes and the despoliation is slowly being reversed.[81]

Newnes Hotel September 2016. Photo by author

The stories of Charlie's siblings

Mary Ann

Continuing with the story of the eldest Noon, Mary Ann, who married Robert McGonigal, a Scottish born miner – after the death of their first child, a second child, named William (Andy), was born in December 1916 and Andy survived into adulthood.[82] Mary Ann gave birth to Mavis, in September 1919, but Mary Ann died the following month as a result of her confinement and a complication due to syphilis.[83] Neither Robert nor anyone else was cited as the father of Mavis. Her brother, George, was the informant on Mary Ann's death record. Mary Ann had contracted the disease four years previously and it is likely it played a part in the relationship breakup. We do not have any information on Robert's health in this regard. Mavis died in August of the following year.[84] The oral history around Mary Ann closed down and nobody seemed to know or was willing to share the story of what had happened to her. One source had heard a story that Mary Ann had died whilst trying to save a child who had fallen down a well. The death certificate, however, is quite clear on the circumstances of her death.

The current owner of the Newnes Hotel told me that the people researching the early society there have concluded the Newnes community was unconventional for the time, with quite a few children born outside the bounds of marriage or where paternity was uncertain. This may have been a by-product of a small inter-connected community in an isolated and, in many ways, idyllic location. Throw into that mix the disruption from men leaving families behind in search of other work in the periods when the Newnes operation faltered. Perhaps also of significance for Mary Ann and Robert was the fact men are reported returning from service in WWI and their return was socially celebrated.[85] A by-product of the war was it had increased the incidence of venereal disease in Australia, with an estimated 60,000 returning soldiers infected.[86] Prior to the general availability of antibiotics after WWII, treatments for syphilis were painful, dangerous and of questionable efficacy. The historical mercury treatment was highly toxic. It was taken orally, topically or by injection. It was replaced in the early twentieth century by the more efficacious, but also toxic, arsenic-based treatment. This later treatment involved slow-acting, painful injections.[87] Another feature of this disease is it has active and dormant phases. The dormant phases give the illusion the patient is cured, but they are still infectious.

George

George, the third son after Charlie and Frank, stayed in the district around Newnes more so than the other male siblings. He and two brothers-in-law were listed as workers at Newnes in the brief revival of 1931–32.[88] The *Lithgow Mercury* reported him as a teenager in fancy dress at skating carnivals.[89]

When he was 23, he married 29-year-old Melbourne-born Irene Daisy Hiam, in March 1919 at Granville in Western Sydney. Irene had a sister living in Granville. Unfortunately, Irene died from the complications of a miscarriage in July 1922.[90] George had been the family member in town when his sister, Mary Ann, died shortly after childbirth in October 1919.[91] For George and the family, these tragic deaths would have seared into their minds the risks women faced from childbearing at that time.

George remarried in June 1927 at Cullen, NSW. His best man was his younger brother, Leslie, and his bride was 28-year-old, Grace Alvina Kirby, who had been born and raised in the Cullen district. Her father was a grazier, running sheep on the family property, *Hillcroft*.[92]

Cullen is a small town about 25 kilometres south-west of Newnes and 20 kilometres north of Lithgow. Currently it is sustained by agriculture, local mines and the Mount Piper power station.[93]

entitlement to property. However, the possibility of unclaimed riches remaining out there, perhaps from his wife's side, is a tantalising thought and this account will not definitively repudiate it.

George and Grace raised a family of seven children. The children born between 1927 and 1945 were Rita, Amy, Charles, Harold, Mavis, Edna and Jeanette. Grace died in Farley Street, Cullen in October 1969. George died in September 1986 at the Campbelltown hospital. He had lived to the venerable age of 91 which was quite a feat considering his career as a coalminer. One of the contributing causes of death, unsurprisingly, was 'chronic obstructive airways disease', which he had suffered from for years.[96] His usual residence was listed as 81 Belmont Road, Glenfield, an outer suburb of South West Sydney. He was buried beside Grace in Cullen Cemetery.

David Cecil (Dick)

When Dick was fifteen years old, he had an accident, resulting in the loss of his left hand. This loss was to trigger episodes of depression, aggravated by the difficulty in finding suitable work. Anecdotally, he was fully conscious when his hand was lost, and some have speculated this affected him profoundly. In his youth, he also appears to have had a character streak that did not endear him to some people. He briefly worked with his older brother, Charlie, in Aramac in Qld. As the story goes, 'he caused some (unspecified) mischief', which particularly upset Lizzie and which resulted in a parting of the ways. This is believed to have happened around 1916 – i.e. after his accident and whilst he was still a teenager. His depression came to the fore during the financial Great Depression of the 1930s. The following newspaper article describes the drama of the situation:

Going to do it, and does so. A sensation was caused at Wolgan early last night, when David Cecil Noon (33), who has been living in the valley for the past two months, is reported to have attempted

George and Grace on their wedding day in 1927[162]

In the days George and Grace lived there, it was a larger community with more widespread mining activity. George is remembered as having ridden his horse from Cullen to Newnes several times.[94] The distance is not so remarkable, but the terrain in sections is challenging. George and family lived at Cullen in their reassembled home for many years, but between 1938 and 1946 the family moved to the Charbon/Kandos area as the work had dried up at Cullen.[95]

Anecdotally, the family suffered a house fire and amongst the other losses, documents were destroyed. George was said to have remarked, it destroyed evidence of the family's claim to half of Parramatta. From available research on known ancestors of George, this is more likely to be evidence of George's sense of humour in the face of adversity than a genuine suggestion of to commit, suicide about 15 yards from where a policeman was standing. Noon is at present in Lithgow hospital in a critical condition. At 6.15 Const. Murphy, the officer-in-charge at Wolgan, was proceeding home, when he was hailed by Noon, who was at the footbridge near the railway station. 'I'm going to do it,' shouted Noon, and the constable was amazed to see him raise his hand and draw an open razor across his throat. Rushing over, Murphy, after a brief struggle, managed to wrest the razor from Noon, from the wound in whose throat blood was flowing freely. A crowd quickly gathered, while the services of Mr. T. Riley, first-aid man at the works, were secured. He bandaged the throat, and prevented the bleeding as much as possible. Noon was then put to bed until the arrival of Lithgow ambulance and Dr. Bamber. Noon, who was now in a semi-conscious state, was given an anaesthetic by the doctor, and several stitches inserted in the gash, which extended for about six inches, running from the right ear. The man was then rushed to Lithgow hospital, the ambulance making a very fast trip, considering the rough nature of the road. Noon has been a resident of the valley off and on for a number of years, and is believed to have attended school there. When he was 15 years of age, he lost his left hand in an accident. Of late he had been very despondent, because of his in-ability to secure employment. He is also well-known in the Cullen Bullen district.[97]

He recovered from his wounds. However, the lack of understanding or sympathy at that time, required Dick to appear in a Lithgow court a week later, on a charge of attempted suicide. He stood in the court with a bandaged neck. The judge did find the charge proved, but mercifully, only sentenced him to the rising of the court.[98] From there he was taken back to hospital.[99] When he did have work, it appears he was a coalminer. His demons re-emerged in the WWII years when he was living at Wombarra Heights north of Wollongong in a small one-roomed, corrugated-iron house. The following newspaper article from December 1944 explains the circumstances:

David Cecil Noon (46), single, for whom police and civilians were searching in the bush on the mountainside at Wombarra Heights on Wednesday, was found in a railway shed near Scarborough late in the afternoon by some railway employees. Noon had been reported missing by his nephew, Thomas Halloran, who had found a blood-stained knife and razor on the kitchen floor of Noon's residence. He also found a note allegedly written by Noon, in which it was stated that he intended to commit suicide. Noon was admitted to Coledale Hospital.[100]

His nephew Thomas was the son of his sister, Amy. Dick did manage to find some peace and happiness. He married Leontine (Leon) Elizabeth Williams in April 1958. He was 60 years old and she was 49. Leon was from South Australia and she had been married twice before in NSW, but she used her maiden name when marrying Dick.[101] Her second husband died a year after marrying Dick, indicating it was initially a bigamist marriage. On her first marriage certificate she listed her profession as bar waitress. Dick and Leon lived at Morrison Avenue, Wombarra. Dick died of natural causes in June 1978 at Coledale and Leon died in December of the same year.[102]

Veta Edna

Veta, 24, married a 38-year-old widower, James (Jim) Victor Mathieson, on New Year's Eve 1924 at Balmain South. He had married Vina Burnett Field on Christmas Day 1915 at Portland, but she had died of epilepsy just five years later at the age of 28.[103] They had had a child, Jean, born around 1917 and so Veta would become her stepmother when Jean was still a young child. Jim worked as a pipe-fitter's labourer in the Wollongong district.[104] He had also been in the newly formed Australian Navy prior to WWI.

James and Veta lived at Tyldesley in the Portland district until around 1936. He had been a miner there. They were living at 58 Main Road, Coledale, in 1937 and moved to 15 Station Road, Corrimal.[105] Veta and James had five children together between 1925 and 1940. Elsie, Leslie Victor, Shirley Melva, James and Gloria. Jim died at the Wollongong District Hospital in 1945.[106]

Veta remarried in 1947. Her new husband was Henry Jennings Leedell, a storeman. He had been born in Nowra in 1906. The couple stayed on in Veta's house in Corrimal. Henry died in 1983 and Veta, in November 1993 in NSW at the grand age of 93.[107]

Three sisters and a brother: Veta Mathieson, Amy Halloran, Frank Noon and Gladys Collins[163]

Aimee (Amy)

We have an account of five-year-old Amy being injured and suffering slight concussion when she fell from the top of the steps at the rear of her father's hall in 1910.[108] The 21-year-old Amy married 48-year-old, Tom Halloran, in Lithgow in May 1925. Tom was a man of many talents and a few vices. He had been a miner in the district that Amy was raised in. Amy and Tom raised Patrick (Pat) (b. c. 1926), Thomas (Mick) (b. c. 1928) and Doreen (b. c. 1931).

The public record Tom leaves projects a sense of a rough but charismatic and energetic man. Family anecdotes add, he could be tough on his kids at times. He was a Master of Ceremonies at an Odd Fellows ball in Newnes, in 1909[109] and again in 1920, at an event to raise money for the establishment of a library.[110] In 1926, he was both the promoter and referee of a boxing exhibition at Cullen.[111] From the same 1909 newspaper reporting his MC duties, he was also up on charges of using indecent language on the Newnes Road and summonsed for having behaved in a riotous manner in the same place on the same day. He was fined a total of £3 2s for the two charges or seven days in the lock-up. He chose to pay the fine.[112] Two decades later in June 1930 and now married to Amy, he is again booked for riotous behaviour at the Royal Hotel at Cullen, incurring a total cost of £1 8s or three days.[113] In November 1931 he was again fined a similar amount for being drunk and disorderly in the same place.[114]

By 1932, Tom starts to get public attention for a completely different characteristic. He is an expert trainer of animals. His job at the mine requires his training skills with horses, but as a sideline and a hobby, he trains dogs to perform tricks.[115] His performing dogs make their stage début in September 1932.[116] He is also reported to have trained chickens, goats and cats, but his dog act grows in reputation and he gets to show it in different localities. He charges the audience sixpence to see the show, which the correspondent lauds as

L: Pat Halloran with the performing dogs and a cat. R: In his boxing act with Bonzer in Christchurch, NZ.[164]

splendid value.[117] A flavour of the entertainment is given by the following *Lithgow Mercury* article from December 1932.

Performances by dogs trained by Mr. Thomas Halloran, of Newnes, were given at Lithgow on Friday and Saturday nights, and the high standard of the shows was the subject of much favorable comment, the opinion being freely expressed that such a show, warranted a State tour. Mate, Cobber and Bonzer display an almost uncanny intelligence, and the latter's three rounds boxing bout with young Pat Halloran was something out of the ordinary. Mr. Halloran and Mr. R. Hyham, who is associated with him in the display, intend to give a performance at Glen Alice tomorrow in aid of the children of unemployed.[118]

Tom was also the president of the Children's Festival Committee at Newnes, where his efforts in that role were praised.[119] At the same time he was recovering in Lithgow hospital from a leg injury.[120] His performing dog act was taken to various Australian states including Tasmania. He ventured to New Zealand with his troupe. Anecdotally, he was on his way to England on a ship with his dogs when WWII broke out and the ship had to come back. Tom died at the age of 66 at Cullen in 1943.[121] In his last fourteen years, he was not able to work in the colliery pit, as he was on the invalid list. He had a stroke about one year prior to his death from which he never recovered.[122]

Amy lived on another fifty years, spending her last thirty in a wheelchair. She married John (Jack) William Urwin, a railway worker, at Thirroul in the early 1950s.[123] Jack's first wife, Elizabeth, died in 1951.[124] Jack was born around 1892 in the UK,

Tom Halloran's fancy billy cart with the big kids at front pulling the little kids at back at Cullen circa 1930.[165]

and he immigrated to Australia around 1910. Jack died in 1971 in the Bulli district.[125] Amy died at Gladesville in July 1994.

Amy's son, Thomas (aka Mick) was living in the Bulli district at the time of his Uncle Dick's second suicide attempt in 1944. Pat and Mick had a reputation for being mischievous in their youth, and they were not to be tangled with. They both got some boxing lessons from Uncle Les. Pat was remembered as a very good southpaw. One story alleges they excavated a large rock on top of a hill overlooking Cullen. It rolled down and knocked a railway truck off the train line. They walked the long way home to cover their tracks, but the local policeman had pinned them as the only, but unproven, suspects.[126]

Gladys May

The 19-year-old Gladys married 24-year-old Charles Harold (Tango) Collins in April 1925

Amy and Gladys Noon in the 1920s[166]

at Lithgow. Their children, born between 1926 and 1941, were George, Alfred (Alfie), Faye, Norman Reginald (Reggie) and Maxwell (Maxie). From 1930 to 1937, Charles was a miner and the family were living at Portland. Addresses include 20 Kiln Street and 3 Williewa Street.

Charles' nickname, Tango, is associated with his days as a bare-knuckle boxer.[127] Charles' appearances in the public record are mostly of the negative kind. Miners faced prolonged struggles at this time. Improvements in safety, wages, benefits and conditions had to be fought for with tenacity and unfortunately some violence occurred. An example of that is the following event from October 1931, where Charles is in company with his brother-in-law, Les, and others:

There was an ugly demonstration outside the Portland court house last night at the conclusion of a case in which four members of the Tyldesley miners' lodge were each fined £1, with 5/- costs, 7/6 damages, and 15/- witnesses expenses, in default five days, on a charge of inflicting malicious damage to Henry Smith's car. The defendants were Wm. Lancaster, Chas. Collins, Kenneth Wilson and Leslie Noon. They were defended by Miss Jollie Smith, of Sydney. The Miners' Federation was represented by Messrs. T. Schroder; and E. Mara. A second charge of throwing stones on a public highway was withdrawn. When Smith and his witnesses, Herbert Teong and Harry Charman, who are working at Tyldesley colliery, which has been declared 'black', emerged from the court, they were greeted with jeers and catcalls from a large crowd. Smith was escorted from the scene under the protection of a police officer. Smith, in evidence, said that while driving to Cullen Bullen on September 21, the defendants, threw stones at his car. The windscreen was broken, and he narrowly escaped injury.[128]

Misbehaviour associated with his drinking, brought him before the police courts on several occasions during his time at Cullen. In 1920, he was charged with riotous behaviour.[129] In 1934, he and two others were charged and fined at Portland for their drunkenness.[130] In 1935, he was charged with four others for being on licensed premises during prohibited hours. They had been in an upstairs room in the Imperial Hotel. Their claim, they had gone there to play cards, was rejected and a fine of 10s and 8s costs was imposed on all of them.[131]

Gladys was remembered as a happy-go-lucky, cheerful soul and for her regular treks in the early days, walking the ten kilometres from Portland to Cullen with young George, her first born, on her hip.[132] The family moved to the Wollongong area around the 1940s and lived at 42 Morrison Avenue, Coledale. Anecdotally, Gladys and the children were visitors to her brother Frank's place at times of domestic stress. Her brother, Les, is also remembered as helping with the family's welfare. Charles died in April 1969 at the Prince Henry Hospital in Little Bay, NSW, aged 68.[133] Gladys died in Bulli in August 1988, aged 82.[134]

Leslie (Les) Raymond

The 24-year-old Les married 18-year-old Laura Challenor in September 1933 at Austinmer, a beach suburb in the Bulli district. Laura was born at Coledale, which is the next beach suburb north of Austinmer. Les and Laura raised two children.

Les has left several references in the public record. They start with him being mentioned as a boxer in a tournament in 1929:

The programme was opened on Friday night by a six-round contest between Al. Brown; of Woonona, and Les Noon, of Wombarra. Noon, who is rather on the 'green' side at present, put up quite a good showing against his more experienced rival. In ringcraft Brown completely outclassed the Wombarra lad, but not before he had felt the weight of some heavy rights sent in his direction. The similarity of tactics deployed by Noon soon became apparent to Brown, with the result that over the concluding stages he had little difficulty in evading the attacks of his opponent, and placing many scoring punches, which earned for him the verdict of the referee.[135]

His nickname from the boxing ring was 'Steamboat'. The story is this moniker was earned because of his rotating arm movements in the ring.[136] He was remembered as stocky and strong and as a formidable fighter.

The next article is the 1931 rock throwing in Cullen with his brother-in-law, Charlie 'Tango' Collins.[137] The most dramatic report, however, is when he is the driver of a car involved in a fatal accident in November 1947 in Austinmer. The following newspaper article from April 1948 summarises the incident and the legal outcome:

Described by police as a man of very good character, Leslie Raymond Noon, Wombarra Heights, was fined £10 at Bulli Court last Friday for negligent driving at Austinmer on November 5. He pleaded guilty. Det. Gallagher said in evidence that at 6.10 p.m. Noon left the hotel at Thirroul and drove his jeep along Lawrence Hargrave Drive towards Austinmer. Passing the crest of Kennedy's Hill at an excessive speed he saw a motor lorry moving in the same direction at a slow speed and two motor cycles approaching in the opposite direction. The motor cycles prevented him from passing the lorry, Det. Gallagher said and the jeep crashed into the rear of the vehicle which was loaded with mill logs. Five persons were in the jeep at the time and one, William Lenham, was fatally injured, and another, Edward Blakney was seriously injured. Blakney had since recovered. Police offered no evidence in a second charge against Noon of driving in a manner dangerous to the public and he was discharged.[138]

A more detailed account of the incident is given in the *Illawarra Mercury's* coverage of the Inquest hearing in March 1948.[139] Les originally faced a charge of manslaughter and was remanded on £200 bail, but the inquest did not provide any finding, which supported that charge.[140]

In April 1950, Les and his family are mentioned when land subsidence on the slopes of the Wombarra-Coledale area caused extensive property damage. The following is an excerpt from a more extensive article:

Another Wombarra Heights resident, Mr. L. Noon who lives there with his wife and two children states that his home has slipped fourteen feet and seems likely to break up. Wombarra Heights residents blame the Coal Board for their plight. They say the coal board put a road above them without building a retaining wall and now the whole hillside is beginning to slide forward.[141]

The house had to be abandoned, as it was uninhabitable. Tree clearing on the slope was also suggested as a factor in the land slippage.[142] Les and his family lived close to some of his siblings at various times. Frank was close by, as were Dick, Amy, Gladys and Syke.

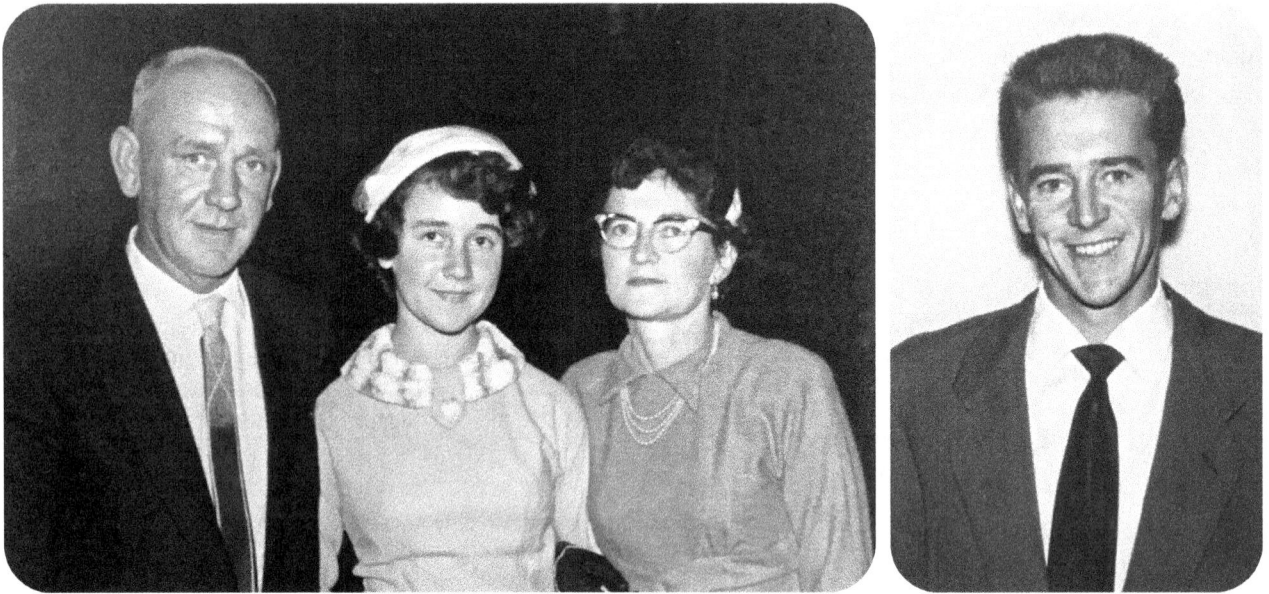

Left: Les and Laura with their daughter circa 1960. Right: Les's son Les Noon

Les' son, Les, generously shared the following insightful memories of his father: Les was a blacksmith when he was young. In the early years of the Great Depression, Les carried his swag, meaning, he was on the road looking for work carrying a few possessions including his bedroll. The story goes, the only time he used his real name was in Armidale. He could get relief rations with a police-authorised form. When he took the form to the storekeeper, he looked at the name *Noon*, sneered and said '*Noon* aye! I suppose you will be *Midnight* in the next town'. At that, Les invited him outside. The storekeeper wisely declined. Later, Les and his brother, Frank, built a two-roomed tin house on the mountainside of the home of Franks' neighbour in Wombarra, Mrs Rumery. That was where he and Laura lived for about four years. Les would catch the train to Port Kembla each day and stand outside with about thirty to fifty other men. The ganger or foreman would select a small group and send the rest away. Les was almost always selected, as he was known for a competitive streak. He would be the first one out of the train and the first one into the showers. If he took something on, then he wanted to be the best at it, whether it be work, sport or drinking.

Les and Laura bought Laura's parents' dairy. From about 1938 to March 1942, the family ran the dairy farm and milked their sixty-plus cows, twice a day. They delivered milk from Austinmer to Stanwell Park twice a day in all conditions. It was hard tiring work, and it could all have ended with the fresh rock falls or slippery precipitous drops on their delivery run.

The family story is, in 1942, when Les was conscripted into the army to fight in WWII, the government took his new Ford utility for the war effort, and he had to sell his business to a man who subsequently made a lot of money from packaging improvements which soon happened to the industry. He went into the army as a craftsman based on his blacksmithing background. He was based in Port Moresby, New Guinea and one of his duties was reported to be 'hosing out' the remains of airmen from the returning aircraft.[143] He was medically discharged in June 1944.

From when he got home until 1945, Les and a mate would cut, split and bag firewood and then sell it and coke from Stanwell Park to Wollongong. Young Les would accompany them and his job was to knock on the back door of houses and ask if any was needed. Les packed it in because of arthritis and then bought a general store and post office shop in Scarborough, which he sold around 1947. He went on to work as a coalminer until 1949. Les ran an odds and evens game whilst in the army and he always had a two-up kit ready for any opportunity. After the war, he ran an SP bookie operation from the Wombarra Heights house.[144] Young Les was the designated cockatoo.[145]

From 1949, he worked as a foreman for Allied Constructions because the owner, Teddy Williams, was an engineer from the steelworks during the Depression era and he remembered Les as a solid worker. His first job was in the Snowy Mountains Hydro Scheme, which apart from being remembered as an iconic post-war engineering triumph, is also remembered for its gambling and drinking culture. It was an almost exclusively male domain, particularly if you disregarded the regular visits of prostitutes. Les was put in charge of the tunnelling jobs. His job descriptions later became engineer and project manager. In those roles, he put a 1511 foot (460.5 metres) deep shaft down Coalcliff Pit in Darkes Forrest. This was claimed to have broken a record for shaft sinking.[146] His boss bought him a new Chevy to show his appreciation. In later years, his work in developing coalmines moved the family to the Newcastle area, and they lived at 25 Pemmell Street, Toronto, NSW. Les died in Newcastle in July 1977, aged 68.[147] Laura died in August 2007 in NSW, aged 92.[148] They are both buried at Toronto, NSW.

A bare footed, Les Noon, front left, working in the 1930s. This photo is from the collection of Les & Julia Noon. It was taken by a professional press photographer, believed to be Sam Hood (d. 1953), and it is also a stock image used by various organisations (e.g. ABC on-line, Ancestry.com) to depict the Great Depression

Arthur Robert (Syke)

The youngest Noon was residing at Portland, NSW in the years 1933–1937. Later, Syke lived at Thirroul in the Wollongong district.[149] In 1943, whilst he was living in the Wollongong district, he was a witness to a fatal road accident. He saw a motorcycle run down a nine-year-old boy as the boy stepped off a bus. The rider of the motorcycle was found not guilty of the manslaughter charge which had been laid against him.[150] Syke was living at Lithgow in 1949.[151] He ventured up to Qld around 1950 where he resided in the Jondaryan district on the Darling Downs. He worked in the Ackland Coal mine there in a managerial role.[152] From around 1963, he moved to 321 Bridge Street, Toowoomba.

Anecdotally, Syke was slight and small of stature and had lung problems from an early age, which held him back in various endeavours.[153] His relatives fondly remembered him as an agreeable man. In 1954, aged 42, he married a 50-year-old widow, Maria Rubi Kajewski (née Volp) at Toowoomba. Maria had been widowed in 1948, when her husband of 27 years, Herman, died. Maria had some children from her first marriage, but none from her marriage to Syke. Syke died in July 1982 in Toowoomba and Maria also died in Toowoomba in January 1986.[154]

Noon's hall and home from near the train station[167]

Endnotes to Chapter 4

1 NSW MC 1885/4025, Mitchell, NSW, 10 May 1885, Lucy Goodwin & Peter Noon
Mitchell, NSW and Mitchell, Qld are different towns. The Qld town is named after the explorer, Thomas Mitchell, whereas the NSW town may have been named after his son Campbell. https://bushwalkingnsw.com/walk.php?nid=795
2 https://en.wikipedia.org/wiki/Sunny_Corner,_New_South_Wales On subsequent certificates, Lucy & Peter stated they were married at Sunny Corner, e.g. NSW BCs 1890/19393, (Charles) 1895/23749 (George)
& NSW DCs 1915/7765, (Peter) 1927/1465 (Lucy).
& Sunny Corner Silver mine, *Sydney Morning Herald*, Fri 26 Aug 1898, page 6 http://nla.gov.au/nla.news-article14156386
& Sunny Corner, *Australian Town and Country Journal*, Sat 14 Feb 1885, page 17 http://nla.gov.au/nla.news-article71023783
& *Australians Events and Places*. Ed: G Aplin, SG Foster & M McKernan Pub: Fairfax, Syme & Weldon, NSW 1987 p221.
3 NSW BC 1867/16739, Spring Creek. Walhallow Stn., Goonoo Goonoo, 19 Dec 1867, Lucy Goodwin.
Goonoo Goonoo, pronounced gunner-gunoo, is approximately 25 km south of Tamworth, NSW.
4 Newnes Good Templars' Lodge, *Lithgow Mercury*, Fri 6 May 1910, page 3 http://nla.gov.au/nla.news-article218490557
& Newnes children entertained, *Lithgow Mercury*, Fri 19 Jul 1912, page 3 http://nla.gov.au/nla.news-article218734420
5 4 Apr 1888 comes from a page in the family bible. Place comes from DC, but the birthplace could have been Portland (Pipers Flat) as that is what was on her son's BC. No Official NSW BC for Mary Ann has yet been found.
6 NSW Land Titles registration, application for lease of land #1889/15006 27 Jun 1889
& Advertisement, *Lithgow Mercury*, Fri 15 Feb 1901, page 5 http://nla.gov.au/nla.news-article219539758
7 Portland was sometimes referred to as the town that built Sydney. It was established to produce Portland cement from the local limestone. Portland cement is named after the similarity of stone on the isle of Portland in Dorset, England. The tramway line adjoined the Noon property – NSW *Government Gazette* May-Jun 1890, page 4356 item 3874.
8 NSW List of Horses and Cattle brands for Quarter Ending 31 Dec 1893
9 Bush fires, *Lithgow Mercury*, Tue 12 Feb 1901, page 2 http://nla.gov.au/nla.news-article219540015
10 NSW Birth Transcription (BT), 1892/20276, Pipers Flat, 23 Oct 1892, Francis Enoch Noon
11 NSW BC 1895/23749, Pipers Flat, 25 Aug 1895, George Noon
& NSW BC 1898/22595, Pipers Flat, 16 Jul 1898, David Cecil Noon
12 Advertising thanks, *Lithgow Mercury*, Fri 27 Jan 1899, page 5 http://nla.gov.au/nla.news-article218624818
13 NSW BT 1900/32633, Pipers Flat, 22 Sep 1900, Veta Edna Noon
& NSW BT – partial, registered 1 Jun 1903, Allen Stanley Noon
14 Family notices, *Lithgow Mercury*, Fri 5 Feb 1904, page 5 http://nla.gov.au/nla.news-article221479528
15 NSW BC 1904/17455, Pipers Flat, 17 Apr 1904, Aimee Noon
& NSW BT 1906/18438, Portland, 10 Apr 1906, Gladys May Noon
16 The 1901 Census identifies Peter Noon living alone at Bridge St, Lithgow.
17 Fire near Piper's Flat, *Lithgow Mercury*, Tue 11 Dec 1900, page 3 http://nla.gov.au/nla.news-article218631577
18 Advertisement, *Lithgow Mercury*, Fri 15 Feb 1901, page 5 http://nla.gov.au/nla.news-article219539758
19 To sell or let, a farm, *Lithgow Mercury*, Tue 2 Aug 1904, page 3 http://nla.gov.au/nla.news-article221483715
20 The late hospital effort, *Lithgow Mercury*, Tue 2 Jul 1901, page 2 http://nla.gov.au/nla.news-article219546545
21 For sale, *Lithgow Mercury*, Fri 20 Sep 1901, page 5 http://nla.gov.au/nla.news-article219551972
& For sale, *Lithgow Mercury*, Fri 27 Sep 1901, page 5 http://nla.gov.au/nla.news-article219546626
22 http://infobluemountains.net.au/rail/upper/wolgan-1.htm
23 Crown land sale at Newnes, *Lithgow Mercury*, Mon 15 Jun 1908, page 3 http://nla.gov.au/nla.news-article219293056
& From the Gazette, *Lithgow Mercury*, Fri 24 Jul 1908, page 6 http://nla.gov.au/nla.news-article219291201
24 Newnes proposed School of Arts, *Lithgow Mercury*, Mon 23 Nov 1908, page 3 http://nla.gov.au/nla.news-article219297263
25 Brevities, *Lithgow Mercury*, Fri 14 Oct 1904, page 4 http://nla.gov.au/nla.news-article221489688
The Temperance Movement aimed to curb the drinking of alcohol.
26 Newnes, *Lithgow Mercury*, Mon 8 Mar 1909, page 1 http://nla.gov.au/nla.news-article218483733
27 Newnes, *Lithgow Mercury*, Fri 1 Apr 1910, page 3 http://nla.gov.au/nla.news-article218498825
28 Newnes, *Lithgow Mercury*, Wed 17 Mar 1909, page 3 http://nla.gov.au/nla.news-article218478656
29 Dramatic entertainment at Newnes, *Lithgow Mercury*, Fri 22 Oct 1909, page 3 http://nla.gov.au/nla.news-article218486934
Mary Ann Noon also had a minor part in the play.
30 Newnes, *Lithgow Mercury*, Fri 14 May 1909, page 3 http://nla.gov.au/nla.news-article218486492
31 Social at Newnes, *Lithgow Mercury*, Fri 2 Apr 1909, page 3 http://nla.gov.au/nla.news-article218482498
32 Wedding at Newnes, *Lithgow Mercury*, Mon 26 Jul 1909, page 3 http://nla.gov.au/nla.news-article218482959
& Wedding at Newnes, *Lithgow Mercury*, Wed 18 Aug 1909, page 4 http://nla.gov.au/nla.news-article218480987
33 Newnes IOG Templars, *Lithgow Mercury*, Fri 18 Jun 1909, page 3 http://nla.gov.au/nla.news-article218484963

34 Newnes, *Lithgow Mercury*, Mon 31 Jan 1910, page 1 http://nla.gov.au/nla.news-article218489065

35 Newnes, *Lithgow Mercury*, Wed 9 Feb 1910, page 3 http://nla.gov.au/nla.news-article218492907

36 Smoke concerts were mainly for men where smoking and chatting and light entertainment occurred.

37 GUOOF – Grand United Order of Odd Fellows

38 Newnes, *Lithgow Mercury*, Wed 2 Mar 1910, page 3 http://nla.gov.au/nla.news-article218497617

39 Distress at Newnes, *Lithgow Mercury*, Fri 2 Apr 1909, page 4 http://nla.gov.au/nla.news-article218482543

40 Newnes, *Lithgow Mercury*, Wed 23 Mar 1910, page 3 http://nla.gov.au/nla.news-article218489310

41 Newnes, *Lithgow Mercury*, Wed 27 Jul 1910, page 3 http://nla.gov.au/nla.news-article218490320

42 Newnes post office, *Lithgow Mercury*, Wed 23 Nov 1910, page 2 http://nla.gov.au/nla.news-article218495663

43 Newnes, *Lithgow Mercury*, Fri 24 Mar 1911, page 3 http://nla.gov.au/nla.news-article219530294

44 Newnes children entertained, *Lithgow Mercury*, Fri 19 Jul 1912, page 3 http://nla.gov.au/nla.news-article218734420

45 Newnes, *Lithgow Mercury*, Mon 11 Feb 1918, page 3 http://nla.gov.au/nla.news-article218473470

46 Skating carnival at Newnes, *Lithgow Mercury*, Mon 31 Jul 1911, page 3 http://nla.gov.au/nla.news-article219531196

47 Newnes, *Lithgow Mercury*, Mon 9 May 1910, page 3 http://nla.gov.au/nla.news-article218490718

& Carnival at Newnes, *Lithgow Mercury*, Mon 8 Aug 1910, page 1 http://nla.gov.au/nla.news-article218490660

48 Skating carnival at Newnes, *Lithgow Mercury*, Mon 13 Jun 1910, page 2 http://nla.gov.au/nla.news-article218498342

& Newnes, *Lithgow Mercury*, Mon 10 Oct 1910, page 3 http://nla.gov.au/nla.news-article218497255

49 Newnes, *Lithgow Mercury*, Wed 27 Apr 1910, page 3 http://nla.gov.au/nla.news-article218499820

50 Newnes, *Lithgow Mercury*, Wed, 29 Jun 1910, page 3 http://nla.gov.au/nla.news-article218491890

51 Newnes, *Lithgow Mercury*, Fri 4 Aug 1911, page 4 http://nla.gov.au/nla.news-article219538941

52 NSW BC 1909/9369, Newnes, 9 Mar 1909, Leslie Raymond Noon

& NSW BC 1912/10806, Newnes, 17 Feb 1912, Arthur Robert Noon

53 Newnes, *Lithgow Mercury*, Wed 8 Dec 1909, page 3 http://nla.gov.au/nla.news-article218484360

54 Newnes band, *Lithgow Mercury*, Wed 15 Sep 1909, page 1 http://nla.gov.au/nla.news-article218479694

& Newnes I.O.G. Templars (inferred), *Lithgow Mercury*, Fri 18 Jun 1909, page 3 http://nla.gov.au/nla.news-article218484963

55 Newnes Good Templar's Lodge, *Lithgow Mercury*, Fri 6 May 1910, page 3 http://nla.gov.au/nla.news-article218490557

56 MP: Member of Parliament & The Post Master General (PMG) was later split into what is now Australia Post and Telstra Corporation.

& Newnes post office, *Lithgow Mercury*, Wed 23 Nov 1910, page 2 http://nla.gov.au/nla.news-article218495663

57 Rival progress associations, *Lithgow Mercury*, Wed 18 Jan 1911, page 2 http://nla.gov.au/nla.news-article219534067

58 Newnes, A lively meeting, *Lithgow Mercury*, Wed 18 Jan 1911, page 2 http://nla.gov.au/nla.news-article219534018

59 Map Village of Newnes 1964, shows a block reserved for the Post Office on the corner of Numietta St & Wolgan Rd. https://nla.gov.au/nla.obj-1629329438

60 RAHS Journal Vol 45 Part 2, A short history of the Wolgan Valley

61 His Son, Anthony S Luchetti, wrote and published an informative account of the oil shale industry in 1976.

62 The Newnes trouble, *Lithgow Mercury*, Mon 13 May 1912, page 2 http://nla.gov.au/nla.news-article218739597

63 The Newnes trouble, *Lithgow Mercury*, Mon 6 May 1912, page 2 http://nla.gov.au/nla.news-article218733720

64 Distress at Newnes, *Lithgow Mercury*, Fri 2 Apr 1909, page 4 http://nla.gov.au/nla.news-article218482543

65 The Newnes exodus, *Lithgow Mercury,* Fri 8 Mar 1912, page 4 http://nla.gov.au/nla.news-article218743739

& The Newnes exodus, *Lithgow Mercury,* Wed 24 Apr 1912, page 3 http://nla.gov.au/nla.news-article218737377

& The Newnes exodus, *Lithgow Mercury,* Fri 28 Mar 1913, page 4 http://nla.gov.au/nla.news-article218663425

66 Newnes skating carnival, *Lithgow Mercury*, Fri 5 Jul 1912, page 4 http://nla.gov.au/nla.news-article218744599

67 Lodge's affairs wound up, *Lithgow Mercury*, Wed 21 Feb 1912, page 3 http://nla.gov.au/nla.news-article218738719

68 In the 1915 Sands Street Index for NSW, a Peter Noon is listed as the occupant of a house on the western side of Clyde St, Granville. His name is second after the 3 cross streets, Redfern, Hudson & Nobbs. A supporting fact is that there are no other recorded contemporary Peter Noons in NSW. The closest is a Patrick Noon who lived in Burwood, Sydney, in the 1890s and died there in 1949. The later connection of George and Granville reinforces the notion that this is Peter Noon of this story. Australia's worst train disaster occurred just near Granville station in Jan 1977. Deaths totalled 83 and 213 people were injured when a train derailed causing a bridge to collapse onto the carriages.

69 NSW DC 1915/7765, Newnes, 8 May 1915, Peter Noon

70 Sudden death at Newnes, *Lithgow Mercury*, Wed 12 May 1915, page 3 http://nla.gov.au/nla.news-article218450931

71 Peter Noon's will, dated 27 Feb 1913, appointed Lucy executor and sole beneficiary.

72 Newnes, *Lithgow Mercury*, Wed 12 Jul 1911, page 3 http://nla.gov.au/nla.news-article219535817

73 Newnes, *Lithgow Mercury*, Mon 24 Jul 1916, page 3 http://nla.gov.au/nla.news-article218731844

74 NSW MC 1917/11524, Lithgow, 19 Dec 1917, Lucy Grace Noon & William Henry Rochester

Although identified as a widower, no record of William's previous marriage has yet been found.

75 NSW DC 1927/1465, Hill End, 25 Mar 1927, Lucy Grace Rochester

76 Tambaroora cemetery, Section B Row 2 Plot 116

77 NSW DC 1936/12835, Lidcombe, 21 Jul 1936, William Henry Rochester

78 What of shale leases? *Lithgow Mercury*, Fri 7 Jan 1927, page 3 http://nla.gov.au/nla.news-article219668044

The story of Cullen Bullen house built from the recycled Newnes hall was validated by Amy & Edna, George's children.

79 http://users.tpg.com.au/newnes/h/histo.htm

80 AS Luchetti, *The oil shale industry, its development, growth and demise*, Lithgow Historical Society, Lithgow, 1976

Tony Luchetti represented the ALP from 1951 until 1975. He succeeded his rival, ex-PM Ben Chifley, in the by-election after Chifley's death.

81 Wolgan Valley now hosts the uber luxurious One and Only Wolgan Valley Resort where 1 night costs around 70 hours of the minimum wage. The Gosper's Mountain mega fire of 2019/2020 burned through Newnes, but spared the Newnes Hotel and surrounding buildings.

82 William married Thelma May Stewart in 1940. Anglican Parish Registers, Sydney 1814–2011

83 NSW DC 1919/024066, Newnes, 25 Oct 1919, Mary Ann McGonigal

84 NSW DT 1920/15105, Newnes, 18 Aug 1920, Mavis Irene Lucy McGonigal

85 Newnes, *Lithgow Mercury*, Mon 18 Mar 1918, page 3 http://nla.gov.au/nla.news-article218473411

86 R Dunbar, *The Secrets of the Anzacs*, Scribe, Brunswick, Victoria, 2014

87 http://www.academia.dk/Blog/syphilis/

88 http://users.tpg.com.au/newnes/h/n_1932.htm

89 Skating carnival at Newnes, *Lithgow Mercury*, Mon 13 Jun 1910, page 2 http://nla.gov.au/nla.news-article218498342

& Newnes, *Lithgow Mercury*, Mon 10 Oct 1910, page 3 http://nla.gov.au/nla.news-article218497255

90 NSW DT, 1922/11164 Lithgow, 9 Jul 1922, Irene Daisy Noon

91 NSW DC 1919/024066, Newnes, 25 Oct 1919, Mary Ann McGonigal

92 NSW DC 1969/42680, Farley St, Cullen Bullen, 18 Oct 1969, Grace Alvina Noon

& oral history from Amy Williams, daughter of George Noon, regarding running sheep on their property.

& A Cullen wedding, *Lithgow Mercury*, Fri 1 Jul 1927, page 7 http://nla.gov.au/nla.news-article219656964

93 https://en.wikipedia.org/wiki/Cullen_Bullen,_New_South_Wales

94 Oral history from George's son Charlie Noon.

95 From Amy Williams obituary 2019. George Noon worked in the Kandos Coomber coalmine.

96 NSW DC 1986/23893, Campbelltown Hospital, 4 Sep 1986, George Noon

97 Going to do it, *Lithgow Mercury*, Fri 6 Nov 1931, page 2 http://nla.gov.au/nla.news-article221844107

98 David would have served his sentence and been released from the dock as soon as the court closed proceedings for his case.

99 Brevities, *Lithgow Mercury*, Thu 12 Nov 1931, page 2 http://nla.gov.au/nla.news-article221854578

100 Searchlight, *Illawarra Mercury*, Fri 1 Dec 1944, page 5 http://nla.gov.au/nla.news-article132648091

101 First married Joseph Gerry Poole in 1929 and then John Joseph Wilkins in 1941.

102 NSW DT 1978/201357, Coledale, 30 Jun 1978, David Cecil Noon

& NSW DT 1978/202575, Coledale, 16 Dec 1978, Leon Elizabeth Noon

103 NSW DT 1920/20790, Lithgow, 14 Dec 1920, Vina Burnett Mathieson

104 NSW DT 1945/6284, Wollongong Hospital, 22 Feb 1945, James Victor Mathieson

105 Commonwealth Electoral Roll NSW

106 NSW DT 1945/6284, Wollongong Hospital, 22 Feb 1945, James Victor Mathieson. His first daughter, Elsie, became Mrs Vennard.

107 Info from NSW BI 1906/6298, NSW DI 1983/202706 & Commonwealth Electoral Rolls

& Ryersonindex.org, Leedell Veta, Death: 10 Nov 1993, age 93, late of Corrimal, *Illawarra Mercury*, 12 Nov 1993

108 Newnes, *Lithgow Mercury*, Wed 9 Feb 1910, page 3 http://nla.gov.au/nla.news-article218492907

109 Language cases, *Lithgow Mercury*, Fri 22 Jan 1909, page 3 http://nla.gov.au/nla.news-article218482854

110 Newnes, *Lithgow Mercury*, Fri 16 Jul 1920, page 3 http://nla.gov.au/nla.news-article218461899

111 Cullen Bullen, *Lithgow Mercury*, Fri 17 Dec 1926, page 3 http://nla.gov.au/nla.news-article224585970

112 Language cases, *Lithgow Mercury*, Fri 22 Jan 1909, page 3 http://nla.gov.au/nla.news-article218482854

113 Portland Police Court, *Lithgow Mercury*, Thu 5 Jun 1930, page 4 http://nla.gov.au/nla.news-article219571565

114 Portland Police Court, *Lithgow Mercury*, Wed 4 Nov 1931, page 6 http://nla.gov.au/nla.news-article221847520

115 Respected resident's death, *Lithgow Mercury*, Wed 18 Aug 1943, page 5 http://nla.gov.au/nla.news-article220791994

116 Newnes, *Lithgow Mercury*, Fri 9 Sep 1932, page 4 http://nla.gov.au/nla.news-article219675397

117 Brevities, *Lithgow Mercury*, Wed 30 Nov 1932, page 2 http://nla.gov.au/nla.news-article219679483

118 Brevities, *Lithgow Mercury*, Mon 5 Dec 1932, page 2 http://nla.gov.au/nla.news-article219682078

119 Newnes Xmas festival, *Lithgow Mercury*, Wed 11 Jan 1933, page 6 http://nla.gov.au/nla.news-article219562076

120 Newnes, *Lithgow Mercury*, Wed 21 Dec 1932, page 6 http://nla.gov.au/nla.news-article219675805

121 NSW DT 1943/22311, Portland Hospital, 11 Aug 1943, Thomas Joseph Halloran

122 Respected resident's death, *Lithgow Mercury*, Wed 18 Aug 1943, page 5 http://nla.gov.au/nla.news-article220791994

123 Funeral notice for her brother, George (4 Sep 1986) identifies her as Amy Irwin, but Amy Urwin fits the records better.

124 Ryersonindex.org Urwin Elizabeth, death 05 Aug 1951 age 61, late of Thirroul *Sydney Morning Herald* 06 Aug 1951

125 NSW DI entries 1971/55890, 1951/22403 NSW MI 1914/2179

126 Oral History from Amy Williams, daughter of George Noon

127 Information was provided by his granddaughter, Jan Fenwick via her niece, Sarah-Jayne Fenwick.

128 Miners fined, *Lithgow Mercury*, Sat 31 Oct 1931, page 1 http://nla.gov.au/nla.news-article221846384

129 Portland police court, *Lithgow Mercury*, Mon 13 Dec 1920, page 2 http://nla.gov.au/nla.news-article218463637

130 Brevities, *Lithgow Mercury*, Thu 27 Dec 1934, page 6 http://nla.gov.au/nla.news-article219604264

131 Portland Police Court, *Lithgow Mercury*, Thu 4 Apr 1935, page 5 http://nla.gov.au/nla.news-article220688952

132 Oral history from Amy Williams, daughter of George Noon

133 NSW DC 1969/1941, Prince Henry Hospital, Little Bay, 16 Apr 1969, Charles Harold Collins

134 Ryersonindex.org, *Illawarra Mercury*, 24 Aug 1988, Gladys May Collins formerly of Coledale Heights (d. 23 Aug 1988)

135 Boxing Friday night, *Illawarra Mercury*, 24 May 1929, page 24 http://nla.gov.au/nla.news-article143122169

136 Oral history from Les Noon, son of Les Noon (b. 1909)

137 Miners fined, *Lithgow Mercury*, Sat 31 Oct 1931, page 1 http://nla.gov.au/nla.news-article221846384

138 Drove negligently, *South Coast Times and Wollongong Argus*, 15 Apr 1948 page 20 http://nla.gov.au/nla.news-article142234443

139 Accidental death verdict, *Illawarra Mercury*, Thu 4 Mar 1948, page 14 http://nla.gov.au/nla.news-article142231984

140 Manslaughter charge remand, *South Coast Times and Wollongong Argus*, Thu 27 Nov 1947, page 3 http://nla.gov.au/nla.news-article142226781

141 Wombarra-Coledale residents evacuate their homes, *South Coast Times and Wollongong Argus*, 6 Apr 1950, page 20 http://nla.gov.au/nla.news-article142870549

142 Oral history from Les Noon, son of Les Noon (b. 1909)

143 Similar stories were heard, from various sources, in my childhood. The victims were most likely to be gunners. Particularly, rear gunners whose exposed position made them vulnerable to attack from most angles.

144 Special Price bookmaker – Illegal gambling. This was the same house that was later damaged in the landslip.

145 Cockatoos were the lookouts and their job was to 'squawk' if the authorities approached.

146 Oral history from Les Noon in combination with: https://www.illawarracoal.com/minebase/minebase-a-c/282-coal-cliff-colliery.html The record has not been independantly verified. There may be some qualification to the claim (eg state or national, vertical, method of construction, etc.). The deepest mine in Australia, Gwalia gold mine, is currently 1.66 km deep. The deepest mine in the world, South Africa's Mponeng gold mine, operates 4.0 km below the surface.

147 NSW DT 1977/104225, Newcastle Hospital, 6 Jul 1977, Leslie Raymond Noon

148 Ryersonindex.org Noon, Laura, Funeral notice, died 11 Aug 2007, formerly of Woonona, *Newcastle Herald*, 18 Aug 2007

149 Commonwealth Electoral Roll

150 Quarter Sessions, *South Coast Time and Wollongong Argus*, Fri 19 Feb 1943, page 2 http://nla.gov.au/nla.news-article142523752

151 Commonwealth Electoral Roll

152 K Greenhalgh, *Ackland – Coal Mine to Tidy Town,* Oakey 2011, page 53 lists Arthur as a coalminer.

153 Oral history from Amy Williams

154 Qld DC 1982/55183, Toowoomba Hospital, 24 Jul 1982, Arthur Robert Noon
& Ryersonindex.org, Noon, Maria Rubi, Funeral Notice, 17 Jan 1986, *The Chronicle* (Toowoomba)

155 JE Carne, *The Copper-mining Industry, and the distribution of copper ores in New South Wales, Sydney, Govt printer 1908* page 235

156 From the collection of Amy Williams

157 Panorama of Newnes Oil Works, New South Wales, 4 [picture] / EB Studios NLA PIC P865/117/3 LOC Nitrate store. The NLA caption this photo as being circa 1930. Similar panorama photos of Newnes exist which form a set and they date from around 1912-1920, therefore I suggest this photo is also from that same set and that same period.

158 Used with permission of Museum of Applied Arts & Sciences — 85/1284-475 Glass plate negative 'Wolgan Valley Railway' depicting a Shay steam locomotive and wagons, by Kerry and Co Sydney NSW, 1906-1917

159 Detail from a Panorama of Newnes township, NSW between 1917 and 1927. / EB Studios, National Library of Australia call number PIC P865/117/1 LOC Nitrate Store, out of copyright and used with permission

160 Photo: GJ Taylor, *Newnes, History of a Blue Mountains Oil-Shale town Australian Railway* Historical Society, Redfern, c 1987 page 1, photo taken from the train station

161 Photo from the collection of Amy Williams. The significance of the photo was not originally known. The provenance of the photo's identity was deduced from the following sources: general information from Amy Williams, a visit to Newnes, matching an image of Mystery Mountain taken from the Noon's land with the rocky outcrop in the photo's top background and the match to the photo in GJ Taylor's book. The resemblance of the older female to the only other known photo of Lucy Goodwin and the resemblance of the others to photos subsequently shared completed the discovery.

162 Photo from the collection of Amy Williams

163 Photo from the collection of Ivy Dare and Brenda Burch

164 Both newspaper cuttings from the collection of Amy Williams

165 Photo from the collection of Amy Williams (Poetic licence: Only juvenile goats are 'kids')

166 Photo from the collection of Jan Fenwick

167 Photo GJ Taylor page 63 - cliff to the left is named 'Old Baldy'.

Chapter 5

Peter No one

The search for Peter Noon's origins

Peter Noon, my maternal grandfather's father, is an enigma. Australian records and family notations suggest he was born in East Kilbride, Lanarkshire, Scotland on 3 August 1859.[1] However, no official British documentation can be found to support this suggestion. Therefore, his birthplace, birthdate and even birth name are by no means certain. He left no record of his parents' names. The impression that I have gained of him is that he was a serious and principled man, and that he is unlikely to have chosen the name Noon to deliberately imply that he has covered his past. If he had chosen the spelling Noone, then I would consider the possibility he was wryly giving us a clue about his past.

What the Australian records say

His death record states his father was a miner.[2] Different sources point to him arriving in Australia aged between 17 and 26.[3] He was possibly on the *Duke of Devonshire*, a steamer, which brought out 571 immigrants in October 1883. An unassisted passenger listed as P Noon, aged 26, disembarked at Brisbane.[4] The age suggests a birth year of 1857. This is acceptably close to the Bible birthdate and is completely consistent with claims regarding his age given at other times.[5]

On one occasion, Peter Noon gave his birthplace as East Kilbride, Scotland.[6] This is understood to be the parish of East Kilbride in the County of Lanarkshire. This contains an old village of Kilbride, centred around the current St Bride's church. In the 1861 census, the parish had a population of 4,062. The modern-day town forms part of the conurbation of modern Glasgow and is about twelve kilometres to the south-east of Glasgow's centre.

Peter Noon, from his 1915 memorial card[66]

One other time, Peter gave his birth location as the County of Ayrshire.[7] At times, his wife, Lucy, gives Peter's birthplace as East Kilbride,[8] East Kilbridge,[9] Kilbride – Ayrshire,[10] East Kilbride – Ayrshire,[11] Kirkilbridge[12] and even as Edinburgh.[13] As well as the East Kilbride in Lanarkshire, there is the small village of West Kilbride on the coast of Ayrshire. These localities are over forty kilometres apart. No Kirkilbridge has been found, but there is a Kirtlebridge in Dumfries and Galloway, which is about one hundred kilometres from Glasgow. Lucy never journeyed outside Australia, so she is simply trying to relate what Peter has told her.

What the Scottish records say

The Scottish Records Office advised Peter is a name paired with Patrick, and then the two are used interchangeably in some families. The birth records for these places mentioned above and further afield have been searched for a Peter or Patrick Noon or Noone, in the period 1855 to 1864.[14] The closest match was a Patrick Noon, born to a Barclay Noon, a shipbuilder's labourer, and Irish-born Mary née Flaherty in Dumbarton, north of Glasgow in January 1857. However, Patrick died in a poorhouse in Dundee in 1917. Interestingly, a Peter Nawn was born in Glasgow to Peter and Ann Nawn in April 1857. The family appears in the 1861 census, but there is no more mention of this family in Scotland after Peter senior's death in 1863. So, this Peter is not eliminated, just sidelined for now.

The search was changed to just look at any Peters/Patricks born in or around East Kilbride. The births of just eleven Peters and eight Patricks were civilly registered in East Kilbride between 1855 and 1864. All of these birth records were examined and none of them resonate with what is known or what is suspected about our Peter. There were just 67 registered male births in East Kilbride in 1859. All of those with a registration date from August on were searched for a birth date of 3 August. No entry matching that date was found.

There were 275 Peters with registered births in 1859 in Lanark, the county containing East Kilbride and there were 39 in Ayrshire that year. A Peter Collins was found who was born on 3 August 1859 in Kirkport, Ayrshire. Unfortunately, it was deduced he died as an infant as he disappears, and another Peter was born to the same family sixteen years later. Searching all of the possible records within those counties without additional clues was not considered prudent or economical.

Census records were also searched and approximately thirty individuals with the surname of Noon were found in 1861. There were seventy in 1871. Most of the families appeared to have some connection with Ireland. Peter's religion is believed to have been Catholic when he arrived in Australia. Peter and Lucy were married in the Catholic church in Sunny Corner. There were four churches to choose from in the town.[15] Many Catholics in Scotland from this time have a connection with Ireland, although there was still a native residue from the old Jacobite days. Noon is a name most commonly associated with Ireland and it is related to the more common Noonan and Noone.

The 1871 census records identified another Patrick Noon born in Glasgow around 1861 to Irish parents, James and Bridget Noon. James was a labourer. By the time of the 1881 census, the name had become Noonan and Patrick was still in Scotland in 1891, confirming he was not the person we are looking for. A few other individuals with the name Patrick Noon/Noone/Noonan briefly appear in the record, but their details (e.g. born in Ireland) push them to the margin of consideration.

The official birth record for the above individual has not been found despite the civil registration of births being mandatory in Scotland from 1855. There was a 20-shilling fine if the birth was not registered within 21 days. Researching various individuals suggests this deterrent was not sufficient to get total compliance as some baptism records from this time do not have corresponding civil registration records.

Amy Williams, granddaughter of Peter and Lucy, said the story she had heard was the Noons came from Ireland to Scotland to escape the Irish Potato Famine of 1845–1852. The father of the family was an ironworker. Other family members thought there was a connection with Wales.[16]

Peter and Lucy's family Bible recorded Peter's birthday. It also lists the birthdate of Lucy's second husband, William Rochester. William's birthdate

identified as, most probably, Lucy's younger sister, Mary Jane, who married James Thompson in New Zealand in 1908. Her cemetery record from East Cape, Poverty Bay, NZ records her as 'Mary (Marie) Jane, blvd. wife of the late James T. Thompson'. She died in October 1964, aged 88 years. She named her first daughter Valerie Marie in 1917. From the records available, this is, by far, the best match and therefore of no help in identifying Peter's original

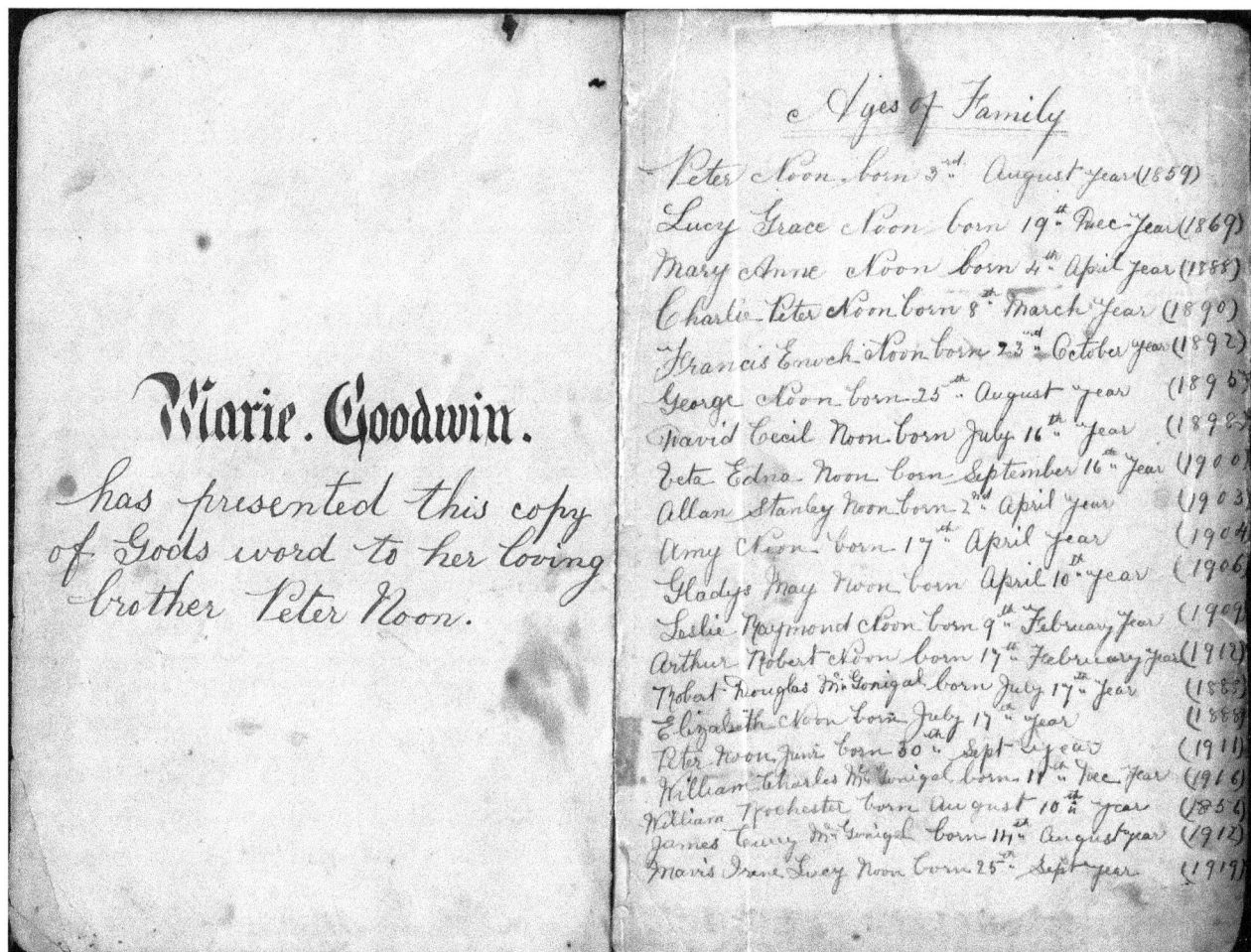

is known to be wrong by four years. Les Noon's birthday is also out by one month. Based on that, there is no certainty Peter's birthdate is accurately recorded. A page adjoining the list of birthdays is also of interest. The two pages are shown above:

If Marie was an actual sister of Peter's, then her details would provide another pathway to explore Peter's origins. Marie Goodwin has been

family because she is a sister-in-law rather than a sister. It is also of note that 'Sister' and 'Brother' were the honorifics Temperance members used when addressing each other.

Peter's first daughter was named Mary Ann, indicating they were honouring Lucy's mother with that choice. Therefore, the choice of Charles Peter as the name for their first son suggests

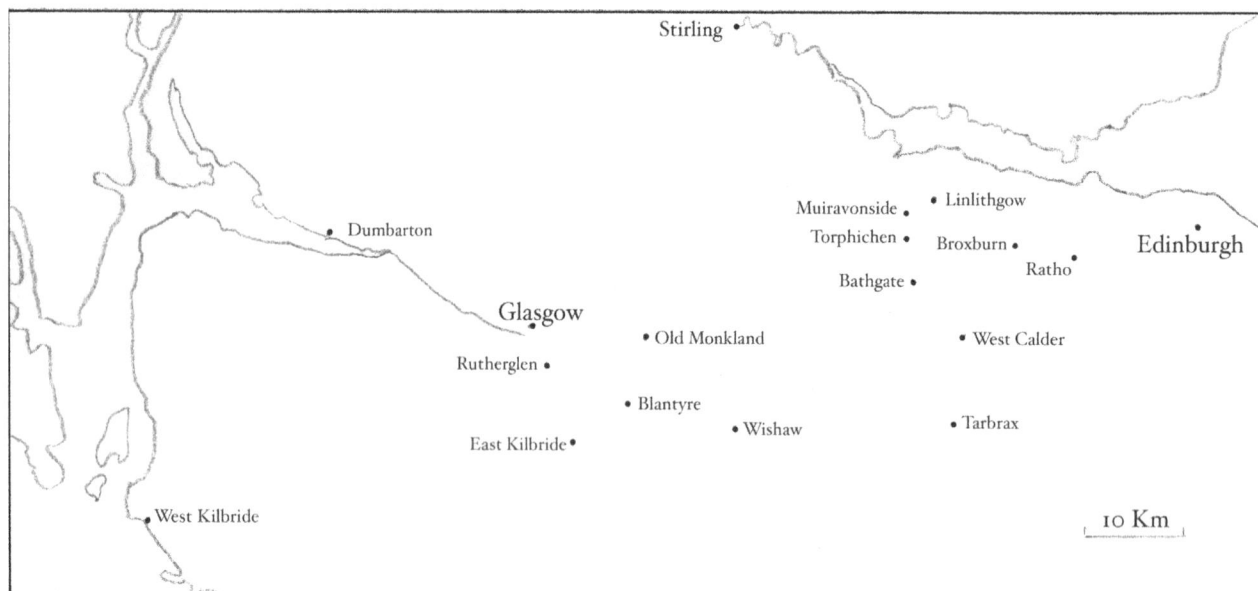

Southern Scotland with placenames significant to Peter Noon's early days and to the McGonigal family

Peter's father's name may have been Charles. A promising Noon family was found in Lanarkshire, with a father named Charles and a son also named Charles about Peter's age. Unfortunately, the son, a glassblower, was eliminated when he was tracked to his registered death (from 'exhaustion') in Scotland in 1899.

When searching Lanarkshire and Ayrshire records in combination with marriages involving a Noon, no obvious candidates were found that could be easily morphed into Peter Noon – e.g. searches were done for all Peters and Patricks born around the right time and likely place which could subsequently have a surname change due to a mother marrying or remarrying. All males born to Noon/Noone families were also examined. So, if the birth was officially registered, then it is likely to be under a different name.

What other records say

Since Peter could not be found in Scotland, attention turned to other places. Peter Noons within England were also investigated and three individuals of about the right age named Peter Noon were examined and all proved to be different to the Peter being searched for. Incidentally, one was a seaman who was charged with murdering his wife, after our Peter was confirmed to be in Australia, so thankfully, he was not the one being sought.

Some identified a Peter Noon, born in Reedy Creek in Victoria to parents, John Noon and Joanna (née Curvel/Kerwin).[17] Just to thicken the plot, the same family had a daughter, Maria, born in 1869 in Growlers Creek, Victoria. They had other children including a daughter, Mary Jane, born in 1871 at Bright. The thinking was, since we were not finding Peter in Scotland, was this our Peter? Whilst Marie Goodwin had not been identified, it was thought Maria could easily be traded for Marie or maybe Mary Jane could be bent into Marie, as was the case with Mary Jane Goodwin. However, quite apart from the problem of Scottish and Australian accent differences, Peter Noon was confirmed as dying in 1937 in East Melbourne, Victoria.[18] That link was therefore confirmed as a red herring.

There was a suggestion Peter Noon may have been an alias, as a family rumour had it that he jumped ship when he came to Australia and may have changed his name. There is also a story, he was a cabin boy and came to Australia in that capacity. If true, then the P Noon on the *Duke of Devonshire* would be someone else.

What the DNA tells us

Attention was turned to the potential of DNA testing. Using DNA to solve genealogical problems is akin to using a metal detector to find a needle in a haystack – i.e. it gives a number of broad clues that have to be combined to get the necessary focus. Y-DNA testing looks at just the Y chromosome fathers pass almost intact to their sons. The Y chromosome includes markers with short tandem repeats (STRs) of genetic code. The count of repeats on these markers provides a set of measures for an individual. Comparing these counts with other test subjects can identify individuals sharing a male ancestor within a relatively short timeframe. The measure of difference is called genetic distance (GD). A validated[19] male Noon descendant[20] was tested at Family Tree DNA[21] and he matched several individuals at close genetic distance. One match was identical with a GD of zero on 111 markers.[22] The next closest had a GD of two on 111 markers[23]. The three[24] closest matches have the surname McCauley.[25] A total of 25 of the top 47 matches have the surname McGuire.[26] No matches with the name Noon were found. All available family trees for the top matches indicate Irish origins for the male line. The Southern Ulster counties of Fermanagh and Cavan figure most prominently.[27] Note: technical detail on the matches is given in the endnotes, but for privacy reasons, names have been reduced to initials or reported in such a way they would be recognised only if someone were to retrace the research.

There are published histories of Irish families telling us the McGuire clan controlled Fermanagh from around 1250 CE.[28] A sub-branch of the clan (or sept) named Awley formed in the south-western parts of the territory (near Cavan) and they started to use the surname McAwley around 1460 CE.[29]

Three of Peter Noon's grandchildren, Peg Ditton, Amy Williams and Les Noon had an autosomal DNA test done with Ancestry.com. That company uses an ethnicity feature for its autosomal DNA tests, which identifies quite specific geographic regions for DNA matches against reference populations of natives of those regions.[30] Ancestry.com says the geographic regions relate to where ancestors lived in the past hundreds of years.[31] This aspect of DNA testing is still developing and not all observers agree this is acceptably accurate. Having said that, all three grandchildren have ancestral regions within Central Ireland.[32] In fact, the results for the three grandchildren are remarkably consistent. No other ancestor at this level[33] for any of these grandchildren is known to account for the matches to those specific regions. Therefore, the DNA evidence points to Peter Noon's ancestry originating in Central Ireland with a male line of McAuleys, probably from the region relating to the Ulster counties of Cavan and Fermanagh.[34]

Ancestry.com also provides information on matches to other people who have taken its autosomal DNA tests and so, by cross comparing the list of matches for the three grandchildren of Peter, we are able to identify the most likely test subjects who are related on the Noon-Goodwin side of the tree. After qualifying matches, approximately thirty potential prospects were identified.[35] Some prospects provide well-documented public family trees, but most do not. Ancestry.com provides a mechanism for contacting the prospects and asking them for information. If the prospects do not know or share the information you seek, then you are limited to the Ancestry.com supplied technical tools, which although useful, are not as good as they could be.

Ancestry.com provided two qualified matches identified as 'shared'.[36] Both had the same individual in their trees – a Patrick McCauley born in 1846 in Blacklion, County Cavan.[37] The strength of one of these matches indicates we are getting very close.[38] It is unlikely to be through Patrick directly, but more probably through his father, Thomas, or less probably through his grandfather, assuming this is indeed Peter's paternal line.[39]

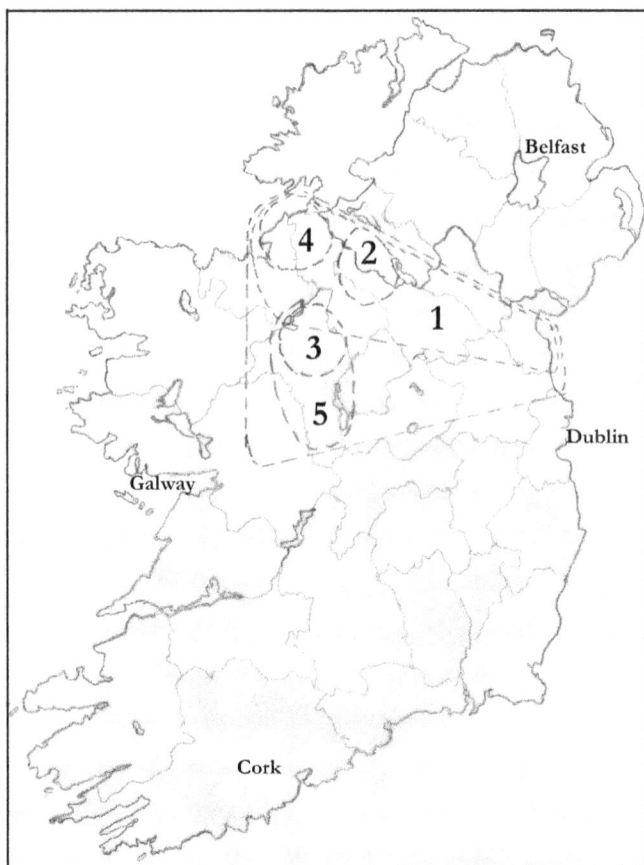

Ancestral regions in Central Ireland as determined by Ancestry.com's analysis of the DNA of three of Peter Noon's grandchildren. Regions 1 (North Leinster and East Connacht) and 2 (Fermanagh and Cavan) were shared by all three grandchildren. Region 3 (North Roscommon) was shared by two and regions 4 (North Leitrim and East Sligo) and 5 (Roscommon) were each identified as an ancestral region for different grandchildren.

Armed with the new DNA clues about McAuleys/McAwleys/McCauleys, the records were searched again to see if anybody with those surnames was born in or near East Kilbride around the time of his supposed birthday. As these are not rare names, some possible matches were found, but more clues would be needed to identify the standout candidates.[40]

The genealogical DNA website, GEDmatch.com allows people to upload their test results from the various DNA testing companies so people who have been tested with the different providers can compare their results. By inference, people using that site are more proactive and willing to share information than the average user of the testing companies. GEDmatch.com provides technical tools which allow for detailed analysis of matches. Using that site, another list of close matches, to the three grandchildren of Peter were validated and collated. The top match and the third top match to Peter's grandchildren were sisters and residents of NSW.[41] One was contacted and asked what they knew of their ancestors.

Because of the strength of the match, the expectation was they would be Goodwin relatives or direct descendants of Peter Noon. This contact had never heard of Noons or Goodwins, but they did identify they had relatives living in East Kilbride between 1847 and 1858, and the father of the family was a lime/cement miner. This contact occurred before the Y-DNA results had been received, and so the analysis was broader than it would have been in light of the Y-DNA results. The initial thought was that Peter Noon may have been born as a legitimate member of that family. The family consisted of a father named Patrick Fallins (sometimes: Fallans, Fallens, Fallons, Falloons, Faland, Follen, Foylen, Fallon, Fallen, Fallaw, Fallance, Valance)[42] (b. c. 1820), Ireland, and a mother named Agnes Burges (b. c. 1824) living in East Kilbride. Three male children born in East Kilbride were Patrick (b. c. 1851), John (b. c. 1853) and Edward (b. c. 1855). Patrick died at the age of twenty in Scotland. Edward and John immigrated to Australia in 1883, as did their sister Agnes (b. c. 1856) in 1885. Our contact was descended from Agnes. Edward and John are fully accounted for, dying in NSW under their own names.[43] A girl, Margaret, was born in May 1859 at nearby Blantyre, meaning the family was no longer at East Kilbride in 1859. There were two more boys born at Blantyre. William was born in 1863 and James in 1864 and two more girls: Bridget in 1861 and Mary in 1867. The family was back in East Kilbride for Mary's birth. William disappeared before the 1871 census, implying he died in infancy, although no death record has been found. James was living at home in 1871 and 1881, but within the next decade, joined his siblings in Australia where he died in 1940.[44] That meant this family was fully accounted for and therefore, not the simple fit the initial discovery suggested.[45]

A check was needed, to ensure the search had not been distracted by a coincidental match on East Kilbride. A check with one of the few relevant public trees available on Ancestry.com showed a qualified and validated match with a person who claimed descent from the youngest daughter, Mary Fallins.[46] Another match, without a public tree, in correspondence, claimed descent from third son Edward.[47] Yet another, in correspondence, claimed descent from youngest son James.[48] These matches confirmed this family was the relevant link to Peter Noon.[49] But just how the link worked was not immediately obvious. The link may have been through the siblings of the parents of these families. Both the Burges family and the Fallins families were examined as well.

The difficulty, however, is we were investigating at the limit of the civil records, which only started in Scotland in 1855. Church records prior to that contain only basic information requiring a combination of speculation and faith to tie individuals into a family tree. The Irish origins also suggest we should be looking at Irish records as well. That was done, but Irish records are notoriously patchy and scant. Only church records are available for the relevant period. Many Irish records were permanently lost due to the bombardment of the Four Courts Building in Dublin in 1922, during the Irish Civil War.

What was discovered was Agnes Burges' mother, Isobel Brown, was Irish born. Agnes had two documented brothers, Francis and John.[50] Francis appeared to have had only one daughter and no sons. John appeared to have had only two daughters and no sons.[51] Looking at the Fallins side, Patrick had a well-documented brother, Edward Fallens (b. c. 1824), married to Mary Gallaher and living nearby in Lanarkshire. Edward and Mary

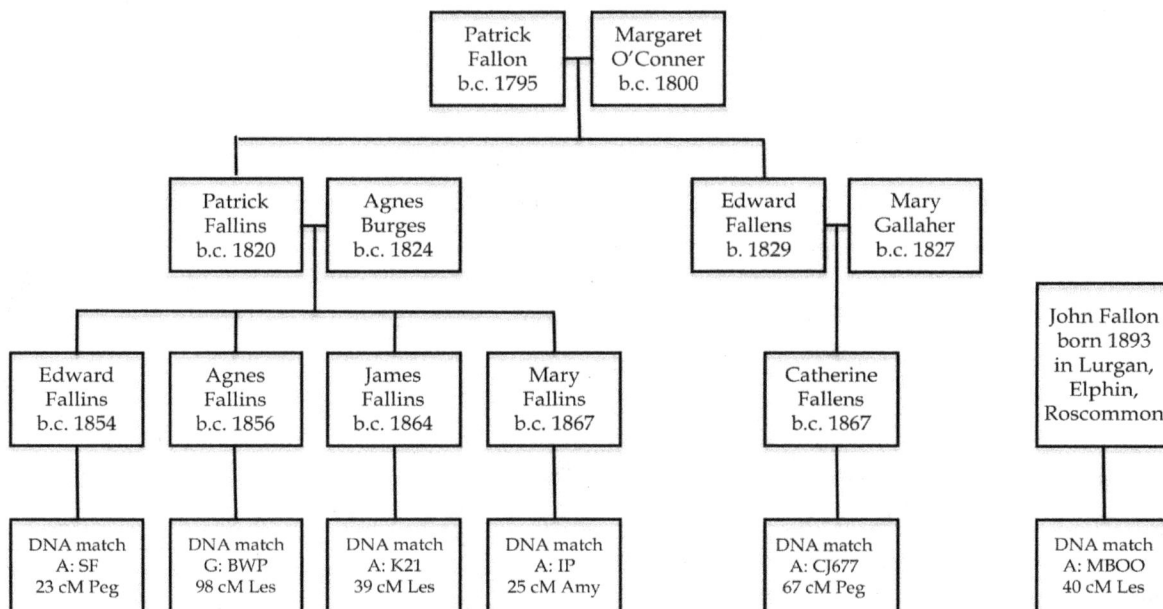

DNA matches that confirmed that Peter Noon had a link to the Fallon family from Elphin, Roscommon. Only the strongest matches are shown for each link - Account names are abbreviated for privacy

had three daughters and a son, Edward (b. 1855), who was completely accounted for.[52] The Scottish records identified Patrick and Edward were born in Roscommon to Patrick Fallens and Margaret O'Konner (O'Connor/Conner). The Irish records indicated the family of Patrick Fallon and Margaret/Marcella/Mary Connor lived on the estate of Ballyoughter House, parish of Elphin, County Roscommon.[53] Irish records identified up to nine other siblings: two Marys, a Bridget, two Catherines, an Honor, a Jeremy, a Michael and a John.[54]

Subsequent contact was made with two more matches. They were triangulated to the matches with the Fallens family.[55] One claimed descent from Edward (b. c. 1824).[56] The other had a relatively recent Fallon family from Elphin parish, Roscommon, within their tree.[57] That strongly suggested the link to Peter Noon is on the Fallon side rather than the Burges side. Concerns about spelling variations need to be put aside as most people from Ireland were illiterate at this time.[58] The spelling ending up on the page was down to what the illiterate informant said, what the scribe heard and the background knowledge of the scribe – e.g. Irish scribes consistently render the name in question as Fallon whereas Scottish scribes seem to pick up on other syllables or accents.

Combining the two clues

Stepping back and considering these two separate DNA clues in combination: The male line was pointing at a McAuley (i.e. in the absence of a Noon) then, given the strength of this match, it implied the Fallon line was most likely supplying the mother of our Peter. Because Peter and Lucy named their first daughter Mary Ann and their second daughter Veta Edna, it suggested we were looking for a Mary/Ann/Veta/Edna. However, the last two names are not common Irish names (Hebrew origins) and represent more of a fashion at the turn of the 1900s. Also keep in mind Mary Ann was the name of Lucy's mother.

There is a Scottish Roman Catholic (RC) church record for a couple from Kilbride, Mary Fallon and Francis McAulay marrying at St Columbkille in Rutherglen in 1855. Rutherglen is less than ten kilometres from East Kilbride.

Francis McAulay & Mary Fallon from Kilbride after due proclamation of banns were married by me in presence of James McArdle & Veronica Daly on the twelfth day of November 1855. John Shaw.[59]

Based on the structure of similar entries, we could infer that both Francis and Mary resided in (East) Kilbride rather than just Mary. This appeared to be the gold we were looking for. From census records, this Mary was probably born circa 1835 in Ireland.[60] Could it be her?[61] As it happened, an Irish baptism record had the second Mary born to Patrick Fallon and Mary Conner in Elphin, Roscommon being born in 1835.[62] She was born in the townland of Clooncullane.[63] This looked promising, as each morsel of information fitted with what was being searched for – i.e. this Mary Fallon appeared to be a younger sister of Patrick and Edward Fallens and a perfect DNA fit for the mother of Peter Noon.

Peter and Lucy's second son was named, Francis Enoch. Enoch was clearly honouring Lucy's father. Was Francis honouring Peter's father? That left us wondering where Charles came from.

A subsequent search found a baptism entry from the same church as the marriage, for a son, Francis McAulay, on the date of 8 September 1856 with parents Francis McAulay and Mary Fallon. There was no equivalent civil registration of the birth despite the law requiring it.[64] The entry read as follows:

Francis x lawful Francis McAulay - Mary Fallon 8 Sept

The 'x' indicates the child was a male and the 'lawful' indicates the birth was legitimate.

The search was renewed, but it was not picking up any other confirmed activity (births, deaths, re-marriage, census or immigration records) for Francis or Mary after the birth of young Francis in 1856.[65] The path goes cold for the family unit, but if the story were to continue, we would need to understand how the hypothesised son, Peter (or did Francis become Peter) and maybe others in the family, then adopt the surname Noon. Did the circumstances of the family change? Did a significant male influence with the name of Charles enter the picture or was that Peter's own given name? Why was Peter so drawn to the Temperance movement? Did he experience any intemperance-related problems? Did the family relocate to Ayrshire at any time?

Thinking through what these scenarios would look like in the records, searches were conducted with that focus. The 1861 census showed seven men aged more than twenty with the name of Francis McAulay (or variants such as: MacAulay, McAully, McAuly, McCaulay) living in Scotland. Searches were also done for young Francis. The best match for the older Francis was Francis McAully, a 26-year-old 'unmarried' Irish-born labourer living in a boarding house in the parish St Quivox, Ayrshire. Not proof, but a possibility. The 1871 census only showed two men of relevant age named Francis McAuley (etc.) and the Ayrshire labourer was not one of them. Similarly, he was not present in 1881. No matching death record explained his disappearance. Perhaps he emigrated.

The results for the young Francis are slightly more interesting. An 1861 census record from Old Monkland, Lanarkshire (not too far from Rutherglen or East Kilbride) showed a five-year-old Francis McAulay living as a son to a Charles and Jane McAuley. There was a brother, Arthur, who was four years old and interestingly, recorded before the older Francis, which was unusual for census recording. The place of birth for all family

Francis (Frank) Noon (standing) with his father, Peter.
From the collection of Amy Williams

members was recorded as Ireland. The age of young Francis matched very well. We could speculate this was a possible outcome if something happened to both of young Francis' parents and 'Uncle Charles' came to his rescue. Listing the older child second implied a bit of an afterthought. Claiming he was born in Ireland might just have made things easier to explain given the younger boy was most probably born in Ireland. Of course, this was just speculation, but it would provide an explanation for the circumstances of young Francis. This family unit could not be found in the 1871 census. Peter named his last son Arthur, which may help point in that direction.

On another possible angle, no clear record for Mary and her hypothesised son, Peter, was found under the surname McAuley, Noon or Fallon. The only interesting record in this regard is one of a 36-year-old Mary McAuley (widow and hostel keeper) marrying a Patrick Noon, 58, widower in Clyde, Glasgow in 1869. However, she gave her parents' names as Patrick and Ann McAuley. This was probably not Mary Fallon. Was she a sister of Francis? Why did she appear to use her maiden name if she was a widow? Was that the tradition then or did she coincidently marry someone with the same surname?

This is the point at which an anecdote from the Noon family is worth retelling. In the version heard, the story was thought to relate to Charlie Noon, Peter's son, but on reflection, it is more likely to relate to Peter himself. The story goes like this: Two women running a boarding house employed the young Noon boy. Some of his duties were to light the fire and start the lanterns of an evening. His employers noticed he used three matches each day. They thought this was a bit extravagant and asked him why he needed three. He said he needed one to light the fire, one to light the lanterns and another to light the candle beside his bed so he could read of an evening. Whether his nocturnal reading was sacrificed in the name of efficiency was not revealed. This frugality is unlikely to be associated with turn-of-the-century Australia, but much more consistent with a nineteenth-century Scotland and gives a glimpse of the motivations for emigration. The story fits in with Peter's passion for reading material, as he was identified as a distributor of reading material at Newnes. Whether this gives a clue to where he spent his childhood is only speculation, but it will be kept in mind in any future searches.

Assessing this disappointing lack of supporting documents, particularly any concrete record of Peter's existence in Scotland, how confident should we be that the marriage record and the birth record for a young Francis referred to above is the key to Peter's origins? This is only slightly better than not being able to find a birth record for a Peter Noon. However, the confidence level that Peter's father is a McCauley/McAulay and his mother is one of the Fallon daughters is extremely high given the strong DNA clues. Mary is the only Fallon girl we have any records for after their baptisms. Those records place her in Scotland (East Kilbride – no less). Catherine, Brigid and the young Honor have not yet been found anywhere and we would expect the name of Peter's mother to be honoured in one of the names of Peter and Lucy's children. This marriage record neatly ties in the Y-DNA result and explains the choice of Francis as a family name. There is the distinct possibility the young Francis McAulay becomes Peter Noon because we cannot find an alternate set of records for young Francis. The overall confidence level is 'a bit more likely than not'. However, the search will continue because new clues or new ideas are bound to keep turning up.

What's the point of all of this?' I can hear people ask. It is simply an exercise in discovering as much as possible about an individual via the most modern of genealogical techniques. Some people like to do jigsaw puzzles. Working diligently for a week or so to produce a complete well-ordered picture which is subsequently broken up and put away. This exercise is similar, except this picture has fuzzy borders, is definitely missing pieces and there is some doubt about how some bits have been put together – but even partially assembled, it can be preserved or worked on for as long as people care about their ancestors.

Endnotes to Chapter 5

1 NSW BCs 1890/19393, Pipers Flat (Charles) & 1906/18438, Portland (Gladys) & Page from a family Bible with names and birth dates is headed by Peter Noon 3 Aug 1859.

2 NSW DC 1915/7765, Newnes, 8 May 1915, Peter Noon

3 His DC stated he had been in Australia 36 years indicating he arrived in 1878/79 at the age of 18–22. There was some oral history he came to Australia as a cabin boy which suggests a young age.

4 Qld, Australia Passenger Lists 1842–1912, P Noon age 26, *Duke of Devonshire*, Cooktown 12 Oct 1883, then Brisbane. This P Noon was not an assisted immigrant, i.e. he paid his own way.

5 His May 1915 DC gives the age of 58 which implies a birth year of 1856/1857

6 On his son, Charles' BC, NSW 1890/19393

7 On his son, David's BC, NSW 1898/22595

8 On her son, Arthur's & daughter, Gladys' BCs, NSW 1912/10806 & 1906/18438

9 On her daughter, Veta's BC, NSW 1900/32633

10 On her son, George's BC, NSW 1895/23749

11 On her daughter, Aimee's BC, NSW 1904/174559

12 NSW DC 1915/7765, Newnes, 8 May 1915, Peter Noon

13 On his sons, Leslie & Allen's birth certificates, NSW BC 1909/9369 & 1903/13262

14 The Scottish records office advised that the names Peter & Patrick are interchangeable in some families and sequences of records for individuals have confirmed that. The name Noon stems from the name Noone and in turn from Noonan.

15 From a historical information plaque displayed in the main street of Sunny Corner, seen 2016.

16 A first cousin remembered that as a story he had heard, but no other detail was available.

17 Name is spelt differently each time it is recorded (Cunavion, Curravion, Currwin, Curvel, Curwin, Curraisons, Kerwin).

18 Victorian DI 1937/4181

19 Autosomal DNA of subject matches all other tested descendants as expected.

20 Charles Peter Noon, son of Peter Charles Noon, son of Charles Peter Noon, son of Peter Noon and the tradition still continues.

21 Only the US-based company, Family Tree DNA, currently offers this test.

22 GD 0 on 111 markers equates to about a 95% chance there is a common ancestor within 5 generations. This particular match records the oldest known male line ancestor as Francis McCauley born Moneenterriff, co. Cavan which is about 10 km SW of Blacklion where the strong autosomal match comes from. The test taker is named 'Ms Warba Minnesota McCauley' This is a reference to Becky McCauley, the person who organised the test for her male double cousin. Becky McCauley is the author of the book *McCauley 'x' is my true name.* {Ref: B. McCauley, *McCauley 'x' is my true name.* Warba, Minnesota, USA self-published 2015 ISBN 151473544X} Becky's autosomal test at Ancestry.com (Beckymccauley63) also scores moderate (11–14 centiMorgans [cMs]) autosomal matches with Peg and Amy but even higher at GEDmatch (33.1 & 24.8 cMs). It is higher because the Ancestry algorithm called Timber, ignores some segments which Ancestry considers 'too matchy'). DNA experts do warn the GD 0 may point to an ancestor further removed as markers can mutate in both directions and so GD 0 may mask movements which cancel each other out on 1 or more of these markers.

23 GD 2 on 111 markers ~ 94% chance there is a common ancestor within 6 generations (& 80% within 4). The test taker was a Dr M W McCauley. A big Y test showed this subject to be the closest match to Charles Noon of anyone who has also undertaken a big Y test as there is a unique Single Nucleotide Polymorphism (SNP) only shared with him and 2 others (at GD 6 & 7). The SNP is R-Y82651 and that is the definite description of Charles' Y haplogroup. It is likely that the even closer match (GD 0) would also share this SNP and haplogroup.

24 The top 2 could be considered the GD 0 and the GD 2 matches at 111 markers.

25 Determining which is the third closest match is a little subjective as there are several measures. Some test subjects did a big Y test where you can determine the terminal SNP. If you share that, then that may make you closer than someone with a lower genetic distance over 111 STRs; using that measure, a person with a GD 6 on 111 markers but with a shared terminal SNP might be considered closer than cases with GD 3 but without the shared terminal SNP.

26 The top 49 are down to a max of GD 6 on 111 markers.

27 These 2 counties share a national border. Cavan is in the Irish Republic and Fermanagh is in the UK.

28 http://mcguire-heritage.blogspot.com – Wikipedia provides the date 1250 CE (Current Era, which was previously referred to as AD).

29 http://www.clanawley.com

30 Autosomal DNA are the chromosomes other than the sex chromosomes (i.e. the autosomes).

31 That is aimed at hundreds of years rather than thousands of years. Other tools trace more ancient roots.

32 Test subjects (grandchildren of Peter Noon) are Amy Williams, Leslie Noon and Peg Ditton.

33 Lucy Goodwin's grandmother, Bridget Evans, was thought to be from the province of Ulster, but this is 2 generations further back. Recent reexamination of the documentary evidence places her in Fermoy, Cork, in the province of Munster.

34 In general, the ethnicity aspects of genetic DNA are controversial and not universally agreed. There is significant variation between the testing companies. From my own observations, Ancestry has improved over the past few years as its reference populations increased by an order of magnitude and is now clearly better at this than the other testing companies particularly for Britain and Ireland. I have found it

impressive enough to include in my discussion of Peter Noon's origins.

35 Qualifying meant removing known or weak matches and noting grouping information supplied by Ancestry.

36 The Ancestry account names of the qualified matches are L D'A (Peg: 112 cMs on 6 segs, Amy: 29 cMs 1 seg, Les: 23 cMs 5 segs) and JD (Peg: 31 cMs 3 segs, Amy: 15 cMs 3 segs, Les 7 cMs 1 seg). Account names partially obscured for privacy reasons. 'Shared' is Ancestry's way of saying they triangulate (share specific DNA segments with each other and with the test under examination). These 2 individuals are second cousins once removed, which in itself provides more confidence of the match than if they were more closely related.

37 Blacklion is a town just south of the border between the Republic of Ireland (co. Cavan) and Northern Ireland (co. Fermanagh). Both Cavan and Fermanagh are in the historical province of Ulster, despite currently being in different countries. The town of Blacklion, Cavan, is on the western edge of the Ancestry.com region marked as Fermanagh and Cavan as shown in the Ancestry.com DNA maps. An interesting article appeared in Melbourne's *Herald Sun* on Sat, 16 Mar 2019, pages 56 & 57 discussing the likely impact of Brexit on the border town communities of Blacklion, Cavan and Belcoo, Fermanagh. The worst-case scenario appears to have been averted.

38 Peg Ditton's match with L D'A was 112 Centimorgans across 6 segments. Ancestry advises this is around second cousin once removed strength and higher than third cousin strength (i.e. quite close).

39 Patrick was too young to be Peter's father and he emigrated to the USA from Ireland in the 1860s. The other test in the triangulated match, JD, identified Patrick's parents as Thomas McCauley & Mary Kerrigan both born around 1820 (or more likely 1810) in County Cavan.

40 These names are within the most common 100 names within Ireland. They are also reasonably common in Scotland.

41 Top unknown match which was shared with either or both Peg and Amy, BWP (matched Les Noon at 98.5 centimorgans (cMs) with a predicted generations to Most Recent Common Ancestor (MRCA) of 3.6 i.e. a 3rd to 4th cousin. BWPs match to Amy was 47 cMs and 40.4 cMs to Peg. Third top MWF matched Les at 69.2 cMs with a MRCA of 3.85. Amy's match to MWF was 23.4 cMs and Peg's was 18 cMs.

42 The family was illiterate, so it was up to the recorder to spell it. The family in Australia settled on 'Fallins'.

43 NSW DC 1931/16051, New Lambton, 1 Sep 1931, John Fallins

44 NSW DC 1940/14023, Kahibah, 15 Jul 1940, James Fallins

45 A hypothesis was one of the Fallon boys became Peter Noon, but they are all accounted for.

46 The match was with Ancestry Account name IP (2 tests, his own & JP) Surname on their records was Fallens.

47 Ancestry account SF (23 cMs match to Peg)

48 Ancestry account k21 test MC (match 39 cMs 3 segs to Les)

49 The assumption was this is pointing to a Peter Noon ancestor rather than a Goodwin ancestor primarily because of the geography. Goodwin ancestors at this level all lived in or around Manchester.

50 Curiously, there is an 1861 Glasgow birth record for Patrick Fallon, father: James Fallon & mother: Ann (maiden surname Burgess).

51 We need a son born around 1855–1863 to be a candidate for the young Peter Noon.

52 Scottish SB 1855 643/92, Kirkton, parish of East Kilbride, 13 Sep 1855, Edward Fallin. & The birth record of Edward says his father was born in Roscommon. Only birth records from the year 1855, the first year civil registration was introduced, record parents' birthplaces.

53 A county of the republic, Roscommon is in the west of the province of Connaught. The parish of Elphin is in the centre of the region named North Roscommon on the Ancestry.com DNA region maps.

54 Irish baptism records – copyright County Roscommon Heritage & Genealogy Company – www.rootsireland.com. When a name is chosen to honour a parent, it is not uncommon for a name to be used again if the first child dies young. This has been seen in other families examined for family history research.

55 Triangulation involves matching segments of DNA to 3 individuals to determine if individuals A, B & C are related to each other because the same segment of DNA of at least threshold size is involved in all of the relationships.

56 Ancestry account CJ677 (64 cMs 6 seg match to Peg)

57 Ancestry account MBOO (40 cMs match to Les)

58 The Stuart kings prevented any popish education in Ireland and so in reality it tended to be only Protestant children that were formally educated – Wikipedia.

59 Catholic Registers Banns and Marriages MP 514120, St Columbkille, Rutherglen, 12 Nov 1855, M Fallon & F McAuley

60 Scottish Census Records 1851 Rutherglen 13/17 Main St., Marey Fallen a 16-year-old farm worker, born Ireland.

61 Another Mary Fallon born Ireland c 1838 married Thomas O'Hara at Rutherglen in 1854. Mother: Catherine.

62 Prefixes to Irish names such as 'O' are often left off Irish records as it was considered an affectation. Mary is often paired with Margaret and in other records the name seems to be recorded as Marcella and Madge.

63 This townland is less than 2 km from the estate of Ballyoughter House.

64 The 8 Sep may be the date of baptism as opposed to the date of birth which does leave the possibility young Francis' birth date was the 3 Aug 1856, which would be 3 years earlier than the date recorded in the family Bible. As a reference, William Rochester's birth date in that Bible was 4 years after his actual birth date.

65 A family with parents Francis & Mary McAulay was found in the census in 1861 residing in Dumbarton. Francis was a shipyard labourer. They had a son, Patrick, of the right age. The 1871 census showed they also had a son, Peter, born in 1862. This was looking very promising until it was noted Patrick & Peter were both recorded in the 1891 Scottish census (i.e. after Peter married Lucy in Australia in 1885). It turned out the mother of this family had the maiden name of Sweeney and was therefore a false lead.

66 Photo from the collection of Amy Williams

Chapter 6

A golden age

Mary Ann and Enoch - Goodwin

Gold was the shot in the arm that completed the transformation of the Australian colonies. Their reputation had gradually moved from penal colonies to a productive agricultural land, providing opportunities for men and women with an appetite for hard work and adventure. The discovery of gold fired up the imagination of many. For a few years, Australia became the most desirable destination on the planet. Gold challenged and disrupted the pastoral industries that the colonies had relied on in their formative years. Over the next five decades, mining drew hundreds of thousands of migrants and fortune seekers to Australia's shores. Experience was not even necessary. A desire to chance your luck was the only qualification required. This chapter is the story of the family my maternal grandfather's mother, Lucy Goodwin, grew up within. Her parents were Mary Ann Smith and Enoch Goodwin.

Enoch Goodwin

Enoch Goodwin was born in Manchester, England, in January 1820. He was baptised at the Wesleyan Chapel in Oldham Street, Manchester.[1] His parents were Samuel Goodwin and Lucy (née Sexstone).[2] His father worked as a sizer.[3] Samuel had been a cotton spinner when he married Lucy in 1802.[4] In the 1841 Census, Enoch was living with his parents and two siblings[5] in Wesley Place in the district of Ancoats. Ancoats has been called 'the world's first industrial suburb'.[6] By 1815, Ancoats was the most populous district in Manchester characterised by rows of back-to-back houses. More than half the dwellings had no plumbing and over half of the streets were not cleaned.[7] At that time, his father's profession was recorded as agent and collector, and Enoch was listed as a 'piecer'.[8] His father also had duties as a lay preacher within the Wesleyan church.[9]

In August 1840, Enoch Goodwin, was convicted of larceny at a court session in Salford[10] and was sentenced to two months imprisonment.[11] At the same session a young man, also charged with larceny, written into the ledger just before Enoch, was sentenced to seven years' transportation.[12] Convict transportation to NSW ended the year of Enoch's trial.[13] After serving his time, Enoch chose to leave for Australia as an assisted immigrant. Even without a blotted copybook, Enoch's prospects in England would have been disheartening. In the 1830s and 40s, the working class were being actively suppressed, which resulted in the Charterist Movement.[14] Enoch embarked on the *Joseph Cunard* on 3 August 1841 at Liverpool. His new employer in Australia, Messrs Aspinall, Browne & Co.[15] paid his £19 passage.[16]

Enoch arrived in Port Jackson (Sydney) on 28 November 1841.[17] The company had acquired significant land holdings in NSW in addition to its trading activity. Therefore, with the job title of 'farm labourer', Enoch was headed for a rural assignment. Enoch's older brother Samuel[18] and his wife, Sarah Smith (née Shepherd) and children had also immigrated to Australia and arrived just a few months after Enoch on 7 January 1842.[19] That family settled in the busy port of Morpeth on the Hunter River.[20]

The first verified discovery of gold in NSW was in 1823. However, as NSW was a penal colony, it was thought best to keep that quiet.[21] Later as NSW transitioned from a 'nest of scoundrels'[22] to a land of opportunity, a reward was offered for discoveries of payable gold. Edward Hargraves[23] claimed the first, officially announced, discovery in Australia in February 1851, at Ophir, about fifteen kilometres north-east of Orange, NSW.[24] Several other gold discoveries quickly followed, including one on the Turon River in June 1851.[25] By the end of 1851, there were newspaper reports of significant amounts of alluvial gold being found at the junction of the Macquarie and Turon rivers.[26] The site was referred to as the Lower Turon. Camps and later settlements spread out from that point in response to where gold was found.

Hill End was established about seven kilometres north-east of the junction. Tambaroora, further to the north, was the most significant settlement in the early days. By 1852, there were 14,000 people on the Lower Turon – 4,000 of them were Chinese. But there were hardly any women.

Enoch Goodwin

Mary Ann Goodwin (née Smith)[139]

One report says there were only three women at the crowded goldfield of Sofala in 1852.[27]

Enoch lived out most of his life in Hill End, as did some of his descendants. We are fortunate in that one of his grandsons, Bruce Goodwin, documented some of Enoch's life.[28] In 1999, Bruce published a book entitled *Lace and Gold,* in which he tells the story of his ancestors, including his grandfather, Enoch.[29] In order to flesh out and enliven the story, Bruce flirts with the historical novel genre. That said, there are charming photos, pertinent personal memories and enough solid information to make the book a valuable source.

Bruce states that Enoch had been living in the Hunter River district and applied for a miner's right in the County of Bathurst on 1 June 1851. This was the first day miner's rights were available.[30] The annual fee was a hefty £18. A newspaper report has Enoch on the Lower Turon with James Marshall, a Scotsman, in the early days. The report went on to say James, an accomplished violinist, and Enoch, a singer of some repute, entertained many of their fellow diggers of an evening.[31]

Bruce had an earlier book about his memories of Hill End entitled *Gold and People,* which dealt with Hill End from the 1920s to the 1960s.[32] I am grateful to Bruce for recording and sharing such useful information. I am also grateful for all the other sources from which I have recycled useful nuggets.[33]

There is no shortage of sources for information about Hill End – e.g. books such as Harry Hodge's detailed trilogy *The Hill End Story*[34] and the more technical *Hill End Gold* by Malcolm Drinkwater.[35] There is also the academic *Hill End* by Alan Mayne[36] and the artistic and entertaining *Hillendiana* by Donald Friend.[37] All these books mention the Goodwin family to some degree. Donald Friend's descent into pariah status will be discussed later in this chapter.

Mary Ann Smith and the romance

In 1855, Enoch married his young bride, Mary Ann Smith. One version of the marriage record has Enoch as a bachelor and another as a widower. No record of any previous marriage has been found. Perhaps he lived in a common-law marriage previously and his partner had died.

Mary Ann Smith had arrived with her parents, James and Bridget Smith, at the Sofala goldfield on the Upper Turon in 1852.[38] For six weeks, they had trekked over the mountains behind a dray drawn by five horses carrying their possessions.[39] The newly established gold mining settlement of Sofala was too crowded to find a suitable claim, so they moved further west and further downstream onto the Lower Turon. On his trip from Klondyke Point to Hill End for supplies, Enoch would pass a settlement at Bragg's Flat near the Turon Crossing. On one of these trips he noticed a young girl. The 35-year-old Enoch made some enquiries about her and a romance developed, resulting in the marriage on 23 July 1855.[40] Enoch was concerned the young girl was in 'moral danger'[41] with all the mostly single male miners swarming over the district.[42]

We can only wonder why Mary Ann's parents agreed to allow their young and only daughter to marry Enoch. The oral history says both James and Bridget were at the goldfields at that time. Perhaps she was genuinely in some danger and they saw Enoch's interest in her would provide her with some security. The Presbyterian minister who married them was the recently ordained Scotsman, Alexander McEwan of Meroo, which was a goldfield near Mudgee.[43] This appears to be one of his earliest visits to the Turon goldfields as only by the following year, 1856, was he identified as a regular visitor.[44] Perhaps visits by any suitable minister were quite rare events and that may have been an impetus for Enoch to arrange the marriage at the time he did. The two witnesses were, uncustomarily, both males (James Elwood and James Lyall), which reinforced the notion females were in short supply in this district.[45]

Marriage of Enoch Goodwin and Mary Ann Smith from 23 July 1855 at Turon County Wellington

The age controversy

Now, this is where there is some controversy. Bruce Goodwin claims Mary Ann was sixteen years old at the time of her marriage, even though the birth date he suggests (October 1840), would make her fourteen.[46] Mary Ann was baptised on 26 January 1845 and on that Church record, her birth date was 11 October 1844. That would give her an age of ten years, nine months and twelve days on the date of her wedding. We know we have the correct baptism record, so there are two possibilities: the baptism record birth date is correct, or it is not.[47] If it were correct, then would the marriage be legal?

From 1275 until 1875, the minimum age of marriage in the English-speaking world was generally considered to be at the age of puberty which was commonly accepted as around twelve for a girl and fourteen for a boy. However, the European tradition acknowledged consent could be meaningful if both were aged older than seven, and therefore historically some marriages were recognised at those ages. This attitude influenced the United Kingdom and its colonies. From 1576 until 1875, UK Law established a two-tiered age of consent for girls. Sex with a girl under ten was a felony and sex with a girl aged ten to twelve was a misdemeanour.[48] Jurists in some colonies, particularly in America, played down the second tier. Importantly, the age of consent did not apply to marriage, as a man could not commit the crime of rape (including statutory) within marriage as consent was assumed.[49] Attitudes of the parties were more significant than age when any matter came before a court. It was only by 1875, when the age of consent in the UK was set at fourteen, that things became clearer and age became critical when determining whether consent was possible. In the UK in 1885, the age of consent and the minimum marriage age were set at sixteen. Australian colonies adjusted their legislation independently, at later dates. Prior to civil registration of births, it was difficult to prove a person's age.[50] It is also true, people at that time and earlier were unreliable sources for their actual age and birth dates, particularly if they were illiterate, as Mary Ann was. Was Enoch and Mary Ann's marriage legal? If someone had challenged it, then probably not. It is of some significance, the marriage records from then did not have a place to record the age of the bride or groom, indicating such issues were nowhere near as significant then, as they would later become.[51]

The other alternative is the baptism record has an incorrect birth date. This was the position Bruce adopted.[52] If we look at documents such as Mary Ann's children's birth certificates, where Mary Ann supplies her age, we see the implied birth year ranges between 1836 and 1841.[53] This puts her marriage age at between fourteen and

The 1845 baptism entry for Mary Ann Smith (at bottom) in context, with a birth date of 11 October 1844

nineteen years.[54] Mary Ann's parents, James Smith and Bridget Evans, were both residents of Prospect when they married in St John's Church of England (C of E), Parramatta, on 10 June 1839. Bruce says James was a carpenter, working for Mr William Lawson (of Blue Mountains fame[55]) when he was building St Bartholomew's Church of England at Prospect (completed in 1841).[56] Mary Ann's baptism register of 1845 at St Bartholomew's has James as a labourer.[57]

Bridget arrived on the *Calcutta* from Cork, Ireland, on 16 October 1838.[58] She met James in NSW. Assuming no paternity issues, that points to an earliest possible birth date of June 1839 and in turn an absolute maximum age of just turned sixteen at the time of her marriage. When providing information for her mother's death record in 1891, Mary Ann implies her own birth year is 1842,

reducing her marriage age to twelve or thirteen.[59] Her death record and her memorial have locked in her birth year as 1839.[60] Mary Ann had no siblings.[61]

In the census of NSW, conducted in early March 1841, there were two men named James Smith living at Prospect.[62] The entry most probably for Mary Ann's parents identifies James as a married man between the age of 21 and 45 living with a married female under the age of fourteen.[63] The female is not named. There are no infants within the household (suggesting Mary Ann was not yet born). James was neither born in the colonies nor did he arrive free. However, his wife arrived free. He was C of E and his wife was RC. He was working in agriculture. They lived in a wooden dwelling like most of his neighbours. This is a reasonable fit for the little we know of James and Bridget and the young age recorded for the person assumed to be Bridget is raising a familiar concern.

A portion of the story Bruce tells tends to support the proposition that Mary Ann was a bit too young to be married at that stage. The story goes, Enoch sent Mary Ann to live with his brother, Samuel, and his family at Morpeth. This was supposedly to get her away from the 'predominantly tough male population that were on the diggings'.[64] If she had been aged around sixteen, then would this really be required? If much younger than that, then this sounds like a plausible scenario.

She was said to have hated her time at Morpeth and did everything she could to make herself unpopular, so she would be sent back to Enoch. It is not revealed how long she spent there, but it is quite telling her first child was not born until June 1860, a full five years after their wedding.

In those times, it is not unusual for someone to alter their age and to have it consistently altered through their life. Enoch shaves between one to six years off his age when he has it recorded on the children's birth certificates. This discussion makes the case that Mary Ann was not truthful when stating her age. Some of the ages she claims are inconsistent, if not impossible. Therefore, she was either sensitive or ignorant or careless about the issue and consequently, we should be wary about her age-related statements.

If we take the following points into account:
◊ Mary Ann was sent to Morpeth, as her young age exposed her to danger.
◊ Her first child was not born until five years after the wedding.
◊ She does not appear in the 1841 census.
◊ She was baptised in 1845 in her local church which had existed since 1841.
◊ The prevailing tradition was a child was baptised soon after birth.[140]
Then on balance, it is likely she was only ten years old on her wedding day.

Left: St Bartholomew's Anglican Church, Prospect (completed 1841). It has suffered vandalism and fire. Restoration commenced in 2000 and at the time of this photo (2009), it was behind security fencing.
Right: The memorial plaque, which is situated on the grave of their son, David Goodwin, at the Hill End and Tambaroora Cemetery. David was killed in a mining accident. That plaque states Mary Ann was born in 1839. This story makes the case the actual birth year was more likely to be 1844. Photo 2009. Photos: author

James Smith and Bridget Evans

What Mary Ann's father was transported for, and when, is difficult to determine because over one hundred convicts, named James Smith, were transported to Australia.[65] The census also revealed James was not currently a ticket-of-leave man, in the government's employment or on private assignment. He was not married under licence, indicating he was not a convict at that time. The young age of his wife may have been as a result of careless census recording or the truth. The age given for Bridget on her 1891 death certificate is a nice round eighty years, suggesting a birth year in 1811. That would mean an age of thirty years at the time of the 1841 census. Mary Ann, the informant, was not able to name her grandparents and she gave nice round numbers for her mother's age at marriage (thirty) and the number of years in the colonies (fifty).[66] She also said her mother's birthplace was County Armagh.[67] Without some corroboration, neither this death record nor the census entry imbues enough confidence to take either suggested birth year as certain.

On page one of *Lace and Gold*, Bruce Goodwin states Bridget Evans, aged 22, a native of Fermagh, County Cork, father, William Evans (profession: tailor) and mother, Bridget Clancy, came to NSW on the *Calcutta* in 1838, with her sister, Jane, and Jane's husband, William Stewart. The original record shows Jane was in fact Bridget's cousin and the town incorrectly written as Fermagh on Jane's record was correctly recorded as Fermoy on William's details. Bridget was a kitchen maid.[68] The parents' details relate to Jane but not Bridget.

Incidentally, Jane did have a sister, Bridget, who was baptised in Fermoy in 1829 and that provides confidence 'Fermagh' (which can't be found on any map) is a misheard mistake. So, given the three sources to choose from regarding Bridget's age, the most reliable is the immigration record, which suggests a birth year for Bridget of 1816 and probably in Fermoy, County Cork.[69] Jane's family was RC as was William's.[70] Jane, a children's maid, could read and write, but William, a coachman, could not. A fair assumption would be, Bridget was the same religion as her cousin.[71]

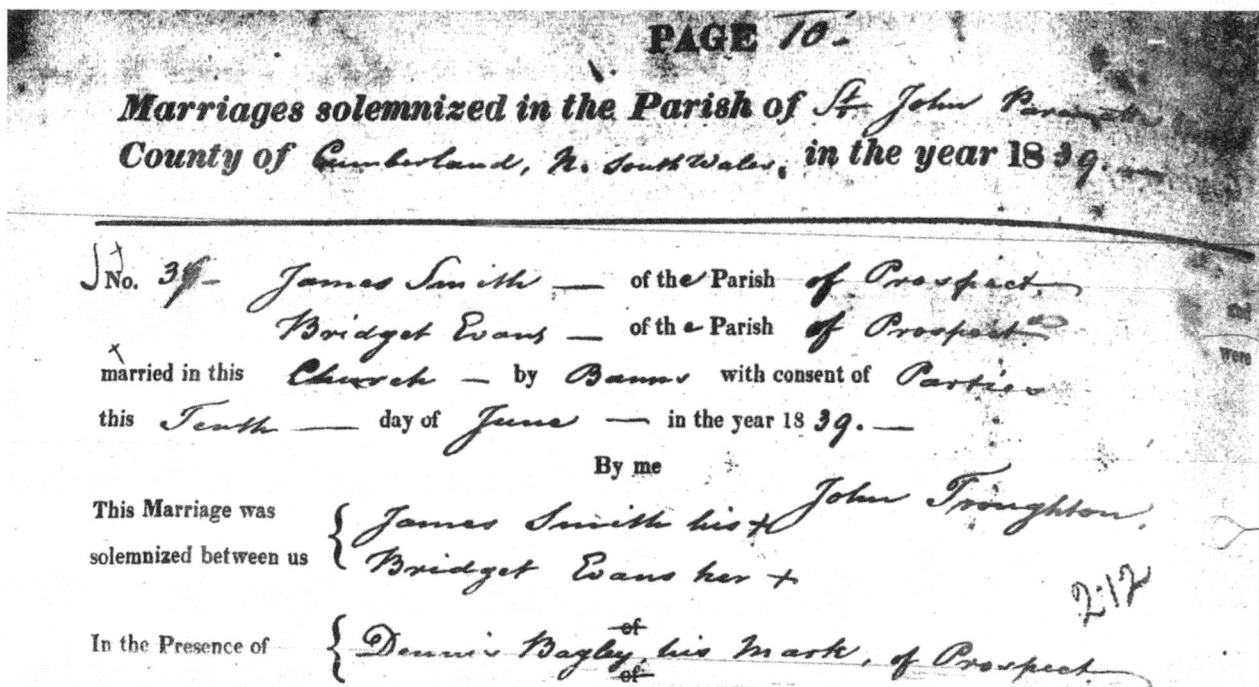

1839 Marriage record for Mary Ann's parents, James Smith and Bridget Evans at Parramatta, NSW

We see from subsequent documents, Bridget signed documents with an X indicating she had not shared Jane's good fortune in acquiring some education. Bridget's husband to be was C of E and it was probably his choice they be married at St John's Anglican Church in Parramatta. Both William and Jane have the notation stating they were brought out by the government. It is not clear what Bridget's status was within the assisted migration regime. She is recorded in the section normally used for dependent children. Bruce wrote that Bridget was sponsored by 'The Gillespies'. No corroborating record has yet been found.

Bruce tells us Bridget remained at Hill End, and after James died, she came to stay with Mary Ann and her family, assisting with the child raising and the housekeeping, especially when Mary Ann was helping Enoch. Bruce wrote: 'Bridget Smith was very superstitious, quite a common thing in that period particularly among the Irish. Mary Ann often recounted stories of the family making very hurried trips home late at night after an outing in town. If they did not get inside before midnight, the little people would be about'.[72]

A report from 1872 states, Bridget Smith came to the attention of the police when she 'threw stones at the doors of the houses of respectable people'.[73] There may have been several Bridget Smiths in Hill End in that boom year, but it would be unsurprising if Mary Ann's mother had some bone to pick with the town's 'respectable people'. Bridget died at Hill End in 1891 from influenza.

The immigration records for Bridget and her cousin Jane Stewart from the *Calcutta* in 1838.

A view of Fermoy, Cork, Ireland from 2007. Barrack Hill, given as the residence of Jane Stewart (née Evans) on her sister's baptism, is just past the church steeple in the distance. Photo: author

No death record has been found for James Smith, so we do not know his fate and it means we lose an opportunity to know something of his origins.[74] He is most likely the first of my ancestors to set foot in Australia, but we know so little about him. Bruce says James was of Irish birth without any reference to sources. He missed the detail that he was most probably a convict. Bruce also states he was still on the goldfields when Mary Ann was married. Mary Ann's death record identifies him as a builder.[75] Whether he was a builder or just another goldminer is not revealed by any sources yet found. However, we can easily see how a transported convict, who spent some time labouring on farms and perhaps as a builder's labourer, would be drawn to try his luck on the goldfields. He was just one of the many who left his employment in relative civilisation for the chance of freedom and riches on the diggings.[76]

The early years together

By about 1856, the easily won alluvial gold was petering out on the Turon. Many of the miners moved onto new fields. Around this time, the Victorian goldfields had over 160,000 people on them and over a quarter were female, indicating the goldfields were becoming almost civilised.[77] However, Enoch decided to stay on at the Turon for a few years. The quieter environment and the end of Mary Ann's maturing sojourn at Morpeth meant the Goodwins could start a family. Enoch acquired a house on the southern slopes of Bald Hill[78], quite close to a good spring of water.[79] Their first child, Samuel, was born in June 1860.[80]

In time, Enoch recognised gold was getting too hard to find with simple methods. The graziers who had been denuded of labour during the peak of the rush started to offer wages and conditions tempting the miners back to more traditional jobs. Enoch and Mary Ann moved hundreds of kilometres north-east to Spring Creek at Goonoo Goonoo. This was briefly a goldfield also, so that may explain how they came to be there. When he appears in the records however, Enoch is working as a shepherd. A shepherd in those days lived with one other shepherd and/or a hut keeper (probably Mary Ann) in simple accommodation remote from the main homestead and its amenities. He would ensure the sheep in his care were protected from the hazards awaiting the flock. Paddocks were not fenced in the Goonoo Goonoo area until the 1880s. His day would begin by releasing the 500 or more sheep in his care from the demountable yards or pens onto an open run. Dogs would assist him, which would give warning of dingos or other threats. He would move the mobile pens to new ground to reduce diseases and parasite infestation. At the end of the day, the flock had to be mustered back into the yards. This daily routine away from other company became notoriously monotonous.[81]

In October 1864, whilst at Spring Creek, Mary Ann gave birth to their first daughter, Rebecca.[82] Around 1866, Mary Ann had a boy who died young.[83] In December 1867, at Walhallow Station, Spring Creek, she gave birth to her second daughter, Lucy.[84] Bruce Goodwin provides an interesting insight into that event in *Lace and Gold*. What follows is a shortened version of his story.

Mary Ann said, on the day Lucy was born, she started to feel the onset of labour pains in the early afternoon. Enoch was working at an out-station some miles from home. She started to plan how she might give birth alone (apart from her two young children who also would need attention). Suddenly there was a knock at the door. Because their hut was so remote, it was rarely visited by anyone, but here was a swagman asking for some food. As was the custom, she prepared some food for him, but her pain became clear and the swagman asked her if there was anything he could do. Mary Ann provided him with instructions and asked him to go and fetch Enoch, to which he readily agreed. A few hours later, both Enoch and the swagman returned, and Mary Ann is quoted as saying 'and everything was alright once he was here'.

This little tale illustrates Mary Ann's stoicism and bravery, contemplating childbirth without a midwife. She would have shared that with all the other women living these remote existences at that time. It also hints at the esteem Mary Ann had for Enoch and tells us a little about their relationship.

Back to Hill End

Around 1868, the family returned to Hill End. They lived in a house on a two-acre block on the southern side of Bald Hill, adjacent to Brewery Creek.[85] Reef mining had been steadily expanding since the first steam battery had operated at Tambaroora in 1861.[86] The gold from the reef was encased in ore and was initially separated mechanically by crushing the ore to powder with a relay of steam-powered heavy cast iron stampers.[87] A new phase for the district began, when rich seams of gold found on Hawkins Hill just to the south of Hill End began to be worked. This phase was initially less frenetic and a bit more ordered than the original rush. It required equipment, hard work and capital.

Initially, Enoch identified a good living was to be had by supplying a service to carry the quartz ore via his packtrain of horses.[88] The horses each carried two hundredweight (101.6 Kg) of ore on the zig-zag tracks from the mine shafts in the central belt, up over the steep side of Hawkins Hill to the Ore Paddock on its crest.[89] From there the ore was carted to the various batteries crushing the ore to retrieve the gold.[90] He charged at the rate of 7s 6d a ton (approximately $8.50 per horse per trip in today's money).[91]

Mary Ann, who was a small woman, spent much of her time tending the horses during their rest periods when they grazed on the Hill End common.[92] She was an intrepid and fearless horsewoman. Her duties included rounding up the horses from the rocky and hilly common. She rode side-saddle and only parted with her lovingly maintained saddle when she was in her eighties.[93]

As well as the proven mining leases, prospectors were sinking shafts all around the town in the hope of making new discoveries. A story from 1869 has the police accusing Enoch of drinking out of hours at the All Nations Hotel. His defence was he 'was waiting for the moon to rise in consequence of so many dangerous holes to go home'.[94] Enoch himself took over the Rose of Australia lease on

1872 view by Henry Beaufoy Merlin of the Hawkins Hill mines from the lookout named after him.[141]

top of Hawkins Hill. It had a shaft down to 120 feet (36.6 m). It was attempting to intercept some of the reefs being worked from the side of the hill. Enoch extended the shaft another thirty feet, but the return was disappointing, with not enough payable gold to carry the venture down further where the best ore would be found. He sold the lease to other miners who had already sunk shafts as much as 900 feet (274 m) deep on their existing leases.[95]

Alan Mayne described the heavily mined Hawkins Hill as an 'ant heap'. By June 1871, over 120 claims had been pegged out there. Hawkins Hill was the most intense part of a 24-kilometre tract of mining stretching either side. The activity peaked in 1872 and this phase was all but finished by 1876. Six batteries around Hill End in 1870 increased to thirteen by 1872. The 'thump thump' of the batteries would go day and night and could be heard all through the town.[96]

After his foray into mining, Enoch started a business dealing in second-hand mining equipment and building materials. The business was situated in two adjoining shops on the eastern side of Clarke Street, two businesses down from the corner with Short Street.[97]

Hill End was changing, with some of the old bark huts being replaced with stronger and more permanent structures. Henry Beaufoy Merlin and his assistant Charles Baylis, photographers from the AA company, captured facets of Hill End around the early 1870s providing a valuable visual record of a significant period in Australia's History.[98] The photos were lost from the public record until being rediscovered in a garden shed in Chatswood in 1951. The old photographic glass plates were originally destined to be recycled in the construction of a glasshouse in the Chatswood garden.[99] The collection is known as the Holtermann Collection,[100] named after Bernhardt Holtermann, the successful German immigrant goldminer who commissioned them.[101] His partner, Louis Beyers, was also a prominent identity.

One of the many memorable images of the Holtermann Collection – an unnamed family with their simple house and neat garden at Hill End circa 1872 – State Library of NSW

Many of the photos show families or groups of people seated or standing outside their houses or place of business. The images convey the sense of the time and place well. The subjects' pose, the style of dress, the design of the houses, the gardens – all tell us a little more about what it must have been like to live in Hill End and indeed rural Australia at that time.

The Family's latter years

Mary Ann and Enoch welcomed another son, Enoch (Enie) in June 1871.[102] Another son, David, was born in May 1874.[103] It is believed he died

shortly afterwards, but no death record has been found. Three girls and another David followed him. Mary Jane was born in July 1875 and Sarah Ann in December 1877.[104] The second David was born in December 1881 and Elizabeth Jane arrived in July 1883.[105] Enoch was an alderman of the Hill End Borough Council from 1878 to 1884 inclusive.[106] He had been appointed trustee of the Hill End and Tambaroora town common in 1881.[107] By the time of the second David's birth in 1881, Enoch described himself as an auctioneer, suggesting he had found a more sedate occupation befitting his age. Enoch died of dropsy on Christmas Day 1885. He had suffering from it for a year.[108]

Eight children had survived him and three had predeceased him. His youngest child, Elizabeth, died aged six, in 1889.

Malcolm Drinkwater's opinion of Enoch was, despite being in the right place at the right time, Enoch had a knack for picking unsuccessful mining ventures and therefore never achieved the wealth that would be suggested by having such a long association with the gold industry at Hill End.[109] Enoch and Mary Ann took the occasional trip to Sydney, as it was reported on 11 April 1875, Enoch had stolen from him £13 in notes and a gold ring set with bloodstone and a lady's ring set with light coloured stones with a pearl in the centre. They were lodging at 150 Castlereagh Street. They had travelled to Sydney with some of their friends from Hill End who were also victims of the theft.[110]

Mary Ann stayed on at Hill End until her death from cardiac issues in 1932.[111] She had spent 47 years as a widow. Her death certificate, from the days of the Great Depression, had the notation 'in receipt of old age pension'.[112] Five of her children survived her. Some of her family also stayed on at Hill End as it faded to a smaller reminder of its glory days. Mary Ann kept the family home going as her children came and went from Hill End exploring opportunities elsewhere.

Alan Mayne described the Goodwin family as an example of the largely self-sufficient families that grew their own vegetables and kept a few farm animals. They could live off the land more easily in Hill End than in most other places.[113]

Snow in Clarke Street, Hill End, 1872 Photo by Henry Beaufoy Merlin – from the Holtermann Collection held by the State Library of NSW

The children, Lucy's siblings

Samuel

Their eldest son, Samuel, married Sarah Ann Alexander in February 1889 at Hill End.[114] Their first child, William, was born in Merewether, NSW later that year. Their next child, Edmund, was born in Katoomba in 1892. The family returned to Hill End and were there for the birth of their daughter, Pearl Emily, in 1895. They were also there in 1897 when their son, Ralph, was born and when he died in 1899. Their son, Edmund, accidently drowned at Hill End in 1898, aged six. They had moved to Blayney by 1900, where their daughter, Ethel May, was born. Ethel died in Newtown, Sydney at the age of twelve in 1912. Their last child, Doris, was born at Erskinville, NSW in 1910. They were living in Sydney at the time of his mother's death in 1932. Samuel died in 1939 at his daughter's home at Ramsgate, Sydney, NSW and his wife, Sarah, died in Wollongong, NSW in 1960.[115]

Rebecca

Their eldest daughter, Rebecca, married Charles Henry Alder of Wickham, in Newcastle in 1889.[116] Their first two children Henry H and Annie Rebecca were born in Newcastle in 1891 and 1892 respectively. The family then moved to Hill End 'after the bank smash of the 1890s' where the following children were born: Rebecca Jane (b. 1894), Arthur Amos (b. 1898), David (b. 1901), Violet (b. 1905), Ivy (b. 1913) and finally Rose (b. after 1919). Charles worked in building and mining activities. Rebecca was the witness on Peter Charles Noon's birth certificate at Newnes in 1911. Peter was her great-nephew. Rebecca nursed her mother, Mary Ann, at the Alder's home near Bald Hill until Mary Ann's death in 1932.

Rebecca was one of the residents mentioned in a 1953 newspaper article regarding Hill End.[117] She was identified as one of the town's oldest inhabitants. She spoke well of Louis Beyers and

how he helped the town's sick and poor and how he planted many of the trees in the public spaces. She lamented there was nothing for the young people in Hill End, but she liked it for herself and the other old-timers. Rebecca died in Hill End in 1955. Charles died there in 1951.[118]

Enoch jnr (Enie)

Enie married Maud Kemshall at Hill End in 1893.[119] All their children were born in Hill End. Starting with Coraline Iris Merle (b. 1896), followed by Edna (b. 1898), Theodora Maud (b. 1901), Doris (b. 1901), Enoch Kemshall (b. 1905), Ivor Howard (b. 1908), Adelaide Constance Lorraine (b. 1911) and lastly Bruce Selwyn (b. 1916). Edna died at the age of three weeks.

Enie spent brief periods working at the Burraga Copper Mine, dredging sand from Narrabeen Lake and investigating a goldmine in New Guinea, but the bulk of his working life was spent in the gold mining industry at Hill End. He was involved with alluvial, reef mining and hydraulic sluicing. He was the foreman and later underground manager of the Reward Mine.[120] This was one of the few mines operating during the early twentieth century. His sons Bruce and Ivor also tried their hands at goldmining in Hill End.

A newspaper article from 1911 reported a comedic episode when two different parties sought to establish a claim on a cancelled ten-acre gold lease from the exact gazetted time when the cancellation became effective.[121] Enie was acting as agent for one of the parties. Neither party was aware of the other's existence until they crossed paths running to complete the pegging required to make the claim. Enie got his application in first, but the warden judged a ballot was needed. Enie's client won the ballot.

Donald Friend's *Hillendiana* has an anecdote from 1887 about Enie finding an escaped circus seal swimming in the Macquarie River.[122] Enie's son, Bruce wrote extensively and affectionately about his parents and family in *Lace and Gold*.

Mary Jane (Marie)

Marie left Australia's shores to marry a New Zealand farmer, James Thomas Thompson in New Zealand in 1908. The family had three known children Ian James (b. 1909), Claude Goodwin (b. 1913) and Valarie Marie (b. 1917). Marie died at Opotiki, in the Bay of Plenty in 1964 and was buried at East Cape, Poverty Bay, New Zealand.

Sarah Ann

Sarah married Harold Lewis Tucker, a labourer, in 1902 at Orange, NSW.[123] Vera Edith (later Lee), (b. 1903) was born in Millthorpe. Amy Still, (b. 1906) was born at Sunny Corner. Daisy Louisa (later Pomering), (b. 1912) and Harold Cyril (b. 1916) were both born in Petersham. Their last child, Gordon Francis (b. 1918), was born in Sydney. In 1937, the family was living in the Sydney suburb of Campsie.[124] Sarah died in Mudgee in 1950 and Harold died in 1956.[125]

David

David married Euphemia Kathleen Robertson in 1903 at Hill End.[126] They had four children, all born at Hill End: Magnus Colin (b. 1904), Norman David (b. 1906), Evan William (b. 1909) and Ronald David (b. 1912). Norman died at Kempsey in 1911. David was a bandmaster and an ardent worker for the Salvation Army.[127] He was killed in a mining accident in 1913, as described in the following report.

Horses and cart bogged in Clarke Street, Hill End, winter of 1872. The *Sydney Morning Herald* described Clarke Street in 1872, as narrow, crooked and filthy. – Holtermann Collection, State Library of NSW.

KILLED BY A FALL OF EARTH. ACCIDENTAL DEATH.
HILL END, Tuesday.

The adjourned inquest on the death of David Goodwin was continued before Mr. Hodge, coroner, at Hill End Court House. Mr. Carthew, mining inspector, was present. Senior-constable Brandon said, in his opinion, the neck and back were broken. The body was brought to Hill End by Mr. Lougher, a distance of seven miles. Mr. Lougher stated that he and David Goodwin were engaged in taking down loam banks, and while David Goodwin was knocking out a pillar, by way of weakening the banks, a lump of earth fell without any warning, and buried him. Witness and the engine-driver, who was standing by, immediately set about getting deceased out, which they accomplished in about five minutes. Witness tried to restore animation, but found life extinct. A verdict of accidental death by a fall of earth was returned.[128]

David's widow, Euphemia, returned with her three young children to her family at Kempsey. The Hill End community raised over £40 to assist her to start a business.[129]

Hill End in later years

Hill End's population peaked at around 8,000 in 1872, which made it the largest NSW town west of the Great Divide.[130] The good times continued until around 1874 when more promising gold strikes were advertised in Qld (Gympie, Charters Towers, the Palmer and the biggest of them all, Mount Morgan).[131] That drew away miners, but more importantly capital, so the mining operations at Hill End were wound down.[132] Another boom, the third, occurred from 1908 to 1924. The last of the stamper batteries finally fell silent in the 1920s. The times before and after this last boom were characterised as 'poor man diggings'.

The bank crash of the 1890s and the Depression of the 1930s saw the population of Hill End increase from one or two hundred permanent people to perhaps double that. The unemployed tried their luck with the left-over alluvial gold, and they could live off the land more easily there than many other places. Rabbits and vegetables flourished at Hill End. By contrast, the nearby town of Tambaroora, which had eclipsed Hill End in the early days, had completely disappeared.[133]

A total of approximately 22,000 kilograms of gold had been extracted from Hill End over its lifetime.[134] Only Cobar, in the state's west, exceeded that total within NSW.

After WWII, several artists discovered the beauty, solitude and restorative powers of the landscape and the small welcoming community. Donald Friend, the war-weary war-artist, and his friend Russell Drysdale led the vanguard. Over the years the visitor list read like a Who's Who of the Australian art world – Brett Whitely, John Olsen, Margaret Olley, Jeffery Smart, Jean Bellette, Paul Haefliger and David Strachan all spent time there and were inspired. Russell Drysdale's painting, *The Cricketers*, is one of the most iconic Australian paintings of the twentieth century. It depicts a bowler, a batsman and an on-looker in an otherwise deserted Hill End street scene.

The artistic flowering contributed to the NSW Government recognising Hill End was indeed special. It declared it a Historic Site in 1967. The NSW Parks and Wildlife service set about managing the conservation of Hill End, catering for visitors and producing an informative and sympathetic set of guides. They utilised some of the Holtermann Collection to explain the context of what remains and what has disappeared.

Hill End is still home to a small community, many of whom are descended from the original mining families. Some still work the creek beds or the old diggings looking for a little extra income. The modern world has come to Hill End, with the consequence its communications, comforts and complexities have changed the nature of the existence in this charming relic of a town.

Donald Friend is now a problem. Undoubtedly talented as he was, he has been, within the past decade, soundly condemned as a paedophile. So much so, that galleries holding even his excellent landscapes, as opposed to his overtly sexual sketches, are reluctant to put them on display. His condemnation is not as a result of any conviction, but largely as a result of his own published diaries and sketches about his life which he compiled whilst living in Sri Lanka and Bali in the 1960s and 70s. There was a continuum of illegality with his homosexuality in conjunction with his attraction to boys. Homosexuality was only made legal between consenting adults in NSW in 1984.[135] His proclivities were probably known and accepted within his artistic circle at that time.

Society's attitudes towards his homosexuality have flipped from a sense of illegal perversion to now being a celebrated social norm, as demonstrated by the passing of the *Australian Marriage Amendment Act 2017*.[136] Whereas the attitudes towards the underage component and the consequent lack of consent have moved from the relative ambivalence the Mary Ann and Enoch situation aroused, to complete condemnation.

Knowledge regarding the profound impact of child sexual abuse has become much more widespread in recent years. In the past, a prudish and censorial society repressed discussion of such issues, which provided a perfect environment for such practices to remain underground. In the more libertine 1960s and 70s, and a few decades beyond, there was a disinclination to condemn fringe behaviours, as there was a revolution against the past repression. That can be demonstrated by the wins in courts against censorship and obscenity laws.[137] It is also of note that certain rock musicians had biographies written about them suggesting their interaction with girls of a questionable age was an accepted part of their stardom.[138] Donald Friend's diaries were made public during that era. Such biographies or diaries would not be published in today's world, as these issues are now taken more seriously. The conjunction of these issues is a good illustration of how morals, the related laws and their enforcement are quickly and dramatically evolving through history.

A scene from Hill End, August 2009; Photo: author

Endnotes to Chapter 6

1 England & Wales, Non-Conformist and Non-Parochial Registers (1567–1970). Enoch was born on 28 Jan and baptised on 5 Mar 1820.

2 Samuel Goodwin: born circa 1783 – died 1857. Birth date is estimated from 1841 census. Death date is from the death record from UK GRO 1857 Jun Qtr. Manchester Vol 08D, page 97, No 162. Samuel is a Collector of Debts aged 74 years in Ancoats, Manchester who died 25 Jun 1857. Informant Daniel Goodwin. Lucy Sexstone, born circa 1782 – died 1842.

3 Sizing in textile manufacturing changes the absorption and wear characteristics of the textiles – Wikipedia.

4 MC (Page 547 [The year 1802] 'No 77 Samuel Goodwin of Macclesfield of this parish, Cotton Spinner and Lucy Sexstone of the same place, spinster, were married in this Church by Barnes this fourth day of May, 1802 by me, Thos Monkhouse curate'. Witnesses Ralph Goodwin & Nancy Rae.

5 Rebecca about 2 years older and David about 5 years younger.

6 Pevsner Architectural Guides: Explore Manchester – source referenced by Wikipedia Ancoats

7 Wikipedia: This is less than 1 km. east of Manchester Cathedral. Ancoats became a cradle of the Industrial Revolution. The first cotton mills were built as early as 1790.

8 The family appeared in 2 entries in the 1841 census on 2 folios of the 1 book. Their street address had not changed. There were subtle differences in what was recorded like ages and one had Samuel's profession as Agent and the other as Collector. The death certificate that is most likely his has his profession as Collector of Debts.

9 From profession recorded on Enoch's NSW death certificate 1885/12146

10 England & Wales Criminal Registers 1791–1892. The centre of Salford is about 3 km west of Ancoats. Salford is also the 'hundred' division of the County of Lancashire which contains Ancoats (and much of Manchester).

11 There is a strong probability this is the Enoch of our story, as the relatively rare name, age and location all line up.

12 Lambert Morton aged 19. He has not been found in the NSW convict register as this coincided with the end of transportation to NSW. At the same session, 2 other defendants were sentenced to 14 years transportation for assault.

13 It continued for a few other colonies, Tasmania (till 1853) and Western Australia (till 1868), but the resistance to the continuation of transportation was growing and this meant a change in sentencing in Britain.

14 The Charterist movement was agitating for universal manhood suffrage and other reforms now taken for granted. The Parliament ignored a petition with over 3 million signatures. Wages were actively suppressed by Magistrates and the Poor Law reforms of 1834 sought to remove relief which the underpaid were previously entitled to. Transportation to NSW ended for several reasons, one because the NSW colony no longer wanted to be the dumping ground for the unwanted and because it was becoming an incentive to commit crime to escape the poor conditions in the mother country.

15 The Sydney branch of the company of merchants based in London and Liverpool. In 1842 the company became Gosling, Browne & Co.

16 The immigration record recorded he contributed a voluntary £2 towards the trip whereas the 'bounty' recorded against his name was £19.

17 http://indexes.records.nsw.gov.au/ebook/list.aspx?Page=NRS5316/4_4782/Joseph%20Cunard_28%20Nov%201841/4_478200034.jpg&No=8

18 Samuel Goodwin: born circa 1809 Macclesfield, Lancashire, UK – died 14 Jun 1874 Morpeth, NSW

19 They arrived on the *Marchioness of Bute* which was also sponsored by the Messrs Aspinall, Brown & Co. Samuel was a labourer and Sarah was a servant.

20 Some identify Morpeth as the second busiest port in NSW around the 1850s, as it was the main port for the Hunter River district. Later Newcastle became the main port for the Hunter region.

21 The discovery was by assistant surveyor James McBrien at Fish River between Rydal and Bathurst – Wikipedia
& D Hill, *The Gold Rush: The fever that forever changed Australia*, Random House, North Sydney, 2011

22 How Lieutenant Ralph Clarke (Royal Marines, First Fleet) described the early days of NSW.

23 John Lister, William & James Tom deposed they found it, but Hargraves had taught them how to look for it and he therefore claimed it. Another, William Tipple Smith, had an earlier claim to having found the same field. – Hill, pages 25–26

24 And about 50 km NW of Bathurst, which was the most significant town in the district.

25 *Australians Events and Places*. Ed: G Aplin, SG Foster & M McKernan Pub: Fairfax, Syme & Weldon, NSW 1987, page 63, 14 Jun 1851.

26 The Lower Turon, *Bathurst Free Press and Mining Journal*, Sat 29 Nov 1851, page 4 http://nla.gov.au/nla.news-article62517155
 Hill End is about 30 kms from Ophir.

27 Pioneer's death, *Mudgee Guardian and North-Western Representative*, Mon 4 Jul 1932, page 4 http://nla.gov.au/nla.news-article160966506

28 Bruce Selwyn Goodwin, born 11 Oct 1916, Hill End, NSW – died 16 Nov 2002 Sydney, NSW

29 BS Goodwin, *Lace and Gold*, subtitled *From Nottingham, Calais, Manchester, Cork & Clunfaele to the Golden River and Hill End*.
 ISBN 1 74018 089 5 Published through Book House PO Box 41 Glebe NSW 2037, 2000,
 Printed by Fast Books a division of Wild & Woolley Pty Ltd – Glebe. www.publishaustralia.com.au, almost certainly out of print.

30 Goodwin, *Lace and Gold*, page 27

31 Goodwin, *Lace and Gold*, states the source as Henry Neary writing in *The Western Times*, 17 Dec 1945.

32 BS Goodwin, *Gold and People : recollections of Hill End 1920s to 1960s*, self-published, French's Forrest, 1992

33 Recycling, but consciously trying to avoid infringement.

34 H Hodge, *The Hill End Story, Books I, II, & III* self-published, Newcastle, 1965 – 1972,

35 M Drinkwater, *Hill End Gold*, Third Ed. self-published, Hill End, 2016

36 A Mayne, *Hill End : an historic Australian goldfields landscape*, Carlton, Melbourne University Press, 2003

37 D Friend, *Hillendiana: A collection of Hillendiana: comprising vast numbers of facts and a considerable amount of fiction concerning the goldfield of Hillend and environs and a commentary both grave and ribald,* Sydney, Ure Smith 1977. In the acknowledgements section of *Hillendiana*, Donald Friend thanks his informants: the Ellis family, the Goodwin family and Miss Gwen Eyre.

38 The obituary gives the year as 1852 but BS Goodwin in *Lace and Gold* says it was 1853.

39 *Mudgee Guardian and North-Western Representative*, Mon 4 Jul 1932, page 4 http://nla.gov.au/nla.news-article160966506

40 From information written by Bruce Goodwin in *Lace and Gold*

41 Between the time when Bruce wrote that around 1998 and today (2020) such a statement has taken on an ironic/cynical hue, which Bruce would not have intended. In other words, attitudes on these matters are still evolving.

42 The populations of non-Aboriginal men & women in NSW in 1856 was 136,712 and 112,570 respectively. – *Australian Historical Statistics* – Ed: W Vamplew, Pub: Fairfax Syme & Weldon Associates NSW 1987. Many of the men on the goldfields would have been emancipated or even escaped convicts.

43 Alexander McEwan was ordained in Scotland in 1853. He was appointed to the Western Goldfields in 1854 – *The Muse*, Journal of the Mudgee Historical Society Inc No 163 Jun 2011.

44 http://hillendfamilyhistory.com/hill-end-tambaroora/hill-end-buildings/st-pauls-presbyterian-church/

45 It was customary to have 2 witnesses of different genders.

46 Goodwin, *Lace and Gold*, page 31. However, on page 6, Bruce argues her birthday was Oct 1840. With her marriage in Jun 1855, those dates would make her 14 at the time of her marriage. Bruce does not provide any proof or justification for his preferred birth date, not even an oral history account of a conversation with Mary Ann. Readers might be more inclined to believe him had he not made so many obvious errors when referencing the available official sources. The tone of the writing is simply, she could not possibly have been the age suggested by the most relevant official document that is available.

47 Mary Ann's DC identified her parents as James Smith & Bridget Evans. Mary Ann was the informant on her mother's (Bridget Smith) DC. No competing alternatives have been identified and there are no other known people who this record might apply to. All known researchers who have independently researched Mary Ann (including Bruce Goodwin) agree this is the correct baptism record.

48 The UK abolished the distinction between a misdemeanour and a felony in 1967. The USA retains it.

49 Statutory rape not applying in marriage: https://www.sunypress.edu/pdf/60840.pdf Rape in marriage: In 1976, South Australia became the first jurisdiction in the English-speaking world to make rape in marriage illegal. https://timeline.awava.org.au/archives/391 Russia had made it illegal in 1922 – Wikipedia.

50 *Children & Youth in History*, Stephen Robertson, University of Sydney. Other sources including: http://www.historyandpolicy.org/policy-papers/papers/the-legacy-of-1885-girls-and-the-age-of-sexual-consent

51 There was a concept of legal parental consent for a minor (under the age of 21) to marry. This applied in England but a bigamy judgement in 1836 in NSW ruled that these laws did not apply in NSW. . The NSW Marriage Act of 1864 did codify such requirements with subsequent amendments being made in 1928. See: *Age at first Marriage and Proportions marrying in Australia 1869-1971* by Peter F. McDonald (Thesis for Research School of Social Sciences, Australian National University) b10142150_McDonald_Peter_F.pdf

52 Goodwin, *Lace and Gold*, page 6. Bruce states: 'Her date of birth on the baptism certificate is 11 Oct 1844, we know this to be incorrect and she was born on 11 Oct 1840. 1844 was probably the date of baptism'. The last statement is incorrect as the context of the baptism record clearly indicates it has the correct baptism date of 26 Jan 1845.

53 NSW BC 1860/12493, Samuel, age 21 in Jun 1860 implying birth year of 1838/1839
& NSW BC 1864/15229, Rebecca, age 26 in Oct 1864 implying birth year of 1837/1838
& NSW BC 1867/76739, Lucy, age 27 in Dec 1867 implying birth year of 1840
& NSW BC 1871/17819, Enoch age 34 in Jun 1871 implying birth year of 1836/1837
& NSW BC 1874/19478, David (I), age 34 in May 1874 implying birth year of 1839/1840
& NSW BC 1875/19853, Mary, age 35 in Jul 1875 implying birth year of 1839/1940
& NSW BC 1877/20868, Sarah Ann, age 38 in Dec 1877 implying birth year of 1839
& NSW BC 1881/21501, David (II), age 40 in Dec 1881 implying birth year of 1841
& NSW BC 1883/24133, Elizabeth Jane, age 43 in Jul 1883 implying birth year of 1839/1840

54 If we assume the day and month are correct but the year is wrong.

55 William Lawson of Blaxland, Wentworth & Lawson fame – the much celebrated trio were the first European settlers to cross the Blue Mountains in 1813. Of course Indigenous folk had been doing it routinely for millennia previously.

56 Wikipedia – St Bartholomew's Anglican Church and Cemetery, Prospect. As explained elsewhere, this may not be Mary Ann's father, as her father is identified as a labourer. If he really was a carpenter, then this would be more likely to be his preferred official profession (implying skill). It could be the other James Smith who was living in Prospect in 1841.

57 Mary Ann's death certificate identifies her father as being a builder. Bruce's father Enoch was the informant. Being a labourer is compatible with being a builder, but it does infer if he was both then he is unlikely to be a skilled builder at the time that he was in Prospect.

58 NSW Assisted Immigrants – NSW State Library – Available via Ancestry.com. Bridget Evans is not recorded in the index associated

with these records. She can be found via the entries for William & Jane Stewart. They are listed as RC, but Bruce said they were Protestant.

59 NSW DC 1891/7326, Bald Hill, Hill End, 24 Nov 1891, Bridget Smith. To be fair, the age she chooses for herself is 49, which advocates for the alternate argument would point out, could indicate a vanity motive.

60 Her obituary in the newspaper and her NSW death certificate have stated she was 92 years old. It was common for elderly people to add a few years to their age. In the case of her memorial this suspect birth year has been cast in bronze.

61 The NSW BI suggested Mary Ann had a brother, Edward, born in 1840 (NSW Baptisms 156 Vol: 61). However, that record belongs to another James & Bridget Smith. The mother's maiden name was Ryan and it appears James was a carrier associated with the army. They also suggested she had a sister, Margaret, born in 1846 (416 Vol: 63). This child was born in Brisbane, which was still part of NSW then. The mother's maiden name was Ryan on that record as well. Interestingly James & Bridget's marriage record from Paramatta has been indexed as Bridget Ryan in an instance seen on Ancestry.

62 The census of 1841 was flawed because of some resistance from the officials who were asked to collect the data, so some returns are less than they should have been.

63 The other James Smith has a wife and 6 children. He is also an ex-convict who is now free and who is on private assignment. There is a chance this James Smith is the carpenter who worked on St Bartholomew's.

64 Goodwin, *Lace and Gold*, page 31

65 There are over 260 index entries for convicts named James Smith in the NSW state archives. That boils down to approximately 110 individuals (based on vessel name and arrival year). Even if we restrict the list to just those who arrived between 1815 and 1837 into NSW then we still have 75 individuals. Further filtering would be possible based on context of the records, but we are likely to be left with between 10 to 20 likely individuals who could possibly be Bridget's husband.

66 53 years would have been more precise.

67 It is possible, she was born in County Armagh and moved to Cork later in life, but people did not tend to move around that much in those times. It also means 2 married brothers would have moved together – even less likely.

68 There is no known town of Fermagh within Cork. There is a County of Fermanagh in the province of Ulster. But it was likely to be referring to Fermoy, which is a sizable town in Cork.

69 An alternate hypothesis is, Bridget was indeed Jane's sister and she was born in 1829 and that would make the 1841 census entry accurate, but this hypothesis requires Mary Ann to have gotten her mother's age wildly wrong, as did the immigration official when recording Bridget's entry to Australia. The relationship of cousin rather than sister is also clearly written. A bit too much of a stretch on the documented facts. Other points in its favour are that Mary Ann was not born until 5 years after the marriage (a delay similar to Mary Ann's own story). It may explain why her parents allowed the marriage to happen. Additionally Bruce may have been using some family knowledge rather than just the documents. (I just wish Bruce had cited his sources.)

70 Goodwin, *Lace and Gold*, page 2: Bruce states, the Evans and Stewart families were Protestant.

71 Irish religious allegiances were of a tribal nature rather than as a result of any considered choice. Bridget and Jane's fathers were brothers. It is highly likely if one were Catholic then the other would be as well.

72 Goodwin, *Lace and Gold*, pages 35 & 36

73 Mayne, page 86

74 NSW DI 1874/7863 from Hill End for James Smith looked promising until the actual document revealed it pertained to a two-month-old infant. Interestingly however, the mother was Eliza Moore and the father was James Smith. The chance the baby's father was Mary Ann's father is considered highly unlikely. A more thorough search by the NSW Registry of Births Deaths and Marriages concluded in August 2020 for the period 1856 to 1875 inclusive found no matching records.

75 NSW DC 1932/11908, Hill End, 2 Jul 1932, Mary Ann Goodwin

76 The story of five horses pulling their possessions to the diggings suggests a level of prosperity that was greater than the average digger so James must have been reasonably successful with his work at Prospect.

77 Hill, page 106

78 *Australians Events and Places*, page 218, Hill End was 'Bald Hill' until c 1867.

79 Goodwin, *Lace and Gold*, page 34

80 NSW BC 1860/12493, Lower Turon, Tambaroora, 7 Jun 1860, Samuel Goodwin

81 *Tamworth and districts early history* produced by Tamworth Regional Council 2006

82 NSW BC 1864/15229, Spring Creek, Goonoo Goonoo, 3 Oct 1864, Rebecca Goodwin

83 Deceased male was mentioned on Lucy's birth record but not on Rebecca's.

84 Walhallow Station was 56,676 acres (in 1840). – *Tamworth and districts early history*.

85 From notes Bruce Goodwin produced before he wrote *Lace and Gold*. He states evidence of the house could still be seen late last century, a couple of hundred metres west from the Merlin's Lookout Rd. In a slight contradiction in a book entitled *Hill End Heroines & Tambaroora Treasures* by Daphne Shead & members of the Hill End and Tambaroora Gathering Group, the Goodwins are mentioned as living on a 2-acre block adjoining the 2-acre property of the Everett family on the western (not southern) side of Bald Hill. The Everett property was 2.5 km from Hill End.

86 Reef mining involved digging into the earth and rocks to chase the veins of gold bearing quartz (reefs). Alluvial gold results from the water eroding the rocks containing the gold and the gold becomes separated from its ore in the riverbed.

87 Steam battery information: Hill, The gold rush spreads, page 244 and https://collection.maas.museum/object/9675

88 Hodge, *Hill End Story Book II*, page 145

89 One imperial hundredweight (Cwt) was equal to 112 pounds, (50.8 kg). 20 Cwt to the Imperial ton.

90 Hodge, *Hill End Story Book II*, page 145

91 It appears Enoch had a monopoly on the horse carting service, but some miners used other means to avoid this expense – e.g. one built a flying fox down to a stamper battery in the gully.

92 One source (a history of James Goodwin) said Enoch and Mary Ann had 82 horses at one stage.

93 From notes produced by Bruce Goodwin prior to writing *Lace and Gold*. She sold the saddle to another woman with the comfort it was going to a good home.

94 Mayne, page 14

95 Goodwin, *Lace and Gold*, page 37. The Star of Peace was the company which bought him out.

96 Mayne, pages 78 & 79.

97 Goodwin, *Lace and Gold*, page 37. The businesses were Betty Emmet's baker's shop and a hotel. Opposite a skating rink.

98 American and Australian Photographic Company. Their photographs form a large part of the Holtermann Collection. Holtermann was a very successful German miner whose company found a famous ore-encrusted nugget which stood to his shoulders. (He was a short man.) The photograph of them shown together is a montage created by Henry Beaufoy Merlin.

99 Drinkwater, Introduction page v

100 Now held by the State Library of NSW

101 Described by Alan Mayne in *Hill End* as 'unlikable' – e.g. he tried to buy the famous gold nugget which was found by his company for £1000. It was worth £12,000 (about $1.5 million today).

102 NSW BC 1871/17819, Hill End, 24 Jun 1871, Enoch Goodwin

103 NSW BC 1874/19478, Hill End, 22 May 1874, David Goodwin

104 NSW BC 1875/19853, Hill End, 2 Jul 1875, Mary Goodwin
& NSW BC 1877/20868, Hill End, 4 Dec 1877, Sarah Ann Goodwin

105 NSW BC 1881/21501, Bald Hill, Hill End, 26 Dec 1881, David Goodwin
& NSW BC 1883/24133, Bald Hill, Hill End, 19 Jul 1883, Elizabeth Jane Goodwin

106 Hodge, *The Hill End Story, Book II*, Newcastle

107 *The Maitland Mercury and Hunter River General Advertiser*, Thu 3 Mar 1881, page 2 http://nla.gov.au/nla.news-article815722

108 NSW DC 1885/12146, Hill End, 25 Dec 1885, Enoch Goodwin
Dropsy is now edema, an accumulation of excess fluid in the interstitium (tissue between the skin and other organs).

109 Drinkwater, page 72 - Observation was reworded.

110 *NSW Police Gazettes*, 1854–1930 14 Apr 1875, page 108 – Residents of Hill End were William Read, George Barnett & John Weal.

111 NSW DC 1932/11908, Hill End, 2 Jul 1932, Mary Ann Goodwin

112 The Commonwealth age pension was first paid in 1909 to men over 65 and extended to women over 60 in 1910

113 Mayne, page 110

114 Sarah Ann Alexander: born 1871 – died 1960

115 Registration district was Rockdale – Information for a brief death notice was in the following newspaper article:
Mudgee district personalities, *Mudgee Guardian and North-Western Representative*, Mon 24 Apr 1939, page 2.
http://nla.gov.au/nla.news-article161935610

116 Charles Henry Alder, born 1867 – died 1951
& Marriage, *Newcastle Morning Herald and Miners' Advocate*, Sat 9 Mar 1889, page 4 http://nla.gov.au/nla.news-article138842164

117 This town has fifty-thousand memories, *The Sunday Herald* (Sydney), Sun 29 Mar 1953, page 12 http://nla.gov.au/nla.news-article18503444

118 Death, *Mudgee Guardian and North-Western Representative*, Mon 3 Sep 1951, page 2 http://nla.gov.au/nla.news-article156466382

119 Maud Kemshall: born 1875 – died 1962

120 Drinkwater, page 72

121 A mining comedy, *Sydney Morning Herald*, Wed 21 Jun 1911, page 15 http://nla.gov.au/nla.news-article15255011

122 Friend, page 32

123 Harold Lewis Tucker, born 1878 – died 1956

124 Australian Electoral Rolls 1836 NSW, Lang, Harcourt

125 Deaths, *Sydney Morning Herald*, Wed 30 Aug 1950, page 32 http://nla.gov.au/nla.news-article18181635

126 Euphemia Kathleen Robertson, born 1873 – died 1955

127 Fatal accident at Hill End, *Mudgee Guardian and North-Western Representative*, Thu 31 Jul 1913, page 27
http://nla.gov.au/nla.news-article157727375

128 Hill End, *The Bathurst Times*, Wed 20 Aug 1913, page 4 http://nla.gov.au/nla.news-article111220191

129 Personal, *The Bathurst Times*, Mon 8 Sep 1913, page 2 http://nla.gov.au/nla.news-article111214469

130 Some sources have stated as many as 50,000 were there. Others have said the district contained about 30,000 people whereas the most credible numbers for the town itself is around the 8000 figure. Alan Mayne in his book *Hill End* argues both the 8,000 and 30,000 are too

high. Most estimates work off Harry Hodges data collected in the 1950 from Mitchell Library sources. The estimates result in the claim that in 1872, Hill End was NSW's largest western town. Bathurst, the town with the largest 'permanent' population had 5000 residents.

131 The Palmer was eclipsed by Qld's Mount Morgan and in the 1890s was the richest goldfield in the world. That same decade, the Western Australian (WA) goldfields were established and they not only overtook the Qld mines but even the earlier Victorian gold discoveries. In time the WA goldfields became the richest in Australian history.

132 Friend, page 21. He states capital raising was subject to a lot of fraudulent activity, so investors were becoming increasing wary of new ventures in the old goldfields.

133 Mayne, page 48–49. Tambaroora had all but disappeared by the 1950s with people struggling to find any trace of the township. Only local knowledge allowed its location to be identified.

134 *Australians Events and Places*, page 218 Hill End. Other records specify 770,000 ounces which is roughly equivalent. Cobar has extracted 3 million ounces since 1870. As of 2019, only approximately 190,000 tons (6 trillion ounces) of gold have ever been mined in the world's history. Two-thirds of that was mined in the last 70 years. Most gold is still accounted for. About 2,500–3000 tons are mined each year. South African mines are the most prolific with 40% of all mined gold coming from the Witwatersrand Basin. Gold.org and Wikipedia.

135 http://www.starobserver.com.au/news/national-news/new-south-wales-news/30-years-since-homosexuality-was-decriminalised-in-nsw/123148

136 The law change followed a 61.6% 'yes' vote in the non-compulsory Australian Marriage Law Postal Survey of 2017.

137 e.g. *The Lady Chatterley's Lover* trial 1960, *Oz Magazine* obscenity trial 1971 (on appeal)

138 e.g. Wyman, Bill, 1990 *Stone Alone*, & Cole, Richard, 1992 *Stairway to Heaven: Led Zeppelin Uncensored*

139 Both photos from Goodwin, *Lace and Gold*

140 Churches encouraged families to baptise their children at the earliest convenience due to the risk of infant death and to give their child the benefit of the baptism if they were to die early. The other entries on the baptism register at St Bartholomew's all pertain to newborn infants.

141 State Library of NSW, Holtermann collection out of copyright. Between 1872 & 1873 Henry documented the goldfields and mining towns of NSW. In 1873, as an employee of Bernhardt Holtermann, he photographed Sydney and rural NSW towns – Wikipedia.

Chapter 7

Running writing

Ellen and Tim – Ditton

In early twentieth-century Australia, just under half the population were living and working away from cities and towns, but then as now there was a pull to the city for the young ones. A decent education helped the process along. A rise in commercial and government services meant there were increasing options to work in offices. The path my grandfather took was to utilise his brain rather than his brawn to make a living. This chapter is the story of the family that raised my father, Arthur (Dit) Cranley Ditton. His parents were Ellen Cranley and Arthur (Tim) Ditton.

Tim's early years

Arthur was born in July 1891 in Mackay, Qld to the unmarried Sarah Jane Barron.[1] No father was recorded on the birth certificate. Her occupation was given as a general servant.[2] According to the oral history, Sarah was living in an orphanage in Mackay.[3] However, historical records say there was no official orphanage in Mackay in 1890.[4]

In March 1891, Abraham Ditton, 51, became a widower when his wife of 27 years, Marion, died in Mackay.[5] They had five surviving children. The older ones had left home. The youngest, Charles, was thirteen years old. Abraham felt the need for a housekeeper, but he stated he 'would rather be married to the woman that slept under my roof'. In November of 1891, Abraham married Sarah and welcomed Arthur into his home also.[6] The family gave Arthur the nickname 'Tim' and that was how he was always informally referred to. Abraham was said to have adopted Tim. There was no formal process in 1891, just an understanding between parties. Subsequent official documents, such as sibling's birth certificates, identify Arthur as a son of Abraham.[7] Although, in the early days, when the official form asked to list 'previous children of relationship', Arthur was omitted.[8] When the form asked, 'Issue living and deceased' Arthur was included.[9] Sarah nominated Arthur as a son of Abraham on Abraham's death certificate.[10] Tim's surname changed from his birth name of Barron to Ditton.

It was originally thought Abraham was his biological father because of the detail on the official records. However, it would have meant Abraham fathered Tim whilst his first wife, Marion, was still alive and in declining health. That threw a slur onto Abraham's character, which as it transpired was completely undeserved. Recent DNA tests identified Tim's biological paternity and when that information was shared with relatives, a considerable flow of new oral and documentary evidence became available. Family sources have confirmed Tim knew Abraham had adopted him, and there are legal documents confirming his brother William was aware of the story.[11] The story of his paternity and the striking correlation of likely inherited talents such as his running and writing ability are covered in a later chapter.

From reading the admission register of orphanages in North Qld around this period, Sarah was probably making an inspired choice in marrying Abraham.[12] Giving up her child to an orphanage was a real prospect as many unmarried mothers, without many options, did just that. The register contains caustic comments about the parentage and circumstances of the children. The orphanage in Rockhampton was likely to have been Tim's new home if not for Sarah's decision to marry Abraham, as that institution took children from the Mackay region. *Neerkol* or *Meteor Park* as it was sometimes called, earned a dreadful reputation for all kinds of abuse before being closed down in 1978.[13]

Tim was raised on the Ditton family farm at Sandy Creek about twelve kilometres south-west of Mackay. He attended Homebush State School.[14] Tim was still residing in the Mackay district in May 1911.[15] He developed into a keen sportsman. In his early years, he was a professional sprinter and an accomplished tennis player.[16] He also dabbled in boxing and rugby.[17] His sons were also able and keen sportsmen with cricket (Arthur and Paul) and golf (Paul) being strong interests.[18] Tim coached a tennis team in Townsville (St Mary's A grade) who were champions in 1915 and 1916.[19] Tim encouraged his oldest daughter, Ursula, to play in social tennis competitions.[20] In later years, Tim took a professional interest in horseracing.

Ellen with first daughter Ursula circa 1916

Arthur (Tim) Ditton circa 1912

132

Tim, centre rear as a Tennis Coach in Townsville with his winning St Mary's A grade team circa 1916.[75]

Ellen and Tim marry

Beside his many documented sporting talents, Tim was also quite the dancer. He won a waltzing competition in Mackay and was later an organiser of dances.[21] By 1913, Tim was present at balls in Brisbane, which the Cranley sisters also attended.[22] Tim married Margaret (Ellen) Cranley in April 1914, at St Stephen's Catholic Cathedral, Brisbane.[23] Ellen, blithely unaware of her own pedigree, described her in-laws as 'a bunch of Ned Kellys'.[24] Ellen was born in Laidley in 1885 to Mary née Barry and her railway employee husband, Patrick Cranley.[25] Both her parents were of Irish descent. Ellen was a milliner by trade and worked in a shop in Brisbane City. She was living in Petrie Terrace with her mother and sisters just prior to her marriage.[26] She played a violin in an amateur orchestra.[27] In those days, Ellen would have been ribbed as being a 'cradle snatcher' as she was five-and-a-half years older than Tim.

Tim had been living at Stanley St, South Brisbane. In October of 1914, Tim and Ellen sailed to Townsville[28] where Ursula was born in November 1914.[29] Their second child, Arthur Cranley (hereafter referred to as Dit), followed in December 1916. Tim worked as a receiver of public monies in the post office in Townsville. In 1917 he was promoted to the Commonwealth Electoral Office for the federal electorate of Herbert.[30] The family was living at Sturt Street in 1915 and Paxton Street in 1917.[31]

Tim moved to the Wide Bay electoral office in Maryborough after his time in Townsville. A shipping record identifies him leaving Townsville in August 1917.[32] Ellen and the two children had preceded him several days earlier.[33] Road travel between the north and the south of the state would not become practical for several decades. The rail connection to the north was not completed until 1924.[34] Whilst in Maryborough, he won a 75-yard handicap race on Labour Day in 1918.[35] He also took part in shooting competitions.[36]

In 1919 it was reported he had lost or had stolen a savings bank passbook and a £50 promissory note.[37] In the early 1920s, he was transferred to Brisbane and later became the Assistant Returning Officer for the federal seat of Lilley.[38] He was appointed a Justice of the Peace in 1923.[39]

The growing family

The Ditton family originally lived in Albion, a northern suburb of Brisbane, but the final family home was established at 34 Cumberland Street, Windsor. Their marriage produced seven children: Ursula, Dit, Mary Marcella, Paul Patrick, Lola Margaret, David Leo and Rita Josephine.[40] The first two were born in Townsville. Mary and Paul were born in Maryborough and the last three were born in Brisbane. David died in January 1925, two days after his birth, and his loss was remembered as affecting Ellen deeply and she became depressed,

around this time.[41] Rita, the last child, was born in June 1926.

Under pen names, such as 'Timo', Tim contributed short stories and verse to various publications in the 1920s and 30s. One of his poems entitled *The North Wind's Children* was published in the Brisbane newspaper, *The Daily Mail* on 15 December 1923 under the pen name of 'King Richard'.[42] The last lines from it may be a reflection on the man he called his father, or it may just be a nod to Brisbane's relatively mild climate.

I am the wind of No Content, the wind of Sally Forth,
My Father is a tyrant wind who dwells far in the North.
He sent us here with furnace breath to burn the country brown.
But I am playing truant, for I like your Brisbane town.

Other contributions using the pen name King Richard include the poems *Sinbad in Moreton Bay*[43] and *The Post Office Clock*.[44] The last lines of *The Post Office Clock* give us some insight into his thoughts.

Dit outside 34 Cumberland Street, Windsor with his WMC company car circa 1948

134

The Ditton Family at their home in Windsor, QLD circa 1940 L to R: Mary, Paul, Ursula, Arthur (Dit), Lola, Margaret (Ellen) née Cranley, Arthur (Tim). Rita, the youngest, may have been taking the photo.

Yet who shall fret for a minute past.
For a man must come to an end at last,
And time will go with an ordered sweep.
Though a man might laugh or a maid might weep,
But thank old Time for a just-missed car
If wives will know where their husbands are.

Anecdotally, he sent contributions to *The Bulletin* under the pen name of 'Timo' and also had some success there as well. Research has not yet validated that.[45] A small selection of short stories and poems survive in family records. One short story was entitled *No Corroboration* and another *Inspiration from a Milk Jug*. *No Corroboration* was the tale of an annoyingly zealous but corrupt Irish-born constable whom his supervisor had posted to remote Hermits Hut to get rid of him. *Inspiration from a Milk Jug* concerned two young men struggling to make their livelihoods as a writer and an artist with one resorting to criminality.

Both stories were written whilst he was in Maryborough and as paper was a bit of a luxury,

they were typed onto public service stationery left over from the *Military Service Referendum Act 1916*. The 'referendum' was PM Billy Hughes first failed attempt to gain popular support during WWI to pass legislation to allow conscripted soldiers to fight abroad. Tim himself did not volunteer. He had only recently been married and a child was expected. A comfortable government job would be another disincentive to enlist.

Tim wrote sporting articles for the Sydney-based publication *Smith's Weekly* and *The Graziers' Review*[46] and other publications such as *The Telegraph*. His *Smith's Weekly* contributions had no by-lines and only his later ones were attributed to 'our Brisbane rep'. Dit had a memory of sleeping on a bench at the Brisbane office of *The Telegraph* after the races (or a boxing match) while his father wrote his story to meet the publishing deadline. Federal public servants could not have other jobs, so he had to use his pen name for his regular sideline. However, he may have got dispensation in later years or it simply became an open secret – e.g. he participated in a fishing competition and he was identified as the

Ursula married Dick Freney in 1938. Dick's sisters (J. & W.) are standing. Ursula's sister Mary is sitting. Arthur (Dit) is behind Mary and the two other groomsmen are W. Binnie and R. Carter

winner of the largest fish sweepstake (a morwong greater than 6lb). He was referred to as being from the '*Smith's Weekly* stall'.[47]

He participated in radio sessions on Brisbane radio station 4BC, at The Wintergarden complex, where he was clearly identified as the presenter. The sessions were advertised as 'Racing anticipations with Mr Arthur Ditton and little Mr Forex'.[48] His obituary also described him as: 'one of Brisbane's best-known racing enthusiasts. The late Mr Ditton was a keen judge of horses and for some years acted as racing representative of *Smith's Weekly*. He was a trusted commissioner and his passing leaves a gap in racing circles'.[49]

Dit remembered his father as quite strict, but he was a bit easier on his daughters. However, Tim vetted their potential suitors with imposing authority. Tim's practice of getting his sons to read aloud from newspapers paid off for Paul. He went on to have a career in radio, working as an announcer at 4BC with a specialty in sports commentary.

Ursula was the first of the children to get married. She married Ernest (Dick) Freney at St Columba's Catholic Church in Wilston in October 1938. Tim was pleased with the union and is reported to have 'celebrated to excess'. Next to marry was Mary, who had to get her mother's permission to marry Alan Roberts, a draper from Kingaroy, as she was not yet 21. They married in September 1939 also at St Columba's.[50] Dit and Lola were the attendants and witnesses at their wedding. Paul had some difficulty finding a woman meeting the approval of his father. As a young man, Paul was in hospital for an appendectomy. Tim and Dit went to visit him and passed a young woman coming out of his hospital room. Tim asked Dit, 'Is that Paul's girlfriend?' Dit replied, 'I don't know'. To which Tim snapped: 'Of course you bloody know. Well, he'd better get over that quickly'. Paul married Dorrie Green at St Bridget's, Red Hill in July 1942.[51]

They were divorced in March 1950 just before Paul's marriage to Joan Esson in Brisbane in April 1950. Rita married Norm Monti at St Columba's in October 1947. Dit married Peg Noon in Mitchell in April 1950. By coincidence, the church in Mitchell was also named for Saint Columba.

Tim was prominent in a campaign to have Brisbane's tram system extended to Grange, a Brisbane suburb just beyond Tim's home in Windsor. The campaign was successful in June 1928.[52] Tim was a member of Tattersalls, a private gentleman's club in Brisbane.[53] During the depression and war years he observed of the membership: 'There were many no-hopers on the scrounge for five bob'.[54]

His wife, Ellen and his mother, Sarah, were very strong on their Catholic faith, but Tim didn't much care for it and tried to sabotage his wife's god-bothering.[55] Anecdotally, he occasionally hid his wife's shoes when it was time for Mass.

He wrote a story or an open letter around the mid-1930s entitled 'Sydney's Sociology' in which he said the family were considering a move to Sydney, as a result of an enticing job offer. He was critical of the society, complaining of the cockney-like accent, the exploitative practices and the locals' constant but unreasoned praise of their newly completed bridge. He did like the harbour, though. The letter gave some insights into his likes and prejudices.[56] He was a product of the times and some of his prejudices, such as anti-Semitism, would not be widely shared or publicly aired today. Although it is instructive that such prejudices were relatively common among the Australian population in this period prior to WWII.

Tim's mother's estate

In 1944, the estate of his mother, Sarah (née Barron), was finally being settled. She had died intestate in 1935 as had her husband, Abraham in 1916. The farm had been taken over by her daughter, Gladys, and her husband Walter (Val) Jewell around 1932. Val had refinanced the farm to settle Sarah's

L: Mary and Alan Roberts' wedding in 1939. Dit and Lola at left.   R: Rita and Norm Monti's wedding in 1947.

Lola Margaret Ditton

Paul Patrick Ditton

estate and it was then valued at £870 and 'after clearing administration costs and expenses' the balance was paid to Sarah's estate. This was an amount of just £8.[57] It was to be dispersed amongst the surviving children of Sarah and Abraham. There was a letter dated 30 October 1944 from a solicitor at the Public Curator's Office to Tim's brother, William (Bill), in which the solicitor wrote: 'A difficulty has, however arisen regarding the share of Arthur Ditton and, on the information supplied to me, I cannot regard him as being entitled to share in the distribution of the Estate'.[58]

William's wish was that Tim receive an equal share, and the solicitor asked the other six beneficiaries affected to write to him to agree to equal distribution. Tim had died two weeks before this letter on 16 October 1944.[59] The next letter from the solicitor stated: 'In the circumstances, no good purpose would be served by the continuance

of my efforts to have the beneficiaries agree to permit him to share in the distribution of the Estate'.[60] A cheque for £1 2s 9p was sent to each of the seven surviving beneficiaries after incidentals and postage were deducted.

Under the relevant *Queensland Act of Succession*, which dealt with intestacy at that time, an illegitimate child was not entitled to share in the estate even of his or her biological mother. If Tim had been the biological son of Abraham, then Abraham and Sarah's marriage after Tim's birth would have legitimised him for the purpose of the Act. Comprehensive formal adoption laws only came into existence in Qld in 1935, but that was too late for Tim.[61] The succession law was reviewed in 1975 and a new act was adopted in 1981, which finally redressed the obvious injustice seen through contemporary eyes.[62]

The confirmation of Tim's promotion to replace the retiring Divisional Returning Officer of Lilley was gazetted three days after his death.[63] He had been provisionally promoted in June. The family remembered Tim's death as a misdiagnosis of a bladder condition, leading to complications. His death certificate nominated congestive cardiac failure and pyelonephritis (kidney infection) as the causes of death.

Sometime after 1949 and before 1954, Ellen moved to 28 Drummond Street, Greenslopes with her unmarried daughter, Lola. Peg remembered Ellen as welcoming, but prim and serious. Ellen lost her mobility in her last two decades and required a wheelchair to move around. Lola stayed on at Greenslopes and became her mother's carer for that time. Ellen died in 1975 a month short of her ninetieth birthday.[64]

Paul suffered a fatal heart attack on the Victoria Park golf course in 1965 at the age of 44. His second wife, Joan Esson, had drowned at Queens Beach, Scarborough, in a scuba diving accident in 1961, aged thirty.[65] Their children were raised by Joan's mother, Jane Esson. Dit's sisters, Ursula, Mary and Rita all raised families. Ursula and Mary died in Brisbane in 1981 and 1996 respectively. Rita had moved to Victoria early in her marriage and she died in Malmsbury in 1997. Lola, the last surviving member of Ellen and Tim's family died in Brisbane in 2005. She was the primary carer for her invalid mother for several decades. Lola was a kind-hearted and generous soul who kept in touch with all fourteen of her nieces and nephews and was a binding force for the dispersed cousins.

The mystery child

DNA testing is a powerful tool for resolving genealogical questions. However, it sometimes throws up questions of its own without being invited to do so. When seeking to solve the riddle of Tim's mother's origins, relevant relatives were asked to take DNA tests to help identify how reported matches might be interpreted. One of the first people asked to do a test was Bob Ditton of Melbourne, a grandson of Robert Albert Ditton, Tim's half-brother.[66]

When Bob was agreeing to do the test, he added the caveat his grandfather had stated when he divorced his first wife in the 1940s that he believed his first child, Leslie (Bob's father), was not his. Furthermore, suspicion was cast towards his half-brother, Tim, for the paternity. Given Leslie was born in 1920 in Cairns and Tim had been 1100 kilometres away in Maryborough for three years, it was thought this was unlikely. However, forewarned was forearmed. The most logical interpretation of

Ellen and Tim circa 1940

139

the DNA test results exonerated Tim and indicated Robert as most probably Leslie's father.[67] However, a seed had been planted with the cast aspersion, suggesting Robert knew something about Tim's behaviour and appetites.

As discussed later, the testing strategy uncovered Tim's biological father and to confirm that link, newly discovered relatives were asked to also do a test. So, inadvertently, a net of DNA results had been set up which would capture something not expected to be captured. A DNA test relating to an individual, 'X', appeared in the net with matches ranging from 'extremely confident' to 'moderate' being reported in August 2018. The matches were with each of the following (in declining match strength order – expressed as relations to Tim) {five grandchildren, a half-niece, a half-first cousin once-removed, a first cousin once-removed, and a first cousin twice-removed}.[68] The presence of a match with the last two, who are descended from Tim's paternal grandparents, implies X is a direct descendant of Tim, as the union between his mother and his biological father starts and finishes with him.[69] In addition, the absence of any match of even low strength with two tested relatives only connected via Ellen's side[70], strongly suggested, Tim fathered a child outside the family.[71] In fact, it is difficult to conjure any other workable hypothesis.

Some progress has been made in unravelling the connection. The current indication is an illegitimate or a birth with an misattributed paternity took place between 1926 and 1932 and therefore most probably in Brisbane. The hypothesis is that Tim fathered one of X's grandparents. Of the four grandparents, the two grandfathers have been rated highly unlikely due to the location and circumstance of the births and the two grandmothers rated possible and probable. The possible is an apparent illegitimate birth in 1926, to a young unmarried mother, but probably in Townsville, whereas the probable is a birth in 1932, to a married thirty-year-old woman already with six children who was living in the same suburb as Tim at the relevant time. The Great Depression had begun a few years before and was still continuing. The woman's husband went bankrupt the year following the birth, and she divorced her husband sixteen years later. The child of that suspected union was still alive until recent times, and a family resemblance has been noted in photos publicly available. Further research is required, but it is made difficult by record access limitations due to the necessary privacy rules.[72] Additional DNA tests of X's relatives would be the surest way of confirming the true connection. Of course, sensitivities must be respected, particularly if a person's paternity proves to be different to what was always thought to be the case.

The revelations from DNA testing present challenging ethical questions, which genealogists are actively debating. Unsurprisingly, the general thrust within that community is that despite the upsets, it is generally better that the truth come out, as people's strong desire to know their origins is asserting itself as a de facto right. In opposition to that is a more established 'right' to privacy.[73] In Qld, adoption regulation has steadily been evolving, trying to balance the rights of the adopted child with the rights of the relinquishing birth parent(s), with lots of forms to manage the rights of each party. A DNA kit has the potential to render all of that as redundant red tape.

In France, legislators have deemed one 'right' superior to the other and recently reavowed their opposition to 'recreational DNA testing', raising suspicion that the legislators feel threatened by the revelation of their own secrets. At 2.8 percent, France has one of the highest rates of misattributed paternity in Europe.[74]

Endnotes to Chapter 7

1 Qld BC 1891/ 8088 5204 Mackay, 25 Jul 1891, Arthur Barron.

2 Qld MC 1891/1410 1168, Mackay, 3 Nov 1891, Sarah Barron & Abraham Ditton

3 Oral history from Delma Haack (née Ditton), daughter of William Ditton (1905–1999)

4 The Mackay orphanage was closed in 1885 and 57 children were transferred to Rockhampton.
https://sites.google.com/site/cqfamilyhistory/articles-indexes/history/orphanages/st-joseph-s-home-neerkol

5 Qld DC 1891/2610 5701, Mackay, 29 Mar 1891, Marion Ditton

6 The marriage produced 10 children. Tim was said to be taller and fairer than his brothers.

7 Qld BC e.g. (Catherine Ditton) 1913/8810 & (Robert Ditton) 1900/7529 8252

8 Qld BC 1896/7363, Ashford near Mackay, 1 Oct 1896, Rupert Ditton (informant: Abraham)

9 Qld BC 1900/7529 8252, Ashford, 18 Jan 1904, Albert Robert Ditton (informant: Sarah)

10 Qld DC 1916/895 9852, Sandy Creek near Mackay, 18 Jan 1916, Abraham Ditton

11 A granddaughter said that based on a conversation with Ellen, Tim and Ellen knew. Her parents also knew but did not disclose it any further. Apparently, Lola did not know, based on her comments when she saw her father's birth certificate.
& Oral history from Delma Haack

12 QSA: http://www.archivessearch.qld.gov.au/Search/ItemDetails.aspx?ItemId=313137

13 http://www.brisbanetimes.com.au/queensland/full-horror-of-neerkol-orphanage-revealed-at-hearing-20150423-1ms5sa.html

14 Queensland Pupils Index QFHS 1903 *Glimpses of the past : Homebush State School Centenary, 1889-1989* by Leonie Fanning

15 Athletics, *Daily Mercury* (Mackay), Wed 26 Apr 1911, page 8 http://nla.gov.au/nla.news-article172439172

16 e.g. Athletics 8 Hour Day, *Daily Mercury* (Mackay), Wed 26 Apr 1911, page 8 http://nla.gov.au/nla.news-article172439172
& e.g. Tennis, *Daily Mercury* (Mackay), Tue 31 Oct 1911, page 9 http://nla.gov.au/nla.news-article170698379
& a winning medal was awared to him in Mackay in 1911 by the HACBS Tennis Club Mackay - held by author.

17 A.A. club's tournament boxing … *The Brisbane Courier*, Sat 27 Jan 1912, page 11, http://nla.gov.au/nla.news-article19728256
& Football, *Daily Mercury* (Mackay), Fri 21 May 1909, page 2 http://nla.gov.au/nla.news-article170781881 Tim played for the Sunflowers.

18 In the sporting spotlight, *The Telegraph* (Brisbane), Mon 20 Apr 1936, page 19, http://nla.gov.au/nla.news-article183386039
& School cricket starts *Daily Standard* (Brisbane), Sat 14 Sep 1935, page 2 http://nla.gov.au/nla.news-article186190437

19 Information from Lola Ditton, Tim's daughter..

20 From information provided by Barbara, daughter of Ursula.

21 Ambulance benefit at Mirani, *Daily Mercury* (Mackay), Wed 2 Nov 1910, page 6 http://nla.gov.au/nla.news-article176277736
& Waratah football social, *Daily Mercury* (Mackay), Sat 13 May 1911, page 6 http://nla.gov.au/nla.news-article172445033

22 Social and personal, *The Telegraph* (Brisbane), Mon 7 Jul 1913, page 11 http://nla.gov.au/nla.news-article175454496

23 Qld MC 1914/14883, Brisbane, 23 Apr 1914, Ellen Margaret Cranley & Arthur Ditton

24 Oral history from her daughter Lola. That was presumably mostly based on news of the exploits of Ernie & Clarry. She did think Tim's half brother Robert (Bob) was quite nice and William and Tim's three sisters would also have been seen in a positive light but there is little record of her meeting her in-laws face to face. E.g. Clarry lived in the same suburb as Tim and Ellen but there is no oral history of any interaction. We can be reasonably certain that Ellen was unaware that her maternal grandfather was a transported convict.

25 Qld BC 1885/7113 4084, Laidley, 7 Dec 1885, Margaret Ellen Cranley

26 Her father, Patrick Cranley, had died in 1910.

27 Oral history from her daughter Lola. The orchestra was possibly the Brisbane Musical Union, or it may have been a church-based orchestra as Lola mentioned Ellen performed at church functions.

28 Late shipping, *The Telegraph* (Brisbane), Wed 7 Oct 1914, page 7 http://nla.gov.au/nla.news-article177943679

29 Qld BC 1914/18220, Flinders St, Townsville, 23 Nov 1914, Ursula Ditton.'

30 Promoted, *Daily Standard* (Brisbane), Fri 5 Jan 1917, page 4 http://nla.gov.au/nla.news-article187078542

31 Commonwealth Electoral Roll, Herbert, 1915 & 1917

32 Shipping arrivals, *The Telegraph* (Brisbane), Fri 3 Aug 1917, page 2 http://nla.gov.au/nla.news-article177902441

33 Shipping arrivals, *The Telegraph* (Brisbane), Tue 31 Jul 1917, page 5 http://nla.gov.au/nla.news-article177902904
Tim possibly left with Ellen and the children, but might have stopped off in Mackay for a few days to see his mother.

34 https://en.wikipedia.org/wiki/North_Coast_railway_line,_Queensland

35 Maryborough celebration, *Daily Standard* (Brisbane), Tue 7 May 1918, page 4 http://nla.gov.au/nla.news-article179401994

36 Sporting rifle shooting, *Maryborough Chronicle, Wide Bay and Burnett Advertiser*, Fri 7 Dec 1917, page 3 http://nla.gov.au/nla.news-article152541422

37 *Queensland Police Gazette*, 10 Apr 1919

38 Senate elections, general elections for the House of Representatives, and referendum held on Saturday the 17th November, 1928. *Commonwealth of Australia Gazette*, (National : 1901 - 1973), 29 Nov 1928,. p. 3272. http://nla.gov.au/nla.news-article232533390

39 New justices, *The Daily Mail* (Brisbane), Sat 6 Jan 1923, page 2 http://nla.gov.au/nla.news-article218978745

40 Ursula Freney née Ditton, born 23 Nov 1914 Townsville, Qld – died 24 Dec 1981, Brisbane, Qld

& Arthur Cranley Ditton, born 20 Dec 1916 Townsville, Qld – died 19 Sep 1972, Toowoomba, Qld

& Mary Marcella Roberts née Ditton, born 9 Dec 1918 Maryborough, Qld – died 9 Dec 1996 Brisbane, Qld

& Paul Patrick Ditton, born 17 Mar 1921 Maryborough, Qld – died 16 Dec 1965 Brisbane, Qld

& Lola Margaret Ditton, born 27 Feb 1923, Brisbane – died 7 Feb 2005 Brisbane, Qld

& David Leo was born on the 27 Jan 1925 in Brisbane and died 2 days later.

& Rita Josephine Monti née Ditton, born 27 Jun 1926 Brisbane, Qld – died 9 Nov 1997 Malmsbury, VIC

41 Qld DC 1925/44938, Cumberland St., Windsor, 29 Jan 1925, David Leo Ditton

42 *The North Winds Children, The Daily Mail* (Brisbane), Sat 15 Dec 1923, page 9 http://nla.gov.au/nla.news-article218967724

We know that this was written by Tim as the original version was within Tim's personal papers.

43 *Sinbad in Moreton Bay, The Daily Mail* (Brisbane), Sat 22 Sep 1923, page 9 http://nla.gov.au/nla.news-article227073342

44 *The Post Office Clock, The Daily Mail* (Brisbane), Sat 11 Aug 1923, page 9 http://nla.gov.au/nla.news-article218950974

45 *The Bulletin* has not yet been digitised by the National Library of Australia.

46 Two articles in *The Graziers' Review* were attributed to Arthur Ditton 25 Jan 1931 pages 960, 962, 1025 & 1026 and 19 Dec 1931 pages 708, 750 & 751. The first was *Future of the Thouroughbred in Queensland*. The second discussed Phar Lap's loss in the 1931 Melbourne Cup.

47 Fish plentiful on Peel Is., *Daily Standard* (Brisbane), Fri 25 Apr 1930, page 8 http://nla.gov.au/nla.news-article179440076

48 4BC-288 metres tomorrow, *Daily Standard* (Brisbane), Thu 11 Jun 1936, page 4 http://nla.gov.au/nla.news-article184486279

49 Death of Mr. A. Ditton, *The Telegraph* (Brisbane), Tue 17 Oct 1944, page 2 http://nla.gov.au/nla.news-article189863081

50 Qld MC 1939/36482, Wilston, 9 Sep 1939, Mary Marcella Ditton & Alan Leslie Roberts

51 It is unknown if the woman was Dorrie. Qld MC 1942/49854, Red Hill, 4 Jul 1942, Dorothy Bessie Green & Paul Patrick Ditton

52 *The North Winds Children, The Daily Mail* (Brisbane), Sat 15 Dec 1923, page 9 http://nla.gov.au/nla.news-article218967724

53 Microsoft Word 365 grammar checker suggested 'strip club' as an alternative to 'gentlemen's club'. Setting aside any judgement of the life experiences of Microsoft employees, to the best of my knowledge, Tattersalls was not then, nor has it ever been a strip club.

54 In a letter from Arthur Cranley to his wife Peg. 'Five bob' was 5 shillings.

55 Sarah: Oral history from Delma Haack. Ellen: Oral history Peg Ditton passed from Dit.

56 *Sydney's Sociology?* – From Tim's personal pages

57 Val Jewell sold the farm to a neighbour in 1975 for $400,000 with an $80,000 tax liability – from a 1976 letter from Val to Bill Ditton – half-brother to Tim.

58 Letter from Public Curator Office Townsville 30 Oct 1944 Re Sarah Jane Ditton I.608 – I/2

59 Qld DC 1944/68218, Cumberland St., Windsor, 16 Oct 1944, Arthur Ditton

60 Letter from Public Curator Office Townsville 23 Nov 1944 Re Sarah Jane Ditton I.1608 – I/2

61 Qld *Adoption of Children Act 1935*. Prior to that act, privately arranged adoptions were recognised via the *Infant Life Protection Act 1905*. Provisions around consent, suitability, formal recording and government oversight were introduced with the 1921 amendments to the *Infant Life Protection Act 1905*.

62 Qld law reform 1975: http://www.qlrc.qld.gov.au/__data/assets/pdf_file/0010/372484/r20.pdf

63 Appointment and retirement of Electoral Registrars (1944, October 19). Commonwealth of Australia Gazette (National : 1901 - 1973), p. 2344. http://nla.gov.au/nla.news-article232756500 Provisional gazette entry gave salary range as £450-£522 p.a.

64 Qld DC 1975/64356, 28 Drummond St., Greenslopes, 4 Nov 1975, Margaret Ellen Ditton

65 Mother drowns in beach dive, *Truth* (Brisbane), Sun, 1 Oct 1961, page 1

66 Robert Albert Ditton, born 9 Mar 1900 Mackay, Qld – died 6 Sep 1991 Laidley, Qld

67 Bob had no match with the Mezger line but did have matches with the Ditton line. The result exonerated Tim, but if still suspicious then his other full brothers may have to be considered. Trying to resolve this with the DNA of the candidate's descendants would be challenging.

68 E.g. My match strength was 346 Centimorgans (cMs) over 15 segments (segs). Ralph's was 206 cMs over 10 segs. My first cousins were both 167 cMs over 10 segs. My sister Anne was 153 cMs over 8 segs. (These are all grandchildren of Tim Ditton.) Tim's half-niece was 121 cMs over 7 segs. Mary, the granddaughter of Tim's hypothesised biological uncle Louis Mezger was 30 cMs over 2 segs. Robert, the grandson of Tim's half-brother Bob Ditton, was 23 cMs over 3 segs and Paul, a great grandson of Tim's hypothesised biological uncle Louis Mezger, was 7 cMs over 2 segs.

69 This is based on the presumption Tim's mother had no further intimate dealings with Tim's biological father. DNA matches with descendants of Ernie, Bob and Bill support this, at least in regards to Ernie, Bob and Bill.

70 Joan E. and Doug H. are both descendants of David Barry and Grace McAlister. Tim's wife Ellen was also a descendant of this couple.

71 Tim's known children are ruled out, as no matches with Joan & Doug are seen, implying there is no Cranley/Barry match in X's DNA.

72 In Qld, birth records are not publicly available until after 100 years, marriage 75 years and death 30 years.

73 In Australia the Commonwealth *Privacy Act 1988* restricts to whom organisations can reveal individual's information.

74 https://isogg.org/wiki/Non-paternity_event

75 Back of Photo reads: Townsville and Suburban Lawn Tennis Association. 'A' Grade Champions St Mary's 1915 & 1916, Holders Association Trophy. Standing A. Barbeler, J. Collins, A Ditton (Coach), A.N. Boniface (Captain) T. Fanning. Sitting: M. Leahy, L. Quaid, M. Quaid, M. Mitchell.

Chapter 8

A tropical blend

Marion, Sarah and Abraham - Ditton

Qld separated from NSW in 1859. Until then, European settlement was mostly confined to the southern regions with no significant colonial settlements on the East Coast further north than the town of Rockhampton (established 1858). The new Qld Government was, famously, completely broke.[1] It needed new sources of revenue. There was a vast untapped area north of the Tropic of Capricorn. New industries were encouraged with outposts established in new ports. Some fleeting gold discoveries initially pushed things along, but it was mostly agriculture driving the settlement further north in the first decade. Port Denison (later Bowen) was the first new port established in the tropics in 1861. Mackay followed in 1862 and Townsville in 1864. This is the story of the blended family my paternal grandfather, Tim Ditton, grew up within. His mother was Sarah Barron and his adoptive father was Abraham Ditton.

Abraham's life in England

Abraham Ditton was born in Woodchurch, Kent, England in November 1839.[2] He was the eighth of ten children born to Abraham Ditton and his wife Lydia (née Wimble).[3] Abraham was destined to have two large families of his own in Australia. The older Abraham was at times a roadman and at other times a farm labourer.[4] The younger Abraham remembered his father as a farm overseer.[5] The Australian immigration record for the younger Abraham listed his profession as a farm labourer.[6] Abraham's forebears had lived in Kent and neighbouring Sussex for many generations.[7] The picturesque village of Woodchurch is a location where hops have been grown since the fifteenth century as they are a vital ingredient of the famous and delicious Kentish ales.[8]

Prospects for farm labourers in the 1850s in England were limited by the attitudes of their so-called betters.[9] The few opportunities for advancement would have been reserved for the family or sycophants of the ruling class, and merit would be only a secondary consideration. One of his father's brothers,

MR. A. DITTON, SENR.,
Abraham Ditton, circa 1912.[154]

Robert, had immigrated to NSW as a free settler in 1839.[10] Abraham was able to read and write and that would have allowed him to a form a favourable view of the opportunities in the colonies.[11]

Records from Woodchurch in 1871 tell us his parents had to rely on the charity of the community in their later years. At that time, Lydia and Abraham were living at 10 Front Road, Woodchurch, and Abraham's grandmother Elizabeth Ditton (née Settertree) ran a small green grocery business next door at number 12.[12]

Abraham's emigration

On 17 June 1858, Abraham, aged eighteen, embarked on the *Alfred* at Liverpool, England. He, like most on board, travelled as a government sponsored immigrant. The ship sailed directly to the Moreton Bay settlement (Brisbane) and arrived on 19 September 1858. There were 437 mostly British and Irish passengers on board. With a tonnage of 1270, the *Alfred* was the largest ship to have sailed into Moreton Bay, up until that time. The *Moreton Bay Courier* described the process of hiring these new workers and the wages Abraham could expect to earn. Between £30 to £40 would be Abraham's expected annual salary.[13]

Oral history has it that his family advised he should go and live with his relative, who was a parson in southern NSW. Abraham was of a different mind, not wanting to live with a parson and so deliberately chose a different destination.[14]

Abraham went north shortly after arriving. The same newspaper reporting the arrival of the ship had stories of gold discoveries at Canoona on the Fitzroy River near Rockhampton and details of how to proceed there.[15] The freedom to choose an adventure in the untamed north is a concept which would be difficult to explain to the siblings he had left behind in England. There, your class would define your expectations, whereas in the colonies, there were few who had any authority over the newcomers, and even fewer would be considered upper class. People like Abraham could even contemplate squatting on large tracts of land. However, the Indigenous people did their best to keep these adventurous spirits in check as they correctly understood the newcomers' intentions were not in their best interests. In this district, the initial goldrush was disappointing and short lived, but it did draw people up into the country for other purposes such as farming, grazing and the services required around those activities.[16]

Numbers 12 (L) & 10 (R) Front Road, Woodchurch, September 2017. Number 12, was known as School House as it was used as a school in the 18th Century and up to 1818. Number 10 is named Church Gates. It was also used as a school between the world wars. All Saints church, behind these houses dates from the 13th century.[155]
Photos: author

Marriage to Marion Stevenson

The next we hear of Abraham is as a 24-year-old when he marries Marion Stevenson, at Calliope Station, 25 kilometres SSW of Gladstone, on 24 June 1864.[17] The thirty-year-old Marion had arrived from Glasgow one year earlier on the *Rockcliff*.[18] Calliope was the first goldfield officially declared by the new Colony of Qld, and in 1864, there were about 800 residents there.[19] Marion and Abraham's first child Isabella (Bella) was born in April 1865 in Gladstone.[20] Back in Scotland, Marion's recently deceased father, Alexander, had been amidst the Industrial Revolution with his profession recorded as 'engine driver' or 'engine keeper'.[21]

This revolution had not reached this corner of the British Empire anywhere near to the same extent. Abraham went bullock driving between Calliope and Gladstone. This was the colonial substitute for steam power. On one of his bullock driving trips, an Aboriginal man speared him whilst he was camped under his wagon near Gladstone. Another bullock driver cut the spear out of his chest. He showed his scar to his children down the years.[22] A 1912 article written about Abraham under the subheading 'Men who blazed the track' states that he arrived in the Mackay district in 1863, just one year after the town was established. It is possible, his bullocking work took him the 450 kilometres from Mackay to Calliope and that is where he met Marion. However, their 1864 marriage record states they both usually resided at Calliope.[23]

Later, Abraham worked as a 'bullock puncher', breaking in bullocks at Pleystowe, about twenty kilometres west of Mackay.[24] To get to

Left: Believed to be Marion Stevenson in Glasgow in 1863. Centre: Believed to be Marion in Mackay in 1884–86. Right: Probably John (Jack) Ditton, Mackay 1884-86. Lyn Murphy, a great-great-granddaughter of Abraham, supplied all three photos from the collection of Allan Ditton. Lyn's detective work identified the photo on the left could only have been taken in Glasgow in 1863. The photo in the centre had some back markings to say it was Lydia Wimble, Abraham's mother, but other back markings indicated it was Marion. There is clearly a similarity between the subject in the 1863 photo and the one in the centre. The photo of the boy was known to be taken in Mackay in 1884–86 by A.B. Clinton.[156] Given the similarity of studio and props, it was concluded the centre photo was most likely of Marion in Mackay from the same time frame.

Photo associated with an article on Abraham Ditton in the book *Early Settlers of Mackay 1860 – 1885*. The photo was captioned 'Abraham Ditton and his bullock team at Palm Tree Crossing, Sunnyside' The photo was found hanging on a wall at the school at Te Kowai, south of Mackay.[157]

Mackay from the Gladstone district, the young family had to cross the Sarina range in a cart. They claim to have been the first family to do that.[25] They encountered snakes and crocodiles along the way.[26] It appears they did more travelling in the cart, as young Bella was reported to have developed a keen scent for water and was able to direct her father to water whilst riding in the cart.[27] Their second child, Abraham (III),[28] was born in Mackay in August 1868.[29] As well as bullock driving, Abraham was initially a 'squatter' and later a 'selector' in the Mackay district.[30] The 1874 *Post Office Directory* listed him as a squatter at *Three Tree Farm*.[31]

In January 1882, Abraham and his family took up residence on their selection about fourteen kilometres south-west of Mackay. The selection comprised 157 acres (63.5 hectares). On the property's northern boundary was Sandy Creek and to the west was BL Creek. In accordance with the land laws of the time, he was required to demonstrate 'continuous and *bona fide* residence' for a period of five years. For this selection, he was to pay annual rent of £4. He was required to pay other charges such as surveying fees and to make improvements. At the end of five years, he was issued with a 'Deed of Grant'.[32]

Abraham had also successfully applied for selection of the neighbouring 84-acre (34 hectares) section to the west of BL Creek. In 1892, he obtained his Deed of Grant for that land after paying ten years' rent at the higher annual rate of £6 6s.[33] At some point he named the joint property

Ashford, after the largest town in the district in which he was born. The farm was referred to as being via Marwood, which is about a kilometre north of the farm.[34] Marwood is another locality in the County of Kent which implies Abraham may have had a part in naming it. Naming a locality is something he could not have dreamed of doing if he had stayed in Kent.

By the mid-1880s, the improvements on this land included a four-room house measuring (in feet) 32 x 24 and a separate kitchen measuring 15 x 12. The buildings had iron roofs and horizontal timber (red cedar) slab walls with pine floorboards and partitions.[35] At this time, Abraham was a 'dairyman' and he also kept several horses. The survey noted the farm had cattle yards and a small dairy shed. The family cultivated one acre of sweet potatoes and sorghum. They had a vegetable garden and grew some fruits. They kept a fowl house. Bella had a memory of her father smoking meat in an open fireplace.[36]

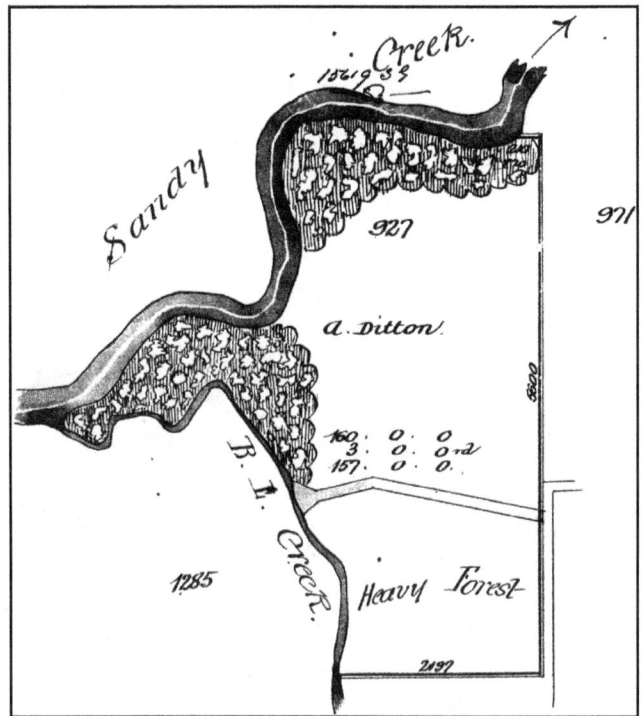

Survey Map showing Abraham's initial selection, (#927) and the later addition (#1285).[158]

In 1885, this farm potentially accommodated and employed Abraham and Marion, their 20-year-old daughter, Bella, their sons Abraham, 17, Alexander (Alex), 15, John, 12 and Charles (Chas), 7. By this time, three children, Alan, Marion and Lydia had died young. The infant girls had each lived for about two years and Alan had only lived one month.[37] The life in this simple rural setting would have been challenging by modern standards. The children had acquired some education, but it is not sure how or from whom. Bella had neat, old-fashioned handwriting with correct spelling.[38] In 1885, the younger Abraham left home driving cattle north, in search of his own independence.[39] Bella left to go working in Brisbane in the 1880s, probably as a seamstress.[40]

Mackay started in 1862 as a sheep and cattle grazing town, but it proved to be less suited than more southerly or dryer locations.[41] From about 1865, some of the farmers in the district had successfully turned to the cultivation of sugarcane.[42] The success was often due to the employment of

South Sea Islanders, then known as Kanakas.[43] These workers were initially forcibly or deceptively 'recruited' and typically employed under exploitative arrangements, which at worst approached the slavery experienced on the Southern USA plantations up until just a few years earlier. The Mackay district was one of the principal centres of this activity. The recruiting practices were moderated after legislation was passed in 1868 following pressure from churches and other nations.[44] Recruiting slowed after 1874 but continued until 1904. Most labourers were on three-year contracts and were returned to their islands at the end of their time. However, a minority, if allowed, opted to stay for another term and some of those continued to work in the district for several decades after.[45]

In 1895, Abraham served on a jury hearing a case of attempted murder of James Barnes by four Kanakas. Despite some serious doubts raised during the trial regarding the guilt of at least one of the accused, the jury took just ten minutes to unanimously find them all guilty.[46]

'Winding Reaches on Sandy Creek at Ashford, Maggie's paddock (at right). Farmhouse on right horizon'.[159]

Abraham was not initially involved in sugarcane growing, but he used his bullock team to bring most of the heavy machinery to the mill at nearby Homebush and to other mills in the district. He had a contract to use his bullocks to turn the rollers to crush the sugarcane at the Midland Sugar Mill. This worked like a horse gear chaff cutter.[47] In 1884, he sold the bullock team when settling on his selection. He turned to butchering and dairying until the parasitic redwater disease, in one year, killed all but forty of his herd.[48] After that, around 1897, he is reported to have become a sugarcane grower for Colonial Sugar Refineries (CSR).[49] He also sold firewood to earn some ready cash.[50]

Oral accounts identify Abraham as caring about the native wildlife and banishing one of his sons after he had shot some koalas that Abraham had been caring for.[51] He had built platforms for them and ensured they had enough feed.[52] Koalas were hunted for their fur in Qld with a penultimate open season in 1919. Bowing to pressure from fur dealers and treasury, but ignoring popular sentiment, the government allowed one final devastating open season in 1927.[53] The Alligator Creek Reserve in Balberra (near *Ashford*) was renamed the Abraham Ditton Reserve in his honour in 2015. The Mackay Regional Council press release stated: 'He was passionate about the care and protection of native wildlife, making him one of the earliest conservationists in the area'.[54]

In March 1913, Martin Ryan made a claim seeking payment of £7 10s from Abraham for fencing work done on his property. Abraham had disputed the terms of the arrangement, particularly using trees as attachment points for the wire instead of posts cut from his property, counterclaiming £14 for materials supplied. The bench found for Mr Ryan requiring Abraham to pay a total of £12 10s including court and witness travelling costs.[55]

Abraham is remembered as being fond of a drink, particularly on his irregular trips to town. If he had an important errand to run, such as registering the birth of one of the children, then he would first quench his thirst. Descendants have said, therefore some of the dates ending up on the children's birth certificates may have been best guesses.[56]

In 1889, Marion started to suffer from heart problems. Bella returned home from Brisbane to nurse Marion. Marion expressed a wish to be near the beach and Bella arranged a place for her where they spent some time.[57] She passed away in March 1891 at Mackay aged 57.[58] Bella left Mackay and visited her brother, Abraham, on the Reid River around this time and moved to Townsville shortly afterwards.[59] Abraham's youngest child, Chas, was now thirteen years old. It is not known whether the middle boys – Alex, 21 and John, 18 – were still helping out on the farm or whether they had started to go their own way. We do know that within a few years, they were no longer at *Ashford*.[60]

Marriage to Sarah Jane Barron

As discussed in the previous chapter, Abraham took in Sarah Barron and her newborn son, Arthur. An arrangement must have been reached between Abraham and Sarah as they were married on Abraham's birthday in November 1891.[61] It was Abraham's 52nd birthday, but he adjusted his age on the marriage record to infer a smaller age gap. Abraham declared himself to be 48 years old. Sarah is thought to have done the same as her stated age of 27 and birthplace of Townsville has her born about one year prior to the first official European birth at Townsville in August 1865.[62] Going into a household shared with young men, to be the

wife of a man with a 26-year-old daughter, would be sufficient cause to fudge her age. Sarah's birth and parentage are a documentary riddle, which is explored in detail in the next chapter.

Sarah and Abraham married in the presbrytery of the Mackay Catholic church. That would have been Sarah's choice. Abraham claimed affiliation with both the C of E and the Presbyterian Church. He had married Marion according to the rites of the Episcopal Church (a Scottish form of Anglicism).[63] That was probably Marion's choice.[64]

The marriage lasted 24 years and produced ten children with seven surviving into adulthood.

The only known photograph of Sarah Jane Ditton (née Barron)- from the collection of Delma Haack.

Sandy Creek horse drawn cane harvest on the Ditton farm.[160]

The children of the two marriages - Tim's step and half siblings

Isabella (Bella)

Abraham's first family moved on over the years. Bella never married and moved to Townsville after the death of her mother.[65] She ran a dressmaking business and at one time employed two young women. Her clientele included leading ladies and the Anglican bishop. In later life, her eyesight failed due to cataracts. An operation to save her sight did not work. She was forced to move from her house when a developer bought up all the houses in the block. She moved in with her nephew, Archie Ditton, and his wife Annie (née Clay) at Charters Towers. After that, she moved to Eventide, Charters Towers, where she died in 1957, aged 92.[66]

Abraham (III)

Abraham (III), his wife, Sarah Ellen (née Smith) and their young family were joined by two brothers, Alex and Chas.[67] The three brothers worked together as drovers. They were living at Reid River about sixty kilometres south of Townsville in the early 1900s.[68] A police gazette from their time there, documents the shooting of two mares belonging to Abraham with suspicion falling on a person known to the police.[69] The house at Reid River burnt down whilst Abraham was away. Annie Ditton claimed it was done to get the insurance money.[70] Abraham had spent years prospecting and contract droving and then settled on Ellenvale Station.[71] Abraham had ups and downs financially. He raised cattle and got good money for them during WWI. The bank provided unlimited money, but when he made some poor choices, he was forced to sell *Ellenvale*.[72] In 1915, he moved to Hinchinbrook Park Station. He was later a member of Thuringowa Shire Council.[73] Abraham's leg was amputated after he broke it in a tangled rope tethering a calf. He moved to Isabella's place in Townsville and died in 1946.[74] His daughter, Hellen Isabella (Helena/Nellie), found herself in a bigamist marriage to Herbert Valentine Palmer, who she 'remained very fond of'.[75]

Alexander (Alex) Stevenson

Shortly after attending his father's funeral in 1916, Alex got a gidyea splinter in his hand. He rubbed raw Condy's crystals into it, but the wound turned septic. Condy's crystals (potassium permanganate) is an effective antiseptic, but it must be used at the correct dilution.[76] Alex died in Charters Towers in 1916 from this episode. It is a good illustration of how relatively simple accidents were so life threating in those days. Alex was 46 years old at the time and he had never married.

John (Jack) Archibald

Jack married Mary Eardly in 1895[77] and raised a family at Mia Mia, a short distance from Mackay.[78] A police gazette cited him for desertion and the non-payment of maintenance. He left the family home in 1913 and went to stay with Bella.[79] He subsequently moved to Darwin where he died in 1939. Mary and the children moved to Windsor in Brisbane and lived a few streets away from her stepbrother-in-law, Tim Ditton. Mary died in 1953.

Left: Abraham III taken on his property at Hinchinbrook Park.[161]
Right: Helena (Nellie) Palmer née Ditton and her aunt Isabella (Bella) at the Townsville show 1941.[162]

Ditton boys: Jack standing and Chas sitting[163]

Ivy May Ditton (later Eastgate)[164]

Charles (Chas) Stevenson

Chas never married. He lived on a property called *Charlesford*. He used to go cattle trucking during the meatworks season. In the off-season he did some fencing and planted fruit trees. He shared his basic accommodation with his nephew, Allen, and quite a few snakes. There were tales of finding death adders under the pillow and under the dinner table. The snakes thinned out when a sow was allowed to sleep in the house. He suffered dementia in his later years and had trouble remembering where he lived. He ended up at Eventide at Charters Towers where he died in 1962.[80]

Ivy May

Abraham II and his new wife, Sarah Jane, continued farming at *Ashford* and went on to have eleven children in all. Combined with the eight born to Marion, Abraham fathered eighteen children and adopted one. In total, thirteen children survived him. After Arthur, came Ivy May in January 1893.[81] She was Sarah's first child with Abraham. Ivy married William Eastgate in 1911 and raised a family in Mackay.[82] Ivy died in 1967 and William died in 1961.

Ernest (Ernie)

The next, Ernie, was born in November 1894.[83] Ernie also had the nickname 'Pompie'.[84] He was a farmer in the Mackay and then Bowen districts. It is fair to say, Ernie was a popular and colourful character with a reckless streak. Societal conventions did not bind him. In 1915, he wrestled with an armed man, David Watt, who was shooting horses that had trespassed onto Watts' unfenced land.[85] He married Margaret Cowan that same year. In January 1921, he was convicted of using dynamite to catch fish in the Pioneer River.[86] He enlisted in the Volunteer Defence Corps (Home Guard) in February 1944.[87]

In September 1946, Ernie shot and killed a man who was armed and threatening him and three women on his farm near Bowen. Two of the women were

Ernie's business partner, Mrs Isabella McLennan, and her daughter Anne Mavis.[88] The rest of that story is related at the end of this chapter. A cousin described the time they went swimming in the creek. Isabella stayed on the bank with a rifle in her lap. Only after the swim did she tell them she was on the lookout for crocodiles.[89]

Ernie died in October 1953[90] and his will left most of his estate to the daughter of Anne Mavis McLennan.[91] His deserted wife, Margaret, challenged the will to win arrears of maintenance for her and her six now-adult children.[92] Margaret died in March of the following year.[93]

The payment of maintenance by a deserting husband was a state-based system, problematic for many, as it required the wives to sue their husbands, and there were cumbersome remedies when maintenance was not paid. The federal Whitlam Government introduced the Supporting Mother's (later Parent's) Benefit in 1973, which addressed many of these problems.[94]

Ernie Ditton[165]

Robert (Bob) Albert

A son, Bob, born in 1900, lived until he was 91.[95] In his long life he was both a health inspector and the Laidley correspondent for the *The Courier Mail*.[96] In his youth he was an accomplished boxer. He held the North Qld Amateur Welterweight Boxing Championship for several years from 1917.[97] He was also an accomplished golfer. He won the Qld Country Golfers Championship title in 1935 by seven strokes.[98] He also became a sports organiser. He was married twice[99] with children from both marriages.[100]

Gladys Elizabeth

Gladys was born in 1903.[101] She married Val Jewell in 1922 and had two boys.[102] Her family took over *Ashford* when Sarah left, and the farm was refinanced in 1944 to resolve Sarah's estate. Val Jewell sold the farm to neighbours in 1975.[103] Gladys died in 1950 and Val died in 1991.[104]

Gladys Jewell (née Ditton) and Bob Ditton[166]

Bill Ditton (seated) with his bride, Louise Evans in 1925

William (Bill) Leslie

The next, Bill, born in 1905, lived for 94 years[105]. He worked for the railways department. His funeral notice referred to him as 'Fishy Bill' (a reference to his love of fishing).[106] Bill married Louise Evans in 1925 and the family moved from Yungaburra on the Atherton Tableland to Brisbane in 1942 and settled in the suburb of Northgate. The move was partly inspired by the desire to avoid advancing Japanese. Bill was known as a keen gardener and stated he had 'gardened since he could walk'. He exhibited his vegetables and flowers. An article in the *Northside Chronicle* from 1991 explained his gardening philosophy and methods.[107] His avoidance of chemicals and use of companion planting would put him in good stead with today's organic gardeners. His daughter remembers Bill as being very fond of his father and mother.[108]

Clarence (Clarry) Isaac

Clarry was born in 1909.[109] He had several well-documented brushes with the law in the Great Depression years of 1931 and 1932. The charges related to the theft of meat[110], use of obscene language[111] and unlawful use of a motor car.[112] The first resulted in a one-month suspended sentence. The second was dismissed on a technicality as the swearing was found to have been done from a vacant lot, which was private property and was therefore lawful. The third offence resulted in six months' hard labour. Clarry cited his need to support his widowed mother (Sarah Jane) and younger sister

(Kath) as motivation for the meat theft. As part of this support, he operated a hire car in Mackay (sometimes without a licence) [113] and had some altercations with his competition, which were at the heart of the obscene language and unauthorised use of a competitor's motor vehicle charges. He and a friend drove the rival's car down to the beach one night after a few drinks where it ran out of petrol. A comedic aftermath of pushing the car back into town was spelt out in the court reports.[114]

Clarry had a few appearances in court over the following years on lesser charges.[115] Clarry married Eileen Conners in 1939 and had three surviving children at the time of his death in 1969.[116] His profession was listed as waterside worker residing in Windsor, Brisbane. Despite his rough edges, Clarry was remembered as a strong advocate for a good education.

Catherine (Kath/Katie) Muriel

The last child, Kath, was born in 1913.[117] Kath was referred to in Sarah's obituary as a 'well known show-rings rider'.[118] She participated in a number of events displaying her impressive horse riding skills.

A children's corner column in a Townsville newspaper identified Kath as a keen correspondent with the paper and other teenagers around 1928 and 1929.[119] The 1943 Electoral Roll listed her as a trained nurse resident at the Mackay District Hospital.[120] She married Colin McDonald and had two sons.[121] She was later matron at the hospital in Boonah in Southern Qld.[122] She had lived at Rocklea and then died in a Hervey Bay nursing home in 1995.[123] Colin died in 1982.

Rupert James, Cecil Francis Roy and Sarah

A son Rupert had been born in 1896,[124] but tragically died eight years later from a sickness which had persisted for two years.[125] The child after Rupert, Cecil, was born in 1898, but survived for just three months.[126] The daughter named for her mother, Sarah, was born in 1902, but only survived a few days,[127] echoing the tragic death of the infant named after Marion 28 years earlier. Sarah, Cecil and Rupert are buried in the same plot as Sarah in the Mackay cemetery. A headstone, remembering Sarah and her three children who died young, was erected in 2017.

Clarry and Eileen at the show[168]

Catherine (Kath) Ditton aged 21[167]

155

Left: Katie Ditton as featured in a publication *Mackay in pictures*[169] Right: Katie Ditton practicing at the farm [170]

The final years

Abraham died at home in January 1916, aged 76. He suffered cardiac failure and had been suffering from 'chronic sprue' (Vitamin K deficiency) for several years prior to his death.[128] The *Cairns Post* of 7 August 1916 cited him as having died intestate. He is buried in Mackay Cemetery in the same plot as Marion in the Presbyterian section. His sons Ernie and Bill and grandson, Kevin, are also listed on memorial plaques which have been erected in recent years to mark the burial plot.[129]

In January 1918, a severe cyclone destroyed the farmhouse, and Sarah and the family had to seek shelter with a neighbour, Jim Paton. Son Bill, remembered the rain was salty despite the sea being eight kilometres away.[130] When they returned to the farm, a pig was standing on a chair with its front hooves on a piano amidst the farmhouse ruins.[131]

Sarah was still living on the farm in 1929[132], but moved to Brisbane Street, Mackay[133] around 1932.[134] Clarry had told a court in 1931 his mother was in poor circumstances. She died at Mackay on 15 August 1935, officially aged 70.[135] Her annual *in memorandum* notices stated she died alone, but was missed by her family.[136] The local paper also praised her skill at growing lucerne as an effective stock food for dairy cattle.[137] The oral history says she was a hard worker. She was remembered as someone who was devout with her Catholic faith. Whenever the priest came to visit, he would be treated much better than her own family with quality food offerings such as a freshly killed roast chicken.[138] It was clear to her children that she had known the priest from her early days. Sarah, like Abraham, died intestate.[139]

Aftermath of the 1918 Cyclone in Mackay[171]

The legacy of Flash Jack O'Hanlon – Ernie's victim

Jack O'Hanlon was a cane farmer at Longford Creek near Bowen, Qld.[140] The neighbourhood knew him as 'Flash Jack' because of his attire and colourful character.[141] In the 1920s, he started to develop a drinking problem. When he was on one of his binges, he became belligerent with his hired help, his neighbours and his own family. He would exploit his three sons for their labour, with promises of future ownership of the farm and in the meantime only pay a pitiful allowance. Any negotiation about pay or inheritance had to be conducted during his sober moments. The documents drafted at these times were typically destroyed during a later binge. He would take a cane knife or a gun and threaten his wife and children. When sober, he would deny the possibility he had behaved that way. A sorry cycle of lucky escapes and subsequent reconciliation continued until 1945 when the sons left to get jobs which paid market wages. Jack had ordered his daughter off the property in 1940, and subsequently pleaded with her to come back. In 1945, a drunken Jack ordered his long-suffering wife, Wilhelmina, off the property. She went to stay with her sister and formally filed for maintenance. She was denied maintenance, as the magistrate ruled she herself had left the marriage. The magistrate suggested they take a holiday together to repair the relationship.[142]

His hired help were likely to be sacked during his binges, but the more resilient ones knew to return when he was sober, and all would be forgotten. His home was well equipped for his habit. He had a demijohn of overproof (OP) rum on a chair near his bed and a case of gin under his bed.[143] His daughter saw him drink two bottles of gin and a bottle of OP rum in one day. On occasion, he would go drinking in Bowen or Proserpine with his neighbours or business associates, but often that ended with fights or accidents, especially if he drove his car home.

Ernie Ditton lived on a neighbouring farm. There was a history of conflict between him and Jack. On one occasion they had a brawl in a train carriage and on another they duelled on horseback using stirrups as weapons.[144] Things did not improve when Ernie gave evidence against Jack in the maintenance hearing.[145] In late August 1946, Wilhelmina went to stay with Ernie and his business partner, Isabella McLennan. Jack heard about that.

On 13 September, Jack fell off his horse and was very unwell. That night he called for his lawyer and frequent drinking partner, John Barry, to come to the farm. Jack asked John to draw up a new will. In that will he left £2 to his wife and each of his children. The rest he bequeathed to John Barry and his family. John Barry believed this was done to maintain Jack's belligerence with the family after his death.[146]

The next morning, Jack declined an offer to be taken to hospital. Instead, he dressed in a khaki shirt with white moleskin jodhpurs, leggings, spurs and a full cartridge belt. The outfit was topped off with a sombrero. Jack downed three big drinks of gin. He then went on horseback armed with a rifle to confront Ernie and to try to get his wife back. Jack dismounted to open Ernie's gate, but had difficulty remounting. Ernie saw Jack first and came up from behind and snatched the rifle off him. Jack rode off and within an hour returned with another rifle. He said to Ernie, 'Say your prayers as you will not live 'til sundown'. He threatened to kill Wilhelmina as well. Ernie said, 'Jack, put that gun down and come and have some dinner'. Jack continued with his threats and dismounted and crouched ready to shoot. Ernie dodged across a doorway and got the gun he had taken from Jack earlier.[147] Ernie aimed the gun intending to wound Jack in the shoulder. Jack fell forward and died instantly. Ernie was charged with murder but acquitted at trial the following year. The jury took five minutes of deliberation to agree he acted in self-defence.

John Barry threatened Jack's children with further ill-fortune if they slandered him or contested the will. He made varying promises of compensation if they let it lie. John Barry's word was not trusted, and in 1950, the will was challenged before Justice RJ Douglas sitting without a jury. Jack's will was upheld, as Jack knew what he was doing, and the will was legally constructed. However, the essence of Justice Douglas' remarks to John Barry were: 'If you ever knew any legal ethics, then you have completely forgotten them'.[148]

John Barry went on to be elected chairman of the Proserpine Shire council.[149] In 1951, he was quoted in the local newspaper giving advice to a local farming board, claiming the way to keep young people on the land was to give the sons an interest in the farm or the crop.[150] A 1953 newspaper details him bestowing the benefit of his financial wisdom upon the visiting Prime Minister, Robert Menzies.[151]

Meanwhile, Jack's family were left to nurse their grudges and reflect on what passed for justice at that time. Jack's daughter had married in 1946. One of Jack's boys had died in an accident in 1947 and in 1954 the other two were finally listed as farmers living with their wives at Longford Creek. They remained there for at least a decade.[152] Wilhelmina died in Proserpine in 1970.[153]

Endnotes to Chapter 8

1 The separation left the new Treasury with only seven pence halfpenny and that was promptly stolen.

2 England Civil Registration BC 1839 #31 App # 3583A – Tenterden Kent, 3 Nov 1839, Abraham Ditton. The surname, Ditton, simply means 'town or place by a ditch or dyke'. There is a locality a few km south of London's centre named, Ditton on Thames. There is also a hamlet in Cambridgeshire named Fen Ditton.

3 Collated from Index England & Wales, Civil Registration birth entries & Ancestry hints.

4 *Woodchurch in 1871. A Kentish village and the Mid-Victorian Census* – Woodchurch Village Life Museum, 2008 page 7

5 Qld MC 1891/1410 1168, Mackay, 3 Nov 1891, Sarah Barron & Abraham Ditton

6 NSW, Australia, Assisted Immigrant Passenger Lists 1828–1896 Vessel: *Alfred*. Arrival: 19 Sep 1858

7 Pedigree information was from many genealogical sources recorded in public trees on Ancestry.com.

8 http://woodchurchinfo.com/village-and-services/history/

9 The rural exodus by Mike Winstanley http://www.bbc.co.uk/history/british/victorians/exodus_01.shtml

10 NSW, Australia, Assisted Immigrant Passenger Lists, 1812–1896 Vessel: *Cornwall*. Date 1839

11 NSW, Australia, Assisted Immigrant Passenger Lists 1828–1896 Vessel: *Alfred*. Arrival: 19 Sep 1858

12 *Woodchurch in 1871. A Kentish village and the Mid-Victorian Census,* page 7

13 … arrival of immigrants, *The Moreton Bay Courier*, 2 Oct 1858, page 2 http://nla.gov.au/nla.news-article3720122

14 Oral history from Delma Haack. Many reasons can be thought of as to why he would not like to live with a parson. He was known to like a drink in his later life, so that may have been one within a list of reasons. Moreton Bay was still part of NSW in 1858, but the relative was thought to be living in what still remained NSW after Qld separated in 1859. The relative may have been on his mother's side..

15 The Canoona goldrush was Qld's first rush, (but not first gold discovery). The rush was finished by 1860. R Cilento & C Lack, *Triumph in the Tropics: an historical sketch of Queensland.* Smith and Paterson, Brisbane, 1959, page 201

16 Wikipedia article on Rockhampton: history https://en.wikipedia.org/wiki/Rockhampton

17 Qld MC 1864/36237 Calliope Station, 20 Jun 1864, Marion Stevenson & Abraham Ditton

18 *Early Settlers of Mackay 1860–1885,* Mackay Family History Society – Abraham Ditton pages 54–55

19 *Australians Events and Places.* Ed: G Aplin, SG Foster & M McKernan Pub: Fairfax, Syme & Weldon, NSW 1987 page 301 Gold had been discovered on the Fitzroy river in 1853 but the Calliope field was the first declared by the new Qld colony.

20 Qld BC 1865/1315, Port Curtis, 16 Apr 1865, Isabella Stevenson Ditton

21 Qld DC 1891/2610 5701, Mackay, 29 Mar 1891, Marion Ditton. Marion's mother was Marion McLeay (1805 – 1884).

22 Family wants pioneer remembered, *Daily Mercury* (Mackay), Wed 2 Jun 1993 – newspaper cutting

23 *The jubilee of Mackay: 1862–1912, Daily Mercury* (Mackay), 1912 http://nla.gov.au/nla.obj-52794186

24 *Early Settlers of Mackay 1860–1885,* P54–55

25 Family wants pioneer remembered, *Daily Mercury* (Mackay), Wed 2 Jun 1993 – newspaper cutting

26 From an account written by Delma Haack

27 From memoirs of Annie Ditton (née Clay) wife of Archibald Ditton, first son of Abraham III. (provided by Lyn Murphy) Pristine water is odourless, but the water Bella smelt was highly unlikely to be pristine.

28 As Abraham (b. 1868) is the son of Abraham (b. 1839) who is the son of Abraham (b. 1800) for the purpose of making a distinction in the story, I have labelled him the 'III'. No one referred to him as that during his life.

29 Qld BC 1868/1644 116, Mackay, 15 Aug 1868, Abraham Ditton

30 Qld State Archives, Series 14033 Items 51827 & 52176 (Selection files)

31 *Bailliere's Directory of Queensland 1874*, Mackay

32 Qld State Archives, Series 14033 Item 51827 selection # 927

33 Qld State Archives, Series 14033 Items 52176 Selection #1285

34 Mackay district development, *Daily Mercury* (Mackay), Wed 21 Aug 1935, page 6 http://nla.gov.au/nla.news-article173211250

35 *Daily Mercury* (Mackay), Wed 2 Jun 1993, A timber, much prized for furniture, was used for external cladding.

36 From the memoirs of Annie Ditton, regarding Isabella.

37 Qld Birth & Death record indexes

38 From the memoirs of Annie Ditton

39 James Cook University archives: http://libserver.jcu.edu.au/specials/Archives/ditton.html.

40 From the memoirs of Annie Ditton

41 JA Nilsson, *Mackay in the Nineteenth Century*, Royal History Society Queensland, 1964

42 *Australians Events and Places.* Ed: G Aplin, SG Foster & M McKernan Pub: Fairfax, Syme & Weldon, NSW 1987

43 Most sources have it as a Polynesian word for men. The men that were recruited were predominately Melanesian. In Australia it is now considered an offensive word, outside of its historical context.

44 Qld *Polynesian Labourers Act 1868* https://www.nma.gov.au/defining-moments/resources/islander-labourers

45 *The south sea islanders of Mackay, Queensland Australia* by Clive Moore

http://www.multiculturalaustralia.edu.au/doc/mmaq01_moore_mackay.pdf

46 Circuit Court, *Mackay Mercury*, Thu 21 Nov 1895, page 3 http://nla.gov.au/nla.news-article168860478

47 From an account written by Delma Haack

48 From an account written by Delma Haack based on her father's memories. The story originally sized the herd at 600, but that herd size sounds very large for the land size he owned at the time. A more careful examination of the context of the memoir and the wording implied that most of the cattle were beef cattle as they were only mustered occasionally and sold to market shortly afterwards. . A dairy herd size around 100 up to 150 would be more manageable for his known land area.

49 *The jubilee of Mackay: 1862–1912, Daily Mercury* (Mackay,) 1912 http://nla.gov.au/nla.obj-52794186

50 Mackay Family History information sheet on Abraham Ditton.

51 *Early Settlers of Mackay 1860–1885*, pages 54–55 (son: Ernie)

52 Oral history from Delma Haack

53 1927 open season on Koalas http://www.archives.qld.gov.au/Researchers/Exhibitions/Top150/126-150/Pages/134.aspx
The lone pine koala sanctuary in the Brisbane suburb of Fig Tree Pocket was opened in 1927 as a response to the slaughter.

54 http://www.mackay.qld.gov.au/about_council/news_and_media/media_releases/parks_named_in_honour_of_pioneers

55 Townsville Bulletin, *Townsville Daily Bulletin*, Fri 14 Mar 1913, page 4 http://nla.gov.au/nla.news-article58177622

56 Oral history from Delma Haack

57 From the memoirs of Annie Ditton

58 Qld DC 1891/2610 5701, Mackay, 29 Mar 1891, Marion Ditton

59 From the memoirs of Annie Ditton

60 From the memoirs of Annie Ditton

61 Qld MC 1891/1410 1168, Mackay, 3 Nov 1891, Sarah Barron & Abraham Ditton

62 Northern development, *Townsville Daily Bulletin*, Sat 29 Dec 1951, page 3 http://nla.gov.au/nla.news-article63397166

63 Qld MC 1864/36237 Calliope, 20 Jun 1864, Marion Stevenson & Abraham Ditton

64 Marion & Abraham are buried in the Presbyterian section of the Mackay Cemetery. The Episcopal Church may have been the closest available to Presbyterian in Calliope.

65 Commonwealth Electoral Roll, Herbert Townsville 1913, 1925, 1949

66 From the memoirs of Annie Ditton

67 Abraham Ditton (III): born 15 Aug 1868 Mackay, Qld – died 16 Apr 1946 Kurukan, Ingham Line, Qld

68 Commonwealth Electoral Roll, Herbert Mirani 1903, 1905

69 *Queensland Police Gazette*, Feb 1906 – two mares owned by Abraham III were shot at Reid river.

70 From the memoirs of Annie Ditton

71 *Ellenvale* was named for his wife whose middle name was Ellen and referred to as Nellie. (Annie Ditton).

72 Paraphrased from Annie Ditton's memoirs. Poor choices included selling breeders and drinking.

73 JCU archives: http://libserver.jcu.edu.au/specials/Archives/ditton.html

74 From the memoirs of Annie Ditton

75 Very fond of him, *Truth* (Brisbane), Sun 14 Feb 1943, page 12 http://nla.gov.au/nla.news-article202384106

76 From the memoirs of Annie Ditton

77 Qld MI 1895/C/1317, 5 Sep 1895, Mary Erdly & John Archibald Ditton

78 Commonwealth Electoral Roll, Herbert, Mia Mia 1903

79 *Queensland Police Gazette* 1915 Mackay summons

80 From the memoirs of Annie Ditton

81 Qld BI 1893/C7203, 04 Jan 1893, Ivy May Ditton

82 Qld MI 1911/C1962 & Qld BI 1912/C8167

83 Qld BI 1894/C7410, 13 Nov 1894, Ernie Ditton

84 Death notice, *Daily Mercury* (Mackay), Wed 18 Nov 1953, page 16 http://nla.gov.au/nla.news-article169661809

85 Horse shooting, *Daily Mercury* (Mackay), Sat 4 Dec 1915, page 6 http://nla.gov.au/nla.news-article172292830

86 Dynamiting fish, *Daily Mercury* (Mackay), Tue 11 Jan 1921, page 4 http://nla.gov.au/nla.news-article188689533

87 http://www.ww2roll.gov.au/Veteran.aspx?serviceId=A&veteranId=115526

88 Longford creek shooting, *Bowen Independent*, Fri 4 Oct 1946, page 1 http://nla.gov.au/nla.news-article195691349

89 Oral history from Delma Haack

90 Death notice, *Daily Mercury* (Mackay), Wed 18 Nov 1953, page 16 http://nla.gov.au/nla.news-article169661809

91 The child born in 1944 was a daughter of Isabella's daughter Anne Mavis born c. 1924. Isabella Graham had married Ewen McLennan in 1913 and lived at Mia Mia near Mackay. She separated from Ewan in 1942.

92 Qld State Archives Northern Ecclesiastical file wills (A17357) 1954 Ernest – Ernie 94

93 Qld DI 1954/C1978, 8 May 1954, Margaret Ditton

94 https://pubmed.ncbi.nlm.nih.gov/12315677/

95 Qld BC 1900/7529 8252, Ashford, Sandy Creek, 9 Mar 1900, Albert Robert Ditton

96 Information from Bob Ditton, grandson of Robert Ditton (1900–1991),

97 Mr. Ditton's departure, *Northern Herald* (Cairns), Wed 11 May 1927, page 7 http://nla.gov.au/nla.news-article149460112

98 Country golf title, *The Telegraph* (Brisbane), Wed 21 Aug 1935, page 2 http://nla.gov.au/nla.news-article180637633

99 Florence Christine Wenck 12 Mar 1924, divorced 1944 and Ethel May Brown Johnston 22 Dec 1945

100 Ditton / Bailey Family Tree http://www.ditton.info/index.htm

101 No Qld BI entry found. Birth year is calculated from age at other events.

102 Qld MI 1922/C3148, 25 Nov 1922, Gladys Elizabeth Ditton & Walter Henry Jewell

103 Jan 1976 letter from Val Jewel to Bill Ditton. Letter in possession of Delma Haack. The farm was sold for $400,000 in 1975 to a neighbour who then owned land 'From Palm Tree crossing to Patons'. He had bought Donald Gun's farm and Hendrick's farm.

104 Qld DC 1950/C4809, Lister Hospital Mackay, 10 Oct 1950, Gladys Elizabeth Jewell

105 Qld BI 1906/C7299, 6 Nov 1905, William Leslie Ditton

106 *The Courier Mail*, Brisbane 2 Jun 1999 Funeral Notices – Newspaper cutting

107 *Northside Chronicle*, Wed 30 Oct 1991, article by Nicole Hawkins – Newspaper cutting

108 Oral history from Delma Haack

109 Qld BI 1911/C7468, 28 Dec 1909, Clarence Isaac Ditton

110 Mackay items, *Townsville Daily Bulletin*, Thu 2 Apr 1931, page 7 http://nla.gov.au/nla.news-article61338596

111 In the courts, *Daily Mercury* (Mackay), Wed 8 Apr 1931 http://nla.gov.au/nla.news-article170417744

112 Summons Court, *Daily Mercury* (Mackay), Tue 8 Mar 1932, page 7 http://nla.gov.au/nla.news-article170756913

113 Summons Court, *Daily Mercury* (Mackay), Tue 6 Jan 1931, page 3 http://nla.gov.au/nla.news-article170747930

114 Summons Court, *Daily Mercury* (Mackay), Tue 8 Mar 1932, page 7 http://nla.gov.au/nla.news-article170756913

115 e.g. In the courts, *Daily Mercury* (Mackay), Thu 27 Dec 1934, page 8 http://nla.gov.au/nla.news-article172972244
& Petty Sessions, *Daily Mercury* (Mackay), Sat 14 Mar 1936, page 9 http://nla.gov.au/nla.news-article172909440

116 Qld MI 1940/C748, 26 Dec 1939, Eileen Ellen Connors & Clarence Isaac Ditton
& Qld DC 1969/10339, Chermside Hospital, 5 Nov 1969, Clarence Isaac Ditton

117 Qld BC 1913/C8810, Alfred St, Mackay, 21 Aug 1913, Catherine Muriel Ditton

118 Personal, *Daily Mercury* (Mackay), Fri 23 Aug 1935, page 9 http://nla.gov.au/nla.news-article173213381

119 Letters …, *Townsville Daily Bulletin*, Sat 15 Dec 1928, page 15 http://nla.gov.au/nla.news-article61053223
& Letters …,*Townsville Daily Bulletin*, Sat 16 Feb 1929, page 15 http://nla.gov.au/nla.news-article60229149

120 Commonwealth Electoral Roll 1947

121 Other researchers have confused her with her distant cousin Kathleen Muriel of Sutton Forest, NSW.

122 Oral history form Delma Haack

123 Ryersonindex.org MacDonald, Catherine Muriel, *The Courier Mail*, 9 Oct 1995

124 Qld BC 1896/7363, Ashford near Mackay, 1 Oct 1896, Rupert James Ditton

125 Qld DC 1904/2396 8036, Ashford near Mackay, 18 Jan 1904, Rupert Ditton

126 Qld BI 1898/C7013 & Qld DI 1899/C3007

127 Qld BI 1902/C7248 & Qld DI 1902/C2889

128 Qld DC 1916/ 895 9852, Sandy Creek near Mackay, 18 Jan 1916, Abraham Ditton

129 Memorial plaque was arranged by Delma & Graham Haack of Melbourne and Barbara Edmonds of Mackay.

130 *Daily Mercury* (Mackay), Wed 2 Jun 1993, Family wants pioneer remembered – newspaper cutting

131 Oral history passed from William Ditton to his daughter Delma.

132 Letters …, *Townsville Daily Bulletin*, Sat 16 Feb 1929, page 15 http://nla.gov.au/nla.news-article60229149

133 Commonwealth Electoral Roll – The street number may have been 30A, as Val Jewell said in 1976, he had 'bought into Brisbane Street' and 30A Brisbane St was his address at that time. (Now a car park)

134 Calculated from Val Jewell's Jan 1976 letter to Bill Ditton where he says he had recently sold the farm and he had been on the farm for the best part of 43 years.

135 Qld DC 1935/ 3205 13592, Mater Hospital, Mackay, 15 Aug 1935, Sarah Jane Ditton

136 Family notices, *Daily Mercury* (Mackay), Tue 15 Aug 1939, page 6 http://nla.gov.au/nla.news-article169825700

137 Mackay district development, *Daily Mercury* (Mackay), Wed 21 Aug 1935, page 6 http://nla.gov.au/nla.news-article173211250

138 Oral history from Delma Haack

139 The Public Curator, *Townsville Daily Bulletin*, Wed 6 May 1936, page 12 http://nla.gov.au/nla.news-article62763453

140 This story about Jack O'Hanlon was published in the *Queensland Family Historian* the journal of the Queensland Family History Society in Nov 2018 Vol 39 Number 4, pages 128 – 129, author Clem Ditton.

141 Bowen Shooting Case, *Cairns Post*, Tue 1 Oct 1946, page 1 http://nla.gov.au/nla.news-article42530446

142 Proserpine will dispute, *Townsville Daily Bulletin*, 11 Sep 1950, page 7 http://nla.gov.au/nla.news-article63095481

143 Third day will dispute, *Townsville Daily Bulletin*, 13 Sep 1950, page 7 http://nla.gov.au/nla.news-article63092530

144 Second day will dispute, *Townsville Daily Bulletin*, 12 Sep 1950, page 7 http://nla.gov.au/nla.news-article63100828

145 Ditton not guilty, *Townsville Daily Bulletin*, 1 May 1947, page 4 http://nla.gov.au/nla.news-article62903959

146 Fourth day will dispute, *Townsville Daily Bulletin,* 14 Sep 1950, page 7 http://nla.gov.au/nla.news-article63091535

147 The murder trial said it was Jack's first gun but the will trial said it was Ernie's gun.

148 O'Hanlon will case verdict, *Townsville Daily Bulletin,* 4 Oct 1950, page 2 http://nla.gov.au/nla.news-article63171619

149 Talks with PM, *Townsville Daily Bulletin,* 20 Mar 1953, page 6 http://nla.gov.au/nla.news-article62485567

150 Interest in farm only way …, *Daily Mercury* (Mackay), 11 Jul 1951, page 2 http://nla.gov.au/nla.news-article172235647

151 Talks with PM, *Townsville Daily Bulletin,* 20 Mar 1953, page 6 http://nla.gov.au/nla.news-article62485567

152 Commonwealth Electoral Rolls, Kennedy Qld 1954, 1963, 1968

153 Qld DC 1970/7444 3744, Proserpine, 30 Aug 1970, Wilhelmina Agnes O'Hanlon

154 Photo *The jubilee of Mackay: 1862–1912*, *Daily Mercury*, Mackay, 1912 page 16 http://nla.gov.au/nla.obj-52794186

155 An unattractive car was parked in the space between the houses, which spoiled a combined photo. Information regarding houses was from J. Chaplin, *A Stroll Around the Green*, Woodchurch Local History Society, Ashford, 2002.

156 AB Clinton, born 1855 – died 1906

157 Picture gives glimpse of pioneering heritage, *The Daily Mercury* (Mackay), Wed 2 Jun 1993 – newspaper cutting

158 Qld State Archives, Series 14033 Item 51827 selection # 927

159 Photo was from the collection of William Ditton (1905–1999). The caption was on the back in quotes.

160 Photo from the collection of Delma Haack.

161 Photo from the collection of Delma Haack

162 Photo from the collection of Allan Ditton

163 Photo from the collection of Allan Ditton

164 Photo from the collection of Delma Haack

165 Photo from the collection of Delma Haack

166 Photo from the collection of Delma Haack

167 Photo from the collection of Maureen Reinders

168 Photo from the collection of Delma Haack

169 *Mackay in pictures 150 years of History* published by the *Daily Mercury* (Mackay) in 2012, page 83. The photo was misattributed as being from the 1980s. The 1930s or possibly the 1920s would be more likely

170 Photo from the collection of Delma Haack

171 Photo from *The Aftermath* by the Mackay Historical Society & Museum Inc. page 25

Chapter 9

Frontier orphan

The search for Sarah Barron's origins

This chapter explores the riddle of the origins of Sarah Jane Barron, who married Abraham Ditton in Mackay, Qld in November 1891.[1] On the marriage record, she stated she was 27 and was born in Townsville to James Barron, a sea captain and Annie (née Laurie). The best match in the official records is the family of James and Anne Barron, who were in North Qld from 1865. They had a daughter named Sarah Jane, born around 1874.[2]

However, this means the following contradictions and issues, need to be addressed:

1. Sarah is possibly 17 at the time of her marriage instead of the recorded 27.
2. Her mother's maiden name is Farley rather than the recorded Lawrie/Laurie.
3. Her father, James, is listed as a 'carrier' rather than the recorded 'sea captain'.
4. All the other children of this family died young. Did this Sarah Jane survive?

The following are some key facts for the documented family of James and Anne Barron.

◊ James states he was born in St John's, Newfoundland, around 1843.[3]
◊ Anne (née Farley) states she was born in County Westmeath[4], Ireland, around 1844.[5]
◊ They were married at St Mary's RC Church, in the four-year-old Bowen on 3 September 1865.[6]
◊ On the marriage record, James was a 'labourer'. Usual place of residence was Bowen for both.[7]
◊ Their first child, William, was born in Bowen on 13 June 1866
◊ William died seven days later of 'convulsions'.
◊ James is recorded as an 'engine driver' and his mark reveals he is probably illiterate.[8]
◊ Their second child, Mary Anne, was born on 15 May 1867 at Conway Station.[9]
◊ On the birth record, James is recorded as a 'labourer'.[10]
◊ James is in the Post Office Directory of 1868 under, Carriers, Carters & Draymen for Conway.[11]
◊ Mary Anne died 15 November 1868, also of 'convulsions', on the Cape River district goldfields.[12]
◊ On the death record, James' profession is recorded as 'carrier'.[13]
◊ A third child, Mary Jane, was born in Townsville on 5 January 1870.[14]
◊ Mary Jane's death is not recorded, but it is implied she died shortly afterwards.[15]

◊ James applied for a Miner's Right for Ravenswood in September 1871 and October 1872.[16]
◊ In December 1872, James applied for a Miner's Right, which covered Charters Towers.[17]
◊ Mary, the fourth child, was born in Townsville on 2 May 1873.[18]
◊ This last Mary dies sixteen days later of 'debility from birth' in Townsville.[19]
◊ James' profession was recorded as 'carrier' on both the birth and death records.
◊ The 1874 Post Office Directory has James as a 'carrier' in Walker Street, Townsville.[20]
◊ An unclaimed letter addressed to James Barron was registered at Townsville in January 1874.[21]
◊ A child, Patrick was born in Cooktown on 24 February 1875.[22]
◊ Sarah Jane was recorded on Patrick's birth record as a one-year-old living sibling.
◊ Patrick died just one day later, also of 'convulsions'.[23]

No Australian immigration record has been found for James Barron or Anne Farley/Laurie.[24] The Palmer goldrush had started late in the dry season of 1873.[25] The wet season (December – March) made the country impassable.[26] It appears the Barrons, like the majority of Townsville residents, left for Cooktown, the access port for the Palmer River goldfields. It would have been wise to stay in Townsville until Sarah Jane's birth and for the end of the wet season. Therefore, they may have left around April 1874 and did not get a chance to register her birth in Townsville.[27] The unclaimed letter implied they may have left in late 1873 to get in early on the rush.

Panoramic view of Townsville's North Shore circa 1890. Kissing Point is the point in the distance at right.[151]

The oral history

Some oral history only came to light in recent years after much record-based searching. According to that oral history, Sarah had been living at an orphanage in Mackay, and Abraham Ditton went looking for a housekeeper after the death of his first wife, Marion. At this time, Sarah was either late in her term or had given birth to her illegitimate son, Arthur.

However, the story about the orphanage does not fit with the recorded history of the orphanage in Mackay. The only official orphanage in Mackay, St Josephs, closed in 1885 and the remaining children were sent to the orphanage in Rockhampton.[28] Sarah's name does not appear on the admission register of any of the North Qld orphanages.[29] However, it was said she had a deep affection for the local Catholic priest. Given the timing, the priest was likely to be Father Pierre-Marie Bucas, who was a highly regarded and influential priest at Mackay in Sarah's time. He was a champion of the underdog such as Indigenous people, Kanakas, escaped ex-convicts from New Caledonia, orphans and the poor. He was also the priest who ran St Joseph's orphanage, Mackay, before it was closed in 1885.[30] He may have assisted Sarah during her predicament. Another clear implication of the story about the orphanage is she was not with her family at this time and it implies she was of a young age. A note in her son Bill's papers[31] claims she was: 'The first white child born at Kissing Point'.[32] This is a rocky headland, a short distance from the early Townsville settlement.[33]

Oral history regarding her parents, had them as Irish. Her father, James, was a sea captain who travelled to Cape Town, South Africa and to India. He died in India when he accidently fell between two ships at dock. He was returning to his ship worse for drink. It is not known when this occurred, but it is likely to have been between 1877 and 1890. Oral history also puts him on the arduous track from Cooktown to the Palmer River gold strike. This is also where we can place the James Barron of the family detailed above. In the oral history version, he turned back when he saw, through his spyglass, Aboriginal men carrying away a European man on a stretcher. The man had one arm pointing straight up, implying rigor mortis. James interpreted the sight as a prelude to cannibalism.[34] There had been many tales of cannibalism in this district printed in the papers of the times and later reports.[35] Subsequent anthropological investigations have questioned whether those reports were correct.[36]

The key document

Extract from Patrick Barron's 1875 birth record from Cooktown, showing Sarah Jane as a living '1 Year' old.[152]

The birth record for Patrick Barron in 1875 in Cooktown, identifies Sarah Jane as a living '1 Year' old.[37] Birth certificates for earlier siblings do not reference Sarah Jane. Sarah Jane has no birth record of her own. What follows is a series of hypotheses which explore how we may be able to link the older Sarah Jane Barron who married Abraham Ditton to this younger Sarah Jane Barron.

Issue 1: The age problem

A simple hypothesis is Sarah Jane's age was adjusted because she was marrying the 52-year-old Abraham, who also adjusted his age to 48 on the marriage record.[38] His first wife, Marion, had died less than eight months earlier at the age of 57.[39] The first recorded European birth in Townsville was on 25 August 1865, which was after the year 1864, which age 27 implies.[40] Perhaps significantly, Abraham's oldest child, Isabella, was born in April 1865.[41] If Sarah's age was adjusted, this may explain the choice of age. In the scenario where a 17-year-

old girl with a newborn child moved to Abraham's farm, then she was likely to be sharing the farm with his sons aged 21, 18 and 13.[42] That could have been a motive to raise Sarah's declared age.

The older family would have known the circumstances of the relationship but may not have been fully aware of the age gap. If it was done, then this was more likely done to preserve Abraham's standing within his family and possibly within the community. It may have also been meant as some deterrence to the two young Ditton men who were older than her – i.e. they were not to treat Sarah as a peer or as a prospect, but rather as a stepmother. The young men were possibly living in the Ditton farmhouse at that time, although we know their older brother Abraham had left home at the age of seventeen.[43] Therefore this may have been partly Abraham's suggestion rather than being Sarah's invention alone.

An observation to accommodate within the hypothesis is that Abraham's age was roughly

Charlotte St Cooktown late 1870s. It was lined with a mile of commercial buildings at the peak of the rush.[153]

correct on records at the end of their child raising, but Sarah's was not adjusted – e.g. on the birth record of Catherine Muriel, their last child, Sarah claims an age of 48 and Abraham was recorded as 75 when 73 would have been more accurate.[44] An official age of 48 for a mother is credible, but starting to get unusual. It must be said, 73 for the father is somewhat more unusual. Marion had her last child with Abraham at 45.[45] On earlier records, Abraham still allows himself some vanity with a two-year downwards adjustment for Rupert James' birth record.[46] We see Sarah recorded as a 32-year-old in March 1900, when 35 would have been more consistent.[47] But these lapses were not common. Was Sarah deriving some benefit from maintaining the deception? It is difficult to think of any particular benefit that could be gained apart from the initial one, or unless the deception needs to be maintained within the family.

Sarah's burial record identifies she was aged 63 when she died in August 1935. That would put her birth year around 1871–72. Her youngest son, the 26-year-old Clarence (Clarry) appears to be the informant for that information.[48] Had she partially 'fessed up' to her youngest children now that Abraham had passed away? If there was a legal issue, it was not related to the age of consent, which was 12–13 in Qld at that time.[49] A large age gap on official records may have drawn more comment and questions from officials, e.g. regarding the circumstances of Marion's death. What may be at play though, is that an age greater than twenty means parental consent to marry is not required.[50]

Sarah was admitted to the Mackay hospital on 13 July 1891.[51] She gave birth to Arthur on 25 July and she was discharged on 8 August.[52] Compared to other admissions for pregnancy to this hospital, stays of one month were not unusual. The minimum time was two weeks. The register, records her age as 26.[53] If this is an invention, then this is when it is first evident, and it implies that

the offer from Abraham is already on the table. It also would be subject to the month-long scrutiny of medical staff, so this is another challenge to the hypothesis. To pull off such a deception she would have to have the appearance of someone aged beyond her actual years. The conditions of pioneer tropical Qld would probably assist with that.

There doesn't appear to be any official advantage in being of a more mature age. The only prospect for Sarah, the orphan, to keep her child would be to have the support of others. There was not yet any government support available for Sarah to keep her child. The only support offered by society was to take the child into an orphanage. Did Abraham stipulate that his prospective bride had to be above a certain age? Was it Sarah's idea

Mackay hospital in 1887. Entries in the records from 1890 for this hospital are the first time that an older Sarah Jane Barron first appears in any records.[154]

alone to raise her age? Adoptions at this stage were informal affairs. The state formally recognised these arrangements in 1905. State supervised legal adoptions were not introduced by Qld until 1921 and then more comprehensive laws were implemented in 1935.[54] As Arthur was staying with his birth mother, no formalities were required in any case. This raises the question as to where Sarah spent her childhood. If it was in Mackay, then pulling off such a deception would be difficult. If she grew up elsewhere, then that would make things easier.

Assuming Sarah retains her actual birthday, but manipulates her age, then in terms of possible birthdays, the adult Sarah appears to celebrate it between 1 October and 3 November.[55] The infant Sarah has an older sister, Mary, born 2 May 1873, and a younger brother, Patrick, born on 24 February 1875, which suggests a possible birth date for the younger Sarah between March and May 1874.[56] If the younger brother was born prematurely, then this could be extended several months, but October is too far. These facts are another challenge to the simple hypothesis. However, it is quite possible Sarah did not know her actual birthday for the reasons explored later, in which case the challenge around the birthday date would be resolved.

The portion of Patrick's record that mentions Sarah

There is evidence officials checked registry entries. Three years after Mary Jane's birth, an official corrected the marriage date and the spelling of Anne Farley's maiden name.[57] They did not seem too concerned with the accuracy of ages however, as James and Anne's ages are not consistent across records. The same ages were claimed for both James and Anne on two birth records more than three years apart.[58]

Sarah Jane appears to be recorded as a '1 year' old on Patrick's birth record. All the dates above would put her as less than a year old. Maybe officials are instructed to record only whole years and that anomaly is resolved. There is a possibility she was born before Mary in Townsville and for various reasons was not recorded at that time and only mentioned once the family had moved to a new locality. The tragic procession of three Marys, who all die, suggests Sarah arrived after that sequence.[59] Having stated that, however, there is a curiosity in the birth record of Patrick. The number of deceased children is understated by one (i.e. three instead of four).[60] Is it at all possible Mary Jane became Sarah Jane? On third Mary's birth record all three prior children are listed as dead.[61] This clearly implies Mary Jane has died although no death record has been found for her. The two other bits of evidence, which suggest this possibility, are her age at death given by her son, Clarry, and the presence of the unclaimed letter at Townsville registered in January 1874, which suggests the Barrons have left Townsville by that time. On balance however, it is difficult to explain away why she is counted as deceased on the third Mary's birth record. Therefore, the evidence is against Mary Jane becoming Sarah Jane, but it remains a distant possibility.

An explanation for the possible deliberate omission from the birth record would be if Sarah Jane's origins were other than the marriage. This could account for up to ten years. The birth would have gone unrecorded until an opportunity presented itself and an attitude had changed. On

Some other 'Y's by the hand of the Cooktown registrar, James C Baird, showing a difference to Sarah's entry

Qld birth records from later decades, the entry for siblings is headed 'Previous Children of Relationship' as opposed to 'Previous Issue'. If that was the intention of recording sibling details, then maybe Sarah Jane did not qualify in the eyes of some prior officials.

Looking closely at Patrick's birth record, there is not a clean entry near Sarah Jane's age. The 'Y' of year extends noticeably higher than the 'Y' of year in most other entries on the page by the same hand. There are a few others which are also high, but this stroke does not look as if it belongs to the 'Y'. All other high 'Y' characters look clean, resulting from a smooth stroke. There is an asterisk like mark below the age. Is this an untidy attempt to record '11'? If so, is it years or months? The singular form of 'year' is chosen rather than the plural, but at the very least there appears to be some interruption or revision in recording of the age of Sarah Jane.

There was clearly some discussion at the registry about some of the facts provided, possibly about the marriage or possibly why their surviving daughter's birth had not been recorded and some reasons why, resulting in some notations being made on the record by the registrar, JC Baird. Patrick's entry is the only one on the page that has the words: 'After declaration duly made according to law'.

If Sarah was born in October 1864, then her age at this time would be ten years and four months. She would have been born in Bowen rather than Townsville, as Townsville had no European residents until November 1864.[63] No births of non-indigenous children were recorded in Townsville until August 1865. Her childhood memories would have included Townsville, as that was where she would have spent several years.

Incidentally, when this record was first provided in 1988 as a typed certificate, the transcriber had typed the name as 'Sarah Janet' with the age of

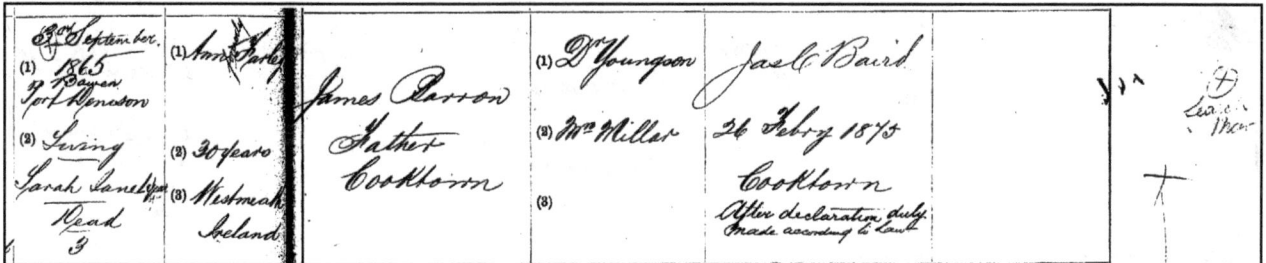

The right hand side of Patrick's registration includes a margin note and the recording of a declaration.

It appears that the registrar was new to his job as he made a number of errors when registering the birth, some of which were subsequently corrected; e.g. incorrectly adding a surname to Patricks name (corrected with a margin note the following year), writing 'formally' vertically before Annie's maiden name and adding Bowen over Port Denison.[62] In addition to the mark beside Sarah Jane's entry, the marriage date has a circled 'X' beside it. There is a note in the margin also with a circled 'X' which appears to be 'Search Mar'. Is that a notation to check on the marriage or to check for Sarah Jane's birth record in March?

'1 year'. This means there were either two uses of the one big stroke or there were considered to be two separate strokes (one for 't' and one for '1'). This demonstrates why it was greatly appreciated when the Queensland Registrar gave the option of providing electronic scans of historical records, rather than just the typed certificates.

The only known photograph of Sarah Jane tends to support the suggestion she survived past the age of sixty, but not conclusively. We are potentially dealing with a person who looked older than her age from her teenage years, and somewhat indelicately, we should also consider the generally poor state of dental health prevailing at that time.[64]

Issue 2: The maiden name problem

Anne Farley was born in County Westmeath Ireland and was illiterate.[65] Laurie and Farley are too dissimilar to consider that there was some consistent confusion based on a thick accent. More credibly, it appears Sarah Jane lost her mother before she had a chance to learn her mother's maiden name properly.

An 'Ann Barron' of the right age, 31, died in Cooktown on 2 June 1876 of alcoholic poisoning.[66]

Contemporary newspaper reports and Hector Holthouse, in *River of Gold,* described how the frontier spirits that were concocted on-site had a diabolical reputation.[67]

The informant was William Hartley, the Cooktown Land Commissioner and prominent local businessman.[68] He was probably not fully 'informed'. The husband would appear to be absent if an unrelated person was being relied upon to be the informant. It is therefore probable this

The death record for an Ann Barron in Cooktown 2 June 1876.[155]

was Sarah Jane's mother as the name, location and age correctly align, and some other details roughly align, but other items conflict. The aligning details were that she had been in the colonies for a number of years (eleven versus seven) and she was married. Her birthplace, 'Kulborough' has not been located anywhere, but it may be an accent-influenced record of 'Kilberry', which is a town in County Meath, a county bordering Westmeath. The conflicting items are her husband was named as 'George' and there were no children living or dead listed in the space provided on the record.

If this was not her, then which Ann(e) Barron was it? No other documented contenders exist. There are also no further records of any other matching Anne/Annie Barron after this event.

There is a George Barron in the Qld electoral records about this time, and he is resident in Charters Towers in 1874–1878, which potentially is a match, given the link via gold mining of the two locations.[69] Indications to date are, he is probably the George Barron, labourer, who died in Ingham in 1929 aged 84 and who was married to Agnes Bruce in 1866, meaning he would be eliminated.[70] The next closest recorded George Barron to him, within a ten-year range, is an older cook in Roma, 1600 kilometres away.[71]

Once again, the oral account of Sarah Jane being an orphan when marrying Abraham is consistent with the scenario of this Ann Barron being her mother.

Perhaps most significantly, there is an evergreen Scottish ballad named *Annie Laurie* which has existed in written down form since 1823. The troops in the Crimea popularised it. Sarah or her carer, quite probably, heard it and therefore it may have inspired the choice of her mother's name, if the real maiden name was not known or correctly remembered. The ballad has its roots in a true-life romance between a couple from opposite sides of the Jacobite conflict. Annie's father was a royalist,

and her suitor, William Douglas, was a supporter of the Jacobite cause.[72]

Evidence this song was enduring and well-known is provided by two early Hollywood movies that dealt with the romance. Lillian Gish played the title role in the first (1927), a silent version, and Ann Rutherford took the lead in the talkie remake (1936).[73] The ballad was sung in the 1945 Hollywood movie, *A tree grows in Brooklyn*.[74] The popular 1970s Scottish folk group, The Corries, have also recorded it.

There is an anecdote from the first year of WWI when British troops in the trenches heard a German voice sing the first verse of this song in perfect English on a still winter's night. The British troops replied with applause. The first verse of the ballad is as follows:

Maxwelton's braes are bonnie,
Where early fa's the dew,
'Twas there that Annie Laurie
Gi'ed me her promise true.
Gi'ed me her promise true
Which ne'er forgot will be,
And for bonnie Annie Laurie
I'd lay me down and dee.[75]

Issue 3: The sea captain problem

A probable explanation for the uninformed informant and subsequent missing details is provided by the *Rockhampton Bulletin*, on 9 June 1876, which reported James Barron was one of six prisoners brought to Rockhampton the previous day by the *Bunyip* and in turn from the steamer *Leichhardt* from up north. James had been 'sentenced by the Cooktown Bench to two months' imprisonment for assault'.[76]

This appears to set up the most appalling tragedy for this young family. James would have been in custody at the time of Anne's demise. Her death, if known about, would have been a mitigating part of his defence. The *Leichhardt* left Cooktown on 3 June.[77] Anne died on 2 June.[78] It is most likely his arrest and trial came before her death. His arrest probably contributed to the situation leading to her death. Whether he knew she had died before he left is not known. The fact the officials recording Anne's death record had not connected Anne with James suggests this communication was missed.

James had been in trouble with the law previously. On 18 March 1875, he faced court over a charge of fowl stealing. The following article suggests James acted without Annie's approval.

James Barron, was charged at the instance of Nicholas Tantovich with having stole one fowl his property. Mr Cooper appeared for the prosecution and Mr Godfrey for the defendant. From the evidence of the prosecutor who resides at the Two-Mile it appeared that on Saturday last, from information he had received he passed at the back of the accused's tent and saw him in the act of plucking a fowl which he identified as his property, and on going to the front and pushing past the wife of the accused found him at the back and a box turned upside down, upon lifting the box prosecutor found his fowl partially plucked and took both box and fowl and placing them outside the tent called a man named Miller who came quickly followed by Mrs Miller, Mrs Sullivan and Mrs Tantovich who all recognised the fowl as the one in question belonging to the prosecutor. The fowl being remarkable for having no tail and its peculiar color, the value was stated at 14s. Prosecutor gave the box and fowl in charge of Miller while he went for the police and when he returned the box was gone, and he was told it was burnt. Henry Miller a neighbour corroborated the evidence of the previous witness, and stated that the wife of the accused came to him and said "how can I help it, it is all his own doing" Miller then went away, he recognised the fowl as belonging to Tantovich. Hester Sullivan, also a neighbour saw the fowl and box in the charge of Miller and identified the fowl as the property of the prosecutor, after Miller had gone away Mrs Barron took both box and bird away and threw them both on to a large fire burning at the back; a little black boy who stays with the accused afterwards took the box out of the fire. Mr Godfrey cross examined the foregoing witness but failed in any way to shake their testimony and the bench considering the offence fully proved, sentenced the accused to pay the value of the fowl 14s, a fine of £5, professional costs £3 3s and 7s costs of court.[79]

The tragic procession of infant deaths was not the only misfortune this family had thrust at them. They were financially drained as well. Miners who returned from the goldfields with little or no money got stranded in a growing crowd of people without sufficient funds to book their passage out.[80] Anyone with money or gold would be welcomed and then fleeced in one of the drinking shanties, opium dens or bordellos lining both sides of Charlotte Street for over a mile.[81] If a miner had no money, they resorted to labouring or thievery.

A Danish immigrant, Thorvald Weitemeyer, described the poor living conditions, the difficulties in obtaining supplies and the nature of people there – many loafers, pickpockets and cardsharpers. He observed, 'the robbing of tents was an everyday occurrence'. He describes Cooktown and the track to the Palmer as being a desperate and desolate place for most.[82] The polymath, David Hill, with the benefit of knowledge of the world's major goldrushes has described the Palmer goldrush as 'one of the wildest, most lawless and dangerous rushes the world has ever seen'.[83]

James was released onto the streets of Rockhampton during July and was not returned to Cooktown.[84] James had some anger management issues, not assisted by his desperate circumstances. The *Rockhampton Bulletin* from November 1876, has the following item:

At the Police Court yesterday, before the P. M., James Barron pleaded guilty to a charge of furious riding in East-street, and was fined £2, in default of immediate payment one month's imprisonment.[85]

What then of the two-year-old Sarah Jane, when Anne dies, and James is imprisoned 1,350 kilometres away? If we assume she has survived, then she would have been in immediate need of care. There appears to be little in the way of community infrastructure. There was one Catholic priest in town but the community was not yet in a position to provide an orphanage.[86] It was probably up to some kind-hearted neighbour to take this child in and give her a home, at least until James could resume responsibility for her. This guardian may have known some details of her parents, which were later passed onto Sarah as she grew up.

If the authorities finally did connect Anne's death and the imprisonment of James leaving Sarah Jane alone, they may have realised they had some responsibility in the matter and taken steps to remedy the situation. There is a vague suggestion from an uncorroborated note in some family papers that Sarah spent some time in the care of nuns in Rockhampton.[87] Of course, if Sarah Jane was twelve years old then her options were greater. At that age, in these times, she could start working for a living and so would not need to rely on charity to the same extent, but she would still have needed a home.

There is one more intriguing mention of a James Barron in the public record of North Qld. In the telegraph news of several newspapers from March 1903: 'The body of James Barron, the pioneer who was drowned while crossing the Barron River in flood, has not been recovered.[88] It was probably swept over the falls'. A subsequent investigation found a Wild River Times article. This is the relevant local newspaper from Herberton and other Atherton Tableland communities, which shows this was a misprint, as the person who drowned was James Robson and the body had been recovered several days later.[89] This news telegram went to several journals as the mistake was duplicated in the remote newspapers. Incidentally, the Barron River was named after Thomas Barron, a Brisbane-based police chief clerk, who is no known relation to James.

Did James unite with his daughter after his time in Rockhampton? The memory of him as a 'sea captain' suggests not, or at least, not for long. All of his activities from 1865 to 1876 indicate James was a land-based carrier rather than some kind of 'sea-going carrier' – e.g. the family's journey from Bowen 190 kilometres south-west to Conway Station, then 300 kilometres west to Cape River

and from there to Townsville via Ravenswood and Charters Towers, clearly demonstrates James was a land-based carrier at this stage of his life.[90] It probably meant that he had a team of bullocks pulling a wagon or dray.

The *Port Denison* (Bowen) *Almanac* of 1868 briefly described the Cape River goldfields that opened up in June 1867, and by October 1867, had '700 to 800 souls' working the diggings. A significant proportion of these were Chinese, who had followed the goldrushes in Australia since the early 1850s. However, this was the first rush in Qld allowing Chinese to participate.[91] A contemporary report described the general assemblage of diggers as being 'the dregs of the southern goldfields'.[92] The warden of the goldfield described it as 'the roughest and toughest goldfield in Australia'.[93] This was the only northern district bushrangers operated in, to any notable extent.[94]

A Jas Barron, presumably this same James, applied for miner's rights to the Ravenswood goldfield in September 1871 and again in October 1872.[95] This implies he was supplementing his carrier work with some gold prospecting. The Ravenswood goldfield had been opened in 1868, and by 1871, it was home to 900 people and primarily a reef mining location, meaning the easily won alluvial or surface gold was in decline. By 1872, the rush had moved ninety kilometres to what became the inland metropolis of Charters Towers.[96] In December 1872, James had applied for a miner's right covering the new field.

In the decade under examination, we see James was a carrier, a labourer, an engine driver and a goldminer or prospector. Even the James Barron from the oral history was not exclusively a sea captain. He was also a prospective goldminer. These two people could possibly be the same.

Perhaps he took to the sea to escape his land-based troubles, but that implies he left his only surviving daughter in the care of others. James states he was born in St John's, Newfoundland, which would almost certainly have involved utilising sea-going vessels. Perhaps his early working life involved working on ships. Further research concentrating on Newfoundland has found families of Barrons (including one named James) owning and operating schooners, brigantines and barques in the 1850s and 1860s.[97] So it is possible James, the carrier, had a fallback profession of seafaring.

Whether James was actually a seafarer or Sarah romanticised her origins, with 'sea captain' used to explain an absent father, the result appears to be the same – i.e. she was effectively orphaned. If she did invent the missing details of her father's life, then this is consistent with how she dealt with her mother's maiden name. Others in her life may have associated her family name with the sea, as there were several Captain Barrons in newspapers of the time and in history.[98]

This research has found several James Barrons in other parts of the world with a connection to the sea, but none with a clear link to Qld or even an Annie. The most promising were as follows: A sea captain, James Barron, born in Dundee Scotland in 1827, perished with nineteen others in the shipwreck of the *St Vincent* off Palliser, New Zealand, on 18 February 1869, whilst sailing from Wellington for Lyttelton.[99] He was described as 'a stranger on the coast'.[100] He had operated in the Australian area for about one year and in the China and East Indies trade for approximately twelve years prior to that.[101] This was initially considered a possibility, but it is unlikely, as the ill-fated voyage originated in Cardiff, Wales.[102] It is not known if he had undertaken any other prior voyages to Australia. Also, no direct connection with Qld or an Annie has been found. His mother in Dundee dedicated a church memorial 'in memory of her husband John Barron, shipmaster who was drowned off Filey Briggs, 28 December, 1849 aged 46 years also of her son James M Barron shipmaster who was drowned in Cooks Strait, New Zealand 14 February 1869 aged 41 years and her

two children who died in infancy'.[103] No mention of a family James left behind. Indications are the religion of this sea captain was Protestant.

There was another sea captain named James Barron, also from Dundee, who operated in Australian waters around the right time. He died at sea aged 40, whilst sailing from Newcastle, NSW, to San Francisco in 1866 on the barque, *Arica*.[104] Prior to that (1858–63), he commanded the barque, *Adriatic*.[105] The identified origin ports for the voyages include: Dundee, Mauritius, Guam, Melbourne and Newcastle.[106] All of the problems with the previous sea captain apply to this one as well: no documented Annie and no documented connection to Qld. Thankfully, there is no James Barron listed amongst the masters of ships that were active in the black-birding (Kanaka) trade that operated out of Queensland at this time.[107]

A fact against James, the carrier, subsequently becoming a sea captain is that he was most probably illiterate or unable to write, given his signing with a mark. Being a sea captain required full literacy.[108]

A whimsical thought was, if we are dealing with a twelve-year-old Sarah born outside of the marriage, then her mother may have told Sarah her (biological) father was a sea captain and so, James Barron, sea captain, could have been an amalgam. In light of all available evidence, this proposition is now rejected, but it would not be without precedent. Female passenger liaisons with sailors of all ranks on the long journey out to Australia have been documented in a number of instances – e.g. the 1866 voyage of the *Bayswater* to Rockhampton from Liverpool ended with a mass desertion of sailors and was followed with the following eyewitness account of their arrest: 'A number of the new immigrant girls were very aggressive. They literally threw themselves at the handcuffed sailors, embraced and kissed them and apparently tried to get them away from the police'.[109] A tyrannical second mate and an ineffectual captain had precipitated a number of incidents during the voyage, resulting in a series of criminal court cases.[110] The deserting sailors had planned to join their loves in the new land, only to be thwarted by the cruel hand of authority. A sea captain would have had more options to control his own destiny.

One of the records found for various James Barrons that could not be eliminated as irrelevant was one found in Victoria. A James Barron, aged 73, died in a Melbourne hospital from kidney failure on 26 October 1900. A policeman found him at the Queens Wharf at Melbourne Docks in severe pain.[111] His death certificate named him as Jas Barren. No details of his mother, father or spouse were recorded on the certificate.[112] This could be Sarah's father.

Issue 4: The infant death problem

If her mother's death in Cooktown was confirmed, its cause would shine light on this sad history of infant mortality, but without hard information it cannot be easily determined how to separate cause from effect. There are death records for four of her siblings, including Patrick, her younger brother in 1875, but none for her as a child. This would suggest, if she did die, then she did not die in the period between Patrick's birth and her mother's death, as we would expect to see a record of it seeing they were resident in Cooktown.

The death of at least five infants within a decade would take a heavy emotional toll on the sturdiest of families. The Barrons were not just strangers to fortune – they were in crisis. The statistics for this time tell us more than one in ten children died before their first birthday.[113] Infant mortality was commonplace, but not as common as this[114], unless there was an underlying medical or lifestyle issue.[115] Accounts of how carriers worked in those days describe the whole family moving as a team, and the women would cook and assist whilst looking after any children.[116] The heat and the insects, the poor food, questionable water and

meagre medical aids would all play their part in this cruel Darwinian contest to favour only robust children. The welfare of children would seem to have been of secondary importance in these times. The pursuit of opportunities to escape the poverty of their origins appears to be a greater driving force.

If the infant, Sarah Jane, was alive when her mother died, then perhaps she moved into the care of someone who maintained an environment and regime more conducive to the survival of an infant. The days on the track may have come to an end. We also need to remember the particular challenges of this time and place. This family moved through some of the most dangerous country in Australia's colonial history. The Indigenous occupants of this territory took violent exception to these interlopers and killed numerous 'pioneers' and, of course in turn, were 'punished' for their resistance. In 1863, an Aboriginal raiding party killed the cook on Conway Station, as described in the memoirs of Andrew Murray, an early squatter and drover in the district.[117] James and Anne were living on this station just four years later.

PR Delamothe's account of Bowen's first hundred years identifies resistance in the area as the most tenacious ever put up by an Aboriginal community.[118] He believed the Bowen region was unique within the continent as it was only there, over a period of ten years or more, where numbers of Europeans killed or wounded exceeded the number of Aboriginal casualties. The Barrons were there at this time.

On the page from Townsville where the last Mary's death is recorded, there is also a record of the death of a William 'unknown' as a result of an Aboriginal attack. The first European to explore this territory, Edmund Kennedy, and three of his companions were killed by Aboriginal inhabitants in 1848.[119] In the Cooktown phase of their life, many miners and carriers succumbed to native attack. Some historians claim, 'thousands of them were killed on the way to the Palmer'.[120] More credible accounts using oral sources claim 'hundreds', with Chinese paying the highest price. Sober academic study using official records and contemporary written reports puts the figure much lower still.[121]

Many hazards faced miners in that challenging environment. A deadlier force than the Aboriginal inhabitants were the desperate rival miners who carried guns. Some of the other hazards in North Qld in the 1870s were some of the world's deadliest snakes, saltwater crocodiles and cassowaries.[122] If you ventured down to the sea, there were sharks, venomous jellyfish and octopus, stonefish and cone shells. Floods and cyclones took a toll, along with the more common culprits of alcohol, opium, disease, starvation, accidents and suicide. If James had tried to return to Cooktown via the inland route he had previously partially travelled, then an undocumented demise may well have awaited him.

Other records considered

A Sarah Jane Barron, aged 14, arrived in Townsville on 6 September 1887 on the *Duke of Devonshire* from Ireland, but then continued onto Brisbane. She was in company with an older Sarah Barron, identified as her mother.[123] Her origin is given as Durham, England. It presents exactly the same age problem. Research established this person as a different Sarah. She was a tailoress who never married and died in Qld in May 1968, aged 95. She spent some of her earlier years (e.g. 1903) in Charters Towers, but her subsequent life was in Brisbane. Her mother, Sarah, died in August 1927, in Brisbane, aged 87. Her father was a miner, named as 'Ino' on Sarah's death certificate and John in the immigration records.[124] A person named J Barron applied for timber-cutting licences for the years 1886 through to 1892, The first application is in Gympie and all later ones are in Charters Towers.[125] This is most likely John, as he has a demonstrated link with Charters Towers around this time.[126]

There is a family of Barrons (Father: James Joseph, Mother: Annie, with children Alice, Ellen, Louise, Agnes and Edith – but no Sarah listed) who arrive from England to Rockhampton on the ship *Scottish Hero* on 29 January 1884.[127] The obvious problems are the absence of Sarah, not being in Townsville or Australia until 1884, and James not being a sea captain (railway stationmaster). James died in 1934 at the age of 84. Annie died in May 1917. Her maiden name was Cox-Poole.[128]

An 1879 death index entry was found in the Indian Records which initially looked to fit in with the oral history.[129] A James Barron died in the port town of Thayetmyo, Bengal, India, aged 37. The actual death record revealed however that this James was a private in the British army and he died of cholera. Those details made it an unlikely fit for the James being sought. Thayetmyo was a trading post on the Irrawaddy River and is now within the nation of Myanmar.

There were six adult James Barrons recorded in Qld in the 1903 Commonwealth Roll.[130] One was the stationmaster. Another James Barron and his wife Jane are buried in Toowong Cemetery, Brisbane. Jane died in February 1898, aged 56 (i.e. b. c. 1842). James died in August 1916, aged 74 (i.e. b. c. 1832).[131] An English-born engineer lived at Wellington Point from the 1880s until his death in 1907.[132] There was a James Barron and Jane Paterson married in Toowoomba in July 1880.[133] They lived on a farm at Westbrook on the Darling Downs. This James was investigated as being a possible new beginning for the James in our story, though it is unlikely, as James was 'a farmer, a bachelor and born in Co. Carlow, Ireland'. It would be difficult to reconcile the farming and accent differences. He also had a brother, Patrick, living nearby. There was a pattern maker at Yeronga in Brisbane and blacksmith at Stafford in Brisbane. None of these appear to be likely reincarnations of the James in our story. The most promising looking one was a commission-agent in Atherton, but he only appears briefly in the record.[134]

Irish born bothers Edmund and Michael Barron were manufacturers of cordial drinks. Edmund started the business in Mackay from 1869. The business moved to Cooktown from 1874 to 1878 where Michael joined the business and they moved back to Mackay after that.[135] They were Catholic and each named a daughter, Sarah honouring their mother. Edmund had Sarah Catherine in 1887 and Michael had Sarah Ellen in 1888.[136] This meant that the small Catholic community of Mackay had at least three Sarah Barrons from 1890. There is no known connection between these Barrons and Sarah Jane, but they are mentioned because they kept appearing in the research and because of the striking coincidence of residence in both Cooktown and Mackay. They were described in *The Aldine history of Queensland* in 1888.[137] On the opposite page of this book was a story about a retired sea captain residing in Mackay. At one point it was considered possible that Sarah Jane had invented a back story and that these pages about Mackay identities may have provided inspiration. That implied that her surname may not have been Barron. In light of other information, that hypothesis has now been discounted.

DNA investigations

With a combination of diligence and luck, DNA has the potential to solve such mysteries once and for all. At least seven descendants of Sarah have had autosomal DNA tests done through Ancestry. com. Raw data for seven tests was uploaded to the third-party site, GEDmatch.com.

As mentioned earlier, the cross matches reported by these tests helped to identify the likely biological father of Sarah Jane's first child, Arthur. The matches were also providing promising contacts for further enquiry regarding Sarah Jane, herself. Several cases who matched tested descendants of Sarah Jane were contacted, and in another case, the presence of the related tests on GEDmatch prompted contact from another researcher.[138]

One of these contacts was particularly fruitful. A kind-hearted researcher in Madison, Wisconsin, did some extra digging and unearthed the following gem published in the Missing Friends section of an 1875 edition of the *Boston Pilot*.[139]

Of JAMES BARRON, son of William Barron and Mary Fleming, of county Kilkenny, who left Halifax, N.S., about 1865; when last heard from he was in Cape River Gold Field, Bowen, Port Denison, Queensland, South Australia.[140] Information of him, dead or alive, will be received by his mother, Mrs. Mary Barron, 6 Houghton Street, Cambridgeport, Mass.[141]

A February 1837 marriage record was found from Inistogue, Kilkenny, which completely matched the details given in the 'Missing Friends' article. In addition, four child baptisms records were found which almost certainly relate to this couple. The first in December 1837, the next in 1840, another in 1843, and a final one in March 1846. The 1840 baptism was for baby James. Irish records from this period are incomplete. Hence, there is no guarantee this is the family of Mary who placed the notice, but the probability is rated highly.

This is yet another challenge as James said he was born in St John's, Newfoundland, around 1843. The end of the baptisms in 1846 fits in with the mass exodus of Irish people for North America, amongst other destinations, in response to the devastation of the Potato Famine which started in late 1845 and lasted for seven years. The exodus, particularly to Canada, was potentially worse than the famine, as many died of disease on what were to become known as the 'coffin ships'. The particular time and destination the Barrons chose was the most dangerous, with one in six dying on or shortly after the journey.[142]

As was seen with James' family, when children were named to honour a parent but those children die, then subsequent children can be given the same name. It is possible a new James was the first child born in their new home, as that would place him at the age of seventeen or eighteen when he married the 21-year-old Anne in Bowen. The alternative is he was aged 25 when he married Anne. He said he was 23. If he was born in Ireland, but said he was born in Newfoundland, then he may have done that because his accent implied a North American beginning and being Irish was unfashionable at that time. But why lower his age? Alternatively, he was born in Newfoundland and he raised his age for some other reason. In an inconsistent episode in May 1873, he gave his age as 25, implying he was born in 1847–48.[143] However, seasoned researchers state age underestimation is the expected norm among illiterate folk, which would support the proposition that James was born in 1840 in Kilkenny.[144]

In addition to the relevant Irish records, more records from 1875 to 1880 were found relating to a Mary Barron in the Cambridge area.[145] In these records, Mary is the widow of William and of Irish birth, which is consistent with the Mary Barron who placed the 1875 advertisement.[146] Cambridge, the home to Harvard, is on the opposite bank of the Charles River to Boston, and Cambridgeport is a neighbourhood within the city. In 1880, the population of Cambridge was 52,669.

These additional details by themselves were only adding more information regarding the James Barron who was identified as the best match in the official records. This extra information helped to make sense of a significant DNA match reported by Ancestry.com. Six of the seven DNA tests of the documented descendants of Sarah Jane were showing a match with another researcher in the USA.[147] She claims descent from William J Barron, son of William and Mary Barron. William J was born in March 1849 in New Brunswick, Canada and was a documented resident of Cambridge, Massachusetts, in 1874–80. William J has a younger brother, Patrick J who was born in 1856 in Hamilton, Ontario, Canada. Both brothers were brass finishers and they both gave their working address as 368 Main, Cambridge, in 1875.[148] In the 1880 census, Mary Barron, a widow born in Ireland, was living with her son Patrick J and his wife at 123 Windsor Street, Cambridge – just 500 metres from Houghton Street.[149]

The clear implication is, this Mary Barron is the same person who placed the advertisement looking for her son, James,

A view near Inistogue, Kilkenny in 2017. The picturesque location has been used as the backdrop to four movies.[156] Photo: author.

Charles River.

A lithograph of the Charles River from the Cambridge Historical Commission. Image donated by Patsy Baudoin

and who is also the mother of William J and Patrick J. The DNA link to this family is compelling evidence that the father of Sarah Jane Barron, second wife of Abraham Ditton, is the James Barron who was on the Cape River goldfield.

Given this James leaves Canada around 1865 and is married in September of that year in Bowen and remains in Bowen for some time, it is difficult to make a case for Sarah being born in Townsville prior to the first officially recorded European birth in August 1865. Furthermore, the official documents clearly relating to this James consistently point to them not being in Townsville until after November 1868 and also to his daughter, Sarah, being born in 1874. James may well have been a seafarer in his earlier career and may have returned to it after his troubles, but the likelihood he was a 'sea captain' would seem a bit of a stretch, given the literacy issue.

I cannot declare that the oral history is wrong, just that it is open to interpretation. Sarah may not have known the truth and may have woven what fragments she did have into a narrative that gave her some comfort.

Overall Assessment

When the initial facts were found, the likelihood that the two Sarahs were one was rated as 'more likely than not'. This was because there were simply no records for the alternate family. That did not necessarily mean that the alternate family did not exist, but it was probable that they did not exist. As the research progressed, the rating rose to 'almost certainly' as the coincidences were very compelling, but the discrepancies still left some doubt. What started this detailed investigation of Sarah's origins was seeing other researchers linking Sarah to other possibilities that did not survive any serious scrutiny. This prompted a methodical approach, documenting all that had been discovered and all that had been considered. The case for the two Sarah Jane Barrons being the same person is now very solid because we can resolve the two James Barrons as the same person due to the DNA evidence and the oral history partially matching (e.g. Townsville, Cooktown, orphan status). Other points of agreement include both being RC with Irish heritage. Of course, there are some details that do not quite match up.

The other difficulties that remain are fitting Sarah's birthday in with the family still being in Townsville, as the window for her birth, given the birth dates of her siblings, is very tight. The undelivered letter in Townsville from early 1874 suggests the family had already departed for Cooktown. James' birthdate and birthplace are also problems thrown up by the evidence. The complete truth has not been uncovered by this research, but the big question has been answered.

With the linchpin of the DNA evidence in place, we have an adequate explanation for the age discrepancy, the maiden name issue and it appears young Sarah was able to survive the frontier. The sea captain claim looks unlikely, but James may have gone to sea in his later years.

In remembrance

Descendants of Sarah erected a simple headstone in the Mackay Cemetery in 2017, as her grave and that of three of her children had previously been unmarked. Abraham was buried with his first wife, Marion in a different section and a headstone had been erected in recent decades. The Celtic cross on Sarah's headstone was chosen to reflect her Irish heritage and Catholic faith. The statement about when she was born was deliberately left with some mystery, as no findings of this research are so definite they should be written in stone. A small gathering beside her grave was held on 26 July 2018 and news of the gathering was shared with Mackay's Historical Society and with the *Daily Mercury*. An article was published regarding the remembrance of Sarah in the Saturday 28 July 2018 edition of the *Daily Mercury*.[150]

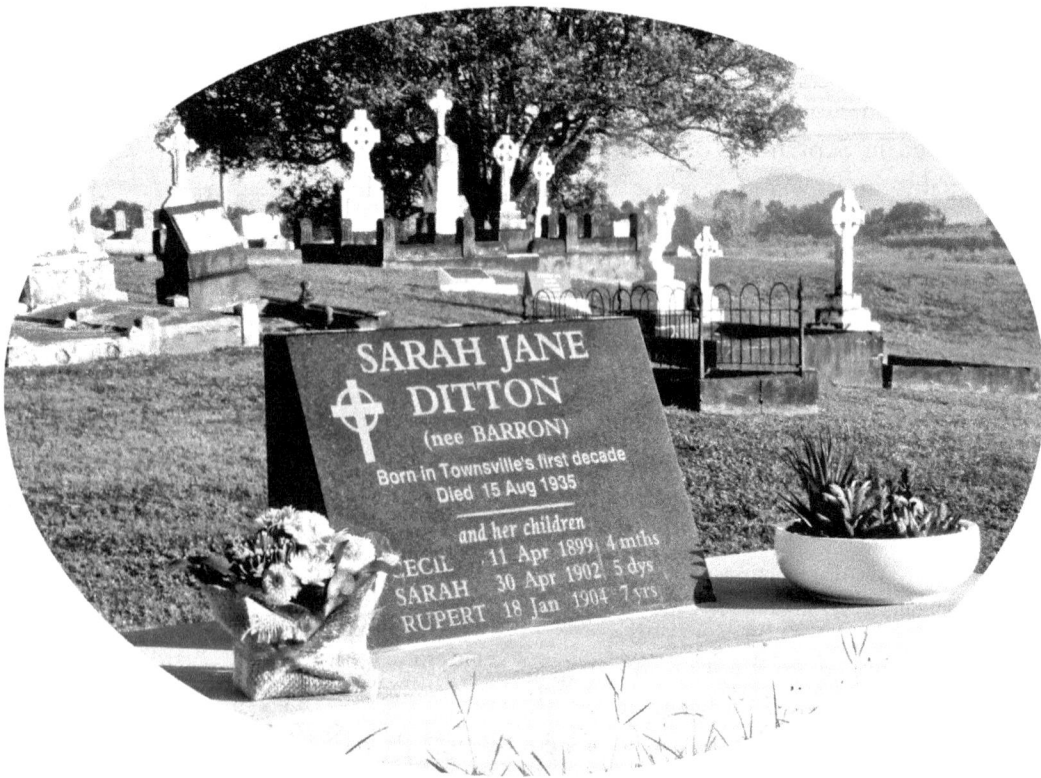

Photo: July 2018 by author

Endnotes to Chapter 9

1 Qld MC 1891/1410 1168, Mackay, 3 Nov 1891, Sarah Barron & Abraham Ditton

2 Qld BC 1875/ 286 22, Cooktown, 24 Feb 1875, Patrick Barron

3 Qld BCs 1867/107 8, 1870/3151 186, 1873/3891 474, 1875/ 286 22

4 One certificate shows Maia, Ireland another shows Meath, Ireland, majority say Westmeath, Ireland.

5 Qld BCs 1867/107 8, 1870/3151 186, 1873/3891 474, 1875/ 286 22

6 Bowen was open for settlement in 1861. Initially named Port Denison, after the NSW governor, by 1865 it had been renamed after George Bowen, the first governor of Qld. – *The foundation of a North Queensland Port Settlement 1861–1880* by Julie Stanley (U of Q Thesis 1984)

7 Qld MC 1865/372 81, St Mary's, Bowen, 3 Sep 1865, Anne Farley & James Barron

8 Qld DC 1866/32 135, Kennedy (Bowen), 20 Jun 1866, William Barron

& The 'X' mark for a signature typically meant illiteracy, but it may only point to not being able to write. He may have been able to read.

9 Conway station was 200 kms south-west of Bowen. *Port Dennison Times Almanac 1868,* pub: FT Rayner, Bowen, 1868

10 Qld BC 1867/73 305, Conway Station, 15 May 1867, Mary Anne Barron

11 *The Queensland Post Office Directory* of 1868 published by Meyer

12 The Cape River goldfields were about 380 kms WSW of Bowen.

13 Qld DC 1868/107 8, Cape River, 15 Nov 1868, Mary Anne Barron

14 Qld BC 1870/3151 186, Townsville, 5 Jan 1870, Mary Jane Barron

15 Qld BC 1873/3891 474, Townsville, 2 May 1873, Mary Barron

16 Qld Miner's Rights & Business Licences 1870–1884 applications on 23 Sep 1871 & 5 Oct 1872

17 Qld Miner's Rights & Business Licences 1870–1884 for Charters Towers, Broughton & Cape River

18 Qld BC 1873/3891 474, Townsville, 2 May 1873, Mary Barron

19 Qld DC 1873/1498 306, Townsville, 19 May 1873, Mary Barron

20 *The Queensland Post Office Directory of 1874*, published by Bailliere

21 QFHS Queensland Unclaimed Letters Index 1860 - 1874. It is not clear exactly, what an unclaimed letter implies. The 1874 Post Office directory lists James as a carrier living in Walker St, Townsville.That may refer to old information by the time that was published. Had he not received mail previously at Townsville or had he moved on? The other point about the letter is that it implies that he has some degree of literacy, he may have required assistance in replying but he possibly could have read his letter..This letter had a colonial origin.

22 Qld BC 1875/286 22, Cooktown, 24 Feb 1875, Patrick Barron

23 Qld DC 1875/241 94, Cooktown, 25 Feb 1875, Patrick Barron

24 The Brisbane flood of 1893 is blamed as an event which destroyed many colonial records including immigration records.

25 JV Mulligan reported his strike at Georgetown, the site of an earlier strike, on 3 Sep 1873.

26 The Palmer, *The Telegraph* (Brisbane), Tue 30 Dec 1873, page 3 http://nla.gov.au/nla.news-article169482538

27 H Holthouse, *River of Gold*, A & R Classics edition, Angus & Robertson, Sydney, 1994, page 24

& D Hill, *The Gold Rush: The fever that forever changed Australia*, Random House, North Sydney, 2011.

& The undelivered letter in Jan 1874 could lead to the hypothesis that Sarah was born in Cooktown rather than Townsville and given the early stage of development of Cooktown, may explain why there was no government scribe to record Sarah's birth.

28 https://www.findandconnect.gov.au/guide/qld/QE00659 site giving history of St Joseph's Orphanage

29 Qld State Archives admission registers for Townsville, Mackay and Rockhampton orphanages

30 *Early Settlers of Mackay* (1860–1885) Mackay Family History Society 2009, pages 124–125

31 Papers were compiled by Sarah's son William Ditton (1905–1999), now in the possession of his daughter, Delma Haack.

32 This undated note implies she is born in a locality previously unsettled. Kissing Point is not far from what was or became Townsville, so the thrust of the note appears to suggest Bill/Sarah is claiming Sarah was the first European child born in the Townsville area.

33 Kissing Point on the NW boundary of the settlement had been named by 1864. – Wikipedia. Several decades later it became a gun battery fortification protecting the port of Townsville. The photo from 1890 doesn't show any housing on the point. Perhaps a vessel was moored off there or tents were erected in the early days.

34 Oral history from Delma Haack

35 Week ending Oct 30, *Queensland Times, Ipswich Herald and General Advertiser*, Sat 6 Nov 1875, page 6 http://nla.gov.au/nla.news-article122071165

& EG Heap, Some Notes on Cannibalism Among Queensland Aborigines, 1824–1900, espace.library.uq.edu.au

& Holthouse provides many more detailed accounts and graphic descriptions from unnamed oral sources.

36 e.g. Aboriginal History 1981 ANU http://press-files.anu.edu.au/downloads/press/p71311/pdf/article024.pdf

37 Qld BC 1875/ 286 22, Cooktown, 24 Feb 1875, Patrick Barron

38 England Civil Registration BC 1839 #31 App # 3583A – Tenterden Kent, 3 Nov 1839, Abraham Ditton

& Qld MC 1891/1410 1168, Mackay, 3 Nov 1891, Sarah Barron & Abraham Ditton

39 Qld DC 1891/2610 5701, Mackay, 29 Mar 1891, Marion Ditton

40 Northern development, *Townsville Daily Bulletin*, Sat 29 Dec 1951, page 3 http://nla.gov.au/nla.news-article63397166 & rootsweb: William Townsville Boyes b. 25 Aug 1865

41 Qld BC 1865/1315, Port Curtis, 16 Apr 1865, Isabella Stevenson Ditton

42 Qld DC 1891/2610 5701, Mackay, 29 Mar 1891, Marion Ditton

43 We know from hospital admission records at Mackay, Charles was resident in the Mackay district in 1897 and John was resident in Mackay in 1903. He had married in 1895 and lived at Mia Mia, not far from Mackay. Abraham III: James Cook University Archives : http://libserver.jcu.edu.au/specials/Archives/ditton.html.

44 Qld BC, Mackay 1913/8810, Alfred St, Mackay, 21 Aug 1913, Catherine Muriel Ditton

45 Qld BI 1880/C3898, 15 Nov 1880, Lydia Wimbell Ditton

46 Qld BC 1896/7363, Ashford near Mackay, 1 Oct 1896, Rupert James Ditton

47 Abraham was the informant; he also appears to confuse some of Marion's history with Sarah's.

48 Mackay, Qld Funeral Notices and Funeral Director Records

49 Until 1961, in Qld, NSW & Vic, girls could theoretically marry at age 12 (boys at 14) with parental consent. Confusingly, in Qld the age of consent was 13 and the landmark *Queensland Criminal Code Act* of 1899 raised it to 14 years, and it had become 17 by 1920. In 1976 it was standardised to 16 across all Australian states. *The Commonwealth Marriage Act 1961* raised the absolute minimum marriage age to 16. Between 16 and 18 a court order was required and was only granted in 'exceptional and unusual' circumstances. Pregnancy was not one of those.

50 Parental consent was required for anyone not yet 21. This was reduced to 18 in the 1970s in line with other changes to the age of majority such as for voting and consumption of alcohol.

51 Qld State Archives Patients admission register, Mackay hospital 1/1/1891–29/11/1899

52 Qld BC 1891/ 8088 5204 Mackay, 25 Jul 1891, Arthur Barron

53 Qld State Archives Patients admission register, Mackay hospital 1/1/1891–29/11/1899

54 https://www.jigsawqueensland.com/history-of-qld-adoption

55 This is based on her reported age on her children's birth certificates and age claims before and upon her marriage.

56 Qld BC 1873/3891 474, Townsville, 2 May 1873, Mary Barron & Qld BC 1875/ 286 22, Cooktown, 24 Feb 1875, Patrick Barron

57 Qld BC 1870/3151 186, Townsville, 5 Jan 1870, Mary Jane Barron

58 Qld BCs 1870/3151 186 (Mary Jane) & 1873/3891 474 (Mary)

59 Irish naming tradition typically honoured grandparents first, suggesting in this instance, Mary was a grandparent's name.

60 Qld BC 1875/ 286 22, Cooktown, 24 Feb 1875, Patrick Barron

61 Qld BC 1873/3891 474, Townsville, 2 May 1873, Mary Barron

62 Bowen had ceased being called Port Denison by the time James and Anne were married. Positioning indicates 'Bowen' was added later.

63 https://www.townsville.qld.gov.au/about-townsville/history-and-heritage/townsville-history/townsville-1770-to-1900

64 Australia's dental generations: oral disease was commonly treated with extraction. https://www.adelaide.edu.au/arcpoh/downloads/publications/reports/dental-statistics-research-series/nsaoh-report.pdf

65 One certificate recorded 'Meath' and another 'Maia' but 3 had Westmeath. All signed with an 'X'.

66 Qld DC 1876/350 386, Cooktown, 2 Jun 1876, Ann Barron

67 Holthouse, page 101, says it was often deliberately adulterated with other dangerous substances. A report from Cooktown described the 'poisonous alcohol vendered by unscrupulous shanty-keepers'. The Palmer, *Northern Argus* (Rockhampton) Thu 10 Dec 1874, page 3 http://nla.gov.au/nla.news-article214286267

68 Footnote 368 in PhD thesis by Peter Albert Ryle (2000) https://researchonline.jcu.edu.au/19585/5/05Chapter_3.pdf

69 Qld State Electoral Rolls 1860–1889 – TDDFHS CD

70 Qld DC 1927/1436, Ingham, 16 May 1929, George Barron

71 *Queensland Police Gazette*, 1866

72 https://en.wikipedia.org/wiki/Annie_Laurie

73 http://www.imdb.com/title/tt0189360/ & http://www.nitrateville.com/viewtopic.php?t=4793

74 https://en.wikipedia.org/wiki/A_Tree_Grows_in_Brooklyn_(film)

75 http://www.lyricsfreak.com/c/corries/annie+laurie_21008677.html

76 Untitled, *Rockhampton Bulletin*, Fri 9 Jun 1876, page 2 http://nla.gov.au/nla.news-article51904408

77 Shipping, *Mackay Mercury and South Kennedy Advertiser*, Sat 10 Jun 1876, page 2 http://nla.gov.au/nla.news-article169855611

78 Qld DC 1876/350 386, Cooktown, 2 Jun 1876, Ann Barron

79 *Cooktown Courier*, 20 Mar 1875, as per The Cooktown Historical Society in email on 26 Jun 2013. Text of article provided 30 Jul 2021. Two mile creek was one of the town's early water supply points, but which became befouled by the activities of mainly Chinese market gardeners. According to a *Cairns Post* article from 2 Feb 1946 " We made our home just outside the town, the "Four Mile," "Three Mile," "Two Mile." You chose at will although the " Two Mile " was the more popular, because of the racecourse opposite. The whole of the locality was used as a camping ground by the teamsters and packers. A little creek meandered casually along through the "Two Mile." There were hotels - it was a good business stand.'

80 Holthouse, Chapter 5, Death in the Mud, pages 51–72

81 The Cooktown and District Historical Society published a booklet *Cooktown Through the Years* in 2009 and on page 33 it states 'Contrary

to popular belief there were no known brothels operating in Cooktown at any time ...'. Holthouse certainly wanted us to believe otherwise. There were documented grog shanties and the Chinese would have had opium businesses for their own countrymen at least.

82 TPL Weitemeyer, *Missing Friends: Being the adventures of a Danish immigrant in Queensland (1871–1880)*, T Fisher, Unwin, London, 1892

83 Hill, photo page after page 242, caption for JV Mulligan's photograph.

84 *Queensland Police Gazette* 1864-1884 QFHS index Vol xiii page 89 5 Jul 1876, 'prisioner to be discharged ... a native of Newfoundland.'

85 PM: Police Magistrate, *Rockhampton Bulletin*, Tue 7 Nov 1876, page 2 http://nla.gov.au/nla.news-article51906508

86 Cooktown was not included in the North Queensland Catholic Diocese until 1877. There was a priest, Father MacGuinnes, in Cooktown from 1874 and a church, St Mary's,.was built in 1875. The Sister of Mercy nuns turned up in 1888. - *Cooktown Through the Years* pages 41 & 42.

87 An unattributed note in William Ditton's papers states: 'Fox's Station, Rockhampton, sister and nun killed by lightning'.

88 e.g. Queensland news, *Morning Bulletin* (Rockhampton), Sat 21 Mar 1903, page 5 http://nla.gov.au/nla.news-article52976178

89 *Wild River Times* Mar 1903, microfilm at John Qxley State Library, Brisbane

90 An 1868 map of the Kennedy District, North Qld in the State Library of Queensland, clearly shows the bush tracks linking the Cape River goldfields to Bowen and to Townsville.

91 https://en.wikipedia.org/wiki/Australian_gold_rushes

92 C Hooper, *North Queensland Deserted Towns Charters Towers – Ravenswood – Cape River,* self-published, NSW, 2014. Page 65, quoting 'Hill'. Warden WRO Hill was referenced in Cilento & Lack.

93 R Cilento & C Lack, *Triumph in the Tropics,* Smith and Paterson, Brisbane, 1959, page 206

94 Hooper, page 65

95 Qld Miner's Rights & Business Licences 1870–1884

96 B McGowan *Australian Ghost Towns*, Lothian Books, Melbourne, 2002

97 Canada, Seafarers of the Atlantic Provinces, 1789–1935 vessel *Antelope* (Brigantine)

98 American Commodore, James Barron, was involved in the infamous *Chesapeake - Leopard* incident in 1807 resulting in his court-martial.

99 Loss of the ship *St. Vincent, Evening Post* (Wellington), Volume V, Issue 7, 17 Feb 1869.

100 Wreck of the ship *St. Vincent, Nelson Examiner and New Zealand Chronicle* Vol XXVIII, 21, Sat 13 Mar 1869

101 Lloyds Register, Sea Captains, State Library of NSW

102 Town news, *Wairarapa Standard*, Volume III. Issue 109, Wed Fri 19 Feb 1869

103 Original reference has not been relocated, but it was copied to and persists in a Rootsweb chat on Barrons.

104 Commercial intelligence – deaths, *The Argus* (Melbourne), Fri 27 Jul 1866, page 4 http://nla.gov.au/nla.news-article5768944

105 e.g. Shipping, *The Age* (Melbourne), Fri 17 Dec 1858, page 4 http://nla.gov.au/nla.news-article154876953 & Shipping intelligence, *The Argus* (Melbourne), Tue 2 Jun 1863, page 4 http://nla.gov.au/nla.news-article6486252

106 Shipping, *The Age* (Melbourne), Wed 11 Nov 1863, page 4 http://nla.gov.au/nla.news-article155021983

107 https://espace.library.uq.edu.au/view/UQ:212739/s18378366_1950_4_3_361.pdf

108 https://www.britishtars.com/2018/01/literacy-afloat.html

109 Quote from Central Queensland History Wiki – site now defunct.

110 *Ferio Tego, The Darling Downs Gazette and General Advertiser*, Tue 13 Feb 1866, page 3 http://nla.gov.au/nla.news-article75516299 & The *Bayswater* outrages, *Northern Argus* (Rockhampton), Wed 31 Jan 1866, page 2 http://nla.gov.au/nla.news-article214407017

111 Public Records Office of Victoria, Victoria Police Report D15759 – Death of James Barron

112 Victorian DC 1900/213717, Melbourne, Oct 1900, Jas Barren

113 https://openresearch-repository.anu.edu.au/bitstream/1885/16791/1/De%20Looper%20Thesis%202015.pdf

114 Infant Mortality in the Australian Colonies, *The Colonist*, Vol III, issue 277 15 Jun 1960

115 An American relative reported several infant deaths in her branch also, possibly related to neuro-muscular disorders.

116 *The memoirs of Andrew Murray, grazier from Central Queensland* History Wiki now defunct

117 *The memoirs of Andrew Murray, grazier from Central Queensland*

118 *Bowen's First Hundred years 1770–1870* Delamothe Collection – Archives

119 https://en.wikipedia.org/wiki/Edmund_Kennedy

120 Cilento & Lack page 203

121 Holthouse says dozens of European diggers and carriers and hundreds of Chinese were killed by the Aboriginal inhabitants. He states: 'Aboriginals preferred the taste of the Chinese to the tobacco chewing Europeans'. In addition, Chinese were not as heavily armed which ensured they were targeted. What is also sometimes forgotten is that Chinese made up two thirds of all the miners that were on the Palmer, so they were much more numerous. Fever, starvation and unpoliced rivalry also took a heavy toll. Retaliation against the Aboriginal population meant they suffered many casualties as well. An academic, Robert Ormston, in his 1996 MA thesis on early Cooktown, *The Rise and Fall of a Frontier Mining Town: Cooktown 1873–85,* disputes the 'hundreds of Chinese' figure and he puts it around 20 based on the written sources, but concedes that an unknown number of undocumented deaths may have occurred. He also makes the general observation that, in his opinion, Hector Holthouse uses exaggerated and sensational claims in the interest of storytelling and selling a book.

122 http://listverse.com/2011/03/30/top-10-most-venomous-snakes/

123 http://data.gov.au/storage/f/2013-05-12T195404/tmpsLxwENImmigration-1848-1912.txt

124 Qld DC 1968/97256, Kangaroo Point, 16 May 1968, Sarah Jane Barron. 'Ino' is probably a mistaken transcription of 'Jno' which is a

short form of John.

125 Qld Timber Licences 1860–1901, Queensland Family History Society

126 State electoral rolls showed family living in Charters Towers before moving to Brisbane.

127 http://data.gov.au/storage/f/2013-05-12T195404/tmpsLxwENImmigration-1848-1912.txt

128 http://www.bennettfamilytree.co.uk/tng/getperson.php?personID=I0543&tree=Bennetts

129 India, Select Deaths and Burials 1719-1948, Ancestry.com

130 In addition the James Barron listed in the Qld death index for 1886 (Qld DC 1886/257, Southwood, 26 Nov 1886, James Barron) is an infant who died on the Darling Downs.

131 Qld DI 1916/103 003861, 3 Aug 1916, James Barron,

132 Qld State Electoral Rolls 1860–1889 – TDDFHS CD

& James Barron, the engineer from Wellington Point was born in Chester England circa 1833 and he had a second wife named Ann Aimes (mc 1861 in England) but only one of his children (Thomas bc 1858 from first wife, Martha Talbot) was living when he died in 1907.

133 Qld MC 1880/276 1701, Toowoomba, 7 Jul 1880, Jane Paterson & James Barron

134 The Atherton based James Barron left little record of his time and had as his address the Barron Valley Hotel indicating a fairly transient existence, which neither helps nor hinders his possible association.

135 http://www.clarelibrary.ie/eolas/coclare/genealogy/don_tran/fam_his/barron_bros/barron_brothers.htm

136 Qld DC 1909/2312 8800, Wood St., Mackay, 22 Aug 1909, Michael Barron. Sarah Ellen was a military nurse in WWI. Neither Sarah Ellen nor Sarah Catherine married.

137 WF Morrison, *Aldine History of Queensland*, Aldine, Sydney, 1888

138 At least 8 descendants of Sarah are known to have taken DNA tests at Ancestry.com

139 Barbara Rex of Madison, Wisconsin – named with permission

140 South Australia is an incorrect reference as it was another colony, separate to the colony of Queensland.

141 *Boston Pilot*, Thu 13 Feb 1875, page 471, Missing Friends – Ancestry Library Edition Database

142 H Litton, *The Irish Famine an Illustrated History*, Wolfhound Press, Dublin 2nd Ed. 2003, Hazards of Emigration page 104

143 Qld BC 1873/3891 474, Townsville, 2 May 1873, Mary Barron

144 Roslaeen Underwood, a professional researcher from Ireland wrote: 'Few people kept their own records so they did not know when they were born. If asked they had to guess, usually wrongly, usually under-estimating their ages. To find someone's age out by 2-5 years is so common it is hardly worth commenting on; 10 years is also quite common ...'

145 Two Mary Barrons were found in Cambridge, one born in Ireland the other in Prussia & married to Herman.

146 US City Directories Massachusetts, Cambridge, 1875 'Barron Mary, widow of William, house 36 Washington'

147 Delma's match was reported at 53 Centimorgans across 4 segments (i.e. strong). The only subject without a match, Ralph Ditton, would expect a match if the reporting threshold was lowered. Sarah Jane Barron is the only most recent common ancestor shared by all 7 test subjects – i.e. it is not associated with Abraham Ditton's line or the Mezger/Bihlmier line.

148 US City Directories, 1822–1995, Ancestry.com, Cambridge 1875. (Their house addresses were 79 Plymouth for Patrick & 34 Union for William – about a block away from each other.)

149 The age given in the census is a nice round 50, which if we take the 1837 marriage makes her 7 at the time of her marriage – starting to see a pattern here. The other challenges are her son, James, is claiming to be born in 1843, which would make her 13 at the time of his birth. If 1847 is more likely then she would be 17 – starting to get more credible. Therefore, either the Irish marriage record is not hers or the family has a tradition of lying about their age. Refer to comments by Roslaeen Underwood in endnote above.

150 https://www.pressreader.com/australia/daily-mercury/20180728/281921658845907

Page 26 in the hard copy version of the paper. The article contained an error: Sarah's son Arthur (Tim) Ditton (1891–1944) was identified as my father when in fact he is my grandfather.

151 John Oxley Library, State Library of Queensland. Image API-057-01-0007, out of copyright

152 Qld BC 1875/ 286 22, Cooktown, 24 Feb 1875, Patrick Barron

153 John Oxley Library, State Library of Queensland. Image APO-008-01-0024, out of copyright. Buildings added a storey in the 1880s

154 Photo from *The Development of the City of Mackay, A Pictorial Time-Line* published by the Mackay Historical Society and Museum Incorporated – The building style closely resembles that of the Lister Private Hospital, Mackay (1907 to 1980).

155 Qld DC 1876/350 386, Cooktown, 2 Jun 1876, Ann Barron

156 Inistogue, Kilkenny in the Republic of Ireland is a picturesque village which has been used as a backdrop to 4 films: *Circle of Friends*, *The Secret Scripture*, *Widow's Peak* and *Between Heaven and Here*.

Chapter 10

Tim's Württemberg connection

A DNA discovery – Mezgers

This chapter explores what is known about Crescentia (Grace) Bihlmaier and her husband Johannes (John) Metzger (Mezger), their children, their origins and their families.[1] Much of the information presented has come from the research and writings of Mary de Jabrun (née O'Neill)[2], a documented descendant of John and Grace via their second son, Louis.[3] Mary's writings extend beyond what is presented here and are recommended reading for those wanting more information.[4]

DNA testing yielded the surprise discovery that Arthur (Tim) Ditton was descended from Grace Bihlmaier. It emerged from the observation, descendants of Tim Ditton were showing significant DNA matches with multiple test subjects in the USA[5] descended from Grace's brother, Vitus Bihlmaier.[6] Tim's birth certificate named Sarah Barron as his mother but no father was recorded in the space provided. In addition to the evidence of DNA matches, oral history and a legal letter[7] indicated Tim's father was not the man who helped raise him, Abraham Ditton (II).[8] Relatives who were proven to be descended from Abraham Ditton were not sharing these Bihlmaier matches. This provided a strong clue in a whodunit mystery – not a murder mystery, but a life-giving mystery.

The administrator of the matching tests in the USA, Joe Bihlmaier, was contacted and asked the question: 'Do you know if you had any relatives who were in Mackay, Queensland, Australia in 1890?' Joe's answer was 'yes', and he nominated Grace and her family. This was the key item of information linking Tim to the Bihlmaiers – i.e. Grace and her family were in the Mackay district at the time of Tim's conception. Grace had no relatives in Australia beyond her immediate family. The candidacy for father would start and stop with the Mezger sons, as it was the mother who was related to the families in America. Therefore, one of Grace's sons must have been Tim's biological father. By 1890, Grace and her husband John, had four surviving sons: William, 23, Louis, 22, Charles, 20 and John, 15.[9]

Nothing is known of the circumstances in which Sarah Barron fell pregnant to one of these boys other than they became part of the Catholic community of the Mackay district and all the boys were still single in 1890. In the years following, they all married women of Irish birth or descent.

William, the eldest, completed a carpenter's apprenticeship.[10] In 1895, he married Irish-born, Ellen Maloney, in Rockhampton, where they lived before and after the marriage.[11] They had four children, of which only one, Nancy, went on to have any children.[12] William was the informant on his father's death certificate in 1892 and his residence at that time was Walkerston. He died in Rockhampton in 1947.[13]

Louis, the second son, stayed on at the family home at Walkerston, where he became the local blacksmith and wheelwright.[14] He earned a reputation as an inventor. He designed and built buggies and coaches. He also designed and built a cane tip wagon. Louis took out patents on his designs. He broke in brumbies and worked with horses, which complemented his interest in horseracing. This was an interest he shared with his father and some of his brothers. He was a steward for the Walkerston Race Club. He married Mary Quillinan from Mirani in 1895. They had three children, all of which went on to have children of their own. The family moved to Mackay in 1911 and he later became a publican running the Post Office Hotel with his wife. In 1915, they sold the licence and then took over the licence for the Pioneer Hotel.[15] The catastrophic cyclone of 1918 extensively damaged the hotel. Louis died in Mackay in 1919.

Charles, the third son, was born 'Michael', but was known as Charles.[16] In time, he showed himself to be quite the athlete. He was an accomplished sprinter,[17] cricketer[18] and cyclist.[19] By 1889, he was working in Mackay at Lamberts Ltd, which was a local department store.[20] He stayed with the firm for 28 years, where he managed the grocery section. Subsequently, he managed the

Mezger family group circa 1907 L to R, back: Louis Mezger, Mary Mezger née Quillinan (Louis' wife), Maggie Quillinan, Grace Mezger née Bihlmaier, Polly Quillinan, Amelia Mezger née O'Toole (John's wife), front: Bill Mezger, May Mezger, Grace Mezger, Jack Mezger, John Mezger jnr, John Andrew Mezger.[64]

Mackay branch of the People's Cash Stores and later still went into business on his own. He married Agnes Catherine Farrelly in Mackay in 1894. Agnes was a Mackay resident of Irish descent. They had five children, but no documented grandchildren.[21] He was the honourable secretary of the Mackay Hibernian Horseracing Club. Charles was a regular anonymous contributor of prose and verse to a Sydney journal.[22] His obituary praised his ability to compose 'topical jingles'.

He was also involved as an organiser in the local Catholic church. He managed a testimonial celebration[23] for Father Pierre-Marie Bucas, the energetic and popular French-born priest who had spent 36 years in Mackay.[24] Around 1927, he moved to Shanghai in China to join his son, Vincent, and his wife, Katia. Vincent worked there as a municipal health inspector. Charles' wife and other adult children remained in Qld. A long and informative letter he wrote to a friend in Mackay described conditions in Shanghai at that time. It was published in the Mackay *Daily Mercury*.[25] Charles died in Shanghai in April 1931 from 'bronchial troubles'.

John, the fourth son, was born 'Andrew', but known as John.[26] He married Amelia O'Toole from Mackay in 1897. He ran a bakery in Mackay, but later sold out to run the Victoria Hotel in Mackay from 1905 to 1907. His wife took over as licensee for 1908.[27] He moved with his family to Marian where he ran the Marian Hotel from 1908 to 1910.[28] He moved back to Mackay before moving to Stanthorpe with his family where he was described as a baker. The family had three children, two of whom went on to have children of their own. John died in Stanthorpe at the age of forty.

In terms of assessing the likelihood of each candidate, we can say suspicion falls most heavily on Charles, because he alone was known to have been living and working in the town of Mackay from 1889.[29] In addition, he shared quite specific traits with Tim. Both Tim and Charles were professional sprinters when young men[30], writers and contributors of anonymous literary works as adults[31] and prominent horseracing identities in their later years.[32] It is possible Tim's mother, Sarah, may have encouraged him in some fields Tim's father excelled at, such as running and writing. There is also the speculative link via Father Bucas who may have been involved in resolving the problem from his youth.

The next in line to consider is William, as he is the oldest and appears to leave the Mackay district for Rockhampton in the early 1890s, which would be a strategy to avoid consequences. However, he was understood to still be in Walkerston in January 1892. In addition, Sarah later named one of her sons William, which suggests this was not a name that had been sullied in her mind. Although it is also the name of her paternal grandfather.

Louis would have to be considered as next in line because of his age. However, two descendants of Louis have been DNA tested and the closest of these matches with four descendants of Tim are more consistent with the strength of second-cousin once-removed rather than half-first-cousin once-removed, although that is far from being an exact science.[33] Further information, which assists Louis' innocence, is his working life is established at Walkerston rather than Mackay.

Lastly, John is least likely, mostly because of his age at the time and the fact Sarah was definitely older than him. Also, in 1890, it is likely he was still attending school and living in Walkerston.

More testing may help validate the hypothesis around the precise identity of Tim's biological father, but since William and Charles have no other known living descendants, it is unlikely it could be resolved by those means alone. I undertook a Y chromosome test and the closest match has documented German ancestry.[34] It also identified my Y haplogroup as G (or more precisely: G-Y20834).[35] The G haplogroup is a relatively rare haplogroup for Europe, but not quite as rare in Germany and Austria. Its main hot

Charles Metzger bottom centre between two priests at a church function at Eimeo, near Mackay in 1912.[65]

spot is Georgia and Armenia in South-West Asia, where more than fifty percent of males share it.

We know Tim and his half-siblings were aware Abraham was not his father, but it is not known if Tim knew exactly who his biological father was. There is some oral history Tim knew his father was of German descent. The story of Tim's paternity was not readily shared with his children or grandchildren, although some seem to have known, whereas others did not.[36]

Kingdom of Württemberg

Both Grace and John were born in the Kingdom of Württemberg, which had existed as a kingdom since 1806.[37] It now sits within the south-western German state of Baden-Württemberg. It borders France to the west, Switzerland to the south and the German state of Bavaria to its east.[38] Even to the current day, it is a Schwäbisch-speaking territory.[39] The people are known as Swabian. They have a reputation amongst Germans of being penny-pinching misers, overly tidy, uptight, hardworking, yet inventive – or as some say, 'The Scots of Germany'.[40]

The residents of this kingdom and the neighbouring kingdom of Bavaria were overwhelmingly RC, whereas the Germanic people to the north were predominantly Protestant. People from these districts had strong regional identities. The kingdom was only absorbed into the new nation state of Germany in 1870, following the actions of Prussia's Chancellor Count Otto Von Bismarck in prosecuting and winning the Franco-Prussian war of 1870–71.[41] When providing her place of birth on official documents, Grace always nominated the 'Kingdom of Württemberg', rather than Germany.

Grace's family came from Heuchlingen,[42] a rural village between Schwäbisch-Gmünd and Aalen. John's family came from Diebach, about 60 Km to the NNW. John's parents were Georg Kasimir Metzger and Maria Anna Spath.[43] Grace's parents were Josef Bihlmaier and Crescentia Rieck.[44]

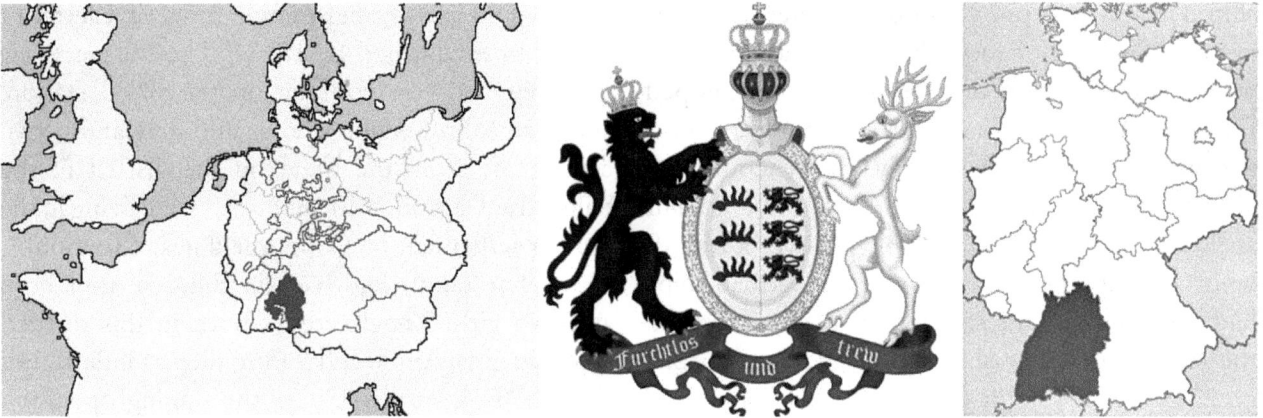

L to R: Kingdom of Württemberg (black), Coat of Arms of the Kingdom, Modern state of Baden-Württemberg

Infant mortality was high in the district with only four out of the eleven Bihlmaier children surviving childhood. John had only a surviving brother – Andreas Martin. From what we know, John's father Georg died just two years after John's birth. It is not known what John's parents did for a living, but we can assume John did not have a prosperous childhood based on his widowed mother's circumstances. The Bihlmaiers were burgers or town people. Josef Bihlmaier was a weaver and one of his other sons, Franz, was a bricklayer and builder.

Grace and John had met in Württemberg and, in 1862, had a baby girl together named Marianna. Sadly, she died at the age of two months. The rise of Bismarck's militarism, increasing population pressures and the lack of opportunities at home played their part in Grace and John seeking a better life on the other side of the world. Grace's oldest brother, Vitus, made his way to America in 1854. John's older brother, Andreas also went to the USA. Grace is known to have had opinions about the direction her homeland was taking under the influence of Bismarck, and she was not in favour of it. The family remembered that she clashed with her brother, Franz, who did support it.

Emigration to Australia

America was seen as the most desirable land to migrate to, but Australia in this period and particularly the colony of Qld were actively seeking emigrants from the Germanic states, as they were considered industrious and hardworking. By 1901, almost eight percent of the foreign-born inhabitants of Qld had come from the Germanic states.[45] Immigration was not a straightforward or inexpensive exercise. John and Grace had to travel north to Hamburg and satisfy the local authorities they had the necessary documentation. They also had to meet the military service requirements and satisfy the local authorities they were not leaving behind debts, wives, dependent children or aged parents who would be a burden to the state. They had to satisfy the Australian colonial immigration agents they were young, healthy and of good character. However, as the agents were paid by the head, the vetting may not have been as robust as was hoped. On some voyages, contagious diseases, which were rampant in Hamburg, took a heavy toll. The American agents had a quite specific list of attributes which would deem a person ineligible for emigration such as: No people who were crippled, blind, deaf, no nauseating or infectious diseases, no unmarried mothers with children, no idiots, fools or half-wits. Time has shown, the last three attributes can emerge spontaneously within a population despite these earlier efforts to vet the breeding stock.

Crescentia and Johannes found passage on the forty-metre-long barque *Johann Cesar*.[46] It sailed from Hamburg on 7 November 1863 with 231 passengers. This would not have been a comfortable journey, as the numbers above suggest a cramped ship. There were reported food and water shortages because the journey took almost six months. This was two months more than would have been hoped for. The food shortages were cited as the reason for two infant deaths onboard. The ship encountered violent storms and gales off Britain, and it sought shelter at Cowes, Isle of Wight, for over a month whilst the winter storms abated. Two German ships had been sunk by the storms, the *Wilhelmsberg* and the *Grassbrook*.[47] The ship arrived in Moreton Bay on 25 April 1864. John and Grace quickly arranged their marriage at St Stephen's Catholic Church, Brisbane for 2 May 1864. He was 37 and she was 31. They described themselves as a 'shepherd' and a 'domestic servant'.[48] Over time, their names would be anglicised from Johannes to John, from Crescentia to Grace and their surname, Metzger was softened to Mezger.

New beginnings in Queensland

The Mezgers had been assigned work at Peak Downs Station, which was a 150,000-acre (607 km²) sheep station inland from Rockhampton. The pastoral leases for this land had initially been issued to the adventurous Archer brothers in the 1850s. They on sold the lease a few years later.[49] The nearby gold and copper mining town of Clermont had been established by 1863.[50] The Mezgers saw out their two-year contract on the sheep station, and then John bought a horse and dray and began carting ore from the mines in the district to the railhead at Clermont. In 1868, they were living in the mining settlement of Copperfield near Clermont.

The family had had six children, four boys and two girls. They were all born in this district. The two girls, Annie and Fanny, died as infants, but all four boys survived.[51] As the mining operation wound down in response to falling prices, the family decided to make the move to the Mackay district about 320 kilometres away.

In 1878, they packed up all their belongings into the dray and walked for three weeks to reach their new home. The boys were aged between four and eleven. They settled in Walkerston, which is a small town about fourteen kilometres west of Mackay.[52] In the early days, the locals called the town Scrubby Creek, or Scrubby for short.[53] John took up a town block consisting of three-acres on the corner of Creek and Dane streets and built a home there, which in 2001 was described as the oldest in the town.[54]

The family planted their allotment with all

A view of Clermont circa 1870 - State Library of Queensland

The intersection of Bridge, Dutton and Creek Streets, Walkerston circa 1915. The prominent building at centre left is the police station.[66]

the varieties of fruit trees known to grow in the climate. They grew vegetables for their own table, and the family story was there was always an abundance of fresh produce and that made them feel prosperous.

John used his dray to cart goods between Mackay and Walkerston and other nearby localities. The economy of Mackay and the surrounding district was heavily based on sugar production, so it is a fair bet John carted many dray loads of sugarcane or even the sugar and its by-products produced from the crushing mills dotted around the district.

John looked after his horses, which pulled his cart, by growing feed for them, and he also raced one of the horses he had bred. In February 1879, John Mezger took the oath of allegiance to the British Queen and obtained his certificate of naturalisation from the Colony of Queensland. He paid 4s 6d for the privilege and this then entitled him to vote. From then on, he appeared on the Qld electoral roll. The four Mezger boys attended the local school, which the family had helped establish through donations and other support.

John died on 9 January 1892 after a long and painful illness, which his death certificate identified as pericarditis.[55] His estate was valued at £37 and his wife Grace was the sole executrix.[56] Grace stayed on at Walkerston where she was well-known for her preserves and dressed poultry, which she often donated to fetes and money-raising activities for the school and church. She also acted as the local midwife and performed nursing duties within the community. Lyall Ford's book, *Poorhouse to Paradise*, mentioned 'Granny Mezger' massaging Eddie Ford's leg with whale oil when he was struck down with polio.[57] He believed that she got him walking again. Her grandchildren remembered her as interesting and entertaining. She was educated, with a good command of English. Throughout her life, she wrote to her sister, Maria Anna Bartle, who had remained in Europe.

The headstone for John and Grace Mezger at Walkerston Cemetery. Photo:author

Detail from the 1912 Eimeo photo with Charles Mezger at centre

World War I

In 1912, Grace's son Louis sold off the land at Walkerston and Grace then went to stay with Louis' family in Mackay. The First World War had broken out in 1914 and people of German birth were automatically treated with suspicion. Grace, however, was of sufficient age to not be considered a threat. She died on 17 December 1916 aged 83 years. Her death record stated she died in Mackay from senility and heart issues.[58] John and Grace are buried together in the Walkerston Cemetery.

The Mezger boys were not exempt from the authorities' scrutiny as their German surnames and descent made them targets of official discrimination via the *War Precautions Act*.[59] Parliamentary debate raged during WWI as to whether naturalised citizens from enemy countries or the descendants of such people, could be trusted to be loyal. That was despite the claim: 'One cannot read any (Australian) casualty list that does not include names of men of enemy origin'.[60] It was the government and not the judiciary who decided who was loyal and who was not. There was no appeal mechanism. Consequently, it was potentially arbitrary as to who was interned and who was trusted. Public service jobs would have been barred to them and anyone who raised suspicion would be put under police surveillance. Graham Freudenberg, the political speech writer, said his German immigrant grandparents automatically had their right to vote stripped from them despite having three sons at the front. All the Mezger boys had married women of Irish descent, which would have helped how they were seen within the local community. Contrary to some perceptions, people of Irish birth and descent served in the Australian Forces at a rate proportionate to their numbers within the general population.[61] In addition, Charles' son Vincent volunteered for the army.[62] Consequently, no Mezger family members were interred. However, for decades after, Australia wide, all things German were distinctly unfashionable. Street and locality names were changed to diminish the memory of Germans immigrants being significant contributors to the development of Australia.

Anecdotes

Around 1985, after retiring from secretarial work, Tim's daughter, Lola, moved to Ashmore and then returned to Brisbane around the year 2000 to be closer to family and friends. She rented a unit at Holland Park, which by coincidence, was owned by Paul O'Neill, a great-grandson of Louis Mezger.[63]

Whilst in Innisfail, in the early sixties, my brother, Ralph, was playing with the son of a Polish immigrant, Mr Dembowski, in their yard. Mr Dembowski looked at Ralph and said, 'You're German. I don't want my son playing with Germans'. To which Ralph replied: 'I'm not German, I'm Scottish'. Mr Dembowski accepted what Ralph said, but he had his suspicions. If there is such a thing as a reasonable prejudice, then this would be an example of one. Mr Dembowski was in the Polish Tank Corp and became a POW after Poland succumbed to invasion in 1939. In general terms, the Germans were cruel masters during their occupation of Poland. When I first shared the DNA news about Mezgers with Ralph, his first words were, 'Mr Dembowski was right. I am German'.

When I travelled through Europe in 1980, I often engaged with Germans and I formed some easy friendships. I was invited to stay in their houses on at least five occasions. I enjoyed their company and their country and lapped up the food and beverages. So, the DNA news did not surprise me on that front. It did make me re-evaluate who I thought I was and to examine if I carried any prejudice towards that heritage. During my childhood, there certainly was a lot of negative feeling towards Germans as a concept, as opposed to individuals of German descent. The only thing I can say for sure is I am pleased I did not have to carry a German surname in my early days, particularly one that translates as 'Butcher'.

Entrance to Walkerston Cemetery - Photo: Author

Endnotes to Chapter 10

1 Crescentia Bihlmaier, born 25 Dec 1833 Heuchlingen, Heidenheim, Württemberg – died 18 Dec 1916 Mackay, Qld

& Johannes Metzger, born 7 Jul 1825 Diebach, Hohenlohekris, Württemberg – died 9 Jan 1892 Walkerston, Qld

2 Mary is descended from, Grace and John's second son Louis Mezger (1868–1916) and in turn from his daughter Mary Veronica O'Neill (née Mezger) (1902–1989). Mary has generously allowed me to reference her earlier writings. In her writings, Mary acknowledges the efforts of her uncle Jack Mezger, who followed up a visit to relatives in Germany in the 1970s, with comprehensive writings about the family.

3 Mary also had a DNA test. It showed a stronger match (3rd to 4th cousin range) to Tim's descendants than did the descendants of Vitus Bihlmier, as is predicted by the hypothesis of Tim's paternity.

4 M De Jabrun, The Mezgers & Bihlmaiers, Blurb, Brisbane 2015 - out of print

5 Test subjects in the USA were those managed by Jim Bihlmier from NYC and included those tests designated as JB (2 separate tests) MB, KT and Jim's. Test subjects descended from Tim included Clem Ditton, Ralph Ditton, Anne Hickey (née Ditton) and cousin Christine. Matches were reported at the 4th to 6th cousin range. Ditton relatives not descended from Tim did not share these matches nor relatives descended from the Cranley or Barry families.

6 Vitus Bihlmaier, born 11 Jun 1825 Heuchlingen, Heidenheim, Württemberg – died 20 Jan 1906 Pennsylvania, USA

7 From oral history provided by Delma Haack (née Ditton), daughter to Tim's half-brother William: A legal letter associated with the winding up of the estate of Tim's mother, Sarah, alludes to the understanding Abraham was not Tim's father.

8 DNA matches also confirmed Abraham was not Tim's father. In contrast DNA confirmed the tested descendants of Abraham and Sarah's marriage were shown to be descended from Abraham.

9 An anomaly with this result is there is an expectation that my own DNA ethnicity profile would have West European markers. Only a slight influence at the range of 0–2% was found, but it was not strong enough to list as a trace. In contrast, my sister, Anne, and my brother, Ralph, have reported West European ethnicity of 28% and 27% respectively. The DNA test confirms the full sibling relationship but questions the accuracy of ethnicity measurement in this instance.

10 William Mezger, born 31 Jan 1867, Clermont, Qld – died 26 Apr 1947, Rockhampton, Qld

11 Qld MC 1895/1836 157, Rockhampton, 19 Oct 1895, Ellen Maloney & William Mezger

12 Nancy Ellen Mezger married Eric Ronald Loch 26/9/1928, Patricia was the only known offspring – further details currently unknown.

13 Initially thought to be an alderman of Mount Morgan from 1894 to 1898. But that was a different W. Mezger namely, William McCarthy Metzger who died in 1902. That William was a native of Sierra Leone.

14 Louis Mezger, born 18 Jun 1868 Clermont, Qld – died 11 Aug 1919 Mackay, Qld

& Advertising, *Mackay Mercury*, Sat 26 Mar 1892, page 1 http://nla.gov.au/nla.news-article167943420

15 http://www.mackayhistory.org/research/hotels/hotels_l_to_z.html

16 Charles Michael Mezger, born 9 Aug 1870, Peak Downs/Clermont – died 29 Apr 1931, Shanghai, China

& Qld Birth Record 1870/2362 298, Beaufort Belyando (Peak Downs), 9 Aug 1870, Michael Mezger

17 e.g. Athletics, *The Capricornian* (Rockhampton), Sat 30 Apr 1892, page 27 http://nla.gov.au/nla.news-article66320483

& United Friendly Societies sport, *Mackay Mercury*, Sat 23 May 1891, page 2 http://nla.gov.au/nla.news-article167941017

18 Cricket, *Mackay Mercury*, Thu 1 Oct 1891, page 3 http://nla.gov.au/nla.news-article167939619

19 Sporting, *Daily Mercury* (Mackay), Tue 15 Jan 1907, page 3 http://nla.gov.au/nla.news-article176289643

20 Personal, *Daily Mercury* (Mackay), Thu 11 Jun 1931, page 6 http://nla.gov.au/nla.news-article170422922

21 Children were: Vincent (1895–1980) married Katherine (Katia) Kossivtzoff in Shanghai – no children,

Roy Charles (1899 – 1940) unmarried labourer lived in Innisfail, Ayr & Mt Isa, no children

Marion Agnes (Marie) (1902–1930) unmarried lived in Mackay, no children,

Kevin Bernard (1905–1951) journalist, married Helen Sayers lived in Charters Towers & Townsville, no children,

Katherine Dorothea (Thea) (1907–1969) – married Harold Corser, lived in Brisbane, no children.

22 Believed to be *The Bulletin*, many people, including Tim Ditton, sent contributions for possible publication, many contributions simply used a pen name to provide anonymity.

23 Father Bucas testimonial, *Daily Mercury* (Mackay), Fri 23 Feb 1912, page 7 http://nla.gov.au/nla.news-article170683273

24 *Early Settlers of Mackay 1860–1885* Mackay Family History Society Inc, pages 124–125

25 Conditions at Shanghai, *Daily Mercury* (Mackay), Mon 14 Jan 1929, page 8 http://nla.gov.au/nla.news-article169775658

26 John Andrew Mezger, born 4 Nov 1874, Clermont, Qld – died 11 Oct 1915, Stanthorpe, Qld

27 http://www.mackayhistory.org/research/hotels/hotels_l_to_z.html#WHITSUNDAY

28 His nephew, John Louis Mezger, was running this same hotel in 1925.

29 Personal, *Daily Mercury* (Mackay), Thu 11 Jun 1931, page 6 http://nla.gov.au/nla.news-article170422922

30 e.g. Athletics, *The Capricornian* (Rockhampton), Sat 2 Jun 1894, page 31 http://nla.gov.au/nla.news-article67940585

& e.g. Athletics, *Daily Mercury* (Mackay), Wed 26 Apr 1911, page 8 http://nla.gov.au/nla.news-article172439172

31 Obituary, *The Brisbane Courier,* Fri 10 Jul 1931, page 13 http://nla.gov.au/nla.news-article21725056

& e.g. *The North Winds Children, The Daily Mail (Brisbane)*, Sat15 Dec 1923, page 7 http://nla.gov.au/nla.news-article218967724

32 Advertising, *Mackay Mercury*, Tue 9 Sep 1902, page 4 http://nla.gov.au/nla.news-article170222053
& Death of Mr. A. Ditton, *The Telegraph* (Brisbane), Tue 17 Oct 1944, page 2 http://nla.gov.au/nla.news-article189863081
33 Mary de Jabrun, Paul's aunt is more closely related according to the hypothesis and she has a match with myself, calculated by Ancestry at 188 centiMorgans (cMs) across 9 segments which is 'virtually 100% conclusive proof we are related via recent ancestors'. (Ralph and Mary match 135 cMs across 10 segments and Anne and Mary match 109 cMs across 5 segments.) This fits right in the second cousin once removed bracket which the hypothesis of a brother of Louis being Arthur's father. However, neither Sonya nor Christine have a significant enough match with Mary to be reported at any level. This highlights the vagaries of DNA testing and the need to test multiple relatives. On Ancestry's calculation, Paul O'Neill's match to myself is 34 cMs over 4 DNA segments. Paul's match to Cousin Sonya is 31 cMs across 2 segments. Cousin Christine only has an 8.4 cMs match on 1 segment as calculated by GEDmatch. All these numbers suggest a match more around the fourth cousin level but could be as close as third cousin.
34 Current closest match is at genetic distance 5 at 67 markers and 3 at 37 markers which suggests the match is beyond the documented genealogical time frame or when surnames were generally adopted. Surname of the closest match is Brunhuber.
35 From the FTDNA website: The G haplogroup was the first branch of haplogroup F outside Africa. G is found mostly in the North Central Middle East and the Caucasus, with smaller numbers around the Mediterranean and eastwards. G-Y20834 is a sub-group under the following nested sub-branches G-L89, G-P15, G-L1259, G-L30, G-L141, G-P303, G-BY28175, G-Z30503, G-Z30520, G-Z30521, and G-Z40458. The G-P15 branch is found most often in Europe and the Middle East.
36 Tim's daughter, Lola was surprised when she obtained her father's birth certificate with its blank father's name. Ursula was Tim's eldest child and her husband Dick Freney is remembered as saying: 'There were Germans in the family'.
37 Originally part of the Duchy of Swabia, it was the County of Württemberg (1083–1495), The Duchy of Württemberg (1495–1803), The Electorate of Württemberg (1803–1806) before becoming the Kingdom of Württemberg in 1806. From 1815 to 1866 (i.e. during John & Grace's time there), it was a member of the German Confederation – Wikipedia.
38 The German states bordering to the north are Rhineland-Palatinate & Hesse.
39 A dialect of German differs in both vocabulary and pronunciation to standard German and is therefore not easily or completely understood by speakers of standard German.
40 https://www.thelocal.de/20161027/new-exhibition-tests-swabian-stereotypes
Albert Einstein, the author Herman Hesse and the astronomer Johannes Kepler are some of the famous Swabian folk.
41 Prior to the nation state, there was a customs union between the separate entities for several decades. German was an ethnicity in a geography which roughly corresponds to the present-day country of Germany, but which potentially included German speakers or speakers of German based dialects in present day countries of Switzerland, Austria, Luxembourg and neighbouring regions of others. The significant point is, English people were likely to classify John & Grace as German, based on their language.
42 It is difficult to locate Diebach on a modern map. John's immigration record from 1863 had his town listed as Disbach, which cannot be found in Württemberg either. There is a sizeable town called Diebach in nearby Bravaria, but the family were clear on him comming from Württemberg. There is a Diebach Lake between Schwäbisch-Hall and Schwäbisch-Gmünd. The location in the text has come from Mary de Jabrun's writings, which in turn has come from contact with living German relatives.
43 Georg Kasimir Metzger, born 4 Mar 1776 Rengershausen, Germany – died 15 Nov 1827, Diebach, Württemberg
However, John's DC (1892/5891) has his father's name as Andrew. Maria Anna Spath died in 1863.
44 Josef Bihlmaier, born 30 Mar 1794, Heuchlingen, Heidenheim, Württemberg – died 12 Jun 1864, Württemberg
& Crescentia Rieck, born 17 Nov 1794, Heuchlingen, Heidenheim, Württemberg – died 17 Jun 1847, Württemberg
45 *Australian Historical Statistics* – Ed: W. Vamplew, Pub: Fairfax Syme & Weldon Associates NSW 1987. In 1901 Qld, there were 13,233 German born out of a total of 174,505 Foreign born. Qld had the highest proportion of foreign-born residents with 35% of the non-Indigenous population. It also had both the highest number and highest proportion of German born immigrants of any state.
46 Rated at 414 tons, built in Hamburg in 1851. A barque has the fore and main mast square rigged and the missen mast rigged fore and aft.
47 The Johan Cesar, *The Brisbane Courier,* Tue 17 May 1864, page 4 http://nla.gov.au/nla.news-article1258521
48 Qld MC 1864/895, St Stephen's Brisbane, 2 May 1864, Crescentia Bihlmaier & Johannes Metzger
49 On the upper reaches of the Capella Creek. Adjoining runs combined to 150,000 acres. http://www.capella.com.au/115
50 R Cilento & C Lack, *Triumph in the Tropics,* Smith and Paterson, Brisbane, 1959, page 206.
& Gold was discovered at nearby Peak Downs in 1861.
51 Annie Mezger, born Maria Anna, 15 Sep 1865, Clermont, Qld – died 13 Dec 1865, Clermont, Qld
& Fanny Mezger, born Frances, Aug 1872, Clermont, Qld – died 23 Jan 1874, Clermont, Qld
52 Walkerston, named after John Walker, who owned a cattle station and boiling down works in the town's current location.
53 A news report from 2021 of a thwarted carjacking included an interview with a man who still refers to the town as 'Scrubby'.
54 LR Ford, *Poorhouse to Paradise: The adventures of a Pioneering Family in a North Queensland Country Town,* Taipan Press, Freshwater, Qld, 2001. This extensive family history states, 'the low-set house on allotment 9 became the Ford family home and a cottage on the Dane St frontage of allotment 10 has the distinction of being one of the oldest (or the oldest) house in Walkerston'. Allotments 8, 9, 10 of section IV running from the corner of Creek & Dane sts in a SE direction towards the corner of Creek & Pound sts. The house was built on allotment 9. John's son Louis subsequently sold off some of his land, including allotments 9 & 10, in half acre lots to a neighbour, Charles Ford.
55 Deaths, *Mackay Mercury*, Tue 12 Jan 1892, page 2 http://nla.gov.au/nla.news-article167947168

& Qld DC 1892/2455 5891, Walkerston, 9 Jan 1892, John Mezger. Inflammation of the peri's cardium, the thin membrane around the heart

56 Notice of probate granted, *Mackay Mercury*, Tue 23 Feb 1892, page 3 http://nla.gov.au/nla.news-article167945085

57 Ford, page 71

58 Qld DC 1917/601 10015, Mackay, 18 Dec 1917, Grace Mezger

59 https://www.legislation.gov.au/Details/C1914A0001

60 Senator Pearce 1918 Parliament House Library website

https://www.aph.gov.au/About_Parliament/Parliamentary_Departments/Parliamentary_Library/pubs/rp/rp1516/WW1Immigration

61 https://www.irishtimes.com/news/ireland/irish-news/irish-in-australia-were-not-shirkers-in-first-world-war-1.1967446

62 Personal, *Daily Mercury* (Mackay), Sat 3 Jul 1915, page 5 http://nla.gov.au/nla.news-article175034885

63 Oral history from Paul O'Neill

64 Photo from the collection of Mary de Jabrun. 'Polly Quillinan' may be misnamed as one questionable source names her as such, whereas another, marks her as unknown.

65 Photo from the collection of Mary de Jabrun

66 Photo from *Poorhouse to Paradise* by Lyall Ford

Chapter 11

Tracks into town

Mary and Patrick – Cranley

Qld was growing up quickly – the southern settled districts were starting to resemble the established colonies of NSW and Victoria. Infrastructure such as railways were spreading out from the population centres. As the colonies were not yet federated, it did not look ahead to the time when such services might be integrated. The three eastern seaboard colonies chose different rail gauges, setting up a problem which has held back the Australian rail network to the current day.[1] This chapter explores the family that raised my paternal grandmother, Ellen Cranley. Her parents were Mary Barry and Patrick Cranley. Patrick worked on the Qld railways.

The early days and the marriage

Patrick Cranley was born at sea in June 1853, on board the *John Fielden* in Moreton Bay. He arrived from England with his Irish-born parents and siblings, who were escaping the devastation of the Irish Potato Famine. By 1857, he was living with his family on the family-owned farm, about one and a half kilometres south of the centre of the fledgling town of Toowoomba. Later, the family moved to their new and larger farm five kilometres to the north of Toowoomba. Patrick was educated locally and participated in the sporting opportunities offered by his community. He played cricket for Toowoomba between 1873 and 1877.[2] He earned some winnings from his running and sack racing at events like the St Patrick's Day sporting carnival.[3]

Mary Barry was born in Drayton, Qld, in 1853. Drayton was just seven kilometres south-west of Toowoomba. She had been orphaned at the age of eleven. It is believed she attended the National School in Drayton which is the oldest continually run school in Qld.[4] The family was RC but the first Catholic school in the Toowoomba district did not open until 1864.[5] Mary and Patrick married in the presbytery of the RC Church in James Street,[6] Toowoomba, on 29 May 1877.[7] Marrying in the presbytery was usually only done if there was some complication to the union from the church's point of view.[8] There was a suggestion, Patrick's father, James had instructed the priest, Father Robert Dunne, to not marry the couple, but it emerged Patrick simply did not seek his father's permission to marry, as he was aware his father disapproved of the match.[9] Therefore, it is presumed it was a love match. Reasons why James may have disapproved of the marriage are revealed in the chapter on Mary's parents.

Family and career

Patrick and Mary were of the same age and probably knew each other as children. They would have lived about five kilometres apart during their childhood. When Patrick married Mary, his occupation was a 'farmer's son'. They lived at Miles for the first year.[10] Patrick registered his own horse and cattle brand in April 1878, and he gave his address as his parents farm.[11] Their first son, Patrick, was born in 1878 at Town View, Hume Street, Toowoomba. Young Patrick was just two days old when he died of bronchitis. His birth was announced in the newspaper on the Tuesday and his death notice appeared the following Saturday.[12]

Patrick was labouring at Four Mile Creek near Stanthorpe when Mary gave birth to their next son, John, in 1880.[13] Patrick applied for a miner's licence in Stanthorpe in October 1881. He was described as a tin miner on his son James' birth record in 1882.[14] Young James died just short of his first birthday. Patrick kept up his farming as in 1882, he won a prize at the Toowoomba Show for the second-best bushel of wheat.[15]

By November 1883, Patrick had joined the Queensland Railways. Trains were the vanguard of the industrial revolution in colonial Australia. As well as moving freight around more economically which boosted trade and therefore prosperity, the railways stimulated the development of other infrastructure and industries. It was now possible for individuals and families to travel significant distances in relative comfort for an affordable fee.[16] Consequently, the

The Cranley family circa 1894. L to R: Patrick, Grace Annie, Mary Ethel, John, Catherine, Ellen and Mary

horizon of every human endeavour was stretched a few hundred kilometres. Country folk could now get a sniff of the big smoke, which accelerated a drift to the cities. The Qld rail network had steadily been expanding since the first train in Qld had run between Ipswich and Grandchester (aka Bigge's Camp) in 1865.

Patrick's first posting was as a porter in Brisbane.[17] He later had postings to Warwick on the Southern Darling Downs and then to Laidley in the Lockyer Valley in 1885. His positions up until 1889 were porter, foreman porter and supervisor. In 1889, he was appointed to the position of stationmaster at Murarrie on the Cleveland line.[18] His annual salary for this position was £120. He held that position until 1903 when he was appointed as a checker working from the city of Brisbane.[19]

Patrick and Mary's family consisted of son John (b. 1880) and daughters Mary Ethel (Cissy) (b. 1883), Ellen (b. 1885), Catherine Patricia (b. 1887) and Grace (Tottie) (b. 1892).[20]

Notable incidents

In 1892, Patrick Cranley was a witness in a trial for a murder which occurred less than a kilometre from the Murarrie railway station. Patrick identified the suspect from a line-up of ten men at South Brisbane. A seventeen-year-old, Frank Horrocks, was convicted and hanged for the brutal murder of a nineteen-year-old recently arrived German immigrant, Rudolph Weissmuller. Patrick had seen his son, John, a mother and her baby and two young men disembark the train at Murarrie on that April afternoon. Horrocks and his victim left the train and headed across a field together. When out of sight, Horrocks dispatched his victim with a tomahawk, recently purchased especially for the deed. Robbery was the motive. They had been staying in a boarding house in Brisbane together. Horrocks 'became the youngest white individual ever to be executed in Qld'. An Aboriginal youth 'named Jago, executed in the 1880s, had been even younger still'.[21]

The last person executed in Qld was Ernest Austin in 1922. In that same year, the reforming government of 'Red Ted' Theodore abolished the death penalty, making Qld the first jurisdiction in the British Commonwealth[22] to abolish hanging.[23] Also in the same year, the trail-blazing government abolished the Legislative Council Chamber, Qld's upper house of parliament, making the unicameral Qld unique among Australian states.[24]

Also, in 1892, Patrick had to attend court for an entirely different matter. He had challenged his father's will, which directly pitted him against his sister, Margaret. Legal proceedings dragged on in that matter for several years. That episode is explored in detail in a later chapter. Some of the things we learnt about Patrick from that episode were that he liked a drink, perhaps too much, and he also took his family to visit his parents in Toowoomba during his annual holidays.

In February 1893, The Brisbane River broke its banks three times as a result of three separate major rain events. The first saw over 907 mm fall on Crohamhurst (in the catchment of the Brisbane River) in one 24-hour period. That is the all-time Australian record. The floods took 35 lives and destroyed the only two bridges in Brisbane that crossed the Brisbane River, including the Albert railway bridge at Indooroopilly. Murarrie was not directly affected, but Brisbane's transport services took years to get back to the pre-flood situation.[25] Another pertinent impact of those floods is that they destroyed many colonial records such as immigration records.[26] The inability to trace some of the early movements of ancestors is a legacy of those floods that we are still living with.

There is an oral history account of an escaped convict coming into the yard of the Cranley's house. It was probably during the family's time at Murarrie. The sound of a violin playing had drawn him into the yard and he had tears in his eyes. The family all played musical instruments and played as a group

199

Albert railway bridge, Indooroopilly in February 1893, after destruction by floodwaters.[38]

at church functions. The story goes, he stayed for several hours listening to the music and talked with the family, but it is not known what his fate was beyond that encounter.

By 1903, the position of checker allowed the family to enjoy the city life. However, his remuneration had declined to seven shillings a day for this position, which implies he had been demoted. His disgrace was complete when he was dismissed from this position in July 1908.[27]

Up until 1916, the family had several addresses in what is now fashionable Paddington and the inner west of the city. In those days, it was a neighbourhood for the working class. They lived at several addresses in Menzies Street, corner of Caxton Street and Church Street, Charlotte Street and Latrobe Terrace.[28] A house which until recently was painted bright yellow, on the corner of Caxton Street and Church Street, very close to Lang Park (Suncorp stadium), is believed to have been their address for about a year around 1905.[29]

The final years

Patrick died in January 1910 of what was recorded as typhoid fever and bronchitis.[30] Typhoid was the most prominent disease that had devastated Ireland in the years of the famine. It was also a disease which struck down thousands of Australian urban dwellers each summer. It was largely a preventable disease caused by bad water, drainage and poor building practices.[31] Patrick's residence at the time of his death was described as *Blackburnie*, Latrobe Terrace, Paddington. His death notice read:

CRANLEY – On the 18th January of Typhoid fever, Patrick beloved husband of Mary Cranley, fourth son of the late James Cranley, Toowoomba, Deeply mourned. May his soul rest in peace.[32]

Mary and her daughters continued to live close to the city. The young women had taken jobs as dressmakers and sales assistants. By 1916, Tottie and Ellen had married. Mary, Cissy and Catherine went to live with John and his family at Church Street (now Bombery Street), Cannon Hill. John and family departed for a new posting at Wynnum around 1930. Mary and Cissy lived on at Cannon Hill. Mary died there in June 1939 aged 86.[33]

Patrick and Mary are buried together in the Toowong Cemetery with just the family name on their grave. Succeeding generations remembered both with affection.

Cranley children - Ellen's siblings

John followed his father into the railways in 1896, where he started as a lad porter earning 2s and 1d a day and by 1910, had attained the position of stationmaster at Linville and later at Cannon Hill.[34] John had married Rachel Ling in 1901. They had two girls, Beryl Rachel (b. 1905) and Joyce (b. 1907). His wife Rachel died in 1932 and John remarried the following year to Susan May Thompson. John died in 1943 and an obituary was published in *The Courier Mail*:[35]

Mr. J. Cranley, 63, station-master at Wynnum for 14 years died on Monday after a brief illness. Joining the Railway Department at an early age, he was stationed at Wynnum as a porter, and became a station-master at 21. The late Mr. Cranley was stationed at Southport, Esk, and Cannon Hill. He was at Cannon Hill for 18 years, before he was shifted to Wynnum. Mr. Cranley was a keen bowler, having recently competed in two finals of pair championships. He leaves his wife and two married daughters, Mrs. Pawley (Sydney), and Mrs. Hill (Brisbane).[36]

Cissy was a dressmaker who never married and lived with her mother until her mother died. Cissy died in Brisbane in 1947.

Catherine Patricia married Harold Matcham Pitt at the age of 42 in Brisbane. There were no children. Catherine died in 1957 and Harold died in 1968.

Tottie married Tom Waters in 1912. They had three children, Joseph Arthur (b. 1913), Maureen Lucy (b. 1916) and Thomas Jack (Jack) (b. c. 1922). Tom died in 1944 and Tottie died in 1952.[37] Following in his father's footsteps, Jack worked at WMC in the post-war period whilst Dit also worked there.

The Cranley family circa 1894 L to R: Cissy, Tottie, Patrick, Ellen, Mary, Catherine and John

Endnotes to Chapter 11

1 Qld & Tas had narrow gauge, NSW had standard gauge. Vic had wide gauge and SA & WA had a mixture – Wikipedia.

2 E.g. From the *Courier* and the *Telegraph*, *The Darling Downs Gazette and General Advertiser*, Wed 12 Mar 1873, page 3
http://nla.gov.au/nla.news-article77085006

& Cricket match, *The Darling Downs Gazette and General Advertiser*, Wed 18 Oct 1876, page 3 http://nla.gov.au/nla.news-article76919546

3 e.g. St. Patrick's Day, *The Darling Downs Gazette and General Advertiser*, Sat 27 Mar 1875, page 1 http://nla.gov.au/nla.news-article212666107

& Caledonian gathering, *The Darling Downs Gazette and General Advertiser*, Wed 3 Jan 1872, page 3 http://nla.gov.au/nla.news-article75529290

& Laidley Jubilee sports, *Queensland Times, Ipswich Herald and General Advertiser*, Thu 23 Jun 1887, page 4
http://nla.gov.au/nla.news-article122820474

4 Opened in 1851 https://draytonss.eq.edu.au/Ourschool/Pages/Ourschool.aspx

5 St Saviour's Primary School, originally called St Patrick's church school

6 The church burnt down in 1880, 1 day after renovations were completed and the present-day St Patrick's Cathedral was erected in its place and completed in 1889.

7 Qld MC 1877/260 1401, James St., Toowoomba, 29 May 1877, Mary Barry & Patrick Cranley

8 Examples of complications were: one of the parties was not Catholic or if the bride was pregnant or some parents objected.

9 Later Catholic Bishop of Brisbane (1882–1887) and then Catholic Archbishop of Brisbane (1887–1912)

10 Civil sittings, *The Telegraph* (Brisbane), Tue 31 May 1892 page 2 http://nla.gov.au/nla.news-article173290349

11 Qld Horse and Cattle Brands 1872-1899,(QFHS index), *Queensland Government Gazette*, Mon 8 Apr 1878, vol XXII No 46 page 867
Later that same year the Qld Electoral Roll identifies Patrick living at Fountain's Camp an old railway navies camp near Murphy's Creek

12 Birth, *Toowoomba Chronicle and Darling Downs General Advertiser*, Tue 26 Nov 1878 p2 http://nla.gov.au/nla.news-article217701143

& Death, *Toowoomba Chronicle and Darling Downs General Advertiser*, Sat 30 Nov 1878 p2 http://nla.gov.au/nla.news-article217699967

13 Qld BC 1880/C/5659 Stanthorpe, 23 Apr 1880 John Cranley. Four Mile Creek was the site of a gold and tin mine in 1880.

14 Qld BC 1882/C/6223 Stanthorpe, 18 Jan 1882, James Cranley. & QFHS Qld Miner's Rights and Business Licences 1870–1884.

15 The Toowoomba show, *The Queenslander* (Brisbane), Sat 18 Feb 1882, page 215 http://nla.gov.au/nla.news-article19782665

16 A second class return ticket on Qld's first train line, Ipswich to Bigge's Camp cost 3 shillings – 75 minutes each way. –
R Fisher *Boosting Brisbane – Imprinting the Colonial Capital of Queensland*, Boolarong Press, Brisbane, 2009 page 76.

17 Qld BC 1884/B/31602 Brisbane, 24 Nov 1883, Mary Ethel Cranley

18 Spelt 'Mooraree' in the 1890s

19 A checker was most probably a ticket checker, but it may have involved checking the rolling stock instead or as well. It was certainly a demotion from Station Master

20 Qld BI 1880/C/5659, 23 Apr 1880, John Cranley

& Qld BI 1884/B/31602, 24 Nov 1883, Mary Ethel Cranley

& Qld BC 1885/7113 4084, Laidley, 7 Dec 1885, Margaret Ellen Cranley

& Qld BI 1888/C/8050, 8 Nov 1887, Catherine Patricia Cranley

& Qld BI 1892/C/9291, 7 Oct 1892, Grace Annie Cranley

21 The Mooraree murder, *Logan Witness* (Beenleigh), Sat 23 Apr 1892, page 3 http://nla.gov.au/nla.news-article163895964

& Boggo Road website names Aboriginal man as Jango aged 17. He was executed in 1883 for a murder near Dingo.

22 Michigan, USA, abolished the death penalty for all but treason, in 1846. Wisconsin, USA, completely abolished it in 1853.

23 https://www.historychannel.com.au/articles/death-penalty-abolished-queensland-leads-way-australia/

24 https://en.wikipedia.org/wiki/List_of_Premiers_of_Queensland_by_time_in_office

25 https://en.wikipedia.org/wiki/1893_Brisbane_flood

26 https://www.qld.gov.au/recreation/arts/heritage/archives/collection/immigration

27 QLD Parliamentary Papers 1909 Vol 2 page 735 (QFHS & SLQ QOPEN Railways appointments and dismissals)

28 Australian Electoral Rolls, Qld, Brisbane, Brisbane North/Toowong, 1903, 1905, 1909

29 Australian Electoral Rolls, Qld, Brisbane, Brisbane North, 1908

30 Qld DC 1910/12022, Brisbane Hospital, 18 Jan 1910, Patrick Cranley

31 *Australians 1888* Ed: G Davison, JW McCarty, A McLeary Pub: Fairfax, Syme, Weldon, Broadway, NSW, 1987, p226

32 Funeral notices, *The Brisbane Courier*, Wed 19 Jan 1910, page 4, http://nla.gov.au/nla.news-article19616104
He was in fact the fifth son.

33 Qld DC 1939/44073, Bombery St., Cannon Hill, 19 Jun 1939, Mary Cranley

34 QLD LA votes and proceedings, 1896 Vol 4 page 368 (QFHS & SLQ QOPEN Railways appointments and dismissals)

35 Funeral notices, *The Brisbane Courier*, Wed 19 Jan 1910, page 4 http://nla.gov.au/nla.news-article19616104

36 Mr. J. Cranley dead, *The Courier Mail* (Brisbane), Wed 17 Mar 1943, page 4 http://nla.gov.au/nla.news-article42030340

37 Qld DC 1952/040685, Evelyn St, Grange, 4 Nov 1952, Grace Annie Waters

38 Photo from the State Library of Queensland 1893 Brisbane Flood

Chapter 12

Transplanted farmers

Margaret and James – Cranley

The Irish Potato Famine was responsible for a wave of displaced people seeking refuge on faraway shores. They came on boats to Australia and other lands. As there were many prejudices regarding the Irish, not all welcomed this disorderly procession, but most refugees found a land which absorbed them and, in time, allowed them to flourish. The lessons of history are easily forgotten and so it is fitting that the history is retold at each opportunity. This chapter is the story of the family that raised my father's mother's father, Patrick Cranley. His parents were Margaret Murphy and James Cranley.

Ireland

James Cranley was born in County Tipperary, Ireland, sometime around 1812. We know little about his parents. The immigration records tell us their names were Timothy and Mary and they were still living in Ireland. James' death certificate had his father's occupation as farmer.[1] James' first child was named Timothy and that is consistent with the Irish child-naming tradition.[2] The best match from the baptism records of County Tipperary has a James Cranley being baptised on 14 January 1813 to parents Timothy Cranley and Margaret (née Ryan).[3] This baptism was in the parish of Anacarthy/Donohill.[4] Local historians say the name Mary was often paired with Margaret and then used interchangeably.[5] The

order in which James and Margaret's children were named also suggests James' mother was formally named Margaret.[6] James had an older brother named Timothy. Their farm was thought to have been in the townland of Gortnacoolagh.[7] The oral history says the Cranleys were of the 'strong farmer class'.[8] Apparently, this did not mean they necessarily owned farmland and this is supported by the following two facts. Firstly, according to the records, the Cranleys of Tipperary were tenant farmers, and secondly, they were Catholics.[9]

By the early 1800s, less than five percent of the farmland in Ireland was owned by Catholics, despite them being eighty percent of the population. Prior to the *Papists Act* in 1778, Catholics were forbidden to own or inherit land. Only after 1782 were they allowed to be formally educated. Prior to that, they were only educated in 'hedge schools', which were clandestine arrangements to provide basic education and religious instruction. Relief from most of the remaining restrictions came with the *Roman Catholic Relief Act* of 1829. Despite that progress, Catholics were still required to pay tithes to the Anglican Church of Ireland until 1838.[10] That requirement only stopped after an increasing number of Catholics refused to pay it. Often that refusal was accompanied by vitriol and/or violence.

There were newspaper reports from the 1830s of mobs setting upon the tithe collectors, and in one case being stripped and thrown in a pond. An 1836 article described an incident near Neagh, Tipperary, where a tithe collector was accompanied by 23 policemen in an attempt to arrest Kennedy of Ballybane against whom a 'writ of rebellion' had been raised because of his non-payment of tithes. The report described how the party was confronted by '200 ferocious looking fellows armed with missiles and various weapons'. The tithe collector and police retreated empty-handed.[11] Earlier in 1834 at Rathcormac, Cork, soldiers had massacred at least a dozen tithe protesters who had hurled rocks at the soldiers. Legal repercussions from that incident led to greater restraint in subsequent efforts.[12] In other cases, forced auctions of defaulters' property prompted pleas to the crowd not to buy the goods if they were intended to collect tithe debts. The protests and the distaste that some authorities had for this work finally shifted sentiment.

An incident that was reported in 1833, gives a sense of how attitudes were changing. A tithe-collecting party including police and soldiers entered a destitute widow's cabin to seize goods to pay for the five shillings outstanding. The only thing of value she possessed was a potato pot. The authorities seized it and started the documentary process of transferring the ownership of the pot, when one of the soldiers intervened and offered six pence from his own pocket and urged others to contribute. The full amount was collected and then offered to the collector who, in his shame, declined the money and returned the pot to the widow.[13] This misuse of power by the ruling class was not the exclusive domain of the Protestants.

When the Catholics were in charge, in seventeenth-century France, they made life hell for the Protestant Huguenots who then fled en masse to other countries.

We have an oral record from granddaughter, Margaret O'Brien, stating James' family was 'upper crust'.[14] The oral record agreed the Cranleys were farmers, but Margaret was of the servant class. This marriage was disapproved of and his parents

Ballyhooly Castle in County Cork, Ireland near the village of Ballyhooly in 2007 Photo: author

subsequently 'threw him out'.[15] If true, then it may have influenced how James later dealt with disappointments with his own children.

Despite the official records[16] identifying James as a farm labourer, oral history[17] expands on this theme and said because of the class difference, Margaret had to curtsy to James when they passed.[18] This seems extreme, but as one family member pointed out: 'This is not the sort of thing that you would make up'.[19] James was a man of strong convictions, a hard and competent worker, but rather intolerant, especially when it concerned his children. By the time of his death, he was in communication with just two of his offspring.

James said he was married in 1840 at Ballyhooly, in County Cork. However, a church marriage record from Ireland puts their marriage date as 22 October 1838.[20] Ballyhooly is a village on the Blackwater River. Margaret Murphy was born into a farming family at a village further downstream on that river at Ballyduff in County Waterford, around 1813 to Michael and Mary Murphy (née O'Brien).[21] After their marriage, James and Margaret moved around Northern County Cork. Their first child, Timothy, was born at Fermoy, Cork, circa 1840 and the two girls, Mary and Margaret (1842 and 1844 respectively), were born at Mitchelstown near the border with Tipperary.[22] The records identify Edward/Edmond was born around 1845, James Joseph in 1847 and John in 1851. From available records they were all born in Northern County Cork.

The landmark survey of Ireland known as Griffith's Valuation 1847–1864 identifies around 1852, a James Cranley occupied a house in the townland of Broomhill, parish of Kilgullane, County Cork.[23] This locality is less than five kilometres west of Mitchelstown. James Gearan owned the house and its annual worth was just one pound.

Life became increasingly difficult, as the staple food of the Irish, the potato, suffered crop failures from 1845 to 1852 due to blight. Other crops, such as corn, were shipped to England because the prices that could be attained in England by the (often absent) landlords were much greater than those attainable as food relief in Ireland. Many factors were at play. Some relief came from various sources, but overall the assistance provided was inadequate and this was made worse by flawed distribution processes.

The Potato Famine was to trigger two parallel disasters, waves of deadly epidemics and almost total economic collapse. It is estimated, during the famine, over one million Irish people succumbed to disease or starvation and around 1.5 million people subsequently emigrated.[24]

Mitchelstown, the birthplace of the girls, was one of the first and most severely affected sites of a deadly fever (typhus) which broke out in 1846 and swept much of Ireland in 1847. It is apparent James and Margaret were much more fortunate than many of their countrymen, as they appear to have lost either none or just one of their children during this time. Although we have no official confirmation of a child's death, the daughter, Margaret, later stated there had been nine children and there is a clear gap in the steady production of children around the year 1849. Whatever work James was doing must have been enough to provide food for the family. It would have kept him and his family out of the dreaded workhouses. In early 1847, the workhouse in Fermoy (birthplace of Timothy) recorded a 24 percent death rate in just over two months.[25]

Income had dried up and landlords were evicting surviving tenants when they fell into arrears.[26] Even if their tenants could pay rent, landlords were motivated to evict their tenants in pursuit of higher profits. There were clauses such as the quarter-acre rule which prevented relief being provided to anyone with more than a quarter acre to farm. This was used to wedge people off their land.[27] Vincent Scully was a notoriously mean landlord who owned the land in Tipperary where

The famine took a devestating toll on the Irish. Few would have been afforded a proper funeral, wake and burial. Photo from Glendalough, Co Wicklow 2007 by the author

Cranley relatives were living, and he was responsible for quite a few evictions.[28]

News of better conditions in the New World would have reached the ears of the landless Irish. In the early days of the famine, many were tricked onto the 'coffin ships' that sailed to Canada, which were at least as bad as the famine they fled.[29] Many Irish fled to Britain, but conditions there were only marginally better. The USA had taken many Irish immigrants since 1820 and this ramped up during and after the famine. Later, many of those immigrants became cannon fodder in the American Civil War.

Australia was actively recruiting immigrants to ease the labour shortage caused by the cessation of convict transportation to NSW in 1840.[30] The lure of the goldrushes in NSW and Victoria in the early 1850s made the labour shortage even worse. Tipperary and Clare were the most common source counties of immigration to Australia followed by Limerick and Kilkenny.[31]

Immigration to Australia

Along with a multitude of their compatriots, the Cranleys made the decision to emigrate. They had managed to survive the famine, but conditions in Ireland were still dire. The Cranleys had made their way across the Irish Sea to England and then booked passage on a ship leaving Birkenhead near Liverpool, bound for Moreton Bay, NSW.[32] James and his wife Margaret along with children: Timothy aged fourteen, Mary twelve, Margaret ten, James eight, Edward six and John two, boarded the immigrant ship, *John Fielden*, in March 1853. Margaret embarked heavily pregnant with her next child, Patrick. Patrick was born at the end of the voyage in Moreton Bay. This would have added an extra measure of discomfort to Margaret's journey.[33]

On 11 June 1853, ninety days after leaving Birkenhead, The *John Fielden* sailed into Moreton Bay. There had been four deaths and seven births on board, and the disembarking immigrants numbered almost 400. The hundred single females outnumbered single males by more than five to one. The Irish outnumbered the British. The single women and girls were to become servants and, no doubt in a short time, they would be married as there was a shortage of women in the colonies. Many of the remaining passengers were married couples, with children.[34] Of the men, most were to become shepherds or labourers working on the large pastoral stations on the Darling Downs, part of the recently opened northern lands in the colony of NSW. The shortage of labour meant pastoralists were desperate to receive these labourers. The wages paid were substantial enough that many such immigrants went on to purchase and settle on their own properties.

The *John Fielden* was rated at 916 tons, which is quite large compared to the ships which had arrived at Moreton Bay up to that point. It was built in New Brunswick, Canada about seven years before this voyage and its dimensions in feet are estimated at 145 x 33 x 22 (length, beam, depth of hold).[35] It required a crew of over thirty to sail it. By any modern-day measure, this would be considered uncomfortably cramped for its crew and human cargo. However, at this time, given the outcome it would simply be judged efficient. The voyage of ninety days was commendably quick and the number of births and deaths nothing exceptional.

An account of the voyage was written by Janet Alexander Tittmarsh (née Adams) and published in *The Fassifern Story*.[36] Janet was a six-year-old at the time of the voyage, so the account may be subject to some exaggeration. The anecdotes include an encounter with a dark and menacing ship that sailed around them, a collision with another ship, *Marc-o-Polo*, the worrisome sighting of an iceberg, the tragic death of a newborn by smothering and details of quartering and rationing on board. She relates, her father reported to the ship's captain some of the ship's timbers were in a poor state with the captain acknowledging he was aware of it. There are also insights into the disorganised

disembarkation process and the primitive state of facilities upon arrival.

Because Moreton Bay was not as well established as other destinations, there were difficulties in coming into port. The ship suffered some damage at the entrance to Moreton Bay during a storm and had to abort its first attempt to land by sailing out to sea again. The ship was not able to negotiate the channel into the bay without pilot assistance, as all of the guiding buoys had again been washed away.

Migration to Moreton Bay was still in its infancy. In 1853 there were just over 10,000 non-indigenous people in the future colony of Qld.[37] Therefore, this one shipload represented an almost four percent increase in this population. By the time of separation from NSW in 1859, the non-indigenous population had more than doubled. In the years to come the population would grow significantly faster. By 1870, Qld's non-indigenous population had grown ten-fold to over 100,000 souls. In contrast it is estimated the Indigenous population living in Qld then stood at about 50,000, down from about 120,000 at the time of Arthur Phillip's arrival in 1788.[38]

Early days in Australia

After James, Margaret and family arrived in Moreton Bay, they would have followed the established route to the Downs. This started with a steamer up the Brisbane and Bremer rivers to Ipswich. From there, it was a bullock wagon up the Range to Drayton – at that time, the gateway to the Darling Downs.[39] When their last son, Michael, was born in 1856, James was employed as a shepherd on a station called *Corranga* (*Cooranga/Coorangah*) some fifty kilometres NNW of present-day Dalby.[40]

The Cranleys may have had some savings from Ireland, but we suspect the likelihood they brought a sizeable 'nest egg' with them from

Ireland as remote, considering the option they chose when they arrived. Indeed, they must have worked hard and saved money, as by March 1857, they had bought twenty acres described as allotment 55, county of Aubigny, parish of Drayton for £45 at a Toowoomba government land sale. At this time James gave his occupation as a farmer and his residence as *Jimbour*. Today, Jimbour is a small country town 27 kilometres NNE of Dalby. Back in those days, it was a squatters' property and had on its north-western boundary, the property of *Corranga* where the last Cranley child, Michael was born. Both these properties were occupied by Bell & Sons, prominent squatters from this time.[41] The older Cranley children would also have been pressed into service to help build the prospects of the family in their new home.

The move to Toowoomba

The Cranley family moved to Toowoomba around 1857.[42] Toowoomba, just a few kilometres to the north of Drayton, was not officially declared a municipality until 1860. Until 1858, it was referred to as Drayton Swamp.[43] It sat atop the Great Dividing Range, several hundred metres higher than the coastal plain, which was directly to the east. The twenty acres (eight hectares) of land bearing James' name is shown on an early map of Toowoomba and Drayton Swamp. The land occupied the southern half of the block bounded by South, Hume, Geddes and Long streets. The present-day McCook Street marks part of the northern boundary of the block. Today there is a Cranley Street that runs parallel to South Street between Hume and Ramsey streets. This street, bearing their name, has the western

Cranley Station (formerly Bremmer's Gates) on the train line from Toowoomba to Gowrie Junction and points west and south. Picture from 1897. The station was mentioned and pictured in an account of the times recorded in letters written by Katie Hume and later collated into a book, *Katie Hume on the Darling Downs*.[79]

half contained within the land that was once theirs. They farmed this land, covered in the rich red soil typical of Toowoomba. It appears the farm was primarily accessed from Hume Street. They sold the farm sometime between 1876 and 1890.[44] In the late 1940s and early 1950s, this land was subdivided into a new housing estate of primarily workers' cottages to cater for the post-war expansion of Toowoomba.

In May 1862, The family bought a property near Toowoomba, which they called *Cranley*. This farm was 104 acres 1 rood 10 perches (40.6 hectares) in size and was bounded on the east by Gowrie Creek and on the south by the properties of Grundy, Thorn and Barnes.[45] They paid £1 an acre for it. They originally purchased 109 acres, but the Commissioner of Railways purchased almost five acres in November 1870, to build a railway line and siding at the eastern side of their property.[46] This divided the farm into two portions separated by the train line.

The farm was in the present-day North Toowoomba suburb of Cranley. The now demolished railway siding was on the Western Line and named 'Cranley'.[47] Up until 1905, this train line was also the southern line as the train to the South first travelled north to Gowrie Junction before turning to Warwick. This railway siding was north-east of the Baillie Henderson Hospital.[48] Construction of this psychiatric hospital, originally known as *Willowburn*, started in 1888 and opened in 1890. It later purchased the farm owned by Thorn on its northern boundary and Cranley's southern boundary.[49] The Cranley farm was offered to the government in 1896 to include within the hospital's land so it could be used for agricultural production by the patients.[50] The sale to the Crown was completed in 1897.[51]

The Toowoomba Second Range Crossing (toll road bypassing Toowoomba) was built between 2015 and 2019. It cuts through much of the land that had been the Cranley farm.

From 1864 to 1866, James was a councillor on the Toowoomba Municipal Council. The newspapers of the day reported the minutes of council meetings. James was not particularly vocal, but it was noted he consistently supported the mayor, William Groom.[52] Groom was an ex-convict who overcame his history to be remembered as a significant founding father of Toowoomba. James Cranley's support for this ex-convict of talent shows, at the very least, he was a practical man.

In early May 1872, newspapers reported James Cranley was charged with feloniously assaulting Agnes Stook, at Toowoomba, on 29 April.[53] The jury acquitted him, without leaving the box. His powerful friends – including William Groom (then MLA[54]), James Taylor, described as 'The King of Toowoomba' and several others – gave strong character references for him.[55] For example, Groom stated: 'No man's character stood higher in the neighbourhood'. The incident involved a woman, Agnes Stook, who was married to a newly arrived German man, John Stook. James had engaged him to work on his farms. The couple had the use of a cottage on the farm, but James had taken advantage of this fresh German with no English and had engaged him to work for him for £15 a year and one ration. Agnes was not part of the labour contract.

One afternoon, about a month into the contract, James had offered some bread and a pint pot of liquor to the woman whilst her husband was away working on another farm owned by James. She had taken some of it and then threw the rest away. This angered James and he grabbed Agnes, which resulted in some bruising to the arm. A subsequent attempt at obtaining compensation from James through an interpreter was met with a firm 'Nonsense!', repeated several times. The Stooks went to the police, which resulted in the charge. Much was made of James' good character, his refusal to buckle to any compensation claim as proof of his innocence, and the terms of the

Left: William Henry Groom   Centre: James Taylor   Right: Mary Klein (née Cranley)[80]

contract the Stooks were by then trying to get out of. This incident gives us several insights into James' character and the prevailing attitudes of the times.

This was not the only incident where James had difficulty with someone of German heritage. His daughter, Mary, had married a German immigrant in 1866. Johann Georg (George) Klein, a Lutheran, had married Mary in the Church of England in Toowoomba. As explored later, James disapproved of the union and then had nothing to do with Mary or her twelve children after that.

James' death

James enjoyed good health and was still active in his later years. John Fahy, who married James' daughter, Margaret, said he worked for James Cranley from 1863 to 1868 and then went bullock driving with James' sons. James quickly gained knowledge of the local conditions for agriculture and did well, as he could afford to pay for labourers when many farmers in the area were unsuccessful. He died at Gowrie Creek on 3 July 1890 after suffering from bronchitis for one week.[56] Up until then, his good health was demonstrated by having ridden 'in from Cranley, about three miles out on horseback' to the chapel at Toowoomba on the

Sunday two weeks prior to his death.[57] James was buried in the Drayton and Toowoomba Cemetery where his towering tombstone states he was '80 years old' and a native of Tipperary. The following obituary appeared in the *Toowoomba Chronicle* on 4 July 1890.

Early yesterday morning news reached Toowoomba of the death of Mr. James Cranley, one of the oldest residents in this district. The melancholy event took place at his residence, Cranley, on Gowrie Creek – from which Cranley siding on the Dalby and Roma railway takes his name – after a brief illness. The deceased gentleman was one of the earliest pioneers of this district and took up his residence here when not more than 200 people were settled in what is now Toowoomba. He has done perhaps more than his share to prove that agriculture can be made a success, and he brought to bear upon his labours a large amount of sound common sense and practical knowledge. In the early days he was a member of the Municipal Council of Toowoomba and joined with others in advancing the district in which he had made his home. He has reared a family, all of whom are now settled in life, one of his daughters being married to Mr. John Fahy, the respected Chairman of the Gowrie Divisional Board. The funeral of the deceased gentleman takes place at two o'clock this afternoon.

James' will left all his farm and personal property to his daughter, Margaret, and all the other children were given 'one shilling each … for their disobedience and folly'. He did not leave anything to his wife of over fifty years but gave instructions in his will for his daughter to look after her. This will was signed on 18 March 1890, just three and a half months before James died. The will was contested by his son Patrick and that episode is explored in detail in the next chapter.

Margaret's death

James Cranley's wife, Margaret, died in January 1896 at Gowrie Junction from senility and old age.[58] She was buried beside her husband in the Drayton and Toowoomba Cemetery.[59] Patrick's first son Patrick had died in infancy and was the first one buried in the plot in November 1878. Margaret and John Fahy were also buried in the same plot as Margaret's parents. Many years later, Margaret Cranley's grandson, Patrick Fahy, died in October 1951 and was buried with her.

Cranley children – Patrick's siblings

Timothy

Timothy was in a business partnership with his brothers James and Edward in Rockhampton, but he voluntarily departed from it in October 1873.[60] In 1874 he married Mary Kearney and later had six children. Timothy had several businesses including running the Crown Hotel. In January 1876, he faced insolvency as a result of the actions of his new partner, carrier and wine and spirit merchant, John Mulvena.[61] He successfully applied for a certificate of discharge in 1877.[62] The hotel licences were transferred to his wife when he had difficulty establishing his own suitability.

He had a rough patch in 1887, firstly in April, when a person to whom he transferred his hotel licence was refused a licence renewal because the hotel was 'filthy' due to Timothy's recovery from an illness.[63] In August, he was cited for deserting his wife, and in September, he faced a charge of attempting to commit suicide.[64] He had fired four shots from a revolver into his head whilst heavily drunk and alone in the house.[65] The glancing bullets had not penetrated his skull, but two had lodged against his skull until a doctor removed them. In his evidence, the doctor attributed that to the thickness of Timothy's skull, which brought laughter to the courtroom.[66] Timothy was present at court with his head bandaged. The charge did not proceed to trial as 'no bill was filed'.[67] The *Queensland Criminal Code 1899* decriminalised attempted suicide, but it was still a crime for many decades to come in other parts of Australia which used Common Law as the basis of criminal law.[68]

Thomas Cranley, Timothy's son, successfully sought exemption from compulsory military service in 1916, as he was the sole support for his aged father.[69] Leading up to the plebiscite in late October 1916, the government used existing legislation to conscript single men, aged between 21 and 35, into the armed forces. The government anticipated the plebiscite would be carried and that would then allow conscripts to be sent overseas to fight. Men could apply for exemption in the courts, and so for several weeks leading up to the failed vote, there were many reports of men applying for exemptions. This pre-emptive call-up was cited as one of PM Billy Hughes' heavy-handed tactics which led to the surprise defeat of the plebiscite.

Kearney descendants, Margaret Szalay and Mary Graham published a book, *Limerick to Queensland*, about the Kearney-Cranley family and others.[70] The book gives more details on this branch and other related topics including all known Cranley family tree details up to 2005.

Mary

Mary married George Klein in 1866 and had twelve children, who in turn had many children of their own. Mary died in Barcaldine in 1912. Ian and Margaret Kelly of Sandstone Point, Qld, wrote a book documenting the over 4000 Australian-born descendants of the Klein family, which arrived in Australia around the same time as the Cranleys. Mary is Ian's great-grandmother. The book was published in August 2006 and is called *Bound for The Downs – The Toowoomba Kleins.*[71]

Margaret

Margaret married John Fahy, a native of Galway in 1869 and had eleven children. James' obituary identified John as 'the respected head of the Gowrie Divisional Board'. They had run a hotel at Gowrie Junction. John died in 1909 and Margaret died in 1913 at Gowrie Junction.[72] Two of her daughters became nuns. Denise Sweeney, a great-granddaughter of Margaret, was intending to publish an account of her branch, but it is not known whether that has happened.

Edward

Edward (aka Edmond) Cranley was a stockman. He was in partnership with his brothers Timothy and James in Rockhampton until November 1873, his brother James having left the previous month. He spent time in the Barcoo and Winton districts. He never married and ended his days in the Dunwich Benevolent Asylum on North Stradbroke Island (Minjerribah) in 1923. He was suffering from a skin condition. Irish skin and Qld sun were often a fateful combination.

James Joseph

James Joseph Cranley married Bridget Devitt in 1881 at Emerald and had two children still alive when he also died at the Dunwich Benevolent Asylum suffering from senility and heart problems.[73] Bridget died in February 1928 at Mount Morgan and is recorded to have had four children from 1892 to 1903 with the surname of Lee, born after the two surviving children she had with James.[74] A 1903 newspaper report of an inquest stated Bridget was living with Michael Lee in Mount Morgan.[75] In 1903, James was registered on the electoral roll as living at Bolwarra Station on the Lower Tate River. His profession was listed as 'stockman'. His death certificate lists him as a 'labourer'.

Shortly after James left his business partnership with his brothers, in October 1873, he joined an expedition to the Palmer to report on the general conditions on the route to the goldfields and the conditions on the goldfields themselves. His informative account was published in several newspapers around the country during that summer.[76] In 1873, there had been a criminal deposition for James Joseph Cranley in Rockhampton on a charge of murder. Details of that deposition are still being searched for. It is unlikely James himself was the subject of the charge, or if he was, then he is likely to have had the charges dropped without a trial, as murder was a capital crime and there are no reports or records of a trial involving James. He died in Brisbane in 1927.

John

John Cranley was a draper and storekeeper in Orange, NSW. He married Elizabeth Bellos McLees in 1877. He was listed as 'a surrender' in the Insolvency Court in 1878.[77] He had two children. His son, William, emigrated to Canada via the UK. A great-granddaughter of John's (via William), Jill Fyffe (née Cranley) of Ontario, Canada has been actively researching Cranleys for some years. John died in Marrickville, NSW in 1924.

Michael

Michael was a stockman in South Australia for many years and never married. He died at Magill Home in Adelaide in 1926.[78] The home was a state-run aged care facility for the destitute.

Endnotes to Chapter 12

1 Qld DC 1890/1424 4545, Gowrie Creek near Toowoomba, 3 Jul 1890, James Cranley

2 First son is named after father's father.

3 Ryan is a very common name in Tipperary – so much so that when I handed in my search request for Cranleys, to the Family History service in Tipperary town, the assistant on duty said: 'They are not Ryans are they? Because that would be hopeless'.

4 Tipperary Family History Research: Baptism Anacarthy/Donohill. The parish is a few km north of town of Tipperary (or 'Tipp Town' as it is called locally).

5 As stated by the assistant on duty at the Tipperary Family History Society, 2007.

6 First daughter is named after mother's mother, second daughter after father's mother. Children were formally named according to this scheme, but they often had pet names or nicknames which were different to their formal names. Priests often refused to baptise a child with a given name which was not a saint's name.

7 Cranleys were in the townland of Gortnacoolagh in 1901 & 1910 and had lived there for several generations. Griffiths Valuation has a John Cranley and a Patrick Cranley residing in this townland as tenant farmers to landlord Vincent Scully. The only 2 other Cranleys in Tipperary in Griffith's Valuation were a tenant farmer in the Parish of Solloghodmore and a widow tenant in Tipperary town. The only land in Ireland owned by a Cranley was some land in Tullamore, County Offaly owned by a James Cranley. Unlikely to be the James Cranley of this story.

8 From a letter by Denise Sweeney (great-granddaughter of Margaret Fahy [née Cranley]) to author, 24 Nov 1991

9 Records: *Griffiths Valuation* 1847–1864

10 Wikipedia – Catholic Emancipation in Great Britain and Ireland

11 Quoting a 'Writs of rebellion' article that first appeared in the *Clonmel Advertiser, Belfast Newsletter,* Tue 19 Apr 1836, page 4

12 https://en.wikipedia.org/wiki/Rathcormac_massacre

13 Tithes – Tithes – The poor widow's pot, *Freemans Journal,* Fri 15 Feb 1833, page 4

14 Daughter of Margaret Fahy, who in turn is the daughter of Margaret Cranley (née Murphy) Denise Sweeney called her 'Margaret III'.

15 Letter from Denise Sweeny to author, 24 Jul 1991

16 e.g. Immigration record from the *John Fielden* 1853.

17 From a great granddaughter, Patricia Conner (née O'Brien) – from a letter from Denise Sweeney to author

18 In a letter from Denise Sweeney to author, 24 Jul 1991

19 That was the reply from Denise Sweeney's first cousin, Fr Pat Connor SVD when she discussed it with him. Both Denise and Pat related, at convent schools everyone had to curtsey to the head nun.

20 NSW BC for Michael Cranley 1856. The birth district would become part of Qld in 1859.

21 Qld DC 1896/1317 5450, Gowrie Junction, 26 Jan 1896, Margaret Cranley. The birth years of both James and Margaret have been estimated from several sources as the immigration records showing James was 28 and Margaret, 26 are almost certainly incorrect. These are 2 of the 6 suspected errors on the immigration records for the Cranleys. When their last child, Michael, was born in 1856, both of their ages were given as 40. Death certificates stretched the birth dates further back in time. Ages are often flexible to suit the audience. Vanity, societal expectations or official limits often come into play, so a range of sources are best collated to get a believable value.

22 Denise Sweeney called Mitchelstown 'the worst town in Ireland'.

23 The survey of County Cork was conducted between 1851 & 1853 – QFHS Irish SIG

24 H Litton, *The Irish Famine an Illustrated History*, Wolfhound Press, Dublin 2ⁿᵈ Ed. 2003, ISBN: 0-86327-912-0

25 Litton, page 75

26 Litton, pages 94–99

27 Litton, pages 77–78 known as the Gregory clause. Also an annual land value less than £5, meant the landlord was liable for taxes.

28 Information from Tom Drohan. In 1852, V. Scully became the member for Cork in the House of Commons in London – Wikipedia & *Irish Examiner,* Wed 12 Apr 1854, page 4, an unfavourable article, but informative on how Vincent Scully was perceived.

29 http://www.historyplace.com/worldhistory/famine/coffin.htm

30 NSW was the first British colony established in Australia in 1788. Convict transportation continued to other colonies such as Tasmania (ceased 1853) and Western Australia (ceased 1868).

31 Wikipedia – Irish Australians and as advised by Qld Family History Society – Irish Special Interest Group

32 Moreton Bay was part of NSW until the official separation of Qld in Nov 1859.

33 NSW Immigration Records John Fielden 1853 http://www.immigrantships.net/v3/1800v3/johnfielden18530619.html
Patrick was baptised on 26 Jun 1853.

34 Shipping intelligence, *The Moreton Bay Courier,* Sat 18 Jun 1853, page 2 http://nla.gov.au/nla.news-article3715998
& NSW Immigrant Shipping records. Margaret Kelly collated the passenger list of the *John Fielden* to provide the summary used.

35 Palmer's List of Merchant Vessels – http://www.geocities.com/mppraetorius/ plus information supplied by Susan Hughes, a descendant of the ships builder Samuel Carson with John Brown at Quaco (St Martins) near Saint John, NB

36 C Pfeffer, *The Fassifern Story: A History of Boonah Shire and Surroundings to 1989*, Boonah Shire Council, Boonah, 1991

37 *Australian Historical Statistics* – Ed: W Vamplew, Pub: Fairfax Syme & Weldon Associates, NSW, 1987, page 26

38 Estimates vary widely according to sources. These are based on medians of various accounts. Aboriginal people were not counted as citizens until after the 1967 referendum. However, there is general agreement, Aboriginal numbers declined significantly over the first century of contact through displacement from their lands, diseases and homicide. A 120,000 figure is provided by *Australian Historical Statistics,* page 4

39 Margaret Kelly of Sandstone Point provided a description of the transport utilised to get to the Downs in 2005.

40 NSW BC 1856/4297, *Corranga* (now in Qld), 21 Aug 1856, Michael Cranley.

41 Information provided by Margaret Kelly of Sandstone Point in 2005. The homestead built on Jimbour in 1874 was the largest, grandest and most expensive private house constructed in Qld in that decade - SLQ.

42 James Taylor, a founding father of Toowoomba, stated on oath in May 1872 he had known James for 16 years. On the same occasion, William Groom MLA said he had known James for 15 years.

43 M French, *Toowoomba: a sense of history: 1840–2008,* University of Southern Queensland, Toowoomba, 1991, preface identifies New Year's Day 1858, as the first time the name Toowoomba was officially used.

44 Queensland Electoral Roll records alternated James' address between Gowrie Creek and Hume St until 1876

45 County of Aubigny, Parish of Drayton, portion 415 (Dept. of Natural Resources, Mines and Environment (dnrme) titles ref: 10005078).

46 Aubigny, Drayton, Portion 415 subdivisions 1 and 4 (dnrme title refs: 10169206 &10169207)

47 Named after him, Ref: obituary in *Toowoomba Chronicle* on 4 July 1890
& e.g. *Australian Town and Country Journal* 12 Jul 1890, page 16 http://nla.gov.au/nla.news-article71179237

48 The railway siding was originally Bremmer's gates and then became Cranley's Gates. The name changed to just Cranley in 1878. *The Darling Downs Gazette and General Advertiser,* Wed 7 Aug 1878, page 3 http://nla.gov.au/nla.news-article75741594

49 http://bailliemuseum.wikidot.com/the-centenary
& Death of an old resident, *Darling Downs Gazette,* Mon 22 Feb 1904, page 2 http://trove.nla.gov.au/ndp/del/article/170475911

50 Toowoomba asylum *Toowoomba Chronicle and Darling Downs General Advertiser,* Tue 6 Oct 1896 page 3 http://nla.gov.au/nla.news-article217654088

51 dnrme title refs: 10169206 &10169207

52 Local and Domestic, *The Darling Downs Gazette and General Advertiser,* 1864–1866 e.g. Thu 11 Feb 1864, page 3 http://nla.gov.au/nla.news-article75512401

53 Friday May 3, *The Darling Downs Gazette and General Advertiser,* Sat 4 May 1872, page 3 http://trove.nla.gov.au/ndp/del/article/75529208

54 Member of the Legislative Assembly (Queensland Colonial [now State] Parliament)

55 http://adb.anu.edu.au/biography/taylor-james-4693

56 Toowoomba, *Australian Town and Country Journal,* Sat 12 Jul 1890, page 16 http://trove.nla.gov.au/ndp/del/article/71179337

57 Civil Sittings, *The Telegraph* (Brisbane), Mon 30 May 1892, page 6 http://nla.gov.au/nla.news-article173296701

58 Qld DC 1896/1317 5450, Gowrie Junction, 26 Jan 1896, Margaret Cranley. The registrar on her DC was the poet, George Essex Evans.

59 In block 10 allot 45 in the RC section

60 Qld DC 1925/C/17875, West St., Rockhampton, 17 Feb 1925, Timothy Cranley

61 Examination in insolvency, *The Capricornian* (Rockhampton), Sat 21 Apr 1877, page 6 http://nla.gov.au/nla.news-article65766009

62 Supreme Court Brisbane, *The Capricornian* (Rockhampton), Sat 27 Oct 1877, page 12 http://nla.gov.au/nla.news-article65762910

63 Rockhampton Licensing Authority, *Morning Bulletin* (Rockhampton), Thu 7 Apr 1887, page 6 http://nla.gov.au/nla.news-article52065800

64 Free trade and protection, *Morning Bulletin* (Rockhampton), Wed 31 Aug 1887, page 4 http://nla.gov.au/nla.news-article52012215

65 In general, handguns have been illegal to own in Australia for many decades even prior to the National Firearms Agreement of 1996. Their use is now strictly regulated. A rare exemption is that antique percussion revolvers can be owned in Qld without a licence.

66 Attempting suicide, *The Capricornian* (Rockhampton), Sat 10 Sep 1887, page 25 http://nla.gov.au/nla.news-article65744941

67 Queensland news, *The Queenslander* (Brisbane), Sat 17 Sep 1887, page 480 http://nla.gov.au/nla.news-article19927317

68 Still a crime in 1965 in NSW, VIC & SA http://classic.austlii.edu.au/au/journals/MelbULawRw/1965/1.pdf

69 Compulsory military service, *Morning Bulletin* (Rockhampton), Sat 21 Oct 1916, page 9 http://nla.gov.au/nla.news-article53405825

70 M Szalay, *Limerick to Queensland: the Kearney family story / our family history as told by Margaret Szalay & Mary Graham, Kearney descendants.* Self-published, Cremorne, NSW, 2006. NLA CiP 929.20994 – It was available via www.cremorne1.com)

71 IM Kelly, *Bound for The Downs The Toowoomba Kleins,,* self-published, USQ, Toowoomba 2006. Coincidently it was discovered whilst writing this book, Ian has published another book entitled *Out Mulga.*

72 Personal, *Darling Downs Gazette,* Fri 8 Aug 1913, page 4 http://nla.gov.au/nla.news-article187362874

73 Qld DC 1927/1550, Benevolent Asylum Dunwich, 24 Jun 1927, James Joseph Cranley

74 Qld DC 1928/717 2597, Mount Morgan, 14 Feb 1928, Bridget Cranley

75 Mount Morgan, *Morning Bulletin* (Rockhampton), Thu 13 Aug 1903, page 6 http://nla.gov.au/nla.news-article52983323

76 The Palmer, *The Telegraph* (Brisbane), Tue 30 Dec 1873, page 3 http://nla.gov.au/nla.news-article169482538

77 Insolvency Court, *Australian Town and Country Journal,* Sat 18 May 1878, page 12 http://nla.gov.au/nla.news-article70613230

78 South Australian DC 1926/284, Norwood, 13 Oct 1926, Michael William Cranley

79 Photo (modified) from Hume Family Collection, UQFL10, Album 3 Page 31. Copyright expired.

80 Left and Centre photos from State Library of Queensland, Right photo from the collection of Ian and Margaret Kelly

Chapter 13

Disobedience and folly

The contested will - Cranley

Patrick Cranley, the fifth son of James Cranley, contested his father's will because he was convinced that the will did not reflect his father's true wishes. He had maintained his relationship with his parents, and in his mind, he had been on good terms with his father. He thought the will was particularly harsh on him. He expressed surprise his father had left a will at all. As time went by, he regarded the whole affair with suspicion. The complete text of James Cranley's handwritten will is as follows:[1]

Now, I James Cranley senior being by the grace of God in sound mind do hereby make such dispositions of my property real and personal as in my deliberate judgement I deem right and proper. I hereby will devise and bequeath to My Second daughter Margaret now Mrs. John Fahey race course road near Toowoomba my farm about 100 acres. Situated on Gowrie Creek three miles from Toowoomba and bounded on the east by Gowrie Creek and the west by Alexandria boundary and the North by a chain road and on the South by Grundy Thorn and Barnes. I also will and bequeath to her all my personal property goods and chattels. In the event of my wife surviving me, she is to go and live with her daughter, Margaret Mrs. Fahy, during life her maintenance is to come from my Estate. I hereby will and bequeath to my sons, Timothy, Edward, James, John, Patrick and Michael and to my eldest daughter Mary all one shilling each to come from my Estate. I will them this small amount on account of their disobedience and folly.
This is my last will and testament if I had made any wills formerly I hereby revoke the same this being my last. I hereby appoint Mrs. John Fahy sole executrix.
Dated at Toowoomba this 18th day of March 1890.
        Signed James Cranley
        Witness Timothy Gleeson
        and James Simpson Junior[2]

A neighbouring farmer, Timothy Gleeson, had written the will. Cranley employed Gleeson to do it, because he thought the lawyers he had previously dealt with were too expensive. Timothy Gleeson knew James Cranley about forty years and lived in Irish Town (now Harlaxton) about half a mile from James for thirty years. Gleeson held onto the will until James Cranley's death in July 1890.

The challenge

As James' daughter, Margaret, was named both sole executrix and principal beneficiary, she petitioned for a grant of probate in August 1890.[3] At the end of 1890, Patrick initiated proceedings and attempted to lodge a caveat on the land transfer. Patrick then proceeded to contest the will. On 29 July 1891, a writ was issued to all parties mentioned in the will. The legal process required he name as respondents his mother and all his siblings, including those who were tarred with the same insult. By this time, all the children were scattered. Addresses were unknown. The summons demonstrated the extent to which the family had lost touch (see box below).

The court ordered the notice be placed in the *Government Gazette*, *The Queenslander*, and in a paper circulating in and around Boulia, as well as a paper circulating in or about Port Augusta, SA.

The Cranley Will Case was well reported in the *Toowoomba Chronicle and Darling Downs General Advertiser*, *The Brisbane Courier*, the *Darling Downs Gazette* and arguably most coherently in *The Telegraph*.[4] The trial was held in the Supreme Court in Brisbane for a week in May and June 1892. A jury of four citizens heard it. The case provides a window into the lives of the Cranley family at that time. The characters come to life. You can hear their voices and understand their anxieties.

When Timothy Gleeson took the stand, he told the court, as Mr Cranley's hand was very shaky,

he guided his hand as he signed the will. Gleeson testified the deceased was sober at the time. James Simpson, a ploughman, who witnessed the will, said the will had already been signed when he witnessed the signature. The court was also told Gleeson had used the words 'on account of their disobedience and folly' earlier when he wrote another will for another person. Other witnesses testified Gleeson and Cranley had a falling out some years before.

Patrick, the plaintiff, said he got on very well with his father and always visited him when he had his annual holidays. He had last seen his father in early June 1890 and parted from him on the best of terms. James gave Patrick a gift of a ham and half a sovereign. James' parting words to Patrick were 'Goodbye, God bless you. I may be down to see you soon'. James had also promised to send him a cow as soon as she had calved. Patrick stated he was the only son who ever visited his father. Patrick's evidence was that, on this occasion, his father did not speak well of Margaret's husband, John Fahy, as the old man said he had lent John some money and could not get the interest out of him.

A witness, Charles Allan, railway guard, deposed the deceased sometimes travelled on the train, which he was in charge of, and he always inquired very friendly after the plaintiff, referring to him as 'my boy Pat'. Patrick told the jury of a conversation with John Fahy on the day of his father's funeral. Patrick's sworn recollection of it was as follows:

◊ Timothy was a carrier at West St, Rockhampton, Qld.
◊ Mary Klein and her husband George Klein, carrier, lived in Alpha, Qld.
◊ John Fahy, gentleman and Margaret Fahy, his wife, lived in Toowoomba.
◊ Edward Cranley, address unknown. (He was a stockman around Winton.)
◊ James Joseph Cranley, address unknown. (He was living in Brisbane at this time.)
◊ John Cranley was a storekeeper in Orange, NSW.
◊ Patrick, the plaintiff, was the stationmaster at Muraree Station (Cleveland line).
◊ Michael Cranley was thought to be living in Port Augusta in South Australia.

Patrick:	I suppose my father died without a will?
John:	No; he made a will.
Patrick:	Who drew it out?
John:	Tim Gleeson
Patrick:	How did he get that old beggar to draw it out?
John:	There's a will right enough Pat, and it does not matter who drew it out. It is all left to you and Mag; and who has a better right to it?

Patrick stated this last statement was repeated several times that night. Patrick was only left one shilling in the will and the evidence was that John and Margaret Fahy were present when Gleeson twice read the will to Cranley, before signing. Margaret Fahy testified her husband had discussed the contents of the will with her. John Fahy testified James Cranley had discussed the contents of the will with him. When questioned on the stand, John Fahy denied he had had the conversation with Patrick. In his defence, he said, Patrick had been drinking that day, as the wake had gone for two nights. When Patrick later asked him why he had told such a lot of lies, he said he did not know any better at the time. Patrick's wife, Mary, gave corroborating evidence there had been such a conversation in her presence.

Patrick's drinking appears to be his Achilles heel. Patrick's job on the railways was a relatively secure, modestly well-paid government job. The defence counsel highlighted an incident seven years earlier during his time in Warwick where an inquiry was held into his conduct. He asked for a shift but was only offered one at reduced wages. He then asked for an inquiry, and as a result he was both demoted from supervisor to porter and suffered a cut in pay. Most damagingly, his sister Margaret testified her father had said Patrick 'had been getting worse and if he left any money to him, he would drink himself to death or lose his billet'. This crucial 'hearsay' statement was probably admitted because James Cranley himself was unavailable to provide it. It would be left to the jury to determine, in light of other evidence, whether it was invented out of self-service, cunning and/or malice or whether it was the significant truth. Unsurprisingly, Gleeson's testimony provided corroboration. Patrick testified on the stand he was not addicted to drink. Unfortunately, his subsequent work history also appears to substantiate the accusation.

The alleged 'will conspiracy' plot thickened when Patrick gave evidence, he had gone to see Timothy Gleeson the day following the funeral about whether his father had made a will. Gleeson, under oath, denied Patrick's version of events. Patrick said Gleeson confirmed there was a will but would not show the document to him, as his asking suggested he 'did not have confidence in him'. Gleeson allegedly said Patrick's share was £50, but that he might get him £100 for it. He related this story to John and Margaret. John laughed and Margaret said Gleeson must have been drunk to think Patrick would only be left £50. Later, after the will's contents were revealed, Margaret said to Patrick, 'If you go to the law they will get as much as you, and I will get as much as any of them'. John Fahy passed by and said: 'Why don't you come to a settlement?' With hindsight, this was the wisest advice proffered. Unfortunately, Patrick ignored it, triggering a spiral of perverse outcomes.

If we believe Patrick's sworn testimony, then we would wonder why Gleeson was deceiving Patrick. What was he up to? How could Gleeson change the will after the testator had died? Had there been a switch? If so, by whom? Was a signature forged? Was his father duped? How much did Margaret and John know and when? The contents of a will seemed so at odds with the impression Patrick had come away with, in the days following his father's death. Suspicion compounded.

217

It emerged there was an earlier draft of the will. The need for a will had been talked about up to four years previously. The draft was from just over a year before James' death and Gleeson also drew it out. The evidence was this was not signed. According to the witness, Daniel Ormond, a neighbouring farmer who was named as executor on the earlier draft, James had left the property to both Margaret and Patrick evenly. Cranley had 'hooted' Gleeson out of his presence when he had presented this will for signing a year before. Ormond testified he saw James Cranley on the day he died, and he said then that he had not settled his affairs and had left no will. The defence tried to discredit Ormond by asserting that he had been told to 'clear out' during the wake. John Fahy admitted in cross-examination that James Cranley had spoken to him about his intentions, and he had indicated at that time he was inclined to leave his property to Patrick. John Fahy confirmed in court Patrick gave him an account of having visited Gleeson and Gleeson would not show him the will.

Solicitor O'Sullivan interviewed James Simpson junior, the second witness to the will, on 3 May 1891. This was in the presence of Detective Officer WA Clark. Simpson refused to sign the record of interview. In his place, WA Clarke attested and signed it as an agreed account of the interview. It stated, on the day of the will signing, he and his uncle were ploughing, and Gleeson called him in and gave him a drink of porter. In the house were Gleeson, his wife, some of his family, Cranley, Fahy and his wife. Gleeson asked Simpson and his uncle if he would witness the will and then read it over. On looking at the document he noticed it had already been signed 'James Cranley' and 'Timothy Gleeson', but he had not seen either write his signature. Before he signed the will, Gleeson asked Cranley to touch the pen. Cranley did so, but the pen did not leave a mark. In contrast to Gleeson's evidence, this record of interview stated Cranley (the testator) was not very sober at the time when Simpson witnessed the will, but Fahy

and Gleeson were quite sober. According to the record of interview, Simpson saw a similar will in Gleeson's possession three years earlier awaiting Cranley's signature. This was consistent with Daniel Ormond's evidence. On the stand, Simpson stated Cranley was sober and he had not seen an earlier version of the will. Simpson's reluctance to fully comply with the legal process and his conflicting testimony would have fuelled Patrick's suspicion of a conspiracy.

John Fahy stated he always got on well with his father-in-law. The deceased's sons, with the exception of John, were not steady, and Cranley told him at some time he had given his sons land or teams, but they had sold them and come back with no money at all. Some had been away for thirty years and had not returned. Margaret had testified her father had said all her brothers, with the exception of John, were 'attached to drink'. In other cases, marriages had been contracted against James' will. John also stated he had paid all his debts to James Cranley with interest.

Patrick stated his wife was always treated well when she visited his father. Adding, 'as far as I know, I do not believe my father retained any anger against me on account of my marriage'. This is the opposite of what Margaret Fahy recalled when she said her father was never on good terms with Mrs Patrick Cranley, as she quoted her father as saying, 'She was not a suitable addition to the family'. There was some discussion about whether his father had approached the Catholic priest, Father Robert Dunne, to prevent the marriage, but Patrick simply said he did not get his father's permission to marry. Patrick related something unspecified happened soon after the marriage, which made James very angry. Margaret Fahy said that Patrick's wife, Mary, was only allowed to visit her because she was Patrick's wife and that her father only recognised her out of respect for his son.

It was also mentioned in court James eldest daughter, Mrs George Klein, had twelve children, but James would not leave her anything, because she had married a man he did not like. Oral history confirms this, and James had nothing or very little to do with Mary after she married George Klein in 1866. Margaret Fahy stated on the stand George owned several bullock teams. This statement may have cast him in the ears of the jury as a bullocky or a drover, which, in those times, had connotations of a rough foul-mouthed under-class. In reality, he was a carrier like some of James' sons. The descendants of George Klein have linked James' dislike of George more to the fact George was a German and a Lutheran. Proud Irish Catholics did not marry German Lutherans in the eyes of men like James.

Thomas Welsby, accountant and 'expert in writing', said in his opinion the person who wrote the will and signed Timothy Gleeson were the one and same person, and that the signature of James Cranley and the body of the will were exceedingly alike. He also stated, the signature on the will was not the same as the railway receipts which had James signature on them, and a railway clerk had confirmed he saw James Cranley sign for them. He provided a forensic analysis of the writing to substantiate his claim.

None of this intrigue had any sway on the jury. After hearing the evidence, the four agreed James Cranley had known what he signed and that it was his signature, although the witness did not see him sign it. Chief Justice Lilley agreed with them, praising them as one of the best juries he had seen in years.

The *Toowoomba Chronicle* (2 June 1892) ended its report with: 'The case concluded this evening, the result being that the will was upheld, and leave was given for the judgment to be moved for before the close of the present sittings'. They had jumped the gun, as the Queensland State Archives holds a petition dated 16 July 1892 which states James Cranley was declared to have died 'intestate', i.e. without a valid will. The petition is from 'The Queensland Permanent Trustee Executor and Finance Company Limited'. The company was 'authorised by Margaret Cranley, widow, who is declared to be entitled to a grant of administration of all of the land, goods, chattels, credits and effects which he then possessed'.

The newspapers from 6 June detail the end of trial where the will was overturned in the final judgment. The *Queensland Law Journal* gives a more legalistic view of the case and identifies the arguments which won the case.[5] It also gives clues as to what Patrick Cranley was trying to achieve in his initial challenge. There were four grounds for the original challenge: (1) undue execution (2) want of sound mind (3) undue influence (4) want of knowledge of the contents of the will. At the core of it, Patrick was trying to win damages in compensation for his meagre inheritance, as he contended it had come about because of 'undue influence'. However, the jury was not at all convinced on this point.

In the final judgment, the will was found to be invalidly executed, solely because the two witnesses had not signed the will following witnessing the signing by James Cranley. This alone did not entitle Patrick to damages as 'undue influence' was not proven. In fact, the judge, Chief Justice Sir Charles Lilley, believed the intention of James Cranley was clear and was reluctant to uphold the challenge as he was critical of the statute and precedents under which it succeeded. He is quoted as saying, 'I am bound by authority. If it had been a matter for me to decide the first time, I would have decided it otherwise'. Margaret Fahy would have taken those comments as evidence that she had a moral right to the inheritance but that she had been thwarted by a questionable legal technicality. That may explain her subsequent actions. Incidentally, the law has since moved on to the point where, in current times, unsigned wills and even unsent text messages have been accepted as valid testaments of intent.[6]

Sir Arthur Rutledge for the plaintiff was a former Attorney-General and an MLA. He had the necessary gravitas to go up against the opposition. John and Margaret Fahy had engaged as part of their legal team, barrister, Sir Samuel Griffith QC,

Left: Sir Charles Lilley, The Judge and former Premier of Qld. Photo: State Library of Queensland
Centre: Sir Arthur Rutledge, for the plantiff, Patrick Cranley - State Library of Queensland
Right: Sir Samuel Griffith, for the defence - Trove, National Library of Australia.

the Qld Attorney-General at the time and author of *Queensland's Criminal Code 1899.*[7] He is still regarded as one of the finest legal minds who ever called Qld home. Both Sir Charles Lilley and Sir Samuel Griffith had previously been Premier of the state. Rutledge and Griffith were political allies and close friends. Sir Samuel Griffith wrote the first draft of the Australian Constitution in 1891 and became the first Chief Justice of the High Court of the Commonwealth of Australia.[8] It should also be said he was popularly known as 'Slippery Sam'.[9]

It was Griffith who scored the telling blow in the trial by inferring with his questioning that Patrick had a problem with his drinking. Sir Samuel himself had a prodigious drinking habit. Historian, Manning Clark wrote of Griffith's fondness for strong drink and his ability to drink all others 'under the table'.[10] His speech, gait and manner gave no clue as to the volume he had consumed. He was lauded as the 'Champion of Burketown' after the locals plotted to get the better of their distinguished but unpopular dinner guest. At daybreak, following an evening of solid drinking, Griffith alone stood to watch the second-place getter retreat on someone else's camel in a direction that was not of his property.[11]

A question which easily occurs to the modern observer is: Why would legal minds of the stature of Griffith and Rutledge be moonlighting from paid public office to provide legal service in a grubby family dispute?[12] A vital clue is given in the final judgment: 'Costs of all parties as between solicitor and client allowed out of the estate'. As is often the case, the real winners were, of course, the lawyers. Although it must be said, there were complications in the defence getting their hands on the costs awarded. Their bill was £275 3s 8d.[13]

Further legal action

This was not the end of the matter, however, as there was a legal mess needing attention. A mess that would allow for even more fees to be extracted from the estate. With the will overturned, probate on James Cranley's will was revoked. Margaret Fahy was initially granted probate in 1890, and she had proceeded to claim her inheritance prior to the challenge. She had the land transferred into her name. She had borrowed £1000 against the land from the Queensland National Bank.

Patrick Cranley's lawyers had tried to lodge a caveat on the land transfer but were one day late according to the deadline set by the Registrar of Titles and the caveat was therefore not accepted. A second caveat in a different form was accepted on Christmas Eve 1890, but that was eleven days after Margaret Fahy had secured a mortgage on the farm. After the challenge to the will overturned it, Margaret Fahy no longer had legitimate title to the land which was the collateral for the loan. The bank then came after her, and in response, she defaulted on the repayment of the principal and interest.

On 19 July 1892, letters of administration of the estate were granted to Patrick Cranley as a result of his court win. Patrick was not awarded the entire estate, but he was appointed to administer the estate according to the intestacy laws.[14] His win entitled him to become the new executor. Because Margaret Fahy had defaulted on her loan repayment, the bank gave notice, on 26 July 1892, of their intention to force the sale of the land. Patrick was then deprived of his land from his win.

On 3 October 1892, Patrick commenced action against his sister claiming administrator's damages. More court action assessed the damages. In November 1892, Margaret Fahy was ordered to pay a sum which had now grown to £1520 10s.[15] She declared herself insolvent on the basis of her property alone – i.e. her husband's assets were not considered in the application.

This was a fairly recent legal development where a wife's financial position could be considered in isolation.[16] She submitted she had no assets at all. Where had the money gone? It isn't known for sure, but there are some clues. The evidence in court at latter proceedings was, 'it had not been accounted for'.[17] The consideration of a wife's financial position separate from her husband's certainly provides a loophole.

Patrick realises his position is hopeless and gives up at this point. The Queensland Trustees then actively administer the estate. They proceed to bring an action against the Registrar of Titles as a nominal defendant. Their claim was, because of the actions of the Registrar of Titles, the estate was deprived of its land, and as a consequence, it is entitled to compensation out of the Government Assurance Fund, which was established to ensure confidence in the Land Titles regime. This is the first time such a case had been heard in the colony. These proceedings were heard by three judges, Harding, Real and Sir Samuel Griffith who by now was the Chief Justice of Queensland. After much legal angst, the Trustees were not awarded the £1520 14s that they sought, but were awarded the amount the bank was owed, £1074 16s 8d, plus costs, which logically could allow the land title to be returned to the estate.[18] It was expressly noted that Patrick was not a party to that action and neither was the bank.

On 5 December 1893, a document from the Queensland Permanent Trustee Executor and Finance Company Limited declared the net proceeds of the Company at £1074 16s 8d and the credit balance of James Cranley's estate of £460 9s 11d.[19] This is a grant of administration to Margaret, widow of James. Patrick's lawyers from the original case and his action in pursuit of his sister in combination with the lawyers for the Trustee would all have been taking their fees out of the estate. Patrick would not have had any significant funds of his own. The balance sheet implies the funds owed to the bank were not paid to it by the estate administrators, and therefore the bank still held a mortgage on the land.[20] Margaret Fahy's name was removed from the land title in August 1893. Nominally, it appears the estate would have title to the land but there was a mortgage issued to a now bankrupt Margaret Fahy. The Administrator's accounts do not include the land. The bank, as mortgagee, was in possession, until the bank sold the land to the Crown in 1897. The bank received around £1040 from the sale, so they would have made an accounting loss on the transaction.[21] By not getting back the land, the estate administrators were foregoing any possible dividend of the value of the land beyond the awarded damages. Maybe that was done because it was easier for the estate as they would have needed to borrow money to make up for that spent on legal fees. By April 1894, the balance of the estate had shrunk to £403 4s 6d.

A further case dragged on into 1894, where Margaret Fahy's solicitors sought advice from the court on how to proceed with claiming their awarded costs from the original trial. The administrators of the estate wanted instruction from the judge as to whether they were required to pay the outstanding £275 3s 8d from the estate. Justice Real said, because Margaret Fahy had not accounted for the £1000 which she acquired whilst she had probate, then neither she, nor her solicitors, were entitled to payment out of the estate.[22] Real justice, perhaps? However, once again, legal fees for that court episode were allowed out of the estate. Whatever value the estate started with was frittered away with legal fees and perhaps a little bit of money spent on the comfort of James' widow. It would also appear that some of the estate was used to erect an impressive memorial to James, Margaret and other family members in the Drayton and Toowoomba Cemetery grounds.

By way of reference, Patrick Cranley's gazetted annual salary in 1892 was £120 per annum. In 1891, the average male farm labourer could expect to earn about £1 15s ($3.50) a week. The early 1890s were depression years accompanied by a bank crash. The Queensland National Bank had only avoided being a victim of the bank crash by fraudulently concealing its insolvency status during 1894-5. It was the bank of choice for the Qld government and when the fraud was discovered the government passed legislation which guaranteed its deposits for a year.[23] Land in this district had had fluctuating fortunes, from bargain to over-speculation and down again. One of the court cases in 1893 discussed whether the land was worth more than the £1000 that had been loaned against it. There was agreement it was, but it would have been worth a lot more at the time of James' death in 1890, which was before the crash.

In 1896 the land was offered to the government to expand the neighbouring hospital, at £10 an acre and it was noted in *Hansard* that in the boom it would have been worth £50 an acre.[24]

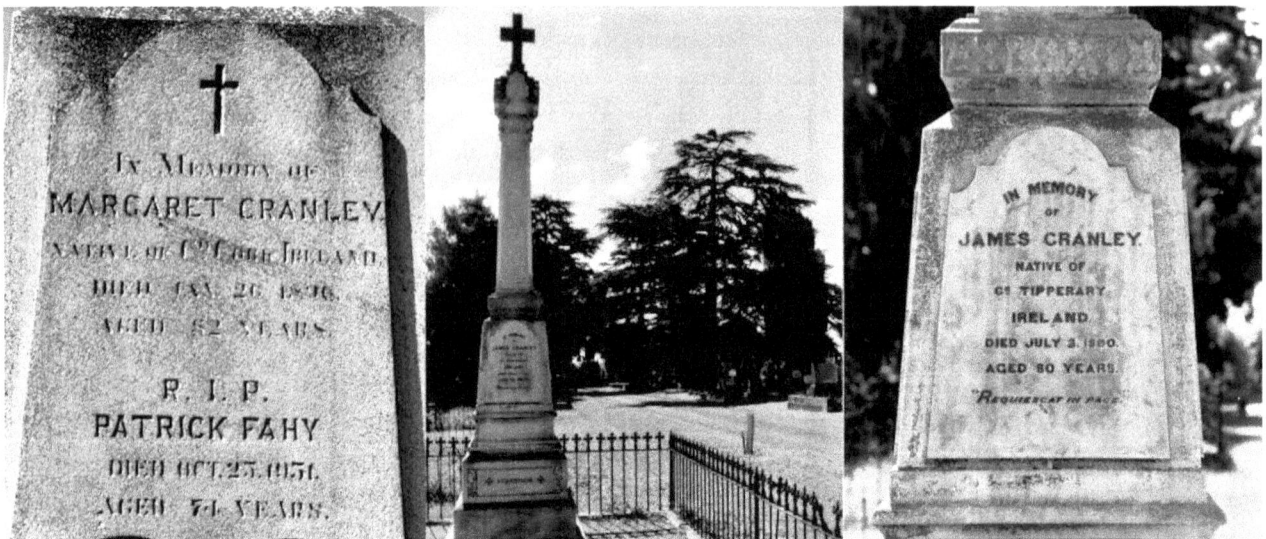

Cranley memorial, Drayton and Toowoomba Cemetery, RC section 1, block 10, allotments 45 & 46. Photo author

In trying to assess how those amounts translate to today's values, a multiplier of 120 has been suggested from official inflation data. However any comparison between what money could buy in 1890 versus 2020 shows how subjective any comparison would be. Land value in general has appreciated more than inflation. Also, interest rates were quite high in the 1890s (around eight percent). The modern price paid for good quality farming land in that district is subject to many different pressures: seasons, markets, environmental considerations and alternate land uses. Suffice to say, James Cranley was a prosperous farmer whose estate was coveted by several. Perhaps so much so, skulduggery was called for to secure a piece of it.

Patrick commenced his legal action during the boom time of the early 1890s, but by the time the first court case was determined, the Depression had reduced the value of the farm by up to eighty percent. Legal fees then consumed more than half of what was left. Even if Margaret Fahy had not taken out the loan against the land and had quietly accepted the result of the case, then because Patrick had not proved 'undue influence', he would have faced a stark choice. He could either take out a mortgage to cover the legal fees or sell the farm to resolve the estate. Finding a buyer during the Depression would be no simple matter. His entitlement at the end of the day would only have been as one of eight siblings after his mother had died. If he took out a loan, how would he service it? Would he need to become a farmer and toil away so that his seven siblings could share in the spoils without lifting a finger. Problems awaited him at every juncture. In the end, Margaret Fahy's financial disobedience and Patrick's legal folly combined to ensure that those particular dilemmas did not need to be faced.

Margaret Cranley's final years

James' widow, Margaret, was still alive through all this and in need of care. Multiple sources indicate Margaret had been in senile decline for some time. A fact which supports this is she was not called to the stand in the will case nor did she provide an affidavit. Patrick's wife, Mary Cranley, quoted her on the stand as saying, 'Oh no, there was no will made'. She was probably not 'in the loop' due to her failing memory. A less likely alternative, which was not fully explored at trial was, she had 'let the cat out of the bag'. The overturned will required Margaret senior live with her daughter and son-in-law, Margaret and John Fahy. It is possible some money went to her and her carers to pay for her needs via the Trustee's grant of administration. If there had been any justice in the process, then any reasonable person would have expected this outcome. In the circumstances, it seems unlikely Margaret Cranley left a will. Certainly, no public record of one has yet been found. It is not known whether there was any cash residue within James' estate that was available to be dispersed to the surviving children.

Oral history does add something here. Some of Patrick's grandchildren regarded the case as the time when Patrick's family were 'diddled out of their inheritance'. Margaret Fahy's descendant, Denise Sweeney, related her grandmother, Margaret O'Brien, daughter of Margaret Fahy, said there was some money left when her unmarried siblings died, but she 'didn't want any of it as it was cursed'. At the time Denise shared that comment (1988) she was unaware of the will case and always assumed the comment referred to money which had come from Ireland. If John Fahy needed to borrow money from James Cranley, then it is unlikely he had significant wealth from Ireland. We can not automatically assume it is referring to the loaned money which had been shifted sideways, but neither can we ignore that possibility given the facts presented in the final court case.

The Fahy oral history says Margaret Cranley, in her declining years, lived with her daughter and thought of John Fahy as her son and her daughter, Margaret, as the interloping daughter-in-law.

Endnotes to Chapter 13

1 With some minor changes (e.g. punctuation) for readability.

2 Qld State Archives: James Cranley's will

3 Probates granted, *The Queenslander* (Brisbane), Sat 6 Sep 1890, page 470 http://nla.gov.au/nla.news-article20285884

4 The Cranley will case, *Darling Downs Gazette*, Mon 30 May 1892, page 3 http://nla.gov.au/nla.news-article170729857
& Tuesday's sittings, *Darling Downs Gazette*, Wed 1 Jun 1892, page 3 http://nla.gov.au/nla.news-article170728687
& The Cranley will case, *Darling Downs Gazette*, Sat 4 Jun 1892, page 5 http://nla.gov.au/nla.news-article170726869
& Judgement in the Cranley will case, *Darling Downs Gazette*, Mon 6 Jun 1892, page 3 http://nla.gov.au/nla.news-article170728638
& The Cranley will case, *Toowoomba Chronicle and Darling Downs General Advertiser*, Tue 31 May 1892, page 3 http://nla.gov.au/nla.news-article220598365
& The Cranley will case, *Toowoomba Chronicle and Darling Downs General Advertiser*, Thu 2 Jun 1892, page 3 http://nla.gov.au/nla.news-article220595660
& The Cranley will case, *Toowoomba Chronicle and Darling Downs General Advertiser*, Sat 4 Jun 1892, page 3 http://nla.gov.au/nla.news-article220595198
& The Cranley will case, *Toowoomba Chronicle and Darling Downs General Advertiser*, Tue 7 Jun 1892, page 3 http://nla.gov.au/nla.news-article220596520
& Supreme Court, *The Brisbane Courier*, Sat 28 May 1892, page 3 http://nla.gov.au/nla.news-article3542541
& Supreme Court, *The Brisbane Courier*, Tue 31 May 1892, page 7 http://nla.gov.au/nla.news-article3542673
& Supreme Court, *The Brisbane Courier*, Thu 2 Jun 1892, page 7 http://nla.gov.au/nla.news-article3542783
& Supreme Court, *The Brisbane Courier*, Sat 4 Jun 1892, page 7 http://nla.gov.au/nla.news-article3542936
& Civil sittings, *The Telegraph* (Brisbane), Sat 28 May 1892 page 2 http://nla.gov.au/nla.news-article173289851
& Civil sittings, *The Telegraph* (Brisbane), Mon 30 May 1892 page 2 http://nla.gov.au/nla.news-article173296701
& Civil sittings, *The Telegraph* (Brisbane), Tue 31 May 1892 page 2 http://nla.gov.au/nla.news-article173290349
& Civil sittings, *The Telegraph* (Brisbane), Wed 1 Jun 1892 page 2 http://nla.gov.au/nla.news-article173290613
& Civil sittings, *The Telegraph* (Brisbane), Thu 2 Jun 1892 page 6 http://nla.gov.au/nla.news-article173287744
& Supreme Court, *The Telegraph* (Brisbane), Sat 4 Jun 1892 page 2 http://nla.gov.au/nla.news-article173289086

5 *The Queensland Law Journal* – Reports {Cases Decided 19 Feb 1890 to 12 Oct 1892}

6 Re Nichol; Nichol v Nichol & Anor [2017] QSC220
https://www.abc.net.au/news/2017-10-09/unsent-text-on-mobile-counts-as-a-will,-queensland-court-finds/9031470

7 Landmark legislation which codified criminal law. Qld was the first Australian jurisdiction to codify its criminal law. It was based on an Italian model. Most English-speaking jurisdictions at that time and many even now primarily rely on British Common Law (law built up via cases and precedents over centuries).

8 https://www.australianconstitutioncentre.org.au/the-writers-of-the-australian-constitution.html

9 R Evans, *A History of Queensland*, Cambridge University Press, Melbourne, 2007, page 115

10 M. Clark, *A History of Australia. Volume V*, Melbourne University Press, Carlton South, 1981 (reprint 1999) page 70

11 *Samuel Griffith: The Great Provincial* by Professor Geoffrey C. Bolton, Clem Lack Memorial Oration, presented on Thu, 21 Mar, 1991 available at espace.library.uq.edu.au

12 By 1892 members of Qld's Legislative Assembly had a salary of £300, which the Griffith Government halved to £150, but it soon returned to its previous level. The average annual salary in Qld was approximately £100.
http://www.qgso.qld.gov.au/products/reports/qld-past-present/qld-past-present-1896-1996-ch04-sec-02.pdf

13 Ecclesiastical jurisdiction, *The Week* (Brisbane), Fri 27 Apr 1894, page 19 http://nla.gov.au/nla.news-article181827837

14 Intestacy laws set out rules of succession, i.e. the entire family would be entitled to some inheritance.

15 Law courts, *The Week* (Brisbane), Fri 5 May 1893, page 19 http://nla.gov.au/nla.news-article183114205

16 *Married Woman's Property Act 1890* (Qld)

17 Petition for advice, *Darling Downs Gazette,* Sat 28 Apr 1894, page 5 http://nla.gov.au/nla.news-article178011514

18 Supreme Court, *The Brisbane Courier,* Fri 21 Jul 1893, page 3 http://nla.gov.au/nla.news-article3563257

19 Queensland State Archive: Will of James Cranley

20 If the land was acquired, then it would have to had sold for an amount exceeding the mortgage and those transactions would have been shown, but the legal fees would have still been outstanding.

21 The bank would have missed out on the 8% interest payments for six years plus administration costs associated with the loan

22 Petition for advice, *Darling Downs Gazette,* Sat 28 Apr 1894, page 5 http://nla.gov.au/nla.news-article178011514

23 https://www.rba.gov.au/publications/rdp/2001/2001-07/1890s-depression.html

24 Toowoomba asylum *Toowoomba Chronicle and Darling Downs General Advertiser* Tue 6 Oct 1896 page 3 http://nla.gov.au/nla.news-article217654088

Chapter 14

Difficult start, tragic end

Grace and David - Barry

Over 162,000 convicts were transported to Australia in the eighty years between 1788 and 1868. Just under forty thousand of those were Irish. In addition, about half a million Irish free settlers made Australia their new home between 1788 and 1921, making Australia the most Irish country in the world outside Ireland.[1] A small sub-set of that group were the four thousand female orphans the Earl Grey Scheme sent out during the Potato Famine.[2] This chapter tells the story of the family my father's mother's mother, Mary Barry, was born into. Her parents were Grace McAlister and David Barry.

Ireland

David Barry, the son of a blacksmith, was born in County Cork, Ireland, around 1817.[3] In Ireland, he had learnt to read and write.[4] He had also learnt his trade as a shoemaker. His life took an abrupt turn in March 1836 when, aged nineteen and single, he was convicted of receiving stolen goods.[5] David was originally charged with burgling 25 pounds of tobacco from the residence of George Thomas Daunt on 2 March 1836.[6] This was a capital offence.[7] George lived in Barrack Street, Cork City.[8] The court established that the tobacco was in David's possession and he knew it was stolen, but they could not prove he stole it. So instead of facing the gallows, David was sentenced to seven years transportation.[9]

He was imprisoned on the hulk, *Surprise*, at Cobh, Cork on 18 May 1836, awaiting transportation.[10] The *Surprise* had earned a fearful reputation since its introduction in 1823. Anne McMahon's *Floating Prisons* described how sick and healthy, boys and men, rivals and allies were all mixed together in the dark and damp hull. Food and clothing were inadequate by careless design and the only antidote to boredom was to make trouble. Following several fires and a serious mutinous riot in 1835, a scathing official report resulted in some order being enforced on board the hulk, but that entailed keeping the prisoners in irons for extended periods of time.[11] The *Surprise* ceased being used as a prison shortly after David's departure.[12]

After enduring seven weeks on the hulk, David Barry, and 227 other prisoners were transported to NSW on the *Captain Cook*.[13] It sailed from County Cork on 5 July 1836.[14] The *Captain Cook* was making its third and last journey to NSW transporting convicts. Almost nineteen weeks later, the ship arrived in Sydney on 13 November 1836, with the loss of just one life. A convict had died from scurvy.[15]

A few days after leaving Cork, the ship's hospital attendant discovered a plot by a group of convicts to initially kill all but the women and three of the crew and sail to America. The remaining three men were then to be made to walk the plank when America was in sight. Thirty-eight ringleaders were clamped in irons after some convicts confessed, but still the remaining convicts seemed to be manoeuvring for mutiny, and so they were handcuffed in pairs for the remainder of the journey. Sixteen of the convicts were transferred to Goat Island upon their arrival in Sydney.[16]

New South Wales

David was put to work, probably as a shoemaker. His first assignment was under the supervision of JR Bunnan of Sydney. He spent some time in Port Macquarie. Its days as a penal settlement had ceased in 1832. Therefore, he was probably on assignment with a local businessman who would have employed him in return for the necessities of life. At the end of his sentence, he would be free to live and work anywhere within the colonies. He obtained his Certificate of Freedom in August 1843. It describes him as 5 foot 6 and a quarter inches, with light blue eyes, brown hair with a ruddy freckled complexion. He sported a scar on the bridge of his nose.[17]

The following Sydney newspaper article from August 1846, and others before and after this time, were thought to be referring to the David Barry of this story.

David Barry, free by servitude, having been found laying drunk and speechless in York Street, on Monday afternoon, was dealt with under the Vagrant Act as a rogue and vagabond, of which he had been previously convicted, and was sent to gaol for two months.[18]

Cobh Harbour. The hulk *Surprise* was moored off Hawlbowline Island, seen here across the channel.[93]
Photo: September 2017 by author

And another from June 1847:

> David Barry, a notorious drunken rogue and vagabond who while out of gaol, generally infests the western side of Macquarie Place between Bridge and Spring streets was again had up yesterday under the Vagrant Act and being convicted of drunkenness, roguery and vagabondism, he was sent to gaol for two calendar months.[19]

However, it appears there was another ex-convict sharing his name.[20] Further reports after this date, such as the following articles from 1848, suggest so:

From May 1848: Vagabonds -Two men were dealt with yesterday under the Vagrant Act; one David Barry, who went into a house near the corner of Park and Castlereagh street to beg and finding the woman alone commenced assaulting her; and was sentenced to three months' imprisonment.[21]

From August 1848: On Wednesday, David Barry, a most notorious skulking thief, was sentenced under the Vagrant Act to three months confinement in Gaol.[22]

Drayton

The David from this story was definitely in residence at Drayton by June 1847.[23] Drayton was a small but important settlement servicing the traffic on the track between Moreton Bay and the Darling Downs. Its first resident was Thomas Alford in 1842. Alford was born in Drayton, Somerset. The settlement was originally called 'The Springs' but became 'Drayton' in 1845 after the sign Alford had displayed on his shop took on general acceptance. Historian, Maurice French, identifies David Barry as one of the earliest businessmen in Drayton, but he was the second shoemaker.[24] In June 1847, Barry, Alford and six others approached the Colonial Secretary to be able to purchase the land on which their businesses stood. The argument was that freehold tenure rather than the payment of heavy fees would encourage the building of more substantial buildings rather than the 'bark gunyahs' which had been built to date.[25]

The court reports of the early days of Drayton point to an unruly and violent society where excess drinking, violent altercations and untimely deaths were common. Drayton had its fair share of brutalised ex-convicts and under-educated refugees from British poverty. Many but not most of the initial businessmen of Drayton had convict origins. It can be assumed a good number of the other citizens and visitors shared those beginnings, because of the demographics of the colonies at that time and the attraction of the frontier for people who were seeking a new beginning or just less scrutiny. There would be adventures and mischief aplenty in the newly opened lands.

David started to behave like his namesake in Sydney. In December 1849, David was fined £2 for assaulting a policeman. A newspaper report from the *Moreton Bay Courier* gives us a sense of attitudes at that time which seem to be quick to victim blame and reflect a remarkably lenient view towards assaulting a policeman. The report is as follows:

David Barry appeared on a summons to answer a charge of assaulting a constable in the execution of his duty. From Constable Glover's statement it appeared that Barry, who is a shoemaker residing at Drayton, cohabits with a very disorderly, character named Jeanette Stuart, alias the 'Bag of Weasels.' On the 7th instant, Constable Glover received information that Barry was ill-treating the woman in a most shameful manner, he proceeded to his house, and there heard the cries of a woman, evidently in great distress; he demanded admittance; Barry opened the door, and, on entering the house, she claimed his protection, and stated Barry had assaulted her; she was in a pitiable plight-her face and body being covered with blood, from cuts which she received on the head. They were both nearly drunk at the time. Constable Glover attempted to bring her to the lock-up, and had her some distance away, when Barry rushed after him, and jostled him so violently that he fell to the ground, and then managed to get the woman back to the hut. The constable procured more assistance, and with some difficulty succeeded in bringing her away. Barry had nothing further to offer in his defence than that he was drunk at the time; he was not aware that he had touched 'one of the officers of the law;' but it was barely possible he might have done so. The Chief Constable stated, that with the exception of an occasional spree, the defendant maintained a very good character. The Bench fined him two pounds, and he was warned not to make his appearance again under similar circumstances, or it might go harder with him.[26]

He again came to the attention of the law when he was in company with William Jones (aka Black Bill) a well-known local pugilist. They were both charged with breaking into a house occupied by James Houston and his wife. Jones had forced entry to the house and made some drunken and facetious remarks to Mrs Ann Houston, but no further offence was recorded. The correspondent stated: 'Barry took no prominent part in the transaction'. The prisoners were discharged by justices Rolleston and Hope.[27]

Grace Anne McAlister

In January 1851, David married another Drayton resident, fifteen-year-old Grace Anne McAlister. Grace had arrived in the colonies from Coleraine, County Derry, Ireland, two years earlier.[28] A Catholic priest in Ipswich conducted the wedding. We know David was RC and Grace is recorded as RC on the marriage document, but under the circumstances we cannot be certain of Grace's religion back in Ireland as some of her family were known to be Protestant.[29]

Grace had a half-sister about seven years older living nearby. Her name was Ellen Smith. Ellen arrived on the *Earl Gray* in 1848 as an 'orphan'.[30] The *Earl Grey* was the first of about twenty ships which brought out more than 4000 Irish 'orphans' in the three years between 1848 and 1850. The girls and young women had been recruited from Irish workhouses, which had overflowed during the Potato Famine. This program was referred to as the Earl Grey Scheme as the third Earl Grey managed the scheme.[31] Most of them landed in Sydney, Melbourne and Adelaide, but several hundred were diverted to northern settlements. We cannot find Grace's arrival details, but at least two ships in the scheme have no surviving passenger manifest.

A sketch of Drayton from 1852 by Conrad Martens.[94] It shows buildings on Brisbane Street from the opposite bank of Westbrook Creek looking north-west. The Barrys owned two blocks of land on that street, one behind the trees in the middle distance at right and a larger one on the left just out of frame. A newspaper report identifies them living on Brisbane Street, most likely at the larger block.[95]

NSW Marriage Record for David Barry and Grace McAllister at Ipswich RC church on 9 January 1851.

The scheme was criticised by some amidst a rising anti-Irish, anti-Catholic sentiment in the colonies. These young females were condemned as 'immoral, unskilled, workhouse sweepings'.[32] If that wasn't harsh enough the *Melbourne Argus* described them as 'hordes of useless trollops thrust on an unwilling community' and went on to add '… ignorant creatures whose knowledge of household duty barely reaches to distinguishing the inside from the outside of a potato, and whose chief employment hitherto, has consisted of some intellectual occupation as occasionally trotting across a bog to fetch back a runaway pig'.[33] Despite this reception and inauspicious beginning, most Irish orphans rose above expectations and went on to lead productive lives and raise a new generation of colonial citizens.

Ellen's father, William Smith, had been a Protestant paymaster sergeant in the military, but he had died when Ellen was young. It is understood Ellen had two other full sisters (Mary Gilligan and Sarah Jane Carr) who also immigrated to NSW on two separate ships.[34] Women, in particular, were encouraged to immigrate to the colonies to redress the gender imbalance. Initiatives other than the Earl Grey Scheme such as that most famously promoted by Caroline Chisholm saw this as a way to civilise the colonies and to give poor women from the British Isles a brighter future, particularly those left behind as a result of their husband's or father's convict transportation.

It appears Grace's parents, John McAlister, a whitesmith, and Mary (née Yates) did not undertake this journey.[35] Mary is believed to have died in Coleraine prior to 1845.[36] We do not know of John's subsequent life, although coincidentally, another John McAllister was to play a part in Grace's story.

As neither Grace nor Ellen were able to sign their names, it is unlikely they had received much formal education back in Ireland, although Ellen's immigration record stated she could read. Ellen first married Owen McGrath, a mail contractor, in Brisbane in 1849.[37] Ellen and Owen were the witnesses at Grace and David's wedding. Owen had a block of land in the centre of Drayton.[38] Ellen was widowed in 1853 when Owen died of a heart attack whilst splitting timber near Drayton. Ellen then married ex-convict, but now Constable William Charington (alias Smith) in 1854 in Drayton.[39] In 1864 she was residing with her husband in nearby Clifton, once again under the name of Ellen Smith.

The family grows

David and Grace's family started to grow with the birth of Mary in February 1853 at Drayton and then followed Ellen in May 1856.[40] Son William was born in June 1857 and finally Joanna Catherine was born in May 1859. A boy died in infancy.[41]

Steven Mehan's Hotel in Darling St, Drayton c 1857.[96] John Oxley Library, State Library of Queensland.

David bought land in Drayton in July 1850 and later two acres of land in Ruthven Street in the neighbouring locality known as 'The Swamp' (later Toowoomba).[42] In October 1854, he bought Lot 3/S14 in the Swamp.[43] His residence and business occupied one of two blocks which he owned on Brisbane Street. One at the intersection of Brisbane Street and present-day Lynch Street. That site is on the other side of Brisbane Street from the Royal Bulls Head Inn and approximately fifty metres away. The impressive Inn dates from 1847 and is now in the care of the National Trust and one of the few buildings in Drayton surviving from the early days. The other block is on the same side of the street as the Inn and about 250 metres south. In 1860 he purchased two more blocks of land, lots 54 and 55 in Toowoomba.[44] One of the blocks that David owned adjoined, on the easter side, land that became the Toowoomba railway station.

David borrowed money for expansion from the prominent storekeeper and neighbour, William Handcock. William was Drayton's first mayor. Business seems to have prospered and David took steps to diversify. In January 1855, he won a tender to provide a mail service between Ipswich and Drayton once a week on horseback for the

DRAYTON IN THE LATE 1860S

The National school is on the left and the Royal Bulls Head Inn is on the right. The shop run by the Lords is just right of centre. As there is no building on the Barry land near the creek it is thought David and Grace's residence and business was most likely on the larger Barry block just to the left of this photo.[97]

annual fee of £210.[45] The following year he won the tender for a twice-a-week service on the same route for £840.[46] This probably complemented his expanding shoemaking business. He purchased horses to support his mail contracting business, but occasionally the horses got away or were stolen, and he offered rewards for their recapture with curious statements like 'Any one showing a better right to the above horse than I, can have him …'.[47] The reward he offered was higher (£5 versus £1) if anyone could prove the horse was stolen.

His shoemaking business employed at least three other journeymen shoemakers. We know this, because in April 1856, one, William Leary, stabbed another, Martin Devine, at the workplace in an argument fuelled by jealousy and alcohol whilst David was absent.[48] Leary believed that Martin was David's favourite employee and he resented it. The incident took place with the three-year-old Mary Barry present. Martin Devine received his deepest wound whilst trying to protect the young child. He was able to struggle outside with Mary. Almost immediately, Grace and William Maynard, another employee, came to their assistance. Martin Devine was recovering from his wounds at the time of the trial. William Leary had confirmed his guilt to the arresting constable by drunkardly declaring he should have killed Devine. Leary was sentenced to seven years of penal servitude.[49]

In January 1859, David was working in his shop at around eight pm when an eight-foot-long brown snake made its appearance. As it made ready to strike at Grace, one of his workers, William Jones, dispatched the unwelcome visitor. A six-foot-long black snake had been killed in their backyard a few hours previously.[50]

David Barry participated in meetings of civic importance.[51] In 1862, he attended a public meeting at Drayton to discuss a vacancy on the first Municipal Council. David Barry was nominated with thirteen others and after a vote of those present, he and five others went through to stand as an alderman for the vacancy.[52] Three candidates subsequently withdrew including David, who withdrew at the last minute. However, there was a controversy when David's name remained on the voting ticket until halfway through the election. His votes were transferred to the colourful candidate who ultimately won, Alderman Rüb, amidst cries of 'farce' from interested observers.[53] Joseph Jacob Rüb was born in Württemberg (Germany). He was a shepherd, a builder and a carpenter and strong headed. He was the last mayor of Drayton. At one time he and William Handcock both claimed to be mayor of Drayton with their own associated alderman with

Map of central Drayton in 1850 showing David Barry's land (bold) and other landowners mentioned (medium)[98]

neither recognising the other. External authorities resolved the situation by recognising Joseph's claim over William's. There had been a violent council meeting previously where tomahawks were brandished, and Joseph was physically thrown out of the council mid-speech. He re-entered through the window and continued his speech before being physically ejected again.

Grace Barry was also reported as a victim of assault by Michael Menehan. He was fined £2. This occurred on the same day David's second round of success with the mail contracting business was reported in the local newspaper.[54] On later occasions, David Barry was fined the sums of £1 and £2 for two incidents of public drunkenness. In 1861 David was fined twenty shillings for assaulting his neighbour, John Vowles.[55]

Tragically, Grace also had a reputation for her 'intemperate habits'. She was not the only female in town with that reputation.[56] On one occasion in 1858, both David and Grace were charged together for being drunk and disorderly and both fined £2 or one months imprisonment. They paid their fines.[57]

David Barry was known to be violent towards his wife. In June 1861, he was confined to the lock-up for 24 hours for being drunk and disorderedly. A constable stated David struck his wife and used bad language. The magistrate went leniently on him because it had been a full nine months since his last similar offence. The magistrate warned him he risked being sent to jail for two years under the *Vagrant Act*.[58] In November 1861 he remained locked up for 48 hours rather than pay the twenty shillings he had been fined for 'assaulting his wife and causing a disturbance in the town'.[59]

The Royal Bulls Head Inn, Drayton is one of the few buildings remaining in Drayton from the time that David and Grace Barry lived there. The Inn was owned and operated by ex-convict, William Horton. It was established in 1847 and extended to its current configuration in 1859. Photo: March 2016 by author.

The tragedy

On the morning of 23 March 1864, events came to a tragic conclusion when Grace took her own life by slashing her throat in her bedroom with a razor.[60] The events occurred as David was attending a court hearing regarding the claim a neighbour, Montgomery Shepherd, had witnessed David Barry throwing rocks at his wife the previous evening. David sent for his daughter, Mary, to give evidence in his favour. Her evidence was interrupted by the news Grace's sister, Ellen, had discovered the tragedy.[61] Ellen confirmed David had been quarrelling with his wife and he was 'cross' with her, but he did not make any threats in Ellen's presence.[62]

Montgomery Shepherd's evidence was more revealing, as he had twice witnessed David beating Grace and had heard many quarrels coming from their house day and night. He made the complaint against David Barry as he said he did not wish to be a witness to a murder.[63]

The newspaper reports of the suicide stated Grace was near her confinement with what would have been her fifth child. However, there was no mention of this condition by the medical witness at the inquest, nor is it noted on her death certificate, and so this point is by no means reliably established. There was evidence about her agitated behaviour the evening prior and about her calm behaviour immediately before the act. The inquest jury laid the blame squarely on David Barry, but the newspaper's correspondent suggested Grace's heavy drinking was at least partly responsible.[64]

Aftermath

David succumbed to 'lunacy'. The *Darling Downs Gazette* reported he 'has given way entirely to habits of intemperance, and the dreadful fate of his wife acting upon an overstimulated brain, has brought on an attack of insanity, the poor man being under the constant impression that his deceased wife is before him'. In late April, Dr Burke ordered he be confined to the Drayton Lock-up as he was 'dangerous both to himself and others'.[65] David Barry died of 'natural causes' just 74 days after his wife's suicide.[66] Grace and David were buried side by side, but their graves within the Toowoomba and Drayton Cemetery are unmarked.[67] At the time of Grace's death, the Catholic Church had a policy of not burying suicide victims in consecrated ground and some relatives have speculated Grace may not have been buried in the RC section of the cemetery. However, we know that her burial was attended by a Catholic priest and so that particular policy may not have applied in her case, particularly in light of the inquest finding.[68]

David had apparently recovered his senses sufficiently to draw up a will in his last week alive. He left his house and various land holdings to his children. His will directed his personal effects and work tools be sold to pay for outstanding

William Handcock, *Leading man of Drayton*

233

debts. William Handcock was the largest creditor with almost £45 outstanding. David's tools were auctioned on two occasions over the following months. The second advertised 'no reserve'. *The Brisbane Courier* reported on David's death and the plight of the children, using the situation to argue the government should establish an 'Orphan's school or Asylum'.[69] Oral history suggests the children were not able to keep the land as they could not pay the ongoing charges and therefore neighbours raised the children and in return acquired the land.

William Handcock took control of David Barry's will from the named executor, Charles Pottinger, which the Supreme Court ratified in September 1864.[70] There is speculation it was William Handcock who took the children into care. If this was so, then they ended up in the home of a disreputable character. Maurice French's article, '*The leading man of Drayton, William Handcock …*' leaves us in no doubt about his failings which would include particular risks for any females in his care.[71] The reaction of his own family provides further evidence of his unpopularity. When his money ran out, his daughter and son-in-law turned him out and his two sisters also refused him. His wife had left him in 1854, 'without explanation'. He died a pauper in 1890 in the benevolent home at Dunwich, North Stradbroke Island.[72]

Context

Even by 1864, Drayton was still just a small community as demonstrated by only 97 residents voting in the municipal election held in 1863.[73] Its newer neighbour to the north, Toowoomba was starting to outgrow it. Drayton was as wild as it was at its inception, keeping policemen and magistrates busy with drunkenness, thievery, assaults and riotous behaviour. Sometimes the criminality escalated to Wild West proportions. The superintendent of nearby Yandilla Station, Charles Owen, was shot dead in 1864 whilst returning from his duties as a magistrate.[74] On the evening of St Patrick's day, one week prior to Grace's suicide, a policeman, David Copely, was drowned in a public well in Drayton. Foul play was suspected, with persons of interest named at the inquest.[75] A few months prior to this, a letter to the editor had noted that policemen appeared to be unwilling to patrol the streets of an evening and complaining of gangs of men and boys throwing rocks at houses and terrorising the population during the night.[76]

Three Barry children L to R: Ellen, William and Mary. The left and centre photos from Doug Hill's collection.

Legacy and connections

The resilience of Grace and David's children allowed them to get on with life. Mary Barry married Patrick Cranley in 1877. Ellen Barry married John Jefferys on Christmas Eve 1874.[77] She gave birth to seven sons between 1876 and 1889. Ellen died in Toowoomba in June 1933 and John died in Clermont in 1900.[78] William Barry married Charlotte Dore in 1883.[79] This marriage produced one girl and eight boys between 1886 and 1902. William died in Pittsworth in 1908 and Charlotte remarried in 1914 and died in 1946 in Emerald.[80] Joanna Catherine never married and died in Brisbane in 1946.[81]

Grace's half-sister, Ellen Smith, died under the name Ellen Charington in 1894 in Brisbane.[82] She had one child with Owen McGrath and five with William Charington (alias Smith). Her parents were William Smith and Mary Yates.[83] Mary Gilligan (née Smith) (b. c. 1821) married Timothy Gilligan (transported in 1835) and was living in New England, NSW in 1849. She had seven living children at the time of her death in 1884 in NSW.[84] Sarah Jane Carr (née Smith) (b. c. 1820) married Charles Carr and was accidently killed by falling into a fire at her home in Forrest Lodge, NSW in 1896. She had one living child at the time of her death.[85]

The foreman of Grace's inquest jury was a 'John McAllister'. This is almost certainly the principal of the Drayton National school.[86] It is highly unlikely to be her father because of the unlikely change of occupation, and this would be a clear conflict of interest even for the standards of 1864. There is no record of her father arriving as an immigrant.

Irish records from the early 1800s are not the easiest to work with due to their lack of detail and the likely possibility they simply don't exist for the family of interest. The family of David Barry back in Cork has not yet been positively identified. The unrelated informant on David's death certificate stated his father's name was David. Identifying a David Barry who was a blacksmith from a family matching the known criteria would be quite compelling.[87] A complicating factor is the family name, Barry, is the fourteenth most common surname in Cork (and 71st most common in the all of Ireland).

Taking the DNA as the primary clue, then the current best match, triangulated from a descendant of Mary and a descendant of William, has ancestors with the surname of Barry from the district around the Northern Cork town of Newmarket.[88] The only clues from David's trial were the offence was committed in Cork City and he claimed to have obtained the tobacco from the nearby town of Midleton, to the east of Cork City.[89] This may be a location he has a connection with. A direct male descendant has taken a FTDNA big Y test, which has confirmed the Barry surname, but there are currently no matches of sufficient strength to establish an ancestral location.[90]

The ancestry of Grace McAlister is a little better understood and this is supported by DNA matches. Unfortunately, no reliable information regarding John McAlister, the Irish whitesmith, has yet been found. However, on her mother's side, a DNA match has been demonstrated with a descendant of Ellen Smith/McGrath/Charington. Grace and Ellen's mother, Mary Yates, is a recorded descendant of James Yates and Grace Dougherty and there are several DNA matches supporting that pedigree.[91] James Yates' family is understood to have come to Derry via Cork with a military regiment. Prior to that, the Yates ancestors had moved to Cork from Lancashire, England in the mid-eighteenth century.[92] This tells us that heritage from one locality is not necessarily locked into that location for all the time beforehand. Occasionally there was migration between diverse districts with intermarriage with locals to help stir the gene pool.

Endnotes to Chapter 14

1 The National Museum of Australia (NMA) site , https://www.nma.gov.au/exhibitions/not-just-ned/family-history/irish/convicts ('Not just Ned'), states that there less than 20,000. However the National Library of Australia (NLA) cites the Irish archives database which contains the names of over 38,000 Irish individuals sent to Australia. see: https://nla.gov.au/nla.obj-919437026/findingaid They were either transported convicts or they were family members who accompanied the convicts to Australia That database is incomplete as it does not contain anyone transported before 1836 unlesss they were the subject of a petition or other official correspondence after 1836. On the basis of the above, I am inclined to accept the information from the NLA.

2 The Earl Grey Scheme operated from 1848–1850. Twenty ships brought out about 4000 'orphan girls' as a result of the Potato Famine https://www.geni.com/projects/Earl-Grey-Irish-Female-Orphans-in-Australia/15952

3 David's DC (Qld 1864 106 393) names his father as David Barry. His mother is not named; however, the Irish child-naming tradition would suggest her first name was either Mary or Ellen. However, given David's first son was William and not David, then it is not clear whether David & Grace were following that tradition whilst in Australia.

4 As evidenced by documents containing his signature and writing such as a will.

5 Irish Convicts to New South Wales 1788–1849 Captain Cook (3) 1836 David Barry (online)
The reason family researchers have concluded that our ancestor David Barry is this convict David Barry is that both were from Cork, both were shoemakers, both were RC, both were born around 1817 and the stated time spent in the colonies also aligns with the convict records. No alternative records fit our ancestor anywhere near as well. E.g. See subsequent discussion on other convicts named David Barry.

6 The court proceedings were reported in 3 different newspapers, but there are remarkable inconsistencies between 2 reports: One report states, 14 and a half pounds of tobacco and 2 others have 25 pounds. One has the date of the theft in late Feb, the other early Mar. One is more concerned with the behaviour of the Bridewell Warden in returning some tobacco to the prosecutor (complainant) prior to the trial's end than with the actual offence committed by David.

7 Cork Assizes, *The Cork Southern Reporter*, Tue 22 Mar 1836, page 2, col. 3 Irish National Library, Dublin.

8 For several decades, it was thought likely the goods received were 'a sheep' because a few days before David's conviction a John Barry, a 23-year-old stable hand, was convicted of stealing a sheep at a different court. A working assumption was John and David were brothers. Subsequent research has determined this is unlikely as the true nature of David's crime was reported in the newspapers.

9 Irish Convicts to New South Wales 1788–1849 Captain Cook (3) 1836 David Barry (online)

10 Despite its spelling, the town's name is pronounced 'Cove' (local advice).

11 A McMahon, *Floating Prisons: Irish Convict Hulks and Voyages to New South Wales 1823–1837* Halstead Press, Canberra, 2017
(Ref chapter 4 *The Surprise*).

12 The last prisoner left in Sep 1836
https://www.echolive.ie/corknews/Maritime-Cork-The-history-and-use-of-prison-hulks-in-Cork-Harbour-d07a1717-c7dc-4e43-8dc2-398c31974a89-ds

13 Originally 236 convicts were embarked, but 7 were put off in English waters.

14 https://www.jenwilletts.com/convict_ship_captain_cook_1836.htm

15 Timothy Buckley, convicted aged 23 died at sea 23 Oct 1836

16 Mutiny on … *Captain Cook, The Sydney Monitor*, 23 Dec 1836, page 2 http://nla.gov.au/nla.news-article32154315
David's name was not on the list of those that were punished for the munity

17 NSW Certificate of Freedom 1843/1385 David Barry 24 Aug 1843

18 *Sydney Morning Herald*, Wed 26 Aug 1846 http://nla.gov.au/nla.news-article12890281

19 Miscellaneous, *Sydney Morning Herald*, Wed 30 Jun 1847, page 3 http://nla.gov.au/nla.news-article12892807

20 e.g. Another David Barry from Cork was transported on the *Mary* in 1819. He was born in 1796. Other David Barrys were transported to Tasmania. According to Alison Alexander's book *Tasmania's Convicts*, about half of the Tasmanian convicts went to the mainland after serving their sentence, but most of those went to Victoria.
A Alexander, *Tasmania's Convicts: how felons built a free society*, Allen & Unwin, Crows Nest, NSW, 2014

21 Domestic intelligence, *Sydney Chronicle*, Tue 9 May 1848, page 2 http://nla.gov.au/nla.news-article31756578

22 Accidents, robberies and offences, *Sydney Chronicle*, Sat 26 Aug 1848, page 2 http://nla.gov.au/nla.news-article31757307

23 M French, *Pubs Ploughs & Peculiar People*, USQ Press Toowoomba, 1992, page 17

24 French, *Pubs Ploughs & Peculiar People*, pages 16 & 17, The first shoemaker was also an ex-convict from Cork named Joseph Harrington.

25 Colonial Secretary (CS) correspondence ref 47/05389 10 Jun 1847 forwarded to CS by Commissioner Rolleston.

26 Drayton, *The Moreton Bay Courier*, Mon 10 Dec 1849, page 1 http://nla.gov.au/nla.news-article3710846

27 Domestic intelligence, *The Moreton Bay Courier*, Sat 19 Jan 1850, page 2 http://nla.gov.au/nla.news-article3709617
It is probable that this William Jones is the same William Jones that is working for David Barry in 1859 - ref: snakes. incident

28 County Derry was officially renamed Londonderry by the British, but as a sign of defiance many locals still call it Derry. Grace referred to it as Derry and so that is how it is referred to in this story.

29 There is a possibility, Grace was a Protestant as Ellen appears to be one. However, her MC states she was RC.

30 It is possible Grace arrived on the same ship, but passenger manifests have been searched with no result as yet.

Difficult start, tragic end

We know that Ellen is a half-sister to Grace because Ellen says that Grace is her 'sister' in an 1864 affidavit. Furthermore a DNA match to a descendant of Ellen at Ancestry.com (16 cM (Anne) and 10 cM (Ralph) to MG) provides further weight to the proposition.

31 Henry George Grey (1802–1894) British Politician. His father was a Prime Minister of England.

32 https://www.historyireland.com/20th-century-contemporary-history/lost-children/

33 Irish orphan immigration, *The Argus* (Melbourne), Sat 13 Apr 1850, page 2 http://nla.gov.au/nla.news-article4764725

34 Ellen's immigration record (*Earl Grey,* Oct 1848) had the notation of 'Sister, Mary Gillingham in New England'.

35 Metalworker who does finishing work on iron and steel. Also, a synonym for tinsmiths – Wikipedia

36 Based on information from Mary Gillian's immigration record

37 NSW RC MC 1849/96 376, Brisbane, 24 Dec 1849, Ellen Smith & Owen McGrath

38 Burnett's plan of Drayton 1850 shows it being on the corner of Brisbane & Darling sts.

39 William was a ticket-of-leave man who was employed in the Queensland Native Police. This was a large and notorious outfit which was utilised to suppress Aboriginal resistance to colonisation. Many of its members were Aboriginal men.

& Family notices, *The Moreton Bay Courier*, Sat 15 Jul 1854, page 3 http://nla.gov.au/nla.news-article3709952

& NSW C of E Marriage 1854/252, Parsonage Drayton, 15 Jun 1854, Ellen McGrath & Thomas Charrington (alias Smith)

40 NSW RC Baptism Record 1853/2659, Parish: Ipswich, Drayton, 23 Feb 1853, Mary Barry

41 NSW BC 1859/6969 233, Drayton, 15 May 1859, Joanna Catherine Barry ('one boy deceased')

42 That block is about 150 metres east of where the Toowoomba railway station was built in the 1860s.

43 Fifty years ago, *The Brisbane Courier,* Sat 5 Nov 1904, page 15 http://nla.gov.au/nla.news-article19343102

& Domestic intelligence, *The Moreton Bay Courier*, Sat 4 Nov 1854, page 2 Drayton http://nla.gov.au/nla.news-article3714181

44 The Downs, *The Moreton Bay Courier*, Sat 24 Nov 1860, page 3 http://nla.gov.au/nla.news-article3723947

45 Government Gazette, *The Maitland Mercury and Hunter River General Advertiser,* Wed 17 Jan 1855, page 1 http://nla.gov.au/nla.news-article697174

46 Fri Dec 28, *The Maitland Mercury and Hunter River General Advertiser,* Wed 2 Jan 1856, page 7 http://nla.gov.au/nla.news-article18647033

47 Classified advertising, *The Moreton Bay Courier,* Sat 31 Oct 1857, page 3 http://nla.gov.au/nla.news-article3717380

48 Brisbane Assizes – stabbing, *Empire* (Sydney), Mon 26 May 1856, page 2 http://nla.gov.au/nla.news-article60248359

49 Domestic intelligence, *The Moreton Bay Courier,* Sat 24 May 1856, page 2 http://nla.gov.au/nla.news-article3710397

50 Snakes, *The Darling Downs Gazette and General Advertiser,* Thu 27 Jan 1859, page 3 http://nla.gov.au/nla.news-article75524215

51 e.g. Drayton, *The Moreton Bay Courier,* Sat 3 Apr 1858, page 4 http://nla.gov.au/nla.news-article3722729

52 Country intelligence, *The Courier* (Brisbane), Mon 22 Sep 1862, page 2 http://nla.gov.au/nla.news-article4608157

53 The Downs, *The Courier* (Brisbane), Tue 21 Oct 1862, page 2 http://nla.gov.au/nla.news-article4608711

& The Downs, *The Courier* (Brisbane), Mon 27 Oct 1862, page 3 http://nla.gov.au/nla.news-article4608845

54 Drayton Police Court, *The Moreton Bay Courier*, 26 Jan 1856, page 2 http://nla.gov.au/nla.news-article3716152

55 Drayton Police Court, *The Toowoomba Chronicle* and *Queensland Advertiser,* Thu 7 Nov 1861, page 5 http://nla.gov.au/nla.news-article212788440

Drayton Police Court John Vowles, a cooper, was David's next-door neighbour. On 19 Oct 1861, John was stabbed by a jealous husband, John Laffery, when Mrs. Laffery was 'stopping' with Vowles. John survived his injury.

56 Ann Houston, the woman that David and Black Bill had harassed at home in 1850, on one occasion in 1863 spent all day drinking with other women. She returned home and abused her husband and her daughter. Her husband retaliated by stripping her, tying her up and beating her severely. He was sentenced to three months jail. - Drayton Police Court, *The Toowoomba Chronicle and Queensland Advertiser* Thu, 29 Oct 1863, page. 3. http://nla.gov.au/nla.news-article212785203

57 Police Office, *The Darling Downs Gazette and General Advertiser,* Thu 26 Aug 1858, page 3 http://nla.gov.au/nla.news-article75527116

58 Fri Jun 14, *The Darling Downs Gazette and General Advertiser,* Sat Jun 15 1861, page 3 http://nla.gov.au/nla.news-article75509709

59 Drayton, *The Courier* (Brisbane), Tue 5 Nov 1861, page 2 http://nla.gov.au/nla.news-article4601986

60 Qld DC 1864/75 363, Drayton, Grace Anne Barry also Qld State Archive Inquest documents

61 Telegraphic, *The Courier* (Brisbane), Mon 28 Mar 1864, page 2 http://nla.gov.au/nla.news-article3169342

62 Ellen Smith's affidavit – inquest Grace Barry, Queensland State Archives JUS/NT 64/63 roll Z2850

63 Montgomery Shepherd's affidavit – inquest Grace Barry, QSA JUS/NT 64/63 roll Z2850

64 Inquests, *The Darling Downs Gazette and General Advertiser*, Thu 31 Mar 1864, page 3 http://nla.gov.au/nla.news-article75512520

65 re *Darling Downs Gazette* 21 Apr 1864, *The Brisbane Courier,* Sat 23 Apr 1864, page 3, http://nla.gov.au/nla.news-article1258077

66 Qld DC 1864/106 393, Drayton, 5 Jun 1864, David Barry

67 Toowoomba, *The Brisbane Courier*, Tue 14 Jun 1864, page 3 https://trove.nla.gov.au/newspaper/article/1259071

68 Both David & Grace's death records mention that their burials were attended by the Catholic priest, Frenchman, Fulgence Hodebourge, which implies neither were denied the rites of the Catholic Church. There were official exceptions to the rule of no funeral and no consecrated burial ground and that was where the suicide was considered 'forced' – e.g. a soldier facing certain death at the hands of an enemy. The priest may have read the inquest finding in that light or he may simply have had more compassion than the hierarchy that set the rules.

69 Toowoomba, *The Brisbane Courier*, Tue 14 Jun 1864, page 3 https://trove.nla.gov.au/newspaper/article/1259071

70 Classified advertising, *The Brisbane Courier,* Mon 8 Aug 1864, page 1 http://nla.gov.au/nla.news-article1260411

& Supreme Court, *The Brisbane Courier*, Fri 23 Sep 1864, page 2 http://nla.gov.au/nla.news-article1262329

71 *The Leading Man of Drayton, William Handcock, Frontier Storekeeper, and the Election of 1859* by Maurice French. https://www.textqueensland.com.au/item/article/2c7922101ee836d340741d8a809e9b2e

72 Traditionally known as Minjerribah in the Jandai language of the people of the Quandamooka country. Handcock's nickname was 'Billy the bull' which alluded to his sexual appetite.

73 Toowoomba and Drayton, *The Courier* (Brisbane), Mon 10 Aug 1863 page 3 http://nla.gov.au/nla.news-article3164956

74 Telegraphic News, Drayton, *The Brisbane Courier*, Mon 2 May 1864, page 2 http://nla.gov.au/nla.news-article1258229

75 "Ferio — Tego" The late inquests in Drayton. *The Darling Downs Gazette and General Advertiser*, Thu 31 March 1864, page 3 http://nla.gov.au/nla.news-article75512520

76 Drayton rowdyism, *The Darling Downs Gazette and General Advertiser* Thu 7 Jan 1864, page 3 http://nla.gov.au/nla.news-article75512093

77 Qld Marriage index (MI) 1875/C/848, 24 Dec 1874, Ellen Barry & John Jefferys

78 Qld Death indexes (DI) 1933/C/3431, 18 Jun 1933, Ellen Jefferys & 1900/C/998, 18 Aug 1900, John Jeffreys

79 Qld MI 1883/C/448, 01 May 1883, Charlotte Elizabeth Dora (*sic*) William Barry

80 Qld DI 1908/C/3718, 22 Jul 1908, William Barry (mother listed as 'Ellen')
& Qld MI 1914/C/1090, 22 Oct 1914, Charlotte Elizabeth Barry & Walter Daniels
& Qld DI 1946/C/2462, 9 Jun 1946, Charlotte Elizabeth Daniels

81 Qld DC 1946/5039, Brisbane, 19 Jan 1946, Joanna Catherine Barry, Informant: Edward Herbert, a nephew

82 At the time of the inquest in 1864, Ellen was staying with a family named Davis. This is understood to be Thomas and Mary Davis who were residents of Drayton and the parents of Arthur Hoey Davis, born 14 Nov 1868 Drayton, Qld – died 11 Oct 1935 Brisbane, Qld, better known by his penname, Steele Rudd.

83 Qld DC 1894/27097, Sheriff St, Petrie Terrace, 16 Jul 1894, Ellen Charington

84 NSW DT 1884/01637, Mary St, Sydney, 6 Sep 1884, Mary Gilligan

85 NSW DT 1896/05371, Forest Lodge, Annandale, 29 Apr 1896, Sarah Jane Carr

86 John was headmaster (and probably only teacher) at the Drayton National School from 1861 to 1866.

87 A family from the townland of Knocknamanagh near Tracton in South East Cork has a father named David Barry. He was a blacksmith based on the advice of local family historians. His wife was Catherine Jeffords. So, there is a name match, but not the more explicable, Mary or Ellen. There were 9 baptisms for the family. A difficulty is other people have claimed descent from this family, and we are not getting any DNA matches with those people. However, beyond second cousin level, there is no guarantee matching DNA will exist. A working assumption is that their claim of descent is valid. So just a possibility.

88 Both a descendant of William and a descendant of Mary triangulate to matches with a USA aunt (Acct: CAL-W) and nephew (Acct: CMK) who claim descent from a Philip Jeremiah Barry born 1831 Tureedarby, Newmarket, Cork. This is not a convincing triangulation but simply the best available. Triangulated means the match shares a specific segment of DNA of sufficient size with the 2 known relatives. Its 'sufficient' size indicates a high probability the segment is identical by 'descent' rather than by 'state' (i.e. by chance).

89 From a report in *The Cork Evening Herald*, Wed 23 Mar 1836, page 1, col. 2. Midleton, Cork is about 20 km east of Cork City and it is home of the modern Jameson whiskey distillery.

90 Doug is the test taker. Current closest match on 111 markers has a GD of 5. Confirmed haplogroup is R-Y13610.

91 James Yates born after 1760, Cork, Cork – died about 1864 Killowen, Coleraine, Derry
& Grace Dougherty born before 1792 in Ireland – died 24 Jan 1830, Killowen, Coleraine, Derry

92 From information provided by a family history researcher in Coleraine Nth Ireland, Orreen Yates.

93 McMahon, page 96, from information provided in a sketch of Cobh Harbour.

94 Original held by Dixson Library, State Library of NSW, out of copyright

95 Toowoomba, *The North Australian*, Tue 29 Mar 1864, page 3 http://nla.gov.au/nla.news-article77435969

96 The Inn in the photograph was owned by Steven Mehan. He had brothers David & James. Michael Meneham the person who assaulted Grace is apparently not related and the similar surnames are just that. On the same day Grace had her complaint heard, Steven Mehan was up on a charge for stabbing his shopman in the eye. He was fined two pounds.

97 Photo from M. French, *Toowoomba: a sense of History 1840–2008*, University of Southern Queensland, Toowoomba, 2009

98 Based on Burnett's 1850 plan of Drayton, Toowoomba City Library

Epilogue

In 1985, I formally aligned my prospects with my partner, Helen Evans. We had met at work in the Department of Social Security in Canberra. Apart from both working in Information Technology, we had many shared interests, which expanded with the birth of our two children. A shared interest that developed with time was family history, and Helen has researched her background with an enthusiasm similar to mine. Our shared interest in travel has meant that we combine the two to visit ancestral localities. That provides a focus for part of our travel and gives us a glimpse of the backdrop to our ancestors' lives, all those years ago.

Helen's origins are predominantly Anglo-Celtic, with migrating ancestors born most prominently in England followed by Scotland, Wales and Ireland. She has identified six convicts coming from both sides of her family, including a wild colonial boy born in NSW who blotted his copybook and then earnt his stripes (or broad arrows) when shipped to Moreton Bay from Sydney. Her roots here are deeper than mine as her earliest arrival was in 1792 and her latest was 1887. Her family settled in NSW and subsequent branches gravitated to South Eastern NSW and just over the border into Victoria. Helen was born in Bega, NSW, which is situated in a picturesque green valley and is now famous for cheese.

Just like my lot, none of her known ancestors were born with silver utensils protruding, but she thinks she may have spotted a threadbare title from Ireland. Some of the searching is a work in progress, as family history tends to be. Many of her forebears worked on the land in South East NSW. The catastrophic fires of 2020 destroyed two wooden ancestral homes in the Eden district that had been built by her great-grandparents and grandparents. Helen had managed to visit the older one during her earlier explorations. Tales of struggle, intrigue, scandal and early tragic death are themes played out

in the stories of her ancestors both in Australia and beyond. Her dabbling with DNA has unearthed some secrets that would otherwise have gone to the grave. Doing her family tree identified distant cousins that she knew socially but not as relatives, which helps to demonstrate the point made in the preface regarding pedigree.

The moment when we discover some profound insight into an ancestor long gone is difficult to describe adequately. Those folks who share this, or similar hobbies, probably understand. That excitement can be addictive. Unfortunately, the big discoveries are rare, and they tend to come out of the blue. Of course, all of the work that was done previously facilitated the big moment. Most days, we are content to just learn a new fact or insight regarding a place and time or minor character. That said, there have been some difficult periods on the journey. The most difficult for me concerns Grace Barry. I can remember where I was when I opened the letter containing Grace Barry's death certificate. I had just retrieved the official-looking letter from my Canberra post-office box and correctly guessed that it was the response to the request for a certificate that I had sent for several weeks before. I walked a few steps and ripped open the letter: Age 27, Cause of death – 'cut throat' … wow! My initial thought was, what was the story behind that? It was a typed certificate and the transcriber may have been applying the official policy of sanitising the original record. What the original record had said was: 'Suicide by cutting her throat'.

It was not until I was able to locate a newspaper microfilm of the relevant paper in Toowoomba, several months later, that I learnt more of Grace's story. It was a heavy blow to read the detail and it took the joy out of family history for me for several years. After some time, my sails reflated and my curiosity was renewed. I tried to discover more from places like the State Archives, which held the stark details of the evidence at her inquest. Trove filled in a lot of the details of her life with David, before the dramatic conclusion. More than a hundred and fifty years have passed since theses events, but they still stir a sadness in me. I was determined to find the positive in the story, which of course had to be the early joys and the renewal shown by the children's resilience. I felt that it was a story that deserved to be told. Being so long ago gave me permission to write up a relatively dispassionate narrative of Grace and David's family. I have never been made aware of any relative knowing about this story from any source other than written records. Mary Cranley named one of her children Grace, but none were named David. Her own daughter, Ellen, chose the name David for one of her sons, which tells me that Mary protected her children from the true story of her parents. Some of the value in relating their story is that people can see the consequence of behaviour that had plenty of warning signs. The harsh convict system may have contributed to David's violent behaviour, but ultimately, the inquest jury got it right. David cannot dodge responsibility for the tragic outcome.

One of the greatest risks in writing a family history is the impulse to write a glowing or even mawkish account of an ancestor. I do admit to having my favourites though, and that will be evident from what has gone before. Where people had desirable qualities, that should be chronicled. However, to be fair and informative, the warts should also be exposed. I do not feel obligated to like my ancestors, but they are due my gratitude for their part in my existence – even if their part was brief, pleasurable and devoid of responsibility, as is suspected in Master Mezger's case. He would argue he was just following biological orders. I certainly hope Sarah was a consenting participant.

I have tried to be as honest as I can without being brutal and stepping on the memories that others may have had of their relatives. There are inevitably sensitivities around certain aspects of any family history and judgement should be exercised when relating it. I have had to apply some discretion in the telling of this story. When details are in the public domain and no closely connected people are still alive, I feel that the story is there to be told. When we do encounter problem behaviour, then the fairest thing we can do is to give it some context. People are a product of their background and environment.

My summary of why I am an Australian is now multi-faceted. In mathematical terms, my foreign ancestry of the past hundreds of years is greater than fifty percent Irish – an ethnicity that was not on my radar before I began my research. Call me fickle, but I am more than happy with that, especially now that being Irish is so hip and fashionable. Not so long ago, the worst Irish jokes typically painted Irish as unintelligent, and pugnacious. They were as wrong as they were lame. Ireland is a wonderful place to visit. All that green beauty, dark ales, charming accents, foot-tapping music and craic ninety. In all humility, I could count myself as a positive outcome of the Potato Famine, given that without it, I would not be here. One of the dispersed and otherwise forgotten credits to apply against the huge debit on the balance sheet.

The Scottish component was always understood and appreciated as a known link to the old country. The line that you can trust the most, the maternal line, is all Scottish as far back as the eye can see. That's currently to about 1729. However, I had wrongly suspected the unknown bits were all English, particularly given my surname and the few other ancestral surnames that I was aware of before my research. As it turns out, my Y chromosome line is solidly Teutonic for several hundred years at least. There is some English, but it is only a few dashes. I did find two convicts, which, despite the misery inherent in that origin, is essentially a positive. It has a prestige akin to aristocracy in the Australian genealogical scene. The broad arrow is the new *fleur-de-lis*. The principal lesson out of convict origins for Australians is that it did not determine the opportunities or achievements of their descendants. The convict stain dissipated quite quickly; by just the next generation, the Currency Children, as they were known, were taller, healthier and more law-abiding than the immigrant free settlers that they lived amongst. Of course, the wild colonial boys were the exception to that generalisation.

My suspicions around the absence of any Indigenous ancestry were borne out. Should I feel guilty about my presence here without such biological heritage? Would the discovery of a dollop of Indigenous ancestry, previously unknown, have suddenly anointed me as Indigenous and absolve me of any need to scrutinise the past? No, on both counts. I feel a slight unease, but no guilt, because I was born here and because nowhere else really feels like home. None of us have any say in our pedigree and some of my ancestors had no say in their migration. Uncovering an unknown biological heritage doesn't automatically make you a part of the corresponding cultural heritage. It might start you on a path of discovery and appreciation and that should be a positive thing. Given the extensive breadth of our pedigrees, it is a certainty that all of us are beneficiaries of past misdeeds, committed by some ancestors or their allies. We live in a current reality born of a past that is never going to be reversed. We do need to be aware that the past is full of pain and injustice, most conspicuously for Indigenous Australians. There is much to be done still to eliminate its continuance. Genuine respect and recognition will make a difference. We will have really matured when we recognise the Indigenous culture and heritage as an integral component of what it means to be Australian, irrespective of our individual biological heritage.

My interest in legal matters, in this story and in my life generally, lead me to the view that legislation is prone to being a blunt instrument and case law is a fuzzy morass. So when real life confronts these constructs in a court room you end up with a percentage game. A contested legal outcome is more likely to be determined by pocket depth and advocate ability than by natural justice and procedural fairness. Litigants become gamblers and are as likely as not to be bitterly disappointed, just like Patrick Cranley. My own limited exposure to legal matters close-up reinforced my belief that there is, thankfully, a healthy bias towards getting the right outcome, but it is often a torturous and close-run thing.

Knowing the past enhances my appreciation of the present. I can have affection for some aspects of the past but that doesn't mean I would want to return to it. I am grateful for living in the current age as the modern products, services and opportunities collectively outshine whatever the past had to offer. We have witnessed many fascinating scientific discoveries and advances, some of which will hopefully help us on the path to identifying and rectifying many previous short-sighted decisions. Of course, there are challenges aplenty ahead of us – not the least of which are the environmental ones caused by ill-considered human activity. Future generations will inherit a greatly stressed and depleted environment which will make many curse the ages when we saw nature only as a mix of resource and adversary.

On an optimistic note, I appreciate the progressive enlightenment of a more educated and diverse population. Even the disruption of the Covid pandemic has many silver linings, most important of which is the clear expression of what society values. This episode has demonstrated that Australia is a relatively sane, sensible and civilised society where health, fairness and cooperation is valued over individual freedoms and profit. It also revealed that distance can be both a tyranny and a benefit. Responses to the pandemic illustrate the point made about laws and regulations being blunt instruments, particularly those that are conceived in haste. It also demonstrates that taking advice from people who are knowledgeable about the science of the issue is greatly preferable to the alternative.

Appendix – Cascading pedigree chart for the author

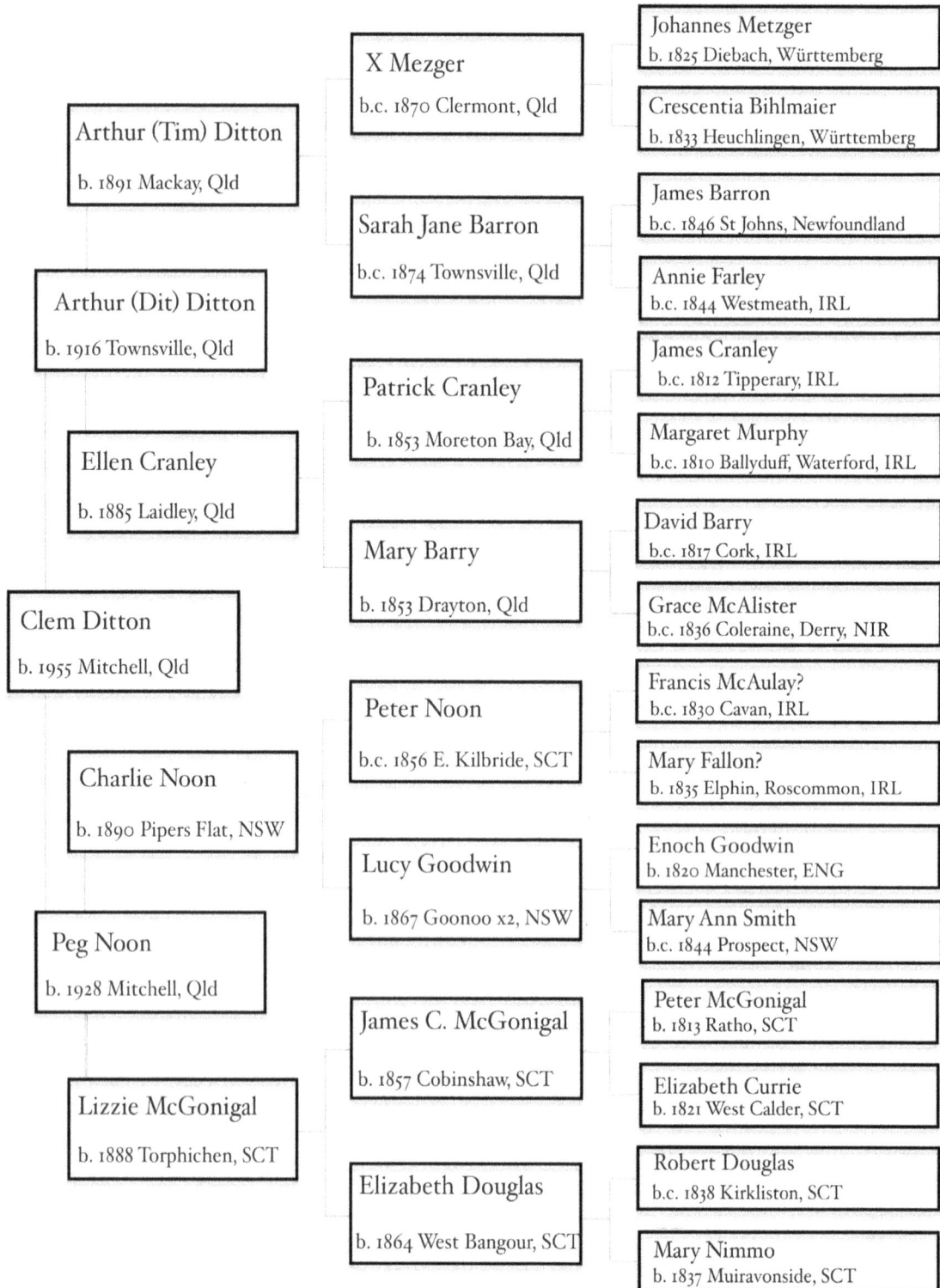

		Johannes Metzger b. 1825 Diebach, Württemberg
	X Mezger b.c. 1870 Clermont, Qld	
		Crescentia Bihlmaier b. 1833 Heuchlingen, Württemberg
Arthur (Tim) Ditton b. 1891 Mackay, Qld		
		James Barron b.c. 1846 St Johns, Newfoundland
	Sarah Jane Barron b.c. 1874 Townsville, Qld	
		Annie Farley b.c. 1844 Westmeath, IRL
Arthur (Dit) Ditton b. 1916 Townsville, Qld		
		James Cranley b.c. 1812 Tipperary, IRL
	Patrick Cranley b. 1853 Moreton Bay, Qld	
		Margaret Murphy b.c. 1810 Ballyduff, Waterford, IRL
Ellen Cranley b. 1885 Laidley, Qld		
		David Barry b.c. 1817 Cork, IRL
	Mary Barry b. 1853 Drayton, Qld	
		Grace McAlister b.c. 1836 Coleraine, Derry, NIR
Clem Ditton b. 1955 Mitchell, Qld		
		Francis McAulay? b.c. 1830 Cavan, IRL
	Peter Noon b.c. 1856 E. Kilbride, SCT	
		Mary Fallon? b. 1835 Elphin, Roscommon, IRL
Charlie Noon b. 1890 Pipers Flat, NSW		
		Enoch Goodwin b. 1820 Manchester, ENG
	Lucy Goodwin b. 1867 Goonoo x2, NSW	
		Mary Ann Smith b.c. 1844 Prospect, NSW
Peg Noon b. 1928 Mitchell, Qld		
		Peter McGonigal b. 1813 Ratho, SCT
	James C. McGonigal b. 1857 Cobinshaw, SCT	
		Elizabeth Currie b. 1821 West Calder, SCT
Lizzie McGonigal b. 1888 Torphichen, SCT		
		Robert Douglas b.c. 1838 Kirkliston, SCT
	Elizabeth Douglas b. 1864 West Bangour, SCT	
		Mary Nimmo b. 1837 Muiravonside, SCT

Select bibliography

Authored books and maunscripts

Cilento, Raphael & Lack, Clem, *Triumph in the Tropics: an historical sketch of Queensland*. Smith and Paterson, Brisbane, 1959

Clark, Manning, *A History of Australia Volume V, from 1888 to 1915*, Melbourne University Press, Carlton South, 1981

De Jabrun, Mary, *The Mezgers & Bihlmaiers*, Blurb, Brisbane 2015,

Ditton, Annie, *Memoirs of Annie Ditton* (née Clay) wife of Archibald Ditton, first son of Abraham III

Drinkwater, Malcolm, *Hill End Gold*, Third Edition. self-published, Hill End, 2016

Dunbar, Raden, *The Secrets of the Anzacs*, Scribe, Brunswick, Victoria, 2014

Evans, Ray , *A History of Queensland*, Cambridge University Press, Melbourne, 2007

Fisher, Rod, *Boosting Brisbane – Imprinting the Colonial Capital of Queensland*, Boolarong Press, Brisbane, 2009

Ford, Lyall, *Poorhouse to Paradise*, Taipan Press, Freshwater, Qld, 2001

Fox, Matthew J, *Fox's history of Queensland: Its people and Industries*, States Publishing Co., Brisbane, 1923

French, Maurice, *Pubs Ploughs & Peculiar People*, University of Southern Queensland Press Toowoomba, 1992

French, Maurice, *Toowoomba: a sense of history: 1840–2008*, University of Southern Queensland, Toowoomba, 1991

Friend, Donald, *Hillendiana: A collection of Hillendiana: comprising vast numbers of facts and a considerable amount of fiction concerning the goldfield of Hillend and environs and a commentary both grave and ribald*, Sydney, Ure Smith 1977

Goodwin, Bruce Selwyn, *Gold and People : recollections of Hill End 1920s to 1960s*, self-pub, French's Forrest, 1992

Goodwin, Bruce Selwyn, *Lace and Gold*, self-published, French's Forrest, 1999

Greenhalgh, Kath, *Ackland – Coal Mine to Tidy Town*, Oakey 2011

Hapgood, West, *Deep Valleys, Tall Trees, Tough Men and Women: Pioneering stories of 'Bulli' and some local History*, Bulli 1992

Hill, David, *The Gold Rush: The fever that forever changed Australia*, Random House, North Sydney, 2011

Hodge, Harry, *The Hill End Story, Books I, II, & III* self-published, Newcastle, 1965 – 1972

Holthouse, Hector, *River of Gold*, A & R Classics edition, Angus & Robertson, Sydney, 1994

Hooper, Colin, *North Queensland Deserted Towns Charters Towers – Ravenswood – Cape River*, self-published, NSW, 2014

Kelly, Ian M, *Bound for The Downs The Toowoomba Kleins,*, self-published, USQ, Toowoomba 2006.

Lehane, Fleur, *Heartbreak Corner*, self-published, Beaudesert, 1996,

Litton, Helen, *The Irish Famine an Illustrated History*, Wolfhound Press, Dublin 2nd Ed. 2003

Luchetti, Anthony S, *The oil shale industry, its development, growth and demise*, Lithgow Historical Society, Lithgow, 1976

Mayne, Alan, *Hill End : an historic Australian goldfields landscape*, Carlton, Melbourne University Press, 2003

McCauley, Becky, *McCauley 'x' is my true name*, self-published, Warba, Minnesota, USA

McGowan, Barry, *Australian Ghost Towns*, Lothian Books, Melbourne, 2002

McMahon, Anne, *Floating Prisons: Irish Convict Hulks and Voyages to New South Wales 1823–1837* Halstead Press, Canberra, 2017

Morrison, W Frederic, *Aldine History of Queensland*, Aldine, Sydney, 1888

Nilsson, JA, *Mackay in the Nineteenth Century*, Royal History Society Queensland, 1964

Pfeffer, Colin, *The Fassifern Story: A History of Boonah Shire and Surroundings to 1989*, Boonah Shire Council, 1991

Stanley, Julie, *The foundation of a North Queensland Port Settlement 1861–1880* (U of Q Thesis 1984)

Szalay, Margaret, *Limerick to Queensland: the Kearney family story / our family history as told by Margaret Szalay & Mary Graham, Kearney descendants*. Self-published, Cremorne, NSW, 2006

Taylor, GJ, Newnes, *History of a Blue Mountains Oil-Shale town*, Australian Railway Historical Society, Redfern c 1987

Weitemeyer, Thorvald Peter Ludwig, *Missing Friends: Being the adventures of a Danish immigrant in Queensland (1871–1880)*, T Fisher, Unwin, London, 1892

White, Patrick, *Flaws in the Glass*, A Self-portrait, Penguin Books, UK, 1983

Edited collections in book form

Australian Historical Statistics – Ed: W. Vamplew, Pub: Fairfax Syme & Weldon Associates NSW 1987
Australians 1888 Ed: G Davison, JW McCarty, A McLeary Pub: Fairfax, Syme, Weldon, Broadway, NSW, 1987
Australians Events and Places. Ed: G. Aplin, S.G. Foster & M. McKernan Pub: Fairfax, Syme & Weldon, NSW 1987
Cooktown Through The Years Ed: J Shay, Cooktown and District Historical Society, QLD 2009
Early Settlers of Mackay 1860–1885, Mackay Family History Society
Katie Hume on the Darling Downs, A Colonial Marriage Ed. Nancy Bonnin, Darling Downs Institute Press, Toowoomba 1985
Port Dennison Times Almanac 1868, pub: FT Rayner, Bowen, 1868
The Aftermath, A tour of Mackay 27 January 1918 Helen Martin & Mackay Historical Society & Museum Inc.
The Development of the City of Mackay, A Pictorial Time-Line Mackay Historical Society and Museum, 2010
The jubilee of Mackay: 1862–1912, Daily Mercury, Mackay, 1912
The Queensland Law Journal – Reports {Cases Decided 19 Feb 1890 to 12 Oct 1892}
Woodchurch in 1871. A Kentish village and the Mid-Victorian Census – Woodchurch Village Life Museum, 2008

Newspapers and Journals Referenced

Australian Town and Country Journal
Balonne Beacon (St George)
Beaudesert Times
Boston Pilot
Bowen Independent
Bundaberg Mail and Burnett Advertiser
Cairns Post
Clonmel Advertiser (Tipperary IRL)
Commonwealth of Australia Gazette
Cooktown Courier
Daily Mail (Brisbane)
Daily Mercury (Mackay)
Daily Standard (Brisbane)
Darling Downs Gazette
Empire (Sydney)
Evening Post (Wellington, NZ)
Freemans Journal (Dublin IRL)
Illawarra Mercury
Irish Examiner (Cork IRL)
Lithgow Mercury
Logan Witness (Beenleigh)
Mackay Mercury and South Kennedy Advertiser
Mackay Mercury
Maryborough Chronicle Wide Bay and Burnett Advertiser,
Morning Bulletin (Rockhampton)
Mudgee Guardian and North-Western Representative
NSW Police Gazette

Nelson Examiner and New Zealand Chronicle
Newcastle Herald
Newcastle Morning Herald and Miners' Advocate
Newcastle Sun
Northern Argus (Rockhampton)
Northern Herald (Cairns)
Northside Chronicle (Brisbane)
Queensland Country Life
Queensland Police Gazette
Queensland Times Ipswich Herald and General Advertiser,
Rockhampton Bulletin
South Coast Times and Wollongong Argus
Sydney Morning Herald
The Age (Melbourne)
The Argus (Melbourne)
The Bathurst Times
The Brisbane Courier
The Capricornian (Rockhampton)
The Catholic Press (Sydney)
The Charleville Times
The Courier Mail (Brisbane)
The Chronicle (Toowoomba)
The Cork Evening Herald (IRL)
The Cork Southern Reporter (IRL)
The Courier (Brisbane)
The Daily Mail (Brisbane)

The Darling Downs Gazette and General Advertiser
The Graziers' Review
The Herald (Melbourne)
The Maitland Mercury and Hunter River General Advertiser
The Moreton Bay Courier
The North Australian
The Queenslander (Brisbane)
The Sunday Herald (Sydney)
The Sydney Monitor
The Telegraph (Brisbane)
The Toowoomba Chronicle and Queensland Advertiser
The Toowoomba Chronicle
The Week (Brisbane)
The West Australian
Toowoomba Chronicle
Toowoomba Chronicle and Darling Downs General Advertiser
Townsville Daily Bulletin
Truth (Brisbane)
Wairarapa Standard (NZ)
Warwick Daily News
Western Star (Roma)
Western Star and Roma Advertiser (Toowoomba)
Wild River Times (Herberton)
Windsor and Richmond Gazette

Index